THE SMALL GIANT

SWEDEN

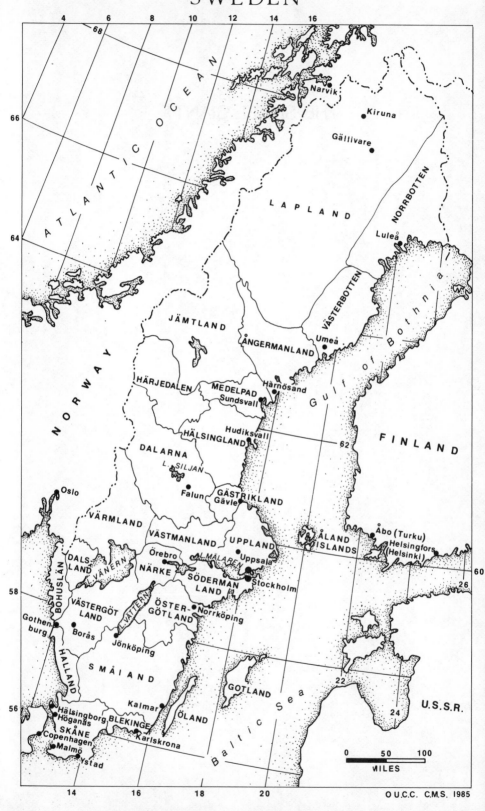

Narvik
Kiruna
Gällivare
NORRBOTTEN
LAPLAND
VÄSTERBOTTEN
Luleå
JÄMTLAND
ÅNGERMANLAND
Umeå
HÄRJEDALEN
MEDELPAD
Härnösand
Sundsvall
Gulf of Bothnia
FINLAND
Hudiksvall
HÄLSINGLAND
DALARNA
L. SILJAN
Oslo
Falun
GÄSTRIKLAND
Gävle
VÄRMLAND
VÄSTMANLAND
UPPLAND
ÅLAND
ISLANDS
Åbo (Turku)
Helsingfors
(Helsinki)
Örebro
L. MÄLAREN
Uppsala
DALS-
LAND
L. VÄNERN
NÄRKE
SÖDERMAN
LAND
Stockholm
BOHUSLÄN
VÄSTERGÖT
LAND
L. VÄTTERN
ÖSTER-
GÖTLAND
Norrköping
Gothen-
burg
Borås
Jönköping
HALLAND
SMÅLAND
GOTLAND
Baltic Sea
U.S.S.R.
ÖLAND
Kalmar
Hälsingborg
Höganäs
BLEKINGE
SKÅNE
Copenhagen
Karlskrona
Malmö
Ystad

ATLANTIC OCEAN
NORWAY

0   50   100
MILES

O.U.C.C. C.M.S. 1985

THE SMALL GIANT

Sweden Enters
the Industrial Era

Carl G. Gustavson

Ohio University Press
Athens, Ohio
London

Library of Congress Cataloging-in-Publication Data

Gustavson, Carl G.
  The small giant.

  Bibliography: p.
  Includes index.
  1. Sweden—Industries—History. 2. Sweden—Economic
conditions. I. Title.
HC375.G83 1986   338.09485   85-25922
ISBN 0-8214-0825-9

*Dedicated
to the Memory of
O. Fritiof Ander*

TABLE OF CONTENTS

PREFACE

Sweden's worldwide image as a model welfare state has tended to obscure the eminently successful industrial powerhouse that has generated the wealth to sustain the costly social advances. *The Economist,* the authoritative business weekly, believes Swedish industry, with more than 600 manufacturing subsidiaries in other countries, to be more strongly multinational than that of any other country (1984). Most of its international companies—AGA, Alfa-Laval, ASEA, Atlas Copco, Bofors, Electrolux, L. M. Ericsson, Husqvarna, Saab-Scania, Sandviken, SKF, Stora Kopparberg, the Swedish Match Co., Uddeholm, and Volvo—emerged to prominence in the fifty years before 1914 or were offshoots of enterprises active just before the First World War.

During that half-century the Swedes, rivaling the Japanese and Americans, had the third highest per capita growth of GNP in the world. Two generations later they entered the 1980s with, at least on paper, the highest per capita GNP ($13,327 in 1981) of the leading industrial powers, and they could also justifiably claim to have the most advanced domestic banking system. The Swedes, who had been a small military giant in the seventeenth century until shattered by their own excess of martial virtues, responded to an era of industrial and technological innovations by emerging, through peaceful conquests, as a small economic giant.

In the American mass media the Swedes tend to be portrayed as somewhat exotic outsiders. They were not our allies in either world war, they have not joined NATO or the EEC, and their geographic location has dictated a diplomatic posture between the West on the one hand and the German Reichs or the Soviet Union on the other. However, the economic position of the country has been quite different. Sweden developed as a province of western Europe and ultimately of the North Atlantic community. It has constituted a not insignificant part of this greater whole, and the history of its industrial and technological achievements can be fully told only within the context of these larger communities.

Sweden usually receives little more than perfunctory mention in the histories of the past two centuries of the European economy. In addition to its smaller size, it has been handicapped by the language barrier. Only a very few writers on the subject, like the great Eli F. Heckscher, were translated before the more recent generation began to present its findings in an international language. Franklin D. Scott, author of *Sweden: The Nation's History* (1977), praised the Swedes as "indefatigable and careful scholars," and the writers on technology, business enterprises, and economic life have been no exception. Unfortunately, much good work that does have relevance to the larger scene is locked up in Swedish-language publications and has therefore seldom passed beyond the national borders. The intent in this book is to tell the story of Swedish industrialization as a coherent whole and within its international context by transmitting into English, in a semipopular style, selected episodes and achievements previously narrated by various Swedish authorities.

Sweden's relatively small population does make it possible to focus on flesh-and-blood persons and to follow their trail of success and failure in the normal human condition as they sought to respond to successive waves of technological innovations. L. T. C. Rolt, in the preface to his *Isambard Kingdom Brunel,* deplored the "curiously impersonal and therefore unreal" writing about the so-called Industrial Revolution that makes it seem "the product of some *deus ex machina* or of some corporate act of will on the part of a whole people." Even though a scholarly history of Swedish industrialization must necessarily be structured by commonly accepted patterns and models, and must be more specifically delineated by means of statistical analyses, constructs, and generalized economic forces (all congenial to our contemporary mode of understanding), the less orderly real world, seen in close-up detail, may surely also be more intimately portrayed in terms of the sustained outpouring of energies and talents by vigorous personalities.

In the role of personalities, the vagaries of circumstantial factors, and the element of chance, the detailed developments bear little resemblance to any *deus ex machina* process. Whether it be in the very ordinariness of some episodes or in the occasional spectacular saga of a heaven-storming career, the unrolling scene seems to offer a fairly typical microcosm of industrial advances elsewhere. Posterity tends to take the legacy of nineteenth-century scientists, engineers, inventors, and entrepreneurs for granted; but, from the perspective of the individual participants, this is approximately how it usually happened. One fundamental aspect of the original industrial transformation—the human response to an accelerating stream of innovations and to the constant threat of obsolescence—does remain as vitally relevant now as then.

A Fulbright travel grant (1970) and two sabbaticals from Ohio University helped to defray part of the research expenses in Sweden. Lengthy and fruitful sojourns at the Wenner-Gren Center in Stockholm were made possible by its director, Claes Grill, and his conscientious staff. The attendants at the Royal Library (Frits Sjöstedt, Per Kjellberg, and others) rendered prompt and cheerful service on innumerable occasions. Alan Booth, Alonzo Hamby, Jack Matthews, Rune Rydén, Lee and Margaret Soltow, and Richard Vedder contributed to the project with timely aid, or friendly interest, often both. Long conversations and warm fellowship with Evert, Åke, Herbert and Ellen, and other relatives permitted me to see Sweden from the inside, not only as a visiting foreigner. I am deeply grateful to Franklin D. Scott for reading the manuscript and for his many helpful comments and corrections. Also to Sig-Britt Sändh for typing the manuscript and rectifying lapses in Swedish-language usage. Needless to say, any errors of fact or judgment are all mine. My thanks also go to Holly Panich and Helen Gawthrop of the Ohio University press for their efficient supervision of the publication process. The maps were prepared by Cathy Steiner of the O. U. Cartographic Center. Finally, as always, I am indebted to Caryl, helpmate and travel manager during the writing of books.

The Small Giant is dedicated to the memory of O. Fritiof Ander of Augustana College, who was indirectly responsible for my embarking upon this exploration of my ancestral homeland.

At Bredablick   CG
Kenora, Ontario
AUGUST 1984

I. PREPARATION

1. THE STEAM ENGINE

Abraham Niclas Clewberg, assistant theater director and minor poet, would at first glance seem a most unlikely person to introduce elements of industrialization into Sweden. His father had been a professor at the academy in Åbo (Turku), the southwestern seaport and capital of a Finland still under the Swedish crown, and he himself was teaching both literary history and natural science at the academy before he reached the age of twenty.

Attracting the attention of the king during a royal visit to Åbo, Clewberg inevitably gravitated to Stockholm and the brilliant court of King Gustav III (1771–1792). The adaptable docent, interested in both science and literature, made his career in this dazzling milieu by playing to the king's cultural interests. A few of his poems were well received, he long served as assistant director of the royal theaters, and he was appointed to the newly founded Swedish Academy. Ennobled in 1789, Clewberg adopted the name of Edelcrantz.

The first native-born sovereign of Sweden since Karl XII (1697–1718), Gustav III had seized power from the dominant political parties the year after his accession and thereafter governed the country in a manner reminiscent of the strong seventeenth-century Vasa kings. During his reign, the Swedes even won a major military victory—their last—in a naval battle against the Russians at Svensksund (1790). His royal court resembled a little Versailles, in which the Francophile king served with graceful flair as patron of the fine arts. For a few brief years in the sunset glow of the century, a galaxy of talented individuals gathered around the polished, charming, and somewhat superficial monarch.

The bubble burst on the evening of March 16, 1792, when, at a masked ball in Stockholm's new opera house, an assassin's bullet mortally wounded the king. Europe went to war against the French Revolution that spring, a war that would engulf much of the continent and would, with occasional respites, continue until 1815. Although Napoleon's armies never entered their homeland, the Swedes, on the periphery of Europe, passed through their own agonizing ordeal of domestic discord, loss of ancient territories, and new political beginnings in these years. The neurotic Gustav IV Adolf (1792–1809), age thirteen when his father died, was crowned in Norrköping on April 3, 1800. It poured rain, mixed with snow, all that day. He had trouble getting on his borrowed horse. When the bedraggled procession passed the animal's home stable, the horse turned in at the gate. After a brief dispute between king and

1

horse, won by the horse, His Majesty, soaking wet, borrowed another steed. His whole life was like that; it never seemed to stop raining on the unfortunate man.

Finland, part of Sweden since the late twelfth century, fell to the Russians in 1808–09. The inept conduct of the war and the need for a scapegoat brought the enforced abdication of the unstable king, who would die in exile in Switzerland under the plain name of Colonel Gustafsson. His uncle, Karl XIII (1809–1818), ascended the throne, the last sovereign of the old dynasty. The constitution of 1809, hurriedly drafted, embodied Swedish realities and traditions so well that it would endure, with some changes, until 1974. At this most unhappy moment in the history of modern Sweden, Marshal Jean Baptiste Jules Bernadotte of France was named crown prince, primarily in the hope that his military ability and Bonaparte connections would result in the reconquest of Finland. However, the general, who assumed the name of Karl Johan, led Sweden into the final great coalition that at long last overthrew the French emperor. Finland remained lost and Swedish Pomerania, a Baltic possession since the Thirty Years War, passed to Prussia. In compensation, Sweden was awarded Norway, a union that, after some skirmishing and much negotiating with the reluctant Norwegians, was formalized as a dual monarchy.

Meantime, what had happened to that minor cultural figure, Count Abraham Niclas Edelcrantz? His was a many-sided personality, a type frequently encountered in the eighteenth century. He was quite capable of playing a succession of roles as academy teacher, courtier, poet, theater director, technologist, entrepreneur, and agricultural expert. After the death of Gustav III came, for those interested in culture, "a whole new era, barren and earthbound."[1] Gustav IV Adolf's interests, as he matured, lay in practical matters, in the material development of his realm. Edelcrantz responded by entering a new career based upon technology and industry—probably closer to his authentic talents anyway. His first achievement took place in the field of optical telegraphy.

The optical telegraph was one of those transitory developments, long since forgotten, in the relay race of technological progress that reflected the growing needs of the modern community and that would later be solved by more fundamental inventions. Claude and Ignace Chappe had just devised a system of optical telegraphy in France by using levered semaphores on high poles; various combinations of bars and arms signaled the letters of the alphabet, and a few often-used words, to an observer with a telescope at the next pole. The first route, between Paris and Lille, was completed in August 1794. That same year Count Edelcrantz worked out his own system of signals in time to put up the few poles necessary to send birthday congratulations from Stockholm to the young king at Drottningholm, some ten kilometers away (November 1, 1794). He contrived a pattern of ten swinging flaps mounted on a rectangular framework; by different combinations of raised and lowered flaps it was possible to make 1024 different signals. Three signs could be sent each minute by the Chappe system, but Edelcrantz claimed up to ten or twelve.[2] The recent 1788–1790 Russian war, revealing the need for rapid communications between Finland and Stockholm, made the government receptive to the plan. Lines of poles, looking a bit like windmills, were set up in the archipelago east of Stockholm, and others were erected near Gothenburg and at the Karlskrona naval base in southern Sweden. Optical telegraph stations at Hälsingborg on the southwest coast and at Helsingör (Elsinore) in Denmark, within sight of each other across the Öresund straits, were intended to speed up communications between the two countries, although the proposed network never was completed. However, the very first message between the stations, on April 2, 1801, was sensational: Horatio Nelson had won the Battle of Copenhagen that day. During the Russian war of 1808–09, approximately fifty stations connected Stockholm with the Åland Islands off the coast of Finland, and another line of stations ran north to the Bothnian seaport of Gävle. (One of Edelcrantz's inspectors, in a project depending upon the use of telescopes, bore the appropriate family name of Venus.) Once the military urgency had passed, most of the system was abandoned, unlike in France, which had close to 5,000 kilometers of optical telegraphy in use by 1845. It did survive in Sweden in some places until the arrival of the electric telegraph. Optical telegraphy reached the count's native Åbo from the east, from St. Petersburg, in 1854, one year before it was superseded by an electric line.[3]

At the end of 1801 Gustav IV Adolf commissioned Edelcrantz to undertake an extensive tour of the continent and England. Though the king obviously was in no position to envision its full consequences, the long-term significance of this tour, in terms of the train of events set in motion, would far exceed the works of his much-vaunted father. The king requested Edelcrantz to study economic life, the market for Swedish iron, and the possibilities for borrowing money abroad. The enthusiastic traveler went beyond his instructions and also observed grain storage, forestry, sawmills, flour mills, distilleries, and much more. He also delivered numerous lectures and eagerly sought membership in continental learned societies, which, as he explained, opened doors for him to study innovations otherwise carefully barred to foreigners. In Germany someone was imprisoned for permitting Edelcrantz to inspect a machine for drying grain. In France he sought out Robert Fulton, then known as an American inventor of a submarine. The count did not much like the French, was strictly objective about the French Revolution, and also managed to irritate Napoleon Bonaparte. He spent too much time with the English in Paris and especially with the family of Richard Lovell Edgeworth, whose uncle, an abbé, had attended Louis XVI at his execution. Napoleon even issued an order for the expulsion of Edelcrantz, but the Swedish envoy succeeded in having it cancelled. Romance, not politics, had drawn the aging bachelor to the Edgeworth household; he proposed to Maria, one of Richard's daughters and a well-known novelist in her own right, but she frustrated her father's enthusiastic approval by rejecting the nobleman's suit.[4]

Edelcrantz arrived in England in the spring of 1803 and stayed for a year, discovering what was, for him, an astonishingly new world of technology and industry. His excitement mounted as he found, in his own words, "improvements in everything that is useful for a country."[5] He never succeeded in penetrating the secret techniques of British manufacture, foreign visitors not being permitted to spy on those invaluable inventions. Nevertheless, he transacted one crucial piece of business in England. He received an invitation to visit James Watt, and out of his burgeoning enthusiasm came the purchase of four steam engines, three from the firm of Fenton, Murray and Wood in Leeds (rivals of Boulton and Watt) and one bought in London. Someone would soon have brought the improved Watt steam engine to Sweden anyway, but it happened to be Edelcrantz who made the opening move and who thereby might be said to have started the chain reaction of nineteenth-century technological change in Sweden. In addition to buying the engines, he also hired expert knowledge in the person of Samuel Owen, whose long pioneering struggle would bring Edelcrantz's vision closer to realization. Owen accompanied him to Sweden on a packet from Norwich to Gothenburg.

Edelcrantz had observed the use of steam engines in distilleries in Scotland, and two of them were installed in crown distilleries on Kungsholmen and Ladugårdsland. A third went to Lars Fresk's textile mill, all three establishments being in the Stockholm area. The Fresk engine was started on Christmas Eve, 1804, the first successful steam engine in a Swedish manufactory.[6] Edelcrantz had intended to use the fourth to run a flour mill of his own, but the engine turned out to be too small so he offered it to the owners of the Dannemora mines for pumping water. Their response was notably unenthusiastic; a Newcomen steam engine had been tried there long ago with indifferent success. The Swedes tended to feel that steam engines were fine for the British, with their abundant coal, but not for the Swedes, who lacked the coal. Four of Sweden's best *mechanici* calculated that to pump out the estimated 1.5 million cubic feet of water at Dannemora would take over seven years and an enormous expenditure of wood for fuel. Samuel Owen assured them that he could do it in a year and a half, and the owners purchased the engine. It took two years and four months to empty the mines of 2.5 million cubic feet, at one-tenth the predicted consumption of wood.[7]

In December 1804 Edelcrantz requested toll-free admission of a fifth, 20-horsepower engine for his flour mill. He was scarcely the first person to realize the advantages of a steam-driven mill for the city. Numerous windmills festooned the heights around Stockholm. In periods of sustained calm no flour was produced, and therefore water-driven mills had been built where the strong current flooding out of Lake Mälaren into Saltsjön, the harbor inlet from the Baltic, offered adequate power. It could happen that low water in the lake brought a reverse current from the Baltic, and if this coincided with a lack of wind, the Stockholmers went without bread. This calamity had last occurred in 1798–99.[8] Edelcrantz put up a large four-story structure at the eastern point of Kungsholmen island, across the water from Gamla Stan (the Old City, well known to tourists) and on the present site of Stadshuset, the elegant Stockholm City Hall. In addition to the flour mill, he also installed linen spinning machinery and a grain-drying machine, which he designed. The inhabitants promptly dubbed it the Eldkvarn, the fire mill. Edelcrantz now also started to become interested in fire insurance societies.

Edelcrantz's troubles had just begun. His problems illustrate the difficulties of introducing technological innovations into a community, where the existing vested interests will naturally react to any threat to their livelihood and privileged positions. A so-called Flour War had been going on between the two rival groups of millers for several decades, ever since some millers began using the water wheel and the windmill operators tried to stop the interlopers. Now both groups joined forces in a ferocious legal attack on Edelcrantz and his Eldkvarn. Furthermore, the count, unlike them, had been granted the right to sell his flour directly from the mill, and this brought the grain and victual guilds, which held a monopoly on the sale of flour to the public, into the fray. The lower courts sympathized with the guilds, but the courtier had enough friends in high places to survive the assaults. Compounding his difficulties, however, an energy crisis struck when wood-laden boats from Finland ceased to arrive during the war with Russia. The government restricted the use of wood for fuel, thereby starving the monstrous appetite of his steam engine. He won partial exemption, but did have to resort to expensive coal for some of his fuel. The epithets flew: Edelcrantz was a careerist, a favor-pandering courtier, and why didn't he go back to the theater where he belonged?[9] His battle finally won, he sold the Eldkvarn in 1815, by which time Samuel Owen had taken over the technological leadership in Sweden. The structure would continue in use until 1878, when a mighty blaze, Stockholm's best spectacle of the year, destroyed it.

Edelcrantz's technical improvements included a safety valve for steam boilers that won a silver medal in London, a cooking apparatus, a drying machine for grain, a lamp, an air pump, an aerometer, and a device for directing heat from a stove to adjoining rooms. He even "invented" a steam engine of dubious utility (1809). He had the exquisite pleasure, after his jousting with the guilds, of being appointed the head of the Kommerskollegium (Board of Trade), which supervised much of the economic life of Sweden (1813). A man with an "almost disturbing manysidedness and unbelievable industry," he devoted part of his apparently inexhaustible energies to the fields and orchards of Skuggan, his estate on nearby Djurgården.[10]

Baron Abraham Niclas Edelcrantz—he was elevated to the rank of *friherre* or baron late in life—is by no means a major figure in Swedish history. Nevertheless, when the processes of the early preparation for industrialization are examined, he does catch the eye, and, indeed, Edelcrantz made a career out of trying to attract attention. Many individuals, including quite a number of his contemporaries, introduced ingredients of industrialization, but Edelcrantz happened to be the right man at the right time to contribute a decisive impulse in the direction that history would move. He was not an isolated figure, a lonely voice in the wilderness; quite the contrary, his importance derives from his specific place in the ongoing processes, of developments reaching far back into the eighteenth century.

On the afternoon of September 17, 1784, the royal family and a large crowd gathered in Stockholm to watch Sweden's first balloon ascension, a spectacle inspired by the successful balloons of the Montgolfier brothers and others in France the year before. The Swedish version, twelve feet in diameter, was filled with hydrogen gas from a chemical reaction of iron filings, sulfuric acid, and water. At 4:45 in the afternoon a rocket was fired, the queen cut the cord, and, amidst a great shout, the balloon, carrying a lone passenger, rose. It was finally located on October 8 on an island in the archipelago east of Stockholm, but its bewildered passenger, a cat, was never seen again.[11]

Sometimes the Swedes could be remarkably quick to emulate innovations elsewhere, as witness optical telegraphy and the balloon. The steam engine, however, required over seventy-five years and about twenty projected or actual attempts before Samuel Owen and Edelcrantz achieved success. The ill-fated early steam engine at Dannemora had been mounted by Mårten Triewald (1691–1747), who seems to have known Thomas Newcomen, after his return in 1726 from England, where he had served as a secretary and then inspector of coal mines for an owner near Newcastle-upon-Tyne. In operation by 1728, it was one of the first Newcomen engines put to use outside of Great Britain. Though Triewald delivered many enthusiastic lectures about technological advances in England, the unsatisfactory performance of the steam engine in pumping water out of the mine, probably due to a lack of proper care, did not encourage more efforts.[12] Not until 1764, by which time almost a hundred Newcomen engines were pumping water in northern England alone, did the owners of another group of mines at Persberg make the attempt. That engine was ordered from the Carron Ironworks in Scotland through the Jennings & Finlay merchant firm in Stockholm; when the parts arrived, no one knew how to install it. The Bergskollegium (Board of Mines) had to send someone to study steam engines in Great Britain. He had it working by May 1768, but its parts were wearing out within two years and it required such huge quantities of wood that Persberg gave up on the experiment.[13]

Johan Erik Norberg, an officer on the mechanical staff of the Swedish navy, worked with the "fire-and-air machines," as they were called, for thirty years. The failures in history sometimes illuminate the true circumstances better than the success stories. Norberg and another man, Johan Fellers, separately made no less than five attempts to use steam engines at Karlskrona between 1771 and 1781, four of these at the naval shipyard. They failed, as did two efforts by a third man. Norberg, the tall, fat, "somewhat adventurous" gentleman, then made two extended visits to Russia, including long travels in Siberia. Back in Stockholm, he succeeded in constructing a Watt-type steam engine, based on the principle of a separate condenser. He received a patent on it, one of the four examiners being a man by the name of Edelcrantz (1796). A few years later Norberg was trying to put a steam engine in the *Jehu,* a schooner owned by the young king, who was much interested in the experiment. Nothing more was heard of the project. Norberg became the first head of the school that in time would grow into the Royal Institute of Technology, but not long thereafter he moved to Denmark, and later Russia. When he refused to leave his work on harbor improvements at Reval (Tallinn) after the outbreak of war in 1808, he was declared a traitor and stripped of his Swedish citizenship. Such can be the rewards for thirty years of labor when they do not come to successful fruition.[14]

Strong opposition from the crews of rowers that served the harbor area may have contributed to his failure in Stockholm. Complaints about the high costs of experimenting, installing, and maintaining steam engines recur in every project from Dannemora on, and the problem of fuel, of course, discouraged their introduction. Very likely, Norberg lacked sufficient technical competence to match his ambitious striving; had he in fact succeeded with the *Jehu,* he might have preempted Robert Fulton's laurels. Torsten Althin, sage historian of Swedish technology, attributed the successive failures to the Swedes' unfamiliarity with steam engine principles and their lack of a tradition of working with such engines.[15] And why not? Because, lacking coal, they possessed an alternative source of energy—cheap and abundant water power.

At Höganäs, a fishing village near the northern entrance to the Öresund straits, Count Eric Ruuth needed steam engines to pump water out of his mines—his *coal* mines. Ruuth had been another favorite of Gustav III, serving as finance minister and later as governor-general of Swedish Pomerania in 1792–96. It had been known since the 1500s that coal existed in Skåne, Sweden's southernmost province, and now, after several years of determined boring, it was found in sufficient quantity to warrant mining on the properties of Ruuth at Höganäs (1793). As water collected in the deepening shafts, the pumps became necessary. Ruuth purchased the old Persberg relic and put it to work. Åkers Styckebruk, an armaments factory near Stockholm owned by Ruuth's father-in-law, was asked to try to make the parts for a steam engine. Skimpy evidence indicates that a couple of steam engines may have been ordered from England, in 1800 or soon thereafter. Ruuth had hired an Englishman, Thomas Stawford (or Stafford, according to one account), as technical leader, and the installation of engines and machinery devolved on him; Stawford claimed, by 1820, to have made some twenty steam engines.[16]

A visitor, Thor August Odencrantz, left a description of Höganäs as it looked in 1806. Two "fire-and-air-machines" were chuffing away, amidst thick smoke, near the road, and horses were pulling wagons along a railway. He saw several smokestacks, a windmill, and a canal to the harbor, where lighters were transporting coal out to anchored ships. Odencrantz was lowered into mine No. 6 in a basket; at the bottom he found several coal shafts and more railways, where ponies were pulling small wagons of coal.[17] It all looked like the real thing, and Count Ruuth must have had high hopes. In a speech in 1813 he painted an imaginative picture of a future industrial center at Höganäs, containing "all sorts of factories, manufactures which can be run by steam engines"; the coal would come cheaply from the nearby mines.[18]

It was not to be. Though coal would continue to be mined at Höganäs, these, the only mines of any consequence in the whole kingdom, produced only relatively small quantities and not of good quality. Sweden would long be handicapped by a domestic lack of coal, one of the basic ingredients of the older industrial revolution. Obviously, Ruuth and Stawford had steam engines in successful operation at least as early as the Stockholm duo, but, failing to develop the anticipated strong coal industry, they were much less strategically located to influence future developments.

Stawford and Owen had been preceded by earlier skilled British mechanics and workers. In 1763 Johan Cahman and Carl Daniel Solander, the latter a Swedish naturalist and explorer then employed at the British Museum, tried to persuade Matthew Boulton, who had not yet entered into his gloriously fruitful partnership with James Watt, to move to Sweden. Cahman, an owner of several iron works who was in the process of setting up a modern foundry in Gothenburg, found his man in Thomas Lewis, who had worked at the newly opened Carron Ironworks. Twice prevented by the authorities from leaving Scotland, Lewis managed to get away on his third attempt. He found five other British workers already employed by Cahman—one small example of the many in this and following decades who, evading official efforts to preserve technological secrets, migrated in order to advance their personal fortunes on the continent. In Gothenburg, Lewis helped Cahman complete his foundry, including a recent British invention, a reverbatory furnace. The Cahman enterprise even made the parts for a steam engine (1769), ordered by some mine owners, but, hearing the bad reports from Persberg, it never was mounted.[19]

8

In 1769 Thomas Lewis secured a *privilegium* or license to found Bergsund on the site of a former tobacco spinnery near the southwest tip of Södermalm, the large southern Stockholm island. Bergsund became Sweden's first *mekaniska verkstad*. A *verkstad* is a workshop; hence Bergsund was, in its most literal meaning, a workshop where mechanics dealt with machinery. Though financially assisted by the merchant Robert Finlay, by the state, and by the Association of Ironmasters, Lewis soon went bankrupt and died while still in his early thirties.[20] A textile manufacturer, Daniel Asplund, acquired the buildings a few years later and maintained its activity for some twenty years. His foreman, Johan Elvius, had worked in Great Britain and allegedly had once stopped Lewis from leaving Scotland by tipping off the authorities. Asplund's successor, Gustaf Daniel Wilcke, who would own Bergsund from 1804 until 1858, hired Samuel Owen in 1806 to take over the technical leadership of his *mekaniska verkstad*.

Samuel Owen (1774–1854) was thinking of moving to the United States, where he thought steam engines more appreciated, when the appearance of Count Edelcrantz changed his plans. Born at Norton-on-Hales (Shropshire), he learned to read and write in one year of schooling before family poverty forced him to go to work. First he tended geese on an estate, then he worked as a farm hand until the age of seventeen. He soon quit a job on canal barges because his companions were too rough; did it cross the mind of the future steamboat pioneer that there might be a better means of transportation than horse-drawn barges? For some years Owen labored as a carpenter while also attending an evening school, after which he was hired as a carpenter with Boulton & Watt, manufacturers of the improved James Watt engine. His foreman, the foundryman Abraham Stoar, gave the eager young worker books to read. Studying a volume about steam engines, Owen discovered his true vocation. Later he moved on to Fenton, Murray and Wood, where Edelcrantz found him.[21]

After setting up the original four steam engines, Owen returned to England to work for Arthur Woolf, an inventor of the compound engine. Edelcrantz soon summoned him back to install his Eldkvarn engine, but when Owen arrived he found Matthew Murray himself there doing the job. Rather than return to England immediately, Owen accepted the position of foreman at Wilcke's Bergsund. During the next two to three years he constructed his first two steam engines and also made a rolling mill for the Kloster iron works in Dalarna. He encountered difficulties with the iron, an ominous hint that all was not well with the Swedish iron industry. In 1809 he purchased the property of Charles Apelquist between a street called Hantverkaregatan and the shore of the lake, and there founded his own *mekaniska verkstad*. Directly to the east lay the Eldkvarn; other neighbors included a glass works and the Kungsholmen distillery which had acquired one of the first steam engines.

This area of Kungsholmen had long been occupied by artisans, tanners, soapmakers, cloth merchants, and other trades; hence the name Hantverkaregatan, the handicraft workers' street. Charles Apelquist (c. 1748–1824) had worked in England for a time, sneaked tools and diagrams back to Sweden, and ultimately, beginning in 1795, erected the buildings bought by Owen. Here he did metal work and manufactured tools and wood screws while also starting a textile mill on a separate location at Marieberg with machinery he made himself; several other textile mills around Stockholm and in Norrköping were equipped with Apelquist machinery.

Samuel Owen gradually over the years furnished the original foundry with steam engines and the standard tools and machinery of the age: lathes, boring machines, planing tools, presses, and rolling mill equipment. Although some workers apparently followed him from Bergsund, he would later lament that no one else knew how to do foundry work, and that he had to train his workers in industrial skills. Wilcke promptly took him to court in a vain effort to prevent the competition. Within a few years Owen was able to strike off in a direction that not only suited his own talents and inclination, but also served as first-rate advertising for the products from his machine shop—the experimentation with steamboats.

He began trying to work out the problems in 1812, five years after Robert Fulton's *Clermont* began its voyages on the Hudson between New York City and Albany. In 1816, after the first practical efforts with a small boat, Crown Prince Karl Johan put a schooner, aptly called *Experiment,* at his disposal. When the boiler burst, Owen bought *The Witch of Stockholm,* a small cargo boat, and installed a steam engine in that. In the first tests the boat moved for a while, then stopped because the engine had exhausted its steam; when the pressure built back up, it moved again. The boiler was too small, and after more work the steamboat functioned better in further tests in November. (The early locomotives in England, in these same years, had the same difficulty.) Owen had brought a second problem on himself by attempting to use a propeller, this being years before John Ericsson and Francis Pettit Smith made them effective. Supposedly, Owen had gotten the idea independently by seeing the blades on a windmill on Lidingö rotating one day; if blades could be pushed by the wind, why not use blades to push against water? However, his first two boats moved much too slowly, so he put paddlewheels, about 2.5 meters in diameter, on *The Witch of Stockholm.*[22]

By 1818 Owen had his first successful steamboat, the *Amphitrite* (named for Poseidon's mate), in operation. Over 19 meters in length and driven by a 6-hp engine (later, 16), it could carry 182 passengers. On August 2, 1818, Owen took it to Drottningholm and back, then began making two trips every Sunday between Stockholm and the island. On weekdays it was rented to excursion groups for cruises. Owen could now proudly claim that the Thames had seen its first steamboat in 1813, the Seine in 1816, and Mälaren in 1818.[23] In September the *Amphitrite* went to Västerås, inland on Mälaren, where a big fair was in progress; people gathered along the shore to watch it pass and, unlike the Stockholmers who were now accustomed to Owen's projects, called it the "fire-ship" and suspected it to be the devil's work. Interest in steamboats was heightened in 1819 by the visit to Stockholm of the oceangoing packet *Savannah*, which had used an auxiliary steam engine for possibly a fifth of the time in crossing the Atlantic in the preceding year. Genuine transatlantic steamship traffic would begin only twenty years later, perhaps best symbolized by that historic day in April 1838 when the little *Sirius*, from London by way of Cork, arrived in New York, followed a few hours later by the *Great Western*, fifteen days out of Bristol, steaming into the harbor.

Owen began building steamboats at his own shipyard and in 1820 launched the *Stockholm* and a smaller craft, the *Upsala. Stockholm*, with a 44-hp engine, made regular trips between Stockholm and Åbo and later between the capital city and Norrköping. Owen kept the *Upsala* and derived a good profit from it. The *Yngve Frey,* constructed at Stora Varvet in Stockholm, was powered by a 22-hp Owen engine and began more or less scheduled visits in 1821 to lake towns as far away as Arboga at the western end of Mälaren. Owen's ultimate contribution to marine development in Sweden included five wooden steamboats, two iron-hulled ships, and thirty marine engines of the total sixty steam engines that he produced. He also tried to get a *privilegium* to make steam-driven land vehicles, like those of William Murdock and Richard Trevithick in England, but nothing more came of that dream. The Owen machine shop produced over a thousand of that era's simple threshing machines, many of which were exported, as well as five rolling mills, pumps, milling machinery, bridges, saws, and ornamental iron articles. Among Owen's several Swedish "firsts" were an iron bridge, a small one, in Stockholm in 1815 and a steam-driven dredge in 1820. Receiving a contract for stronger pumps for the Höganäs coal mines, where a new effort to extract more coal had started, he delivered two large pumps run by 150-hp engines, and also two small engines and six boilers (1832).[24]

Over on the opposite side of Mälaren at Bergsund, Wilcke was not happy over Owen's success. Unable to compete, Bergsund had fallen back largely on the manufacture of such articles as pots and pans, tinware and stoves. Owen's fame obscured the career of Wilcke, who did not suffer his fate in silence. He, too, had ambitions; an uncle of his, Johan Carl Wilcke (1732–96), had published enough on the characteristics of electricity to merit, perhaps, mention as a forerunner of Michael Faraday. In 1830 the proprietor of Bergsund, trying to set the record straight, was writing that Bergsund had been Stockholm's first iron foundry, and he personally took the credit for arranging Owen's construction of the two steam engines and the Kloster rolling mill. Later workshops devoted to the mechanical arts, he insisted, had sprung from Bergsund, where the new processes had first been tested. Then, sinking the harpoon deep, Wilcke added that *he*, Wilcke, had *sent* Owen back to England to improve his skills and had continued to pay him while he was doing so.[25]

If it was any solace to him, Wilcke outlasted Owen. Profits at the Kungsholmen workshop were good for the first twenty years, but increasing competition from new rivals worsened Owen's financial position. Having trained several hundred men in what, in effect, had become Sweden's first practical school in modern technology, Owen now saw them spread out in other enterprises that competed with his. An eternal optimist and genius of sorts, he compounded the difficulties of unfavorable economic conditions by his incessant zeal for conducting experiments without regard to costs. A long iron bridge in Stockholm, never completed, cost large sums without any financial rewards. The *Oscar,* one of his own ships, went up in flames. So did his pride, the large *Josephine,* which could carry 600 passengers. Owen had exceeded himself on this one, and the combination of his imaginative ideas resulted in a singularly awkward construction. On its maiden voyage in 1824, a screw fell into the machinery, stopping the whole works. On a trip soon thereafter the passengers were entertained, or alarmed, by seeing a fountain of water spurting from the smokestack. One man had full-time employment running around and dousing the flying sparks. One day, just after leaving Strängnäs, a fire went out of control and that was the end of *Josephine.*[26]

Despite financial help from the state and the Association of Ironmasters, this precursor of modern Swedish industrial development went bankrupt in 1843. Owen later worked at Åkers Styckebruk for a few years as a foreman. Three years before his death in 1854 he visited the London World Exhibition, and as he wandered among the industrial displays in the Crystal Palace the aged expatriate must have had some long, long thoughts. An early account of his life, interestingly enough, devoted far more space to his work on behalf of temperance and Methodism than his technological contributions.[27] His third wife, who devoted her widow years to drinking tea and reading English books, was an aunt of August Strindberg (1849–1912). Thus, by marriage, Samuel Owen, the steamboat pioneer, became an uncle of Sweden's future immortal playwright.[28] Strindberg was no great admirer of steam engines.

A few years after the bankruptcy, the Crown bought the property and moved the Swedish mint there, a location it would retain until 1974. Its yellow and white buildings, now occupied by others, lie alongside a short and narrow street, the Samuel Owen Gata, which inadequately perpetuates his memory. Industry having long since departed Kungsholmen, the area now serves in part as a lair for Sweden's omnipresent bureaucrats. On the Mälarstrand end of

Samuel Owen Gata, small lake boats raise their quiet masts, a scene more reminiscent of the days of sail than of the smoke and noise of Owen's steamboats.

Sweden had a population of about two and a half million in 1815, a figure that increased to another million by midcentury and passed five million before 1900. In 1800 only six cities possessed over 5,000 inhabitants; Stockholm had 73,000 and Gothenburg 12,000, followed by Karlskrona, Norrköping, Gävle, and Uppsala. Approximately four-fifths of the inhabitants were dependent upon agriculture, and 72.4 percent would still be gaining their livelihood directly from the land in 1870.

Handicraft workers comprised the second largest occupational group, the rural craftsmen now growing more rapidly in numbers than those in towns and cities. In 1830 about 12,000 handicraft workers were employed in manufactories, scattered among no less than 1,857 enterprises. That is, with a few exceptions, they were tiny. They included the many small iron works, textile and paper workshops, dyeworks, sugar refineries, and tobacco spinneries. Some textile mills, especially in Norrköping, and a few other enterprises might by then be considered semi-industrial in scope, but in most of them the labor force worked with little or no machinery. In addition, cottage industry—linen, wool, cotton, glass, and wood articles—existed over much of Sweden, with special concentrations in parts of Småland and Dalarna, where they would survive the period of industrialization, and in the Borås region of Västergötland.

The guild system, with the usual restrictions on freedom of occupation, prevailed in urban areas; to prevent competition, many articles were not allowed to be made in the homes. The guilds had spread to the smaller towns in the later eighteenth century, but their monopolies brought bitter protests and widespread violations of the law. Their restraints, however, would not much hamper the beginnings of industrialization. In 1739 the government, in order to encourage manufacturing, had ordained that "factories" (*fabriker*) need not be subject to guild regulations, and this law was so loosely implemented that manufactories in general were exempt even if the work was largely handicraft.[29]

Later Swedish generations would look back to the earlier nineteenth century as a time of poverty and stagnation. The smaller towns tended to be self-sufficient and by no means played the role in economic life that they would later. Visitors to Sweden commented on the lack of goods-carrying wagons on the often wretched roads; most freight, where feasible, was shipped along the coastal waters or on the inland lakes.[30] Nor was there much interchange between the town and the countryside, the peasants having little to sell and not much money with which to buy town commodities. Purchases tended to be limited to salt, herring, iron, and the so-called colonial wares, such as sugar and tobacco. Stores were still rare in the towns, annual markets and fairs continued to be held, and peddlers made their rounds among the country people. The village peasantry, living in their wooden red houses with white trim and sod or thatched roofs, largely depended upon their own resources. They spun their own flax or wool and wove their own clothes, and they might build their own houses and make their own wagons and tools; however, certain local citizens often specialized as tanners, shoemakers, millers, smiths, and carpenters. The condition of the harvest continued to be by far the most important factor in the lives of the people.

An agrarian revolution necessarily preceded the large-scale transformation of industrial production. Only the replacement of communal villages, where each family cultivated numerous separate strips of land, by compact individual farms would enable a sufficient increase in productivity to sustain a growing population. The number of strips had been somewhat reduced in the eighteenth century, and small individual farms did already exist in the heavily forested areas of Sweden. Strongly supported by King Gustav IV Adolf, laws in 1803 and 1807 provided for a more systematic redistribution of the land (*enskifte*) in southern and much of central Sweden. By 1827, however, this reform had been implemented only in Skåne and in some portions of the farmland south of Lake Vänern in Västergötland. In that year another law initiated a much more widespread redistribution, a process basically (but by no means entirely) completed by 1860.

Between about 1820 and 1860 the amount of cultivated land more than doubled, much of the added acreage consisting of former meadows that often first had to be drained. An effective rotation of crops, replacing the ancient system of leaving at least a third of the land fallow, increased productivity. Less grazing land reduced the amount of livestock, but Sweden began exporting grain in 1829 and continued to do so into the 1880s. A big increase in the potato crop offered a new means of subsistence, though peasants were also permitted to make *brännvin* (hard liquor) out of grain or potatoes, a practice that created serious social problems. The added acreage and improved methods of farming enlarged the food supply, gradually brought some purchasing power to the countryside, and stimulated the growth of machine shops by increasing the demand for farm tools and machinery.

The agricultural revolution did not, however, solve the problem of an excessive number of mouths to feed. The breakup of the communal system destroyed the security of the poor, and, since Sweden as yet had no state relief for the poor, many people had to be apportioned small cottages and occasional labor, a condition that could never amount to more than barely subsistence living. In 1870 the crofters, cotters, household servants, and day laborers numbered 1,288,000, almost as many as, counting family members, the 1,396,000 owners and renters of farm acreage. Until industry could draw off this surplus labor, the inhabitants of the countryside, starting in the 1840s, would emigrate in large numbers, the overwhelming majority to the United States. About 1.3 million Swedes ultimately left the kingdom; about 200,000 later returned.

In addition to about 9,000 estates held by nobles and gentry, the country, after land redistribution, had approximately 200,000 peasant proprietors, a figure that remained comparatively stable. These landowning peasants would in time become relatively prosperous, but for the others the prospects were bleak. Inheritance was by primogeniture, which meant that younger sons and unmarried daughters had to look elsewhere for their sustenance. As the cultivation of grain for export expanded, the owners, needing unencumbered ground, tended to evict their tenant farmers, another fertile source of emigrants. The famine years of the late 1860s and their aftermath took their toll, and industrialization sent some handicraft workers on their way. This mobility had started *before* the decades of mass migration. Lennart Jörberg says that the Swedes were "a wandering folk" long before the great emigration began, that there had been substantial population movement within the country as individuals tried to improve their lot.[31] Even during the migration decades, many first looked for work in the cities, then decided to leave their nation altogether. Primarily, the pressures of overpopulation in the countryside, coinciding with the improved transatlantic and American railroad transportation and the available farmland in North America, became irresistible to the landless individuals, who long made up the great majority of the emigrants. Nor was the American frontier completely alien to a people already involved in the "internal colonization," in the doubling of agricultural land by clearing forests and draining the swamps.[32]

The new political dispensation of 1809 had entrenched the position of the bureaucracy, centered in Stockholm. The king governed the country, with the advice of his ministers, and shared legislative power with the Riksdag. This parliament, however, continued to be made up of four estates—nobles, clergy, burgesses, and peasants—and the difficulty of passing legislation or amending the 1809 constitution tended to leave the direction of affairs in the hands of the king and of the bureaucrats. At least Sweden did have a parliament and a constitution, unlike most continental states at this time.

Mercantilist policies prevailed far into the century. After the end of the Napoleonic wars, the government, confronted by an unfavorable balance of trade and fearing the dumping of goods by countries trying to restore their prewar commerce, enacted a strongly protective tariff. Literally hundreds of articles were barred from importation either directly or by prohibitively high duties, and about fifty types of goods could not be exported (1816). Textile and agricultural products, particularly, were protected, while iron ore and pig iron were reserved for domestic use. The Navigation Act of 1724 (the Produktplakat), somewhat modified, remained in force, a measure intended to strengthen the Swedish merchant marine by permitting foreign vessels to bring to Sweden only goods from their own country and its colonies. Nor was the Swedish riksdaler stable until after a drastic devaluation in 1834 and the resumption of silver redemption.

Presiding over economic affairs were the Kommerskollegium (Board of Trade), founded in 1651, and the Bergskollegium (Board of Mines), dating from 1637. The domestic economy was minutely supervised by strictly enforced regulations. Iron works and sawmills produced according to specific annual quotas, and the founding of new enterprises entailed a time-consuming procedure of applications, hearings, and sometimes investigations, resulting in, perhaps, final approval.

For persons of initiative, Sweden might well have seemed "a little country of civil servants . . . a country which seemed atrophied in old forms . . . well protected from life-giving impulses from the outside. . . ."[33] A dark picture, but very much an oversimplified one. Arthur Montgomery, in *The Rise of Modern Industry in Sweden* (1939), cautioned that the "outward semblance of immobility and stagnation" was "partly illusory." New and disintegrating forces had appeared that in the 1830s and 1840s became quite clear and that in the 1850s would bring "almost an economic revolution."[34]

A lengthy, often acrimonious struggle between liberals and conservatives reflected the stirrings of new energies in the land. Pressures mounted for the elimination of paternalistic policies and bureaucratic restraints on the economy. Never officially abolished, the navigation laws ceased to be implemented as the government, to avoid reprisals, found it necessary to negotiate treaties with various countries waiving its regulations. (The first treaty had been considerably earlier, with the newly independent United States, in 1783.) Three of the four estates of the Riksdag voted for freedom of occupation in 1823, only to have it blocked by the fourth. In the same year, state forests began to be turned over to private hands, largely to the peasantry; the quota system on sawmill production was dropped in 1842, and controls on the iron industry were being progressively relaxed.

The Swedes had entered the nineteenth century with a respectable legacy of technological and scientific achievement. Their metallurgical techniques for a time, thanks to their copper and iron industry, had ranked second to none. Mechanical skills had been nurtured there and in armament works, whose cannon were widely exported. A number of men eminent in science or related fields had appeared in the eighteenth century. Christopher Polhem (1661–1751) stands at the beginning of the list, a many-sided inventor and engineer. Carl Linnaeus (1707–1778) devised a universally accepted classification of plants, and several of his students made further contributions in botany. Emanuel Swedenborg (1707–1778) made notable scientific discoveries before becoming absorbed in the psychic and spiritual. Anders Celsius (1701–1744) originated the centigrade scale of measuring temperature that still bears his name. Carl Scheele (1742–1786) has been called the greatest experimental chemist of his time; the discovery of oxygen, independently of Joseph Priestley, is one of his numerous achievements. The optical telegraph had been made possible by better telescopes, and John Dollond's improved telescope in England had in part resulted from the studies of achromatic light by Samuel Klingenstierna (1698–1765). Torbern Bergman (1735–1784) helped to pioneer chemical analysis, and Jöns Jacob Berzelius (1779–1848) was, when this story begins, working out the system of chemical formulation that would henceforth be used by all chemists. In 1818 he published a table of the composition of chemical compounds.

Seen in historical perspective, the crucial factor for the Swedish economy derived from the beginnings of industrialization in Great Britain that inexorably rendered obsolete the prevailing technology and modes of production. A new wave of fundamental innovations thrust Sweden, relatively well advanced in some respects within the context of previous circumstances, into the position of being forced to catch up. A new terrain had to be explored and conquered, an adventure the Swedes would share in the coming years with other peoples of western Europe and North America.

Voicing the national shock over the loss of Finland, Esaias Tegnér (1782–1846), perhaps Sweden's greatest poet, had written that Finland must be regained within the confines of Sweden, that the fatherland must be restored to greatness within more limited borders. In a territorial sense the Swedes would do so by reclaiming farmland in Sweden's remaining provinces. Viewed in another dimension, however, Sweden would acquire new terrain through the peaceful conquest of the forces of nature. Winning new sources of energy, deploying various types of machinery, and harvesting from new bases of industrial production would be a slow and difficult process. It would entail many campaigns, much trial and error, and numerous failures and triumphs in which other Clewbergs would be ennobled with memorable names.

2. WATERWAYS AND STEAMBOATS

Protocol called for a warship passing the Danish fort at Helsingör (Elsinore) on the Öresund to fire a sixteen-gun salute, whereupon the Danes would respond with a similar salute. Baltzar von Platen, temporarily in command of the *Bellona,* duly fired sixteen times, and the Danes responded with—fifteen. No one knew whether it was accident, malice, or the work of a humorist gunner, but, since Danish-Swedish relations were in their customary rancorous state, the Swedish commander cleared his ship for action. The Danes hurriedly sent a suggestion that they repeat the ritual; this time the Danes would fire sixteen times and the Swedes could answer with fifteen. When news of the incident reached the Swedish admiralty, opinion was sharply divided between promoting or cashiering Baltzar von Platen. He was, finally, promoted.[1]

Controversy accompanied the gruff naval officer throughout his career. He had been born in 1766 on the island of Rügen in Swedish Pomerania; his field marshal father became governor-general of that province in 1796, succeeding Count Eric Ruuth. After attending the naval academy in Karlskrona, the son served on merchant vessels and then in the navy, where he fell prisoner of war to the Russians. Though complaining regularly about his slow promotions, he achieved permanent command of a warship before he was thirty. Five years later, in 1800, he quit the navy, completely exasperated by its bureaucratic mentality and tired of being, as he put it, "crucified" for his nonchalant disregard of formal regulations.[2]

Predictably, the vigorous captain found life much too peaceful on his newly purchased lakeside estate near the southwestern end of Vänern. Elected to the directory of the company that had just completed the construction of the Trollhätte Canal, he discovered something in the company archives that would absorb even his impatient energies for most of the rest of his life. The find consisted of two plans for a canal from Vänern to the Baltic Sea prepared a few decades earlier by Daniel Thunberg and Elias Schweder. The proposal was far from new. A plan had been submitted to King Gustav Vasa (1523–1560) by Bishop Hans Brask of Linköping, and even that had not been the first time the idea had been broached. With mounting enthusiasm, von Platen began a campaign on behalf of a Göta Canal, a "blue band" across Sweden to "unite the seas," the Kattegat and the Baltic. In 1806 he published a 64-page treatise outlining the arguments for building it: traversing the canal would be shorter than the distance around southern Sweden, it would safeguard traffic from possible enemy action in wartime, the payment of the Öresund dues to the Danes would be avoided, and it might attract the transit traffic of foreign merchandise. By spurring economic growth along its course, argued von Platen, the Göta Canal might even in the long run finance itself. Coming in the years when Swedish fortunes had reached their nadir, the challenge of a large, constructive undertaking might reinvigorate the national morale.[3]

The dream of a Göta Canal had tantalized the Swedes for so long that its realization had, it would seem, become almost a compulsion within the national consciousness, a tangible goal leading on toward a brighter future destiny. That the Swedes should focus their efforts on an artificial waterway was quite natural, since their vital arteries of communication consisted so largely of waterways. Four lakes—Mälaren, Hjälmaren, Vättern, and Vänern—very nearly bisect central Sweden, the heartland of the country. The medieval kingdom had emerged around these lakes. Stockholm, Västerås, Eskilstuna, Örebro, and Jönköping were located on or close to one or another of them, and nearby Norrköping had an outlet to the Baltic; flowing out of Vänern, the Göta Älv, a river, entered the Kattegat at Gothenburg. Sweden's other waterways followed the coastline. Northward from Stockholm lay Gävle, a thriving seaport for several centuries, and beyond it a string of coastal towns at the mouths of streams rarely navigable but convenient for the floating of timber. South from the capital another series of towns extended past Kalmar and the naval base at Karlskrona to Ystad, then the principal terminal port to Germany. Hälsingborg and Malmö, the latter not yet of much importance, fronted on Denmark, with which they had close economic ties. Nearly all Swedish towns of any consequence had access to water transportation.

This was the final great period of canal building. Thomas Telford was supervising the work on the Caledonian canal in Scotland, completed in 1822, and the Erie canal in the United States was being dug in the years 1817 to 1824. The St. Quentin in France opened in 1810. The first leg of the Trollhätte Canal along the Göta Älv between Gothenburg and Vänern had been finished in 1752, following a plan for a waterway across Sweden sketched by Christopher Polhem. Surmounting the six falls at Trollhättan and a water drop of more than a hundred feet posed far greater problems, however, and the work, bogging down until 1793, was not completed until 1800. Much of the money for construction came from merchant houses in Gothenburg, which would greatly benefit from the easier transportation of iron and wood from the Värmland northern shores of Vänern, the shipping of agricultural products from northern Västergötland on the southern side, and the easier movement of consumer goods from the western seaport into the interior.

The Riksdag authorized the creation of the Göta Canal Company, not without strong opposition, and Baltzar von Platen, chairman of its directory, was put in charge of construction. Having early joined the group that came to power in the palace revolution of 1809 and having also supported the candidacy of Bernadotte, Count von Platen, who sat on the State Council until 1812, occupied a strong position. He would need it during the coming vicissitudes, and Bernadotte, as crown prince and then as king, remained a tower of strength for the strong-willed canal builder. The sale of company stock brought in about 3.1 million riksdaler for construction, of which about 1 million came from Stockholm sources and nearly 1.25 million from Gothenburg.

Thomas Telford himself arrived with two assistants to stake out the route, following virtually the same course as that proposed by Thunberg and Schweder. In six fast weeks they did the work, including the sites for locks and the measurements along the way (1808). One link would start at Sjötorp on Vänern and emerge at Rödesund on Vättern; from Motala on the lake's eastern shore the canal would run crosscountry to connect with three successive small lakes—Boren, Roxen, and Asplangen—on its way to the Baltic at Slätbaken near Söderköping. When completed, the actual canal would be about fifty-four English miles in length, divided into links, and entailing no less than fifty-eight locks.

Construction, supposed to take ten years, began in 1810. The Swedes had dug canals before, and even now, under the supervision of Major Erik Nordewall, another company was excavating for a canal from Lake Mälaren south past Södertälje to the Baltic, a route later used by Göta Canal boats approaching or leaving Stockholm. The much more ambitious project, however, would strain the country's resources in poor economic times and reveal deficiencies in the technical knowledge and equipment necessary for the task. Baltzar von Platen, as a naval officer, originally assumed that the mechanical corps of the navy, accustomed to marine construction, could cope with the difficult engineering problems. Thomas Telford, whose letters conveyed both technical counsel and moral support, strongly recommended the employment of experienced British foremen, and the director, worried by early delays and mistakes, heeded Telford's advice. By 1817 thirteen British engineers, nearly all from Scotland, were supervising the project, their high wages repeatedly being denounced in the Riksdag. These men in turn complained that they were *poorly* paid, and the behavior of two or three of them gave the stern director cause for concern. Swedes were gradually trained to replace them, a few being sent on to England for further study under Telford. Lacking an able and willing labor force, the authorities resorted to soldiers for most of their workers, a common practice in many countries in peacetime. The original expectation that skilled local people could be recruited never was realized. Soldiers who had been properly trained were encouraged to continue working beyond their military tour of duty; they later returned to civilian life with valuable proficiency in such occupations as masonry and carpentry. The total work force varied from about 500, when the soldiers were called back for military duty during the final Napoleonic war, to approximately 4,000 in the peak year.[4]

As many as sixteen sections of the route were sometimes underway simultaneously. The director was apt to turn up unexpectedly anywhere along the route. In physical appearance he was not impressive, rather short and thin, but everyone learned to keep a wary lookout for a man wearing a long gray coat, gray trousers, a black hat, and a white scarf. Seen close up, that eagle nose, determined chin, and protruding lower lip could be vastly intimidating. One writer says that his eyes were blue, another thinks that they were brown, but the two agree that they were fiery.[5] His temper could be volcanic. On at least one occasion, however, the count was on the receiving end. A busily digging soldier, becoming irritated by von Platen and other officials standing around watching, lost *his* temper and shouted up to them, "Behold the ant, you sluggards!"[6]

The money derived from the sale of stock did not begin to cover the costs, and the Riksdag had to come to the financial rescue, amidst anguished lamentations from some of its members. The English connection, particularly, drew broadsides from those not in a position to understand its necessity. Critics charged that the canal authorities did not know enough about either canal building or available Swedish skills. The company leaders were falsely accused of making profits at the expense of the state, while opponents of the regime frequently sniped at von Platen, who, as a member of the governing group, was particularly vulnerable. The embattled director had to defend the Göta Canal through seven Riksdags. In 1815 Mikael Ankarsvärd was complaining that after five to six years of work, only one lock had been completed. When someone taunted him about his German-accented Swedish, he shot back that his family had *earned* its citizenship by three generations of service to the Swedish crown. Gustaf Mauritz Armfelt slashed the deepest wounds: von Platen had all the lubberly graces of a common sailor, he was a selfish, despotic anthropophagus, and he even lacked the competence to get himself hired at an ordinary shipyard! Count von Platen did lack skill in financial matters and money was undoubtedly wasted, but he nevertheless hit the mark when he once retorted that those who complained the most about expenses were motivated by purposes other than saving money. Collisions even occurred between the iron-willed admiral (since 1815) and the hot-tempered Karl XIV Johan. When the angry king on one occasion threatened to withdraw his support, von Platen told him that he should reflect most soberly before plucking out one of the gems from his crown. His Majesty stared at him for a moment, then coldly admonished, "Be careful, be *very* careful, Count von Platen!"[7]

By concentrating the work for a few years, the link between Vänern and

THE SMALL GIANT

Vättern was completed in 1822. Ten years later, after a total of twenty-two years and at a cost of nearly ten million riksdaler, the full stretch was opened to traffic on September 26, 1832. Baltzar von Platen had left the scene before that. Worn out by the long struggle and the heavy criticism, he had been appointed governor-general of Norway in 1827 and died there two years later. The dedication by the king took place before huge crowds at the eastern terminus of the canal and at nearby Söderköping. Two grenadier regimental bands played, the flags flew, the bonfires flamed, and important dignitaries crowded the festive tents. A banquet brought 330 celebrants, some of them uninvited. Rumors had it that seventeen persons had fallen into the canal and that the bass drummer, who had been freely imbibing all day, had drowned.

Trips between Stockholm and Gothenburg took four to five days and seem to have been relaxed affairs. A traveler in 1837 described in lyrical language the changing pastoral scene of meadows, grainfields, woods, farm cottages, manor houses, and churches. Often, at the locks, the passengers would get out and walk, sometimes led by a fiddler playing a merry tune. Women and children met the boat, selling melons, blueberries, strawberries, and cookies. Canal boats tied up at night, and the passengers were entertained by music, dance and other performances.[8]

The Göta Canal, however, did not fulfill the original high expectations. An international transit traffic never materialized on a canal measuring, at its smallest, 7 to 8 meters (about 24 feet) in breadth and 2.82 meters (9 to 10 feet) in depth, and which could not accommodate craft longer than 32 meters (105 feet). Tsar Nicholas I, fearing a renewed British intrusion into the eastern Baltic, forcefully dissuaded the Swedes from allowing their boats on the canal. The abolition of the Öresund tolls in 1857 encouraged domestic shipments by the sea route. Nor did the canal much enliven economic life along its course. Instead, as in other countries, the railroad would preempt the projected functions of the canal, rendering it largely obsolete within a few decades. There has recently been talk of rejuvenating the canal at an estimated cost of 160 to 175 million kronor. About 6,000 small craft use the canal annually and about 50,000 persons travel on it. The now state-owned company maintains a summer schedule of tourist-bearing passenger boats traversing the 380 English miles between the Riddarholm quai in Stockholm and Lilla Bommen in Gothenburg.

That the Swedes would respond to the beginnings of an era of technological change by constructing this monument to waterways was both fitting and natural. That an arduous enterprise almost beyond Swedish means and technical abilities required British assistance was also natural; most of the impulses leading to the economic and technological transformation of Sweden would long flow from England. Though the canal may not have paid for itself in anticipated ways, its unforeseen consequences as an early beachhead for more advanced engineering and mechanical techniques would indeed contribute to a brighter future destiny.

In 1822 Count von Platen was in England buying a dredge from Bryan Donkin & Co. This was a relatively new development, for the first successful steam dredge had been put into use in England in 1804. Samuel Owen, who had just made one, put in a bid at the Göta Canal project, but the director preferred to buy it from the British, having learned to distrust Swedish construction during the early years of canal building. Installations had been needed for the fifty-eight locks and the thirty-five bridges, as well as such other auxiliary equipment as cranes and pumps. The Owen machine shop was too far away and its prices too high. Drawbridges were ordered from the Finspång iron and armaments works near Norrköping; its facilities were small, its deliveries delayed, and its prices swiftly rose, once its management learned the true costs of their manufacture.[9] Attempts to use other nearby iron works miscarried entirely. A few of the bridges and gates for the locks, made of iron, were ordered in England, and many others had to be constructed of wood, necessitating early replacement. Each purchase in England drew snide comments and protests in the Swedish parliament that it violated mercantilist principles. Another solution had to be found.

That steam dredge seemed to require an astounding amount of maintenance. A repair shop had been established at Motala, using money contributed by the Association of Ironmasters (1822). A workshop, a large shed, and a forge containing three hearths appeared, as well as two iron lathes bought during the England trip; all this, on the face of it, to take care of the dredge and to do general repairs on current equipment. Only a few people understood that this was a camouflage for von Platen's real intent, to create a full-fledged engineering works where iron bridges and iron gates for the locks might be conveniently and relatively cheaply produced. He carefully veiled the true nature of the Motala venture from even the directors of the company, already much disturbed by lack of dividends and mounting expenses.

When the dredge had been purchased, Telford had sent along Daniel Fraser to set it up. Like Samuel Owen in similar circumstances, Fraser would remain in Sweden to become one of the pioneering technicians. Born in Scotland in 1787 as the son of a constructor of flour mills, he had worked at Bryan Donkin & Co. for many years before being hired by von Platen. A trained expert in hydraulic engineering machinery, Fraser's arrival gave the long-suffering director the awaited opportunity. Though another repair station elsewhere on the route had been in use for some years, von Platen considered Motala the best location, and he put Fraser in charge of building and operating the workshop. The structures were put up between the new canal and the stream that flowed from the lake at this point. Water power was available from the river, in fact a number of mills and forges were already using it, and more power could be added by sluicing additional water from the higher level of the canal. Iron could easily be shipped across the lake from two small iron works, and wood for fuel came from forests assigned to the company by the original grant. "In this unpretentious fashion was founded Motala, the later well-known *mekaniska verkstad.*"[10]

Soon Baltzar von Platen began to regard the infant workshop as more than an auxiliary for the canal; it became a goal in itself, and under his aegis it started making goods not directly concerned with the canal at all. He visualized Motala as a future *national* workshop, not only essential for the operation of the canal, but contributing to the naval defense of the realm and to the mining industry of Sweden. Motala would in fact help to stimulate more Swedish advances than the Göta Canal, but in the meantime it was sorely expensive. The directors had long since lost hope of any financial returns on their investment, but one faction, in the years after Count von Platen's departure, hoped to eliminate the spiraling costs of Motala by selling it.

Berndt (B. H.) Santesson (1776–1862) adamantly opposed the sale. A Gothenburg merchant and holder of the single largest number of company shares, he had been von Platen's most vigorous supporter throughout the construction period. As a member of the Riksdag most of the time between 1809 and 1835, he spoke for the commercial interests of his city and led the supporters of the canal.[11] Even after the directors decided to sell Motala, over Santesson's strong (and correct) belief that it had finally reached a position to produce profits, no buyer could be found. Santesson himself, highly vulnerable to the charge of a conflict of interests, was forced out of the canal directory in the late 1830s. Finally, in 1840, a new company, organized for the express purpose of buying it and headed by the son of Baltzar von Platen, purchased Motala at a ridiculously low price.

The second largest holder of canal company stock was the Ekman family, also of Gothenburg. In 1800, that crucial year when the then Captain von Platen left the navy, moved to the vicinity of the Trollhätte canal, and began to focus his interests on canal building, he married Hedvig Elisabeth Ekman. This opens up an interesting vista on the pattern of influences within the inner circle of the canal builders and helps to explain, even if it does not justify, some of the rancorous voices in the parliament.

When Motala passed under new ownership, the original twenty-two workers had risen to about two hundred. Among the earliest had been some Russians, former prisoners of war who had refused to return home, and a gang of carpenters from a district in Västergötland, led by "Old-herring-foreman Lars." Fraser, who apparently never bothered to learn much Swedish and who was called "Mäster" by the work force, managed to turn these and others into good machine operators. He had the assistance of a succession of British foremen and engineers, of which at least one, Andrew Malcolm, stayed on to run his own machine shop. The workers, usually hired on a three-year contract, lived in adjoining dwellings and worked a thirteen-hour day, starting at five o'clock in the morning.[12]

Sweden still lacked schools for civilian technical training, though two were started in the 1820s, the Falun School of Mines (1822) and Chalmers' slöjdskola in Gothenburg (1829). The Institute of Technology (Teknologiska Institutet) in Stockholm, founded in 1798, was reorganized and somewhat improved in 1825–26. In addition, the military war college at Marieberg, the most professional, was training some officers as engineers. At Motala, students were admitted for a learning-on-the-job education that stretched over a full five years. They received free room in the company dwelling quarters and were paid (in 1838) 20 riksdaler a month during their first year, more the following.[13] Former Motala workers and students, the "Motaliter," moved on, like so many of Samuel Owen's trainees, to other enterprises, and thereby disseminated the new mechanical skills and techniques to various parts of the country.

Alongside the Göta Canal, like canals everywhere, ran a path, the trälväg or slave trail, where slowly moving draft animals or human beings drew on the towing lines of barges and sailing vessels. The advent of the steamboat would seem neatly timed for the opening of the canal, and Count von Platen early saw the connection. Already in 1822 he was trying to stir up interest in organizing a company to inaugurate steamboat passenger service, but "remarkably enough, this invitation earned little applause in the land."[14] Steamboats evoked little public confidence as yet, quite aside from the suspicion that anything involving the canal would be a likely financial loser. Another ten years elapsed and the canal had to be completed before the passenger steamboat Sleipner appeared, followed a bit later by the Amiral v. Platen. Both were built at the Hammarsten shipyard in Norrköping and equipped with steam engines made at Motala. Craft laden with freight, however, continued to be towed by muscle power.

Churning paddlewheelers made awkward vehicles for the narrow, shallow canal and more graceful conveyance had to wait a few more years for the screw propeller, just then being perfected in England. However, Swedish inland lakes and the comparatively calm waters of the Baltic, like the American rivers, offered the best possible circumstances for the fragile early paddlewheelers, and Owen's first steamboats were being joined by others. Captain Olof Hammarsten, owner of Gamla Varvet (the Old Shipyard) in Norrköping, had a hand in three early ones. The schooner Norrköping, equipped with a steam engine, began making regular trips to Stockholm, and the Carl Johan shuttled between Skåne and the capital city (1820f). The latter, four-masted, had been

25

built to transport cattle to market and, to save room for the quadruped passengers, had only one 22-hp Owen engine. Neither ship made a profit and both were turned into engineless vessels to carry freight. The *Norrköping* sank in the English Channel at the end of 1826 and the *Carl Johan* suffered shipwreck on the island of Guernsey. In 1825 Captain Hammarsten, a colorful figure who sometimes swore back at his more vocal passengers, launched the *Ormen Lange (Long Serpent)*, which thereafter plied the route between Norrköping and Stockholm.[15]

Meanwhile, two paddlewheelers using Owen engines, *Svenska Lejonet (The Swedish Lion)* and *Preussiska Örnen (The Prussian Eagle)*, had been constructed at the Karlskrona naval yards to be used on the mail run between Ystad and Stralsund, the former Swedish seaport on the German Baltic coast. The first Gothenburg steamboat, *Braut Anund,* had its share of adventures. Since Owen had been too busy to make the engine, the owners procured one from Thomas Stawford at Höganäs; it turned out to be a stationary engine not in the least adapted to propelling a ship. Then, equipped with an Owen engine, it had the distinction of being the first steamboat to use the Göta Canal, going as far east as Lake Boren, the end of completed construction in 1826. On another occasion, two of the few existing steamboats managed to collide at midnight off of Essingen outside of Stockholm. One of them was *Braut Anund,* and, adding spice to the excitement, it had on board the members of the peasant estate of the Riksdag, returning from an excursion to Drottningholm.[16]

Stockholm boasted eight steamboats in 1830. Passenger service expanded steadily, to the Åland Islands and to Finland, to Gotland, and in 1837 to Lübeck. Also in 1837 the *Norrland* steamed northward, inaugurating faster connections with the coastal ports along the Gulf of Bothnia.

Not everyone in those towns, where the building of sailing vessels was a major industry, cheered the arrival of the steamboat. The sailors, shipbuilders, and fleet owners might well see it as an evil omen. And, in Sweden as elsewhere, some worried about its effect on human beings: "Let us contemplate a sailing vessel! What resolution in judgment, what speed and strength has been instilled in its crew! On the contrary on a paddling steamer—what wretchedness, one or two half-cooked boiler firemen!" This writer went on to say that Sweden should delay the coming of the steamboat as long as possible because passengers were being freighted like pack goods, the steam engine required neither understanding nor strength, and machines would kill public judgment, energy, and well-being.[17]

Any change from established ways is likely to bring mingled apprehension and exhilaration. Timorous folk chose not to set foot on these infernal vessels with their fiery, smoking engines and clanking machinery. Not for nothing were prayers sometimes formally declaimed, upon embarkation, for a safe arrival.

Accidents could and did happen, not least the danger of fire, as witness the fate of the *Josephine*. The paddlewheel fell off the *Norrköping* on one trip, no doubt accompanied by lurid Hammarsten language. Due to faulty air conduits, the *Rosen*, a Motala boat, announced its presence by a continual, uncontrollable whistling. All steamships retained their sailing gear until the 1850s in case steam engines or machinery broke down; also to save fuel, should a favorable wind arise. Imported coal raised costs, but the less efficient wood reduced cargo by taking up much space on board ship. Cargoes had to be limited, anyway, because paddlewheels did not function well when the weight sank them deeper into the water. Passenger traffic therefore increased much more rapidly than freight transportation, though the development of the screw propeller did solve this particular problem.

For steamboat advocates and builders, each of the early vessels represented a constructive triumph, a sign of progress and a challenge to solve new problems brought on by the innovations. An individual ship, as in the days of sail, had its own characteristics and, seemingly, its own personality for the crew and those that traveled on it. Sometimes their names were deliberately evocative of the adventurous Viking seafaring spirit: *Sleipner, Ormen Långe, Yngve Frey, Braut Anund,* and *Odin*.

At the helm of the *Norrland* on its first voyage to the northern ports was a young man still in his twenties, Captain Otto Edvard Carlsund, who would become Sweden's greatest shipbuilder of the century. The rector of his school had doubted that he would ever amount to anything and advised him to become a manual laborer.[18] He was the youngest child in a large seafaring family in Karlskrona, where most people earned a living, directly or indirectly, from the sea. He would ever afterward despise academic work and diplomas, but he did finish school and then, at the insistence of Anton, an older brother, studied law at Lund University. By 1832, however, he had escaped to Motala to become a student of shipbuilding. At the age of twenty-four, in 1833–34, he captained the whistling *Rosen*, the second ship built at Motala.

Its first one, appropriately named *Motala,* had been ordered in 1827 by the postal service, the second in 1829 by the merchant John Swartz of Norrköping to be used on the Norrköping-Stockholm route. *Motala* carried one 60-hp steam engine, *Rosen* two engines of 30-hp each. Anton Carlsund, who had been trained at the naval shipyard and studied shipbuilding abroad, supervised the construction of both vessels, then a few years later was responsible for the navy's first two steamboats, *Odin* and *Gylfe*. Suddenly, tragedy. Major Anton Carlsund was struck down in the great cholera epidemic of 1834 and died.

Otto Edvard, nine years his junior, stepped into his brother's shoes and carried on the work. A third brother, Clas, had, with Anton, started a shipyard at Kolboda, south of Kalmar. Here O. E. Carlsund directed the building of the *Norrland,* distinguished by direct transmission of power from the steam

27

engine and by machinery only one-half the size of the earlier steamboats, thereby leaving more space for goods.

Altogether he had built or drafted plans for six ships before he went to England at the end of 1839. He found a job at Braithwaite & Co., first as a worker, then as a draftsman, and finally as a constructor. On one ship he worked with James Nasmyth, just then in his most productive years as an inventor of machine tools, including his famous steam hammer.[19] Having learned the most recent developments in English shipbuilding, Carlsund returned to Sweden to take over the one position where he could best use his genius.

Motala had built no more ships after the first two, until the takeover by the new company brought vigor and firm leadership to its management. A new shipyard at Norrköping, giving deep-water access to the Baltic, made possible the construction of larger ships. (In 1856 it purchased the Hammarsten properties.) Two years after Samuel Owen had launched Sweden's first iron-hulled ship, Motala built the second, the *Scandia* (1842). When Daniel Fraser retired in 1843, the younger Count von Platen and Count Adolf Eugène von Rosen, both influential members of the Motala directory, summoned Carlsund to become its technical leader and manager.

John Ericsson, Swedish emigrant, had patented an effective screw propeller in England in 1836. Carlsund returned to Sweden as a propeller enthusiast and quickly built at Motala the propeller-driven *Flygfisken* (*The Flying Fish*), incorporating his innovation of direct transmission of power from the engine (1843). This was followed by *Linköping* and *Jönköping*, both for the Göta Canal traffic. The advent of the *Linköping* in 1846 marked the solution of steamboat navigation problems on Swedish canals. It was captained by a bishop's son who had, among other places, spent some time in the United States, and who bore future Sweden's most formidable family name—Wallenberg.

Both vessels were iron-ribbed. Three partially iron ships were built at the Nyköping engineering works in these same years. It fell to Carlsund to launch Sweden's first all-iron ship in 1859, the *Chapman,* named for Fredric Henric af Chapman, Sweden's greatest shipbuilder of the preceding century. Merely to mention Carlsund's role in specific innovations does not do full justice to him. It has been suggested that his lack of full academic schooling and his contempt for classroom learning may have left him more open to formulating his own creative ideas. He was a master of hydrodynamics, creating vessels driven by steam that moved gracefully with minimum water resistance. Some were models of elegant beauty, perhaps helping to reconcile some devotees of the sailing vessel to the success of the steamship. In his years at Motala he was responsible for 270 steamships, and he tried to make no two alike. Under his strict, sometimes brusque, guidance, Motala also continued to set the pace in other areas than shipbuilding as Sweden's foremost engineering works. *Gubben* ("the Old Man"), as he was affectionately if apprehensively known by his workers, would remain active long enough to launch the world's first ship to be driven by a (primitive) steam turbine.[20]

In 1850 the Swedes owned the largest number of steamboats in continental Europe, being surpassed only by the British and Americans. Fifty-four were in use in 1840 and sixty-seven in 1850. Once the steam engine had been perfected, favorable geographical circumstances encouraged, virtually drove, the Swedes to its use in inland and coastal transportation. Adapting the steamboat to their own needs, the Swedes had brought themselves, within the limitations of their own situation, abreast of recent industrial and technological developments in maritime navigation.

Two very bright boys, sons of a construction foreman on the Göta Canal, attracted the attention of Count Baltzar von Platen during his tours of inspection. Even as a small boy in Värmland, where his father was then an inspector of mines, John, the younger brother, had shunned childhood play in order to make drawings and models of mining and sawmill equipment. At the canal John and Nils Ericsson were constantly exposed to technical talk and to the "new world of mechanical interest" by the British and Swedish engineers who boarded in their home.[21] At the age of thirteen John became an assistant leveler on the project. Von Platen arranged for the brothers to be enrolled as cadets in the navy's mechanical corps, where they would be educated as engineers.

John Ericsson, however, tired of the steady routine. He went to the count, accompanied by Nils, to tell the great man that he was leaving. Von Platen felt betrayed, as he usually did when someone after being carefully trained abandoned his precious Göta Canal. The countess, working in the next room and overhearing the conversation, knew her man, knew that the volcano was about to erupt, and hurriedly pushed over her sewing table. Von Platen stopped in mid-sentence and rushed to her rescue. Thus interrupted, the canal director never did resume his tirade, and the young men, except for a parting shot that John could go the devil, escaped unscathed.[22]

John enrolled in the Jämtland Field Chausseurs, and Nils stayed at the canal. Military life in turn began to pall on the young lieutenant after he invented his first version of a hot air engine, an idea that would be a goad and a frustration for him for much of his life. Why not use hot air as the motive power in the cylinder instead of steam, with its constant danger of explosion? The Swedes had scarcely learned how to make a steam engine properly when John began trying to perfect a successor. In 1826, he borrowed a thousand riksdaler and went to England, taking the hot air engine with him.

It had worked fine in Sweden, with charcoal, but, using coal in England, the high heat melted the parts. Ericsson had bumped up against a common limiting factor in the process of making practical inventions: that they are often dependent upon advances in more than one line of development, in this case heat-resistant metals.[23] He would return to his hot air or so-called caloric engine time and again, including trying to use it on a ship, the *Ericsson* (1852), but he finally had to settle for a somewhat successful small caloric engine capable of running printing presses, sewing machines, small boats, and pumps.

During his thirteen years in England he patented thirty inventions; by 1863 he would claim an even hundred.[24] In 1828–29 he and John Braithwaite, owner of an engineering works at New Road in London, brought out a steam fire engine, replacing the hand-operated ones, and capable of shooting jets of water to the top of high buildings. This was the first modern fire engine, and it proved its value at several big fires in London. However, the rowdy fire brigades, their jobs threatened, defended their prerogatives so roughly that Braithwaite stopped making the new engines.

In October 1829 George Stephenson demonstrated his mastery of the steam locomotive by driving *The Rocket* to victory in the famous Rainhill Trials. History usually disregards the "also-rans," one of whom at Rainhill was John Ericsson. John designed and Braithwaite built *The Novelty,* incorporating the fire engine steam boiler, in seven weeks. Ericsson's copper and blue locomotive went the fastest, a mile in less than two minutes, and, according to some, was the more technically advanced of the two, but mechanical defects, caused by hasty construction, prevented *The Novelty* from completing the course on any of its three runs. Stephenson said that it lacked "guts," that is, was not powerful enough to fulfill the functions of a locomotive. Two later Braithwaite locomotives were equally deficient.[25]

Instead of winning fame and fortune in England, John Ericsson went to debtor's prison in the spring of 1832 for not being able to pay the large debts incurred on his inventions. Still in prison the following Christmas, he was visited that day by brother Nils, who was on a business trip to England. John's newly developed steam engine was at Maudslay's being tested; if successful, he would obviously get out of prison, and John's nerves were badly frayed. Nils himself came away with the feeling that his opportune arrival may have saved his brother's life. The two brothers never met again.

John also lost out on the screw propeller in England to (Sir) Francis Pettit Smith, British inventor who patented one in 1836, the same year as Ericsson. The next summer the Swede proved the efficacy of his propeller by towing the lordships of the Admiralty on the Admiralty Barge with a propeller-driven tugboat; the lords, as usual balking at anything novel, refused to believe the evidence of their own eyes. The British would largely use Smith's version, while the Americans and the French often used Ericsson's. By 1843 there were forty-one steamers equipped with Ericsson's types. At the Göta Canal, his invention helped to fulfill his "betrayed" mentor's early vision.

The *Robert F. Stockton* was launched in July 1838, ordered by an American naval officer of that name. The small iron vessel, built by Messrs. John and MacGregor Laird, was equipped with Ericsson's patented spiral propeller. Destined for canal duty in New Jersey, it was taken by a five-man crew, by sail, across the Atlantic. On November 1, 1839, Ericsson followed the *Stockton*, traveling on Brunel's famous steamer *Great Western*, to settle permanently in New York City as an American citizen.[26] He left his British affairs in the care of Count Adolf Eugène von Rosen, who had often helped him during these bitter years.

He had emigrated from a Sweden not yet ready for his inventive genius. Nor did this flawed genius find any easy success for his technological innovations in England or the United States. He was incessantly buffeted about by those who opposed techniques that violated established wisdom and threatened current vested interests. He was equally imposed upon by those who sought personal advantages or glory from his inventions, or who misused them. The prototype of a compulsive inventor, a demonic spirit, he left himself open to many of his problems by financial improvidence, an unworldly failure to reckon with the ways of the world, and his fuming, embittered reaction to the bureaucrats. He followed too many interesting problems, unable to resist "a myriad of sidepaths" that beckoned. Undeniably he had, in the words of Ruth White, an "unhappy attraction for sudden, unforeseeable disaster."[27] An inspired, dedicated apostle of technological change, he did not inspire confidence among those who considered him "a rash and impractical visionary," but, in his own words, he lacked patience with those who could only "see things as they are, and not as they ought to be."[28]

The Swedes would continue to hear, with mingled pride and alarm, about the adventures in the United States of this knight errant of technology. And Nils, the brother who stayed home? More prosaic, more proper, more responsible, he would spend a lifetime—in the shadow of an illustrious brother who built engines, ships, and locomotives—working with canals and harbor installations; then, near the end of his career, he would receive an assignment comparable in scope and significance to that of his early mentor, Count Baltzar von Platen.

3. MERCHANTS AND MONEY

Gothenburg (Göteborg) was founded in the early seventeenth century as Sweden's gateway to the West, and to this day there is a striking contrast in outlook between Sweden's second largest city and Stockholm; Gothenburg is more open to influence from the North Sea and Atlantic, whereas Stockholm much more reflects a Baltic viewpoint. The Dutch, being good traders, fellow Protestants and sometimes allies, were encouraged to participate in its founding; Pieter von Egmont, Rolof Jansson van Schotingen, and Jakob Huefnagl sat alongside Torsson, Svensson, and Andersson on the 1621–22 council of magistrates.[1] Gothenburg long retained its original Dutch imprint.

Royal policy gave the infant town an oceanic role from the beginning. It served as the home port for ships of the Southern Company (*Söderkompaniet*), a Dutch-led enterprise chartered to trade in "Asiam, Africam, Americam and Magellanicum." When New Sweden (Delaware) was colonized in 1638 the company received the Swedish tobacco monopoly in return for the use of some of its ships in the transatlantic traffic. During the brief existence of the American settlement (1638–1655), Gothenburg had fairly regular contacts with the New World, and place names in the colony—Nya Göteborg, Älfsborg, and Mölndal—reflected the Gothenburg influence. The city's formal participation in the founding decades of the North Atlantic community did not last long, however, for Sweden's attention continued to be focused on the Baltic regions, to the neglect of other ventures.

In the eighteenth century Gothenburg became the home port and, until the last decades, the headquarters for the Swedish East India Company, founded in 1731. Gothenburg and Stockholm merchants were heavily involved, and the family names of some company directors and supercargoes will reappear repeatedly in these pages: Alströmer, Arfwedson, Chalmers, Grill, Santesson, Tham, Tranchell. Its real founder, however, had been Colin Campbell (1687–1757), a Scottish participant in the Ostend Company, an attempt, under the aegis of the Holy Roman Emperor, to break the monopoly of the British and Dutch East India companies in Far Eastern trade. When British-Dutch pressure forced the emperor to suspend its activities, some of its merchants sought alternatives at Altona in Germany and in Denmark. Campbell found his opportunity in Sweden.

He may have been drawn to Sweden by conversations with Niklas Sahlgren of Gothenburg, who happened to be visiting Holland and Flanders, in which the two men discovered mutual advantages in the formation of a Swedish trading company. Campbell went to Stockholm and, keeping a low profile himself, found a good front man in Henrik König, who had already, with some partners, secured reluctant permission to send two ships to the Indies. The government was even more dubious about the proposed company, in view of the fate of the Ostend venture, but, with the help of an enthusiastic Riksdag, the Swedish East India Company received its charter on June 11, 1731. Endowed with the title of minister plenipotentiary, Campbell, who had been there before, made three highly profitable trips to Canton in the 1730s. On his first voyage, the *Fredericus Rex*, the company ship, was stopped and taken into Batavia by the Dutch, but the diplomatic cover persuaded them to release the vessel.[2] The Swedish flag joined that of other European nations in the foreign colony at Canton, flying over a "factory" run by a resident supercargo. In Gothenburg, Niklas Sahlgren managed the preparations for each voyage and the marketing of the imported wares by auction.

The company prospered until the last two decades of the century. During the time of the first charter (1731–48), the *Fredericus Rex* made five of the twenty-five voyages. Over forty different ships served the company at one time or another between 1732 and 1809. A few went to India, most of them to Canton. For a time the leadership fell to Dublin-born Robert Finlay (1719–1785), an iron exporter who had married into the wealthy Plomgren family in Stockholm. Chinese imports, as elsewhere in Europe, strongly influenced Swedish culture, and wealthy families would later continue to cherish porcelain, lacquered boxes, and other heirlooms from the China trade. When, for example, Anders Arfwedson came home on the *Cron Prins Gustaf* in 1769 he brought back as his personal acquisitions coffee and tea service sets, vases, punch bowls, mother-of-pearl inlaid boxes, and silk and cotton cloth.[3]

Among those who traveled to China on a company ship was Stockholm-born (Sir) William Chambers, future architect of Somerset House and builder of the China pagoda at Kew Gardens; his father, then a Gothenburg trader, was also trying to collect full repayment on debts owed him by the Swedish government. William went out in 1748 on *Hoppet (The Hope)* and remained for a time as a supercargo at the Swedish factory.[4] Another man, Jacob Wallenberg, went out as a chaplain on the *Finland* and wrote a widely read account of his journey. A century later his brother's grandson and leading Swedish banker, A. O. Wallenberg (one-time captain of the *Linköping*), could be seen going through a daily ritual. After breakfast he would unlock a little casket, take out a teacup and saucer brought from China by Jacob, have a cup of tea, carefully wash the heirloom, and replace it in the casket.[5]

Outward-bound company ships usually carried iron goods for sale at Cadiz and other ports; the Spanish piasters, acceptable as currency by the Chinese, were used to buy tea, porcelain, silk, and other wares, but especially tea, which usually amounted to about half the cargo. Foreign merchants would purchase at least 90 percent of the tea, normally of the cheap Bohea kind, at the Gothenburg company auctions for re-export to continental ports. Here it would be passed on to smugglers, experts in illicit entry into Britain and its steadily increasing demand for the popular beverage. The combination of British East India Company monopoly and extremely high import duties created an irresistible temptation for smugglers and a lucrative sales outlet for the Swedish company and the counterpart Danish East Asiatic Company (chartered in 1732), as well as for Dutch and French opportunists.[6]

Finally, at long last, the younger William Pitt overcame governmental stupidity or inertia and lowered the imposts on tea drastically, thereby cutting the ground out from under the smugglers (1784). The fortunes of the well-organized and smoothly run Swedish company thereafter deteriorated, made worse by the frequent seizure of its ships during the wars after 1792. The Swedish East India Company went into bankruptcy in 1809, although it lingered on in name until 1813.

Niklas Sahlgren (1701–1776) made a good thing for himself out of the East India Company. Son of a Gothenburg businessman, he and a brother had founded the city's first sugar refinery in 1729. Out of these activities and a substantial export of iron, he built up, in terms of the day, a "colossal fortune." Totally devoted to business, he avoided public affairs but made up for it by donating money for the building of the Sahlgrenska Hospital. It bears his name to this day.[7]

The two daughters of Niklas Sahlgren married the sons of Jonas Alströmer (1685–1761), whose ambitious projects excited much contemporary attention. He had gone to England in 1707 and, after working as a bookkeeper, started a successful business firm. Convinced by sizable Swedish purchases of British cloth that a market for it existed at home, he returned to establish a textile manufactory at Alingsås, northeast of Gothenburg. He used smuggled Dutch looms, English methods and some English workers, and, more important, his venture happened to coincide with the mercantilist policies of the governing political party, the so-called Hats. By claiming that Alingsås served as a model and a school for additional manufactories, he obtained prolonged state subsidies, beginning in 1726–27. Alströmer kept his subsidies until the Hats lost power in 1765–66, but his high prices, mediocre quality of products, and overly ambitious expansion kept Alingsås from becoming a financial success. A disastrous fire in 1779 terminated the venture. Once considered a precursor of industrialization in Sweden, Alströmer and his manufactories have long since been demoted from that exalted position. Alströmer's enduring monument may be that omnipresent Swedish dinner staple, the humble potato; he was not the first in the country to grow it, but he seems to have introduced it as an article of food (1724).[8] It took the hunger years of crop failure in 1771–73 to convince the peasants of its virtues, and the discovery that it could be transformed into inebriating hard liquor (*brännvin*) to speed its proliferation.

William Chalmers (1748–1811) also left an enduring monument, a technical school that bears his name and that celebrated its sesquicentennial in 1979. His father had arrived in Gothenburg as the agent for a British company, then had set up his own business in iron and timber. The son went out to China as supercargo in 1783 and, including a stay in Calcutta, did not return until 1793. During the following years he and Peter Bagge, who had acquired much of his money in shipping and in the sale of smoked fish, led the successful drive to complete the Trollhätte Canal. Bagge's proposal that construction be completed by a canal company was accepted by the government and later served as a model for the Göta Canal Company. Chalmers, in charge of the campaign to gather enough subscriptions for the canal company to cover the costs, was particularly anxious to enlist financial support in the Vänern ports and in Värmland to counter the accusation that the canal would benefit only the Gothenburg merchants.[9]

Chalmers fought a losing battle to keep the East India Company afloat, and he followed it into bankruptcy. His house burned down in 1802, in one of the city's five devastating fires between 1792 and 1804, and he replaced it with an ostentatious mansion, which must have contributed to his financial troubles. At his death in 1811, his fortune was willed to the establishment of an industrial school for poor children, the future Chalmers technical school, but, because of the bankruptcy, the will remained in litigation into the 1820s. Berzelius, viewing this munificence through the eyes of a contemporary, once facetiously remarked that since Chalmers had been unable to drink up all of his huge fortune, he willed some of the remainder for a school.

A lively mercantile scene would not in itself ensure the adoption of modern machinery and the factory system, but its absence would certainly prevent their introduction except as they were sponsored by the state. The existence of an active group of merchants and their vigorous entrepreneurial spirit was a requisite for the later developments. Some were strictly merchants, others combined trade with investments in manufacturing establishments; Sahlgren had his sugar refinery, and Chalmers invested in a mechanical cotton spinning mill at Lerum (1797). The Gothenburg mercantile group consisted of a healthy blend of Swedes and foreigners, the latter mostly but not exclusively British, who were drawn to the city by the large Swedish export of iron to British iron works, by the sale of forest products, and by the Swedish market for sugar, tobacco, and cotton. And, at times, by opportunities for smuggling. The British brought in their own business methods and a disposition to introduce, for their own profit, new technology that would stimulate commerce and industrial development in the city and its environs during the following half-century.

The Hall family attained fabulous wealth as exporters to England of iron and timber. John Hall, a member of the sizable contingent from the town of Hull in Gothenburg's British colony, established, with John Wilson, the merchant firm of Wilson & Hall (1758). A nephew of the same name worked for Sahlgren and Alströmer, then founded John Hall & Co., which in time eclipsed the Sahlgren commercial ventures. He bought several iron works and sawmills in Värmland and Dalsland and ultimately controlled nearly one-half of the city's iron exports and over half of the foreign trade in wood products. This second John Hall (1735–1802) owned the finest house in town and a princely estate, Gunnebo, but the taciturn man took little part in the city's social life.[10]

King Gustav III once asked to borrow a hundred thousand riksdaler from him; trapped, Hall gave it to him, and probably with some very British thoughts about enforced benevolences, instructed his bookkeeper, within hearing of the king, to enter it in the losses column of the financial ledgers. He was unintentionally cremated when the church in which his coffin was resting burned down in the 1802 fire. Misfortune assailed his son and successor, a third John, from the beginning. Skägg-Hallen ("the Bearded Hall"), as the Swedes called him, had no business qualifications whatsoever and seems to have been mentally handicapped. Though left such a fortune that his father believed him secure for life, Skägg-Hallen went bankrupt after five years and in time became a forlorn, disreputable figure wandering the streets of the city. In 1830 he was found in one of northern Stockholm's worst dives, frozen to death.[11]

The Carnegie family rose on the ruin of the Halls. George Carnegie had fought at the Battle of Culloden on the side of Bonnie Prince Charlie (1746), and thereafter necessarily absented himself from Scotland. His father, the Earl of Southesk, had also suffered for the Stuarts, having lost his title for participating in the 1715 rebellion against the Hanoverians. One story has George fleeing out to sea in a small boat and being picked up by a ship that happened to be sailing to Gothenburg. A more likely one asserts that he went to London disguised as someone's servant and there took ship to Gothenburg. "Here he hung up his knightly sword in the business office he established," and for the next twenty years exported bar iron and timber while importing grain, coal, and other goods.[12]

Leaving the firm in the competent hands of Thomas Erskine, George returned to Scotland in 1769. The enterprise was ultimately inherited by George's son, David, born near Montrose in Scotland. David was dispatched to Gothenburg at the age of fourteen to be trained by Erskine, by now British consul and later to become the ninth Earl of Kellie. When David took over the firm (with a partner, Jan Lambert), it became known as D. Carnegie & Co. (1803), a name that would figure prominently in Swedish economic life during the following decades. David Carnegie (1772–1837) also engaged to carry on the foreign business affairs for Skägg-Hallen. When the bankruptcy occurred, Carnegie was one of the men appointed to straighten out the affairs of the company, and at the auctions he and others bought up the Hall properties at shamefully low figures. Hall sued Carnegie, accusing him of an unpaid loan of a thousand pounds sterling and of having sold Hall company iron abroad on his own behalf. Hall's lawyer accused him of theft, deceit, and false bookkeeping, so complex a case that court proceedings dragged on from 1809 until 1828.[13] Whatever the truth in all this, Carnegie had undoubtedly been in a key position to take over the property and business of the doomed Hall firm.

In Scotland the eldest line of the Carnegies regained its noble title in the reign of Queen Victoria. The Earl of Southesk and Andrew Carnegie, the great American industrialist, called each other "cousin," but it was only in fun. Andrew's immediate ancestors had been lowly weavers. No blood relationship can be proven, though both families did trace their origins to the same small village.[14]

Anyone from the British Isles was English to the Swedes, and England was synonymous with the United Kingdom, though Campbell, Chalmers, Erskine, and Carnegie all hailed from Scotland, as did several others not yet mentioned. Gothenburg had a Scottish trading colony in the seventeenth century, and names like Hamilton, Douglas, Sinclair, and Ramsay testify to the presence of Scots in the Swedish army and nobility in the 1600s.[15] Scottish ties now became important to Swedish industrial and technological development. James Watt and Thomas Telford were, after all, from Scotland. The Carron Ironworks, mentioned earlier, was located in Scotland and so was the New Lanark cotton spinning mill. Steamboats were in use on the Firth of Clyde and along the west coast by 1812. The Scots arriving in Gothenburg and other cities came out of a community that by 1780 was undergoing industrial transformation, and they would automatically transmit the attitudes and behavior characteristics of the new era.

In a sense, some of the contemporary Swedish entrepreneurs in Gothenburg were also migrants. They or their parents had come from towns like Marstrand, Uddevalla or Vänersborg, drawn, like the British, by the location and opportunities of the young city. Santesson's family, however, had originated in the province of Småland. Berndt Santesson, champion of the Göta Canal, had inherited his father's fleet of ships and his herring fisheries; alive until 1862, he became the last living ex-director of the defunct East India Company. Peter Bagge (1743–1819), Trollhätte Canal company director, stemmed from several generations of Marstrand traders; he managed thriving fisheries, an important Gothenburg industry in the eighteenth century, and established a shipyard. A son who served Count von Platen as an engineer in the early stages of the canal building drew "much and pungent" criticism.[16] Herring (*sill*) also contributed to the rise of the Ekman family, which would overflow with talent for several generations in various fields of endeavor. Descended from a line of royal bailiffs and counselors, the founder of the Gothenburg family exported wood and imported grain. His son of the same first name, Peter (1740–1807), in addition to importing grain ran a dozen locales for the salting of herring. In the third generation, Gustaf Henrik (brother-in-law of Count von Platen) in turn founded Ekman & Co. in 1802, which would grow into the largest exporter of iron in Sweden for a time under *his* son, Janne. For the Ekmans, who had also bought the Lesjöfors iron works in 1813, the long crisis in the Swedish iron industry would be a matter of financial life or death, and Janne's brother, Gustaf, would become the famed hero of the ultimate triumph.

Jonas Kjellberg (1752–1832), an orphan educated by the Herrnhuters, secured a job with Berndt Santesson's father, then started his own business. He prospered during the Napoleonic period from an import trade and probably also handled transit goods. Combining good business sense with a deep religious mysticism, Kjellberg became one of the legendary figures in Gothenburg history and founded a long-enduring patrician family. His nephew, Jonas Anders, served as an agent in iron and wood exports, then later bought Lo and Kramfors sawmills. He and his son, Carl Ossian, would both be deeply involved in the beginnings of industrialization. So would Carl Fredrik Waern (1787–1858), whose Norwegian father of Danish descent had acquired the Billingsfors iron works in the province of Dalsland. The son founded a company in 1813 and survived the postwar period to become a successful export agent for a number of iron works. In 1823 he purchased Bäckefors, another iron works, where he, too, would play a role in solving the crucial problems of the Swedish iron industry. Later, he and his son would support the building of railroads and advocate liberal reforms in the Riksdag.

An English visitor, just off his ship at the anchorage (the inner harbor was too shallow for anything bigger than canal or coastal vessels), walked into Gothenburg one day in 1808. He found "a long, badly maintained road, neither pleasant for the feet, which wandered in deep dirt, nor for the eyes. . . ." Once in town, he did not enjoy the hotel either. Perhaps he did not make allowances for the fires that had ravaged the community. Two years later, Richard S. Smith, newly arrived American consul, did like the city, population of about 15,000, or 20,000 if the nearby suburbs were counted. The narrow streets without sidewalks were full of lively, loud, prosperous-looking people shouldering their way helter-skelter among the wagons, carts and carriages. Unlike the Englishman, he met many English-speaking individuals, among them a number of American sea captains. Gothenburg was in its halcyon years when British and neutral traders evaded the French Continental System by using the city and some southern Swedish ports to sneak their goods into French-dominated territory across the Baltic.[17]

Nearly two million kilograms of coffee were unloaded in 1810, and not even the coffee-addicted Swedes were ready, yet, to consume such quantities. Sugar imports sextupled between 1807 and 1810. Foreign sea captains suddenly became Swedish citizens with a minimum of formality, and foreign ships sprouted Swedish flags. All the coffee, sugar, tobacco, and cotton had, so it seemed, come from neutral America, not Great Britain. Privateers came sailing in to auction their booty. Suddenly wealthy, the city rose from its ashes, in the words of Carl Tiselius, "like a new Phoenix," and the citizens who could afford it, remembering the fires, now built in stone.[18]

Sweden made peace with France in 1810, the price being a formal and unfought state of war with Great Britain. The harbor emptied while nearby smugglers took over, then in the middle of 1812 Sweden joined the coalition against Napoleon. Imports of colonial wares hit new records in 1813, not even counting the widespread smuggling. By 1816, with the war over, Gothenburg sea traffic was back to prewar levels. Some merchants, lucky or farsighted, made and then kept their fortunes, while others were ruined. The end of the war found overstocked warehouses and brought collapse to temporarily prosperous firms.

Most of the speculators and opportunists decamped. Among those who stayed were the Dickson brothers. They hailed from "quiet Montrose," birthplace of David Carnegie, and which had earlier sent a number of migrants (Fyfes, Guthries, and others) to Sweden in the 1600s.[19] Robert and James Dickson arrived in time to do extremely well in the transit trade; Robert, however, was caught by the end of the blockade and suffered financial disaster. James survived to found James Dickson & Co. in 1816, later joined by his brother. They exported timber, imported cotton from England and the United States, and made such profits from the increasing demand for cotton that James could buy sawmills and large forest tracts in Värmland. The Dicksons were on their way to much wealth—and much future notoriety—in the lumber business.[20] The brothers are described as quiet, reserved men totally devoted to business and to the accumulation of money, which, however, they later freely disbursed as generous philanthropists. In other words, they were Scots.

Quiet Montrose also contributed the Kennedys. The father arrived at the turn of the century, and over the years the family acquired its money from tobacco imports and from fire insurance, which sold well in Gothenburg. Thomas (1818–1892) had a "harem," and when the pastor remonstrated that he ought to get married, he responded, "Very willingly, but which one of them, in the devil, should I take!" In old age he constantly complained about his heavy business losses, and at his death the impoverished Scot's estate only amounted to 1,343,015 kronor. And 68 öre (pennies). Illustrative of Gothenburg's wide horizons, he could claim one Kennedy relative (Thomas Francis K.) as a noted Whig member of the House of Commons and another one (John Pendleton K.) as a twenty-year member of the U.S. Congress and Secretary of the Navy.[21]

Mendel Elias Delbanco (1780–1862) was one of the Jewish contingent who stayed. Jews, nearly all from Germany, had started arriving in Sweden after King Gustav III lifted the bars against them (1782). Small Jewish communities soon existed in the larger towns, where they were permitted to settle; the synagogue in Gothenburg numbered 215 persons by 1815.[22] Delbanco, with a member of the Leman family, established a branch agency for the Michael Leman merchant house of Hamburg, which also had outlets in London and Amsterdam (1809). The Gothenburg agency closed in 1815, but Delbanco, after two brief sojourns in London, bought part of an oil works (oljeslageri) in Mölndal. The enterprise, which usually dominated the industry in Sweden, remained in the family until 1929.

Three men remain to be mentioned, a family triumvirate that helped to move Gothenburg toward industrialization. William Gibson of Arbroath in Scotland arrived at the age of fourteen to work for James Christie, an exporter of iron. Having accumulated a little capital, he opened a shop for the preparation of vinegar, then later founded a rope mill, a weaving mill, and a foundry. In the 1830s some of the enterprises were assembled in one place at Jonsered outside of Gothenburg, where a sail and rope factory had been started by Alexander Keiller (1804–1874). This man, member of an important Dundee merchant family having trade connections with Sweden, came to Gothenburg in 1826 and would become one of Sweden's leading industrialists, instrumental in introducing elements of industrialization and founding the ultimately giant enterprise later known as Götaverken.

It was Keiller who saw the possibilities in using the rapids at Jonsered for water power and who bought the site. The two were brothers-in-law, both having married sisters of the wealthy Swedish merchant, Olof Wijk. The two did not get along together very well, however, and in 1839 they parted company, Gibson retaining Jonsered while Keiller founded Gothenburg's first enduring engineering works (1841). Located on the Göta Älv and later moved across the river to Hisingen, Keiller's mekaniska verkstad grew into the third largest in Sweden, after Motala and Bergsund. Here he installed the first steam-driven hammer forge in the country and an iron plate works. Its ideal location at the harbor, with the growing sea traffic, offered opportunities in maritime supplies and ship repair, as well as in the construction of new ships for use on the canals, inland lakes, and coastal traffic. A variety of manufactured goods would later flow from Keillers: machinery for paper mills, pumps, cranes, hydraulic presses, bridges, washing machines, and farm implements.

Far-sighted, iron-willed, restless, always hatching more plans, Keiller finally overextended his commitments by buying too many mines and iron works, and suffered bankruptcy in 1867. A hard man with his workers, he also reputedly did not have the heart to fire anyone. When his Irish was up (an Irish ancestor had migrated to Scotland), he could be a handy man with his fists. If excited or exasperated, he would shout "Tusan Fan!" ("thousand devils," the more evocative word being pronounced "*fah-uhn!*" in this then-common Swedish expletive). This man with the Scottish-accented Swedish, a model of the old-time patriarchal factory owner, also trained a generation of novices in the running of machinery and the discipline of the factory system.

Son of a ship captain, Olof Wijk (1786–1856) was sent to sea by his father at the age of twelve, but, not having inherited any taste for a sailor's life, Olof soon went back to solid ground to take a job as an errand boy. Then he secured a job at Christie's, working alongside Gibson. When Christie died in 1806, Wijk, at the age of twenty, continued to run the business with competence and finally became its owner. In the depressed years after 1815 he was in a position to pick up much property cheaply. He exported iron and timber products, imported colonial wares, ran a fleet of merchant ships, and financially supported his brothers-in-law. Wijk was influential in bringing about the dredging of the inner harbor in the 1830s to permit seagoing vessels (including his own) to come all the way into the harbor.

As a young errand boy, Olof, in his spare time and on his own initiative, gathered bent nails, straightened them, and sold them, producing his earliest capitol. Or so went a later legend, accompanied by a popular Gothenburg verse that, in one of several variations, ran as follows: "*Olof Wijk, räta spik, så han blef rik.*" ("Olof Wijk, straightened nails, so he became rich.") Undoubtedly originating because as a merchant he later sold nails, the myth did, as myths about well-known figures usually do, reflect public opinion of him. A hard taskmaster for his employees and well known for paying low wages, this Swedish Scrooge also sat on the city council and ultimately served as a hardline conservative in the Riksdag. A trip to the United States exposed him to American temperance societies, and he returned to demand that some of the Gothenburg saloons be closed. Wijk's "certain combination of brusqueness, arrogance and ambitions" may have been abrasive, but, as a noted town character, he was generally popular. He married the most beautiful girl in town; his son of the same name, who later guided the firm with skillful hand, married the richest heiress, Caroline Dickson.[23]

Within this interrelated, tightly knit upper bourgeoisie class, the typical early nineteenth-century merchant code prevailed. In the days of poor banking facilities and communications, the personal element tended to be decisive. The merchants knew each other intimately, sent their sons to be trained in their friends' firms, and were well enough acquainted with the younger staff of other businesses to know whether to extend credit when one of them started his own enterprise. Money on credit was the life blood of commerce in the city as well as in the international network of friends, acquaintances, and clients extending to London, Hamburg, Amsterdam, and sometimes to the United States. Their word had to be their bond. It was generally understood, says Ernst Söderlund, that one "never leaves either his debtor or his creditor in the lurch" if it could be avoided.[24]

Bayard Taylor in the 1850s found Gothenburg "more energetic and wide-awake than Stockholm," having more wealth, proportionately, as well as more public spirit.[25] The people of Gothenburg liked to refer to their city as "Little London." The seaport, to reiterate, was peculiarly open to influences from the West and the sources of industrialization, while simultaneously its merchants increasingly looked up the Trollhätte Canal and across Vänern to the iron works and sawmills of Värmland and adjoining provinces. Through their imports of cotton and other colonial wares and their export of iron and timber products, for so long the staple commodities of Swedish foreign trade, they possessed ample contacts abroad for borrowing both money and technology from more industrially advanced countries. The city also imported liberal political views, its so-called *Rabulism* expressed in terms of abolition of guilds, lower tariffs, and a more democratic parliamentary system. Gothenburg in the 1840s, and 1850s reportedly had more than forty millionaires. Capital was being accumulated and the merchants were reinvesting a considerable portion of their profits from export-import trade. An aggressive pattern of entrepreneurial initiative was very much evident, a spirit, to use Lennart Jörberg's phrase, of "rational economic thinking."[26]

This profile of development in Gothenburg does not imply that the city was the sole beachhead for the spread of new ideas and techniques. Far from it. It only illustrates in some detail that Sweden, with a foreign admixture, possessed a class of businessmen quite capable of founding and developing industrial enterprises whenever opportunities presented themselves. That this was not limited to Gothenburg will become fully evident in the following chapters.

In Stockholm reigned the so-called Skeppsbroadel, a group of some twenty rich merchant families living in the Skeppsbro harbor area of the city, constituting an aristocracy (*adel*) of the bourgeois merchants, deriving its wealth from commerce, shipping and finance. The Skeppsbroadel of Stockholm, the merchants of Gothenburg, and the ironmasters, financially interrelated groups, had, by the end of the eighteenth century, replaced the older landed aristocracy as the most influential in the kingdom. The iron and timber country had, before the increasing Gothenburg challenge, been largely the preserve of the Stockholm merchant houses, which served as intermediaries for the export of iron and timber products. In the absence of better banking facilities, the mercantile establishments also usually performed some of these functions. As the only major source, except for the state itself, of sizable amounts of credit, they extended loans to enterprises and in return controlled the sale of the borrowers' goods.

The ironmasters had much of their capital tied up; transport was expensive before railroads, and the iron was likely to lie unused for many months before being cast in the hearths and again before going to the forges. Hence, they were often in need of credit from the merchants, who extended it as a service, making no profit on the loans but reimbursing themselves on the export sales. They also gained financially by selling colonial wares to the iron works communities and their surrounding countryside; the Stockholm merchants customarily imported coffee, tobacco, and other items through Hamburg, and much of their foreign credit was tied in with that city. When needed, however, the merchants could usually get money from banks in London or Amsterdam. They built up their own businesses on foreign loans only to a small extent in the 1800s, but they made a vital contribution in securing foreign credits on coming deliveries for the iron works.[27]

Sawmill owners, too, needed the merchants for their export sales, and they also required periodic credit. The small sawmills in Värmland, Dalsland, and northern Norrland were especially dependent upon them, while the larger ones in time began to acquire their own agents abroad. Textile mills also had much of their capital tied up in the form of imported raw cotton. The merchants often became owners of iron works themselves, were active in starting sawmills, and gave assistance to technicians founding small machine shops. Kurt Samuelsson called the Stockholm and Gothenburg merchant houses "the one main dynamic factor" in the Swedish economy in the eighteenth and early nineteenth centuries.[28]

Probably the single most important merchant house in the capital city at the turn of the century was Tottie and Arfwedson, which was serving as agent for no less than forty-five iron works. The Totties, from Scotland (1688) but of Lancashire origin, started with a tobacco workshop in Stockholm, branched out to the making of snuff, playing cards, and stockings and jerseys, and from these moved on to shipping, export of iron, tar and wood, and the financing of iron works.[29] The Arfwedsons were originally involved in Baltic and North Sea fishing, then began an import-export trade with their own ships. They acquired an arms factory at Norrtälje and the Schebo iron works, the latter to be the scene of experiments during the iron crisis. Carl Christopher Arfwedson and Anders Tottie, cousins, joined forces in 1771 to found the larger merchant house of Tottie and Arfwedson. The Totties, however, moved to London in 1804, where Carl Tottie would be the central figure among its Swedish residents as Swedish consul-general for over fifty years.

Carl Christopher (1735–1826) and his son Carl Abraham Arfwedson

(1774–1861) were prominent, as merchants and financiers, in Swedish economic life for about a century. They also figured in several footnotes to history, one of them false. Carl Abraham, according to some older accounts, had a youthful romantic interest in Desirée Clary, who later, as the wife of King Karl XIV Johan, became queen of Sweden. According to this story, the young man worked for a time for her father, Francois Clary, a banker in Marseilles, and betimes a hint of romance occurred between the young Swede and the girl, later engaged to an artillery officer by the name of Napoleon Bonaparte and still later married to General Jean Baptiste Bernadotte. A lovely story, but not true, although it appears in the standard biographical works. Arne Munthe, in a history of the merchant family, punctured that anecdote: Arfwedson did not work for Clary, was in Marseilles for only three weeks, and was there in the early autumn of 1798, some months after Desirée had married Bernadotte. The romantic allusion surfaced in 1862 in a memorial to Carl Abraham after his death, possibly suggested because a grandson had worked in Marseilles for a couple of years.[30]

He was also involved in a freak episode with the British minister to Sweden. Temporarily short of funds, Lord Bloomfield, former secretary to King George IV, borrowed a thousand riksdaler from Arfwedson. When he came to the merchant's house to pay back the debt, Arfwedson was reading a Bible. Bloomfield had just placed two 500-riksdaler bills on the table when a servant suddenly called Arfwedson away on an errand. When Bloomfield returned to ask for his promissory note, Arfwedson responded that he first wanted the money; the baffled minister did not get his note back until he had handed over another thousand riksdaler. Arfwedson's side of the story, with its obvious implications, went the rounds in Stockholm, and the minister was recalled in disgrace (1832). The first Lord Bloomfield received no more diplomatic appointments. Many years later someone chanced to riffle the pages of the ancient Bible, and there lay two old 500-riksdaler bills.[31]

The Arfwedsons appear in another footnote to history, the minute Swedish presence in the West Indies. In 1784 the French ceded St. Bartholomew, an eight-square-mile speck of land in the Leeward Islands, to King Gustav III. Carl Christopher, a director in the East India Company who had been sending ships to the Caribbean, became a director in the Swedish West Indies Company. Count Eric Ruuth, later Höganäs proprietor, served as the government representative in the directory. Founded in 1787, the company's plan called for trade with the West Indies and North America and for slave trade with Africa, but the profits were so slight that the company dissolved itself in 1805. The war between France and England brought repeated seizures of ships by both combatants and rendered difficult an effort to make Gustavia, named for the king and the only town on the island, an effective neutral port for transit trade. Admiral Dackworth briefly occupied the island in 1801–1802. Its population,

458 whites and 281 blacks in 1784, rose and fell sporadically, reaching a high of perhaps 5000, as military and economic circumstances changed. In 1796 and again in 1811 over 1,700 vessels, mostly small, entered or left the harbor. When the British banned American ships from their colonies in 1826–31, many of them came to Gustavia to trade with vessels from the islands. After that, the economy shriveled, though St. Bartholomew exported small quantities of fruit and vegetables, straw hats, cigars, goat skins, and cotton. The slaves, numbering 523 in a population of 2,683, were emancipated in 1846–47. St. Bartholomew passed back to France in 1878.[32]

Another Stockholm merchant house, Schön & Co., had been established by the intermarried and confusingly similarly named Schön and Schwan families. The Schöns originated with a Lübeck coppersmith, the Schwans from a miller in the province of Östergötland. Johan Schön (1753–1805) became a leading member of the Skeppsbroadel. His grandson, Johan Gustaf Schwan (1802–1869), as a merchant displayed a keen interest in improving Swedish transportation facilities. He took the risk of initiating a new company for the rebuilding of the Trollhätte canal and locks (1838–44) and derived a good profit from it, thanks to the good fortune of having Nils Ericsson, an expert canal builder, in charge. In 1837 Schwan joined Abraham Rydberg (1780–1844), whose vessels were bringing in colonial wares from Latin America, in starting steamship service to Lübeck. Their ships, beginning with the *Gauthiod* and *Svithiod*, plied this route until the railroads drew off the customers. Schwan, meantime, had had the foresight to advocate building railroads, and his company participated in the first railroad loan secured from abroad.[33]

Schwan's ostentatious luxury, high living, and hard-handed business dealings, as well as seemingly reckless speculation, drew caustic newspaper criticism and virulent public disapproval. He was accidentally killed, after leaving a lady of dubious reputation, when he slipped and fell down a flight of stairs. This final exploit, at the age of sixty-seven, was not out of character. Some years earlier he had taken the Motala-built steamer, *Svea*, on its maiden voyage with only Rosina, an American girl, and her party on board; the Stockholmers called it, using the English words, "the wedding trip."[34]

Several of the preceding stories are from the scurrilous pen of Lazarus, a journalist whose real name was Carl Fredrik Lindahl (1841–1911). Originally published in his column, *Rikt Folk (Rich People)*, in a Stockholm newspaper, he later collected them (1897–1905) in book form under the title of *Svenska millionärer (Swedish Millionaires)*. He found enough rich Swedes to fill ten volumes, and in the process, by insinuations and innuendo, provided much entertainment and satisfaction for those who were jealous of their betters.

Anecdotes do have a function in bringing the past to life. Formal and institutional sources of information about the founders tend to portray them as paragons of wisdom and morality, and anecdotes, however unfair they may sometimes be, serve as a crude corrective for such hagiography. One nasty story may suddenly illuminate and make more credible the contemporary scene and its actors. Economic history, after all, is made by flesh-and-blood individuals, however much obscured by the scholarly quest for sound impersonal generalizations. Gossip may, surely, be peeked at as *possibly* conveying an otherwise unacknowledged aspect of the whole picture, but, without detailed evidence, any evaluation had better be left to the judgment of St. Peter. These stories do reveal contemporary moods and the public perception of personality traits of important individuals in the community, whether or not the specific narrative had any factual basis.

A third merchant house, Godenius & Co. (founded in 1812), owned an oil works, Gustafsbergs porcelain factory, and Marma sawmill, and then in 1866 would make the mistake of buying Nyhammar and Fredshammer iron works in association with N. M. Höglund, another merchant firm. The consequence would be a monumental business disaster. Another merchant house, Michaelson and Benedicks, was founded by two Jewish families from Germany. Starting as court jewelers, they ran their establishment largely as a banking business, though they also acquired the Gysinge iron works. Michael Benedicks had access to international finance through such men as Salomon Heine (Hamburg) and the Rothschilds (London, Paris, Frankfurt, Vienna), a service that he often used to help the Swedish government. Gustav IV Adolf, not otherwise friendly to the Jews, made an exception for Michael Benedicks.

Carl, Michael's son, earned a footnote in history at an early age. In 1824–25 the government attempted to dispose of five old warships to Simon Bolivar and to Mexico, using the Benedickses as intermediaries. When the tsar, acting on behalf of the Holy Alliance, reacted violently to the prospect of aid to the Latin American rebels against Spain, Kark XIV Johan hastily cancelled the deal. Tipped off early, Michael sent Carl, aged fifteen, racing across Sweden ahead of the royal courier, and the first two ships cleared Hälsingborg harbor before the courier could order them back to the Karlskrona naval base. When the ships reached Cartagena in Colombia, the financial intermediaries of Bolivar refused to pay, and they ended up in New York City, where they were sold at auction. The adventure had turned into a humiliating setback for Sweden, underlining its subservience to Russia, and as for the Benedicks, they lost large sums of money on this international imbroglio.[35]

One more major figure will suffice for this prefatory glimpse of Stockholm business life. Baron Martin von Wahrendorff (1789–1861) went over entirely to industrial life. His grandfather, member of a Westphalian noble family, had acquired a large fortune in commerce after migrating to Sweden in the middle of the eighteenth century. Martin became a diplomat, serving as a secretary in the Swedish delegation to the Congress of Vienna and later as legation secretary in London. Two events changed his life—the inheritance of the family-owned Åkers Styckebruk and the sudden deaths of his young wife and infant daughter. He gave up social life and lived an austere existence in order to use his money to build up the Styckebruk. He may have been following a natural inclination, judging by his friendship with men like Samuel Owen (who briefly worked for him at the end of his career), Eric Ruuth, Carl Abraham Arfwedson, and Adolf Eugène von Rosen.

The factory, southwest of Stockholm, derived its name from the "pieces" (*stycke*), the cannon, produced there since 1654. It had prospered in the years of the many Swedish wars and had also sold large numbers of them abroad. Wahrendorff restored the deteriorating workshop and resumed making artillery, using the C. G. Helwig model at first, with the assistance of the eminent metallurgist Erik Thomas Svedenstierna. Aware that the government had brought an Englishman to Sweden to devise a breech-loading cannon, he himself set out to manufacture one. Patents on the so-called Wahrendorff cannon were first secured in 1837, followed by later improvements, and Wahrendorff traveled all over Europe to advertise and sell it; he even sent some to Garibaldi as a gift. At the suggestion of Major Giovanni Cavalli, whose Sardinian government was a good customer, Åkers Styckebruk, with Cavalli's help, began making *rifled* barrels (1846).[36]

Though Baron Wahrendorff gained an international reputation by his pioneering work with breech-loaders and rifled barrels, his last years were embittered by controversy. A Swedish lieutenant had invented a cannon that Wahrendorff claimed was practically a copy of his own, but influential army officers, who had always resented the amateur's intrusion into their professional interests, sided with their comrade. At this point, Anders Moberg, engineer at Åkers Styckebruk when the breech-loading cannon was first being developed, claimed that he was the true inventor, that the shot had come out of both ends of the barrel until he had figured out how to tighten the breech. Shortly before Wahrendorff's death the critics were charging that his cannon had failed tests in several countries and that they had been delivered to Swedish forts before being properly tested.

Åkers Styckebruk ceased making cannon in 1866 anyway, because the old cast iron (and bronze) cannon had become obsolete when Alfred Krupp began turning out cast steel artillery in the 1850s. Thereafter its most important production consisted of rolling mill equipment for iron works, which had been started in the early 1830s when the Iron Office (Jernkontoret) of the Association of Ironmasters had selected it as most qualified in Sweden to make them. One relic of Wahrendorff and Åkers Styckebruk is still visible on the midtown horizon of Stockholm, the lattice-work iron steeple on the Riddarholm church. After the old spire had burned in a dramatic 1835 fire,

THE SMALL GIANT

Samuel Owen proposed a steeple that would not burn, one made of iron. Anders Moberg, a former student of Owen, made it, and the steeple still remains, a rather feeble invocation to the heavenly powers above.[37]

4. APPRENTICED TO MODERN INDUSTRY

Sven Magnus Sunnerdahl, proprietor of one of the two biggest paper-making establishments in Sweden, had a problem. Most of his product was being sold in nearby Denmark, and now a rival Danish firm, Strandmøllen, had installed a Bryan Donkin paper-making machine. Johan Christian Drewsen, whose family had owned Strandmøllen since 1718, put in a steam engine (1821), then the Bryan Donkin machine (1829), and in fifteen years his output would more than quintuple.

Due to the very nature of handicraft methods, Sweden's ninety-one paper-making shops could not be large, and Sunnerdahl's Klippan in 1829 made 6.9 percent of the Swedish paper.[1] Klippan, where paper had been made as early as 1573, was located in a stony area about forty kilometers east of Hälsingborg, which in turn lies across the narrow straits from Denmark. Its name derived from the Swedish word for a rock or cliff, Sweden is well endowed with them, and hence Klippan, "the Cliff," is apt to recur in various localities.

Sunnerdahl visited Strandmøllen, north of Copenhagen, to inspect the technological wonder, and, knowing that he would otherwise lose his customers, quickly made a decision. He, too, must acquire such a costly machine, however, formidable its financing and the expense of constructing a new building to house it. He applied for a loan from the state, using the often effective plea that this would introduce a needed technological innovation into the country. Approved by the Board of Trade, Sunnerdahl received 15,000 riksdaler and toll-free admission of the machine. It was in operation by the middle of 1832, powered by a water wheel, and an Englishman, William Howard, served as shop foreman over the five, later six, Swedish workers.[2]

A paper-making machine had originally been invented by Louis Robert in France, then sold to his employer, who took it to England in 1800. The English engineer Bryan Donkin devised the first model that worked (1804), and the resulting Bryan Donkin & Co. at Bermondsey in London constructed progressively improved models for the British market. His machine began to be used in Germany in 1818, and in France four years later; the one at Klippan was number 96. Mr. Donkin also made a fool of himself by his criticism of the Brunels during the digging of the Thames tunnel, but that is another story.

At Klippan six or seven persons were now accomplishing as much as twenty-five had formerly, although other phases of the work employed additional laborers. Production increased steadily, more than tripling in the next twenty years.[3] From being itself threatened, Klippan now endangered other paper-making shops. They had to buy Bryan Donkin machines or, lacking the financial means, go to special kinds of paper that could not yet be made by machine. Or close their shops. However, had Sunnerdahl not been forced to respond to his particular circumstances, someone else would have bought such a machine within a few years. Economics and opportunity demanded it.

That someone might have been Henrik Munktell, whose family had founded (1740) the Grycksbo paper mill in the Bergslagen mining region; its annual production in 1830 ran slightly higher than that of Klippan. Henrik was more than a technician, having attended Uppsala before serving in the civil service for some years; preparatory to taking over the family enterprise, he studied the new industrial production of paper in continental countries (1828–30). The second Bryan Donkin machine in Sweden went into operation at Grysksbo in 1836.

Two other machines followed in the same year, at Holmen in Norrköping and at Lessebo in the province of Småland; the three of them were installed virtually simultaneously. Holmen had borne one of the most illustrious names in the Swedish economy since the seventeenth century. Started by the Crown on some small islands in the river for the purpose of making cloth, it was chartered to Louis De Geer and Willem de Besche, Walloons from the Liége area. (A *holm* is a small island.) It manufactured uniforms for the Swedish army during the Thirty Years War, and also made some paper in that century. Declining after the death of Louis De Geer, it was burned in a Russian foray in 1719. With Holmen's purchase in 1817 by Norrköping's domineering mayor, Lars Magnus Trozelli, the venerable enterprise entered a new period of growth, eventually including cotton spinning and weaving factories as well as becoming one of Sweden's largest paper-making mills.

When the resumption of paper-making was planned in the mid-1830s, Trozelli ordered a Bryan Donkin as a necessary part of a modern plant; he also installed a steam boiler, but continued to use a water wheel, to which Holmen had owed much of its earlier success. Swedish workshops needing power had usually been placed to take advantage of one of Sweden's best resources, rapidly moving water, and the adoption of modern machinery in one aspect of work by no means persuaded owners that steam engines were also necessary. Production in the new paper mill rose tenfold, forcing the handicrafts shops in the region to close, and Holmen was soon making about 10 percent of all Swedish paper.[4]

Lessebo, far out in the countryside, presented a very different picture than Norrköping, Sweden's most industrial city. Lacking the fertile agricultural land of Skåne to the south, the hard-bitten, toughened people of Småland, scrabbling desperately for meager rewards, had little of anything except *brännvin*, the potent liquor brewed from their own grain or potatoes. They did have clear, running water, essential for the making of paper, and of the 154 known papermaking shops however briefly in existence in Sweden from the sixteenth century until 1850, fifty-one were in Småland.[5]

Running six paper mills, several iron works (*bruk*), and a copper and nickel mine with crews of these people was no mean achievement. Johan Lorentz Aschan (1772–1856), doctor by profession, did it with such style that he became a legendary figure in the province. He may have faced his hardest test when he went to ask for the hand of his chosen bride, Katharina, daughter of Rike Nilsson ("Rich" Nilsson), owner of a dozen *bruk* and a fearsome reputation to match. Wearing his best clothes and driving along in a nicely cleaned buggy, Aschan encountered a dirty old tramp by the roadside who asked for a lift. The doctor genially let him into the buggy, and the ragged old man stayed with him all the way up to the door of Katharina's stately home. Aschan was introduced to the girl's numerous relatives and then, finally, to the tramp, who turned out to be Rike Nilsson himself. Having passed the test (and possibly forewarned), the good doctor acquired a wife and a handsome dowry, with which the next year he bought Lessebo (1802).

Lessebo had usually lost money for successive proprietors. Aschan made it pay. He was up and working at four o'clock in the morning, and so were the laborers. Or else. According to Johan Alfred Göth, in his sometimes entertaining biography, it was not always easy for even Aschan to terrify the Smålanders (Smålänningar) into working, but things did get better. Göth quotes an aged Lessebo hand, who said that a regular caste system existed in Aschan's time: Aschan beat the inspector, the inspector beat the foremen, the foremen beat the workers, and the workers beat up on the oxen, the horses, and each other. The doctor, "the orneriest Smålander yet," was regarded "with respect, with affection, with both childish and superstitious fear." However, Aschan also set up schools and a hospital, diligently vaccinated people against smallpox, opposed coffee as being injurious to the health, and fought a lifelong crusade against *brännvin*. When a party among the workers became too boisterous or lasted too long, a deputy would hurry over to warn them that Aschan was coming, which was enough to scatter them rapidly. His wife, whose money had started him on his way, held the opinion that she was responsible for his success; one day he handed her the sum total of the original dowry, plus 6 percent interest, and suggested that she shut up about it.[6]

Dr. Aschan may have lived deep in the woods, but he kept an alert eye on industrial developments in Sweden and elsewhere. His original interest in buying Lessebo had been its iron works, rather than the paper-making.

Klippan, however, lay perilously close to his own marketing territory, and so a Bryan Donkin arrived on this unlikely scene.

A fifth paper-making workshop, Korndal, would be of importance in the next phase of development, and under the name of Papyrus would continue to be one of Sweden's major paper mills. It had originally been started in 1763 at Mölndal, a short distance south of Gothenburg, where fifteen small waterfalls and a drop of 150 feet in elevation created ideal conditions for water power. The name Mölndal itself means "Valley of Mills," and here, by the 1700s, various mills were located: flour, dyeing, paper, textiles, and sugar. Korndal was partially mechanized with equipment from England in 1832, by 1855 boasted the largest production in Sweden, and by 1870 was manufacturing nearly one-half of all Swedish paper, much of it exported.[7] In 1856 Korndal became part of the growing D. O. Francke business empire; a major figure in early Swedish industrialization, Francke will be met repeatedly later.

A paper-making machine had been mounted at Korndal in 1849 by the preceding owner. However, Korndal, like all paper-making shops, had been confronting, in an increasingly acute form, a difficult problem: the need for new raw materials as the demand for paper, domestic and international, rose rapidly by midcentury. Elementary schooling became compulsory in 1842, increasing the need for paper and textbooks. The growth of newspapers, an improved postal service (postage rates for the country were equalized in 1855), and the growing number of business companies all contributed to an expanding market for paper.

Most of the handicraft shops had been located close to towns in central and southern Sweden, near to both the market and the principal sources for paper, old rags and scrap paper. While the amount of paper manufactured steadily increased, thanks to the new machinery and growing demand, the supply of rags and scrap paper remained strictly limited. Efforts to solve this bottleneck had been made in several countries by experimenting with various alternatives; Carl Arosenius at the Gryt paper mill in Norrköping, among others, had tried to make paper out of straw. The invention of the Voelter wood shredding machine in the early 1840s in Germany could scarcely have come at a more opportune moment. Francke promptly bought Voelter's patent for Sweden, and, since the water power at Mölndal was insufficient for this project, placed the mill on Önan island at the Trollhättan falls (1857). Sweden's first, and the world's sixth, wood pulp mill went into operation the next year, thereby inaugurating one of Sweden's most important industries. The Swedes in time would make their own innovative contributions to it, and the industry would become a major source of exports.

One single machine in its successive improvements, the Bryan Donkin, had revolutionized paper-making. The Pontifex & Wood vacuum cooker had the same effect in the refining of sugar. The handicraft system used all over Europe, simply put, consisted of mixing the raw sugar in limewater and boiling in an open pan. The boiling continued until the sugar crystallized; about one-half of the original raw sugar, aside from impurities, was lost as wasted syrup.[8] Pontifex & Wood had secured a patent on machinery for vacuum cooking, using steam, and, although the apparatus was expensive to buy, the process resulted in a higher yield of sugar.

In 1836 David Carnegie the younger (nephew of the earlier David) bought the Lorentska refinery in Gothenburg, which had originated partially out of American sugar, cotton, and slaves. Two brothers, Abraham and Paul Lorent of Hamburg, having become wealthy in the United States, divided their efforts, Paul remaining in Charleston, South Carolina, while Abraham went back to Europe. Here he drove a transit trade out of neutral Copenhagen, where he also started a refinery to profit from blockaded Europe's sugar famine. This splendid idea went awry when the Danes declared war on the British (1807), whereupon Lorent crossed to still-neutral Sweden to continue his transit trade and to start another refinery. His new one at Gothenburg's Klippan, the largest of five in the area, brought a few years of prosperity; then came the end of the war and of profits. Paul returned from the Carolinas to take over the ownership, and the two of them, with brother-in-law John Nonnen, struggled on for years. They owed money in London, Hamburg, Copenhagen, and Mannheim, and finally the refinery had to be put up for auction.[9]

How could David Carnegie turn this obviously losing proposition around? By introducing new techniques and machinery, by securing an exclusive ten-year Swedish right to the Pontifex & Wood patent, thereby giving him a big advantage over competitors. Going into production in 1839, D. Carnegie & Co. upset the equilibrium in the Swedish sugar industry, in fact dominated it during the next decade. Since the technique produced only medium-quality sugar, rivals might survive by concentrating on high quality, but a number of refineries had to close. The owners of two Gothenburg enterprises gave up and joined a new, reorganized Carnegie company. One of these, Eduard Magnus, was the son of a Jewish immigrant from Germany who had started with an open market booth and ended up with one of the most lucrative businesses in the city. As for the younger David Carnegie, he went back to Scotland after 1845; unlike many other Scots, the Carnegies did not settle permanently in Sweden.

When the ten-year lease expired, new competitors appeared promptly, among them D. O. Francke with a mechanized refinery in Mölndal. Carnegie responded with improved pumpers and boilers from Pontifex & Wood, sufficient to permit repeated lowering of prices. More serious competition came from Landskrona in southern Sweden, where a refinery in existence for a century was refurbished with Pontifex & Wood machinery and new company organization. Known as the Skånska Sockerfabriks AB, it ultimately replaced D. Carnegie & Co. as the largest in Sweden. Meantime, the consumer benefited as sugar, once a luxury, came to be considered a necessity, which in turn vastly expanded the sales market for the refineries.

In the years around 1840 the Landskrona refinery had gambled and lost on another promising innovation, this one brought in from Prussia and France. Why go to the expense and trouble of importing sugar cane when, by processes developed during the Napoleonic wars, sugar beets grown in Sweden might be used? (Carnegie raw sugar cane was largely imported from Brazil on company-owned ships.) The Landskrona plant went over partially to beet sugar, and so did three other refineries in southern Sweden. Too many people tried to crowd in on a good thing, a wave of speculation followed, the methods of production still needed improving, and, as had happened on the continent when the blockade ended, sugar cane drove out the beet sugar. Landskrona was the last to abandon the attempt (1847). Not least of the problem was that Swedish farmers showed little disposition to grow sugar beets, and not until American grain entered the market at the end of the 1870s, with devastating effect on prices, did the farmers begin to adopt the new crop. By 1900 Sweden was growing nearly all its own sugar.[10]

These developments in paper-making and sugar refining illustrate in simple form the basic pattern wherever an innovation intruded upon earlier means of production. An entrepreneur with the financial means to introduce new or improved machinery and techniques thereby gained the advantage and in the process furthered the progressive, step-by-step advance of industrialization. Competition in the marketplace sooner or later eliminated obsolete methods of production and crudely selected the most efficient of new models. For the handicraft shops, a single invention came as a shattering bombshell, forcing them to go to industrial production themselves, adjust to making specialized sugar or paper, or shut down. In both industries the machines, responding to a growing market, created a greater demand for raw materials, thus starting a new cycle of experimentation with alternatives.

Sweden was still very much the borrower of the ingredients of industrialization at this time. Unless seen within the context of international developments, the ripples of change in this one country may seem chaotic and haphazard. As a province of western Europe, Sweden was one sector within a much larger community, sharing, with local variations, an experience common to a number of countries in this period. A survey of the industrialization of textile manufacturing should reveal more of the basic coherence of the overall pattern.

A double theft made possible Fredrik Hummel's mechanical cotton spinning mill in Sävedalen near Lerum, northeast of Gothenburg. On visits to

Copenhagen in 1792 and 1793 he became fascinated by the machinery in a new textile factory there. Its proprietors had managed to smuggle out the secrets for making British spinning and weaving machines, then had them reproduced in Copenhagen. Hummel's estate near Lerum did have a stream for water power, so why not use it for a similar enterprise? Exactly how the transaction was handled remains obscure, but he persuaded C. H. Strimberg, a worker, to memorize the details of the machinery, then come to Lerum to construct similar ones (1797). Possessing a building site, water power, and valuable technological secrets, Hummel apparently had no difficulty in obtaining financial help from William Chalmers and other businessmen.

One of the four main buildings spanned the water to an island in the Säve River, and here a water wheel was mounted that drove the carding and spinning machinery. Another of the buildings was devoted to cotton handicraft weaving. Although Hummel died in 1809, a nephew continued the operation, and the original work force of about 15 grew to about 120 by the 1830s.[11] Strimberg remained as foreman for some years, then moved on to Sjuntorp near Trollhättan where he constructed a second set of machines for a cotton spinning mill there.[12]

When Gustaf Ferdinand Hennig started the Mariedahl and Rosendahl textile mills, later owned by D. O. Francke, in Mölndal (1826–1834) he obtained his machinery from two sources. He bought one set from a Danish spinnery that had closed, and the other from John Cockerill in Liége; the Cockerill enterprises manufactured most of the early cotton spinning machines that were imported into Sweden. They were of British design, and Hennig brought in British experts to teach his workers the current techniques in carding and spinning. Swedish workers learned how to make yarn from American cotton in his factories, and, according to Gösta Bodman, it was Hennig, above all others, who was instrumental in making the Swedish transition to the new epoch of cotton spinning.[13]

Antenor Nydqvist, future manufacturer of Swedish locomotives, and his brother worked for Hennig at Rosendahl and watched new machinery being put into place. Later, by 1836, they saw other textile machinery in Berlin while on their work-study tour in Germany. At the Haubholtz textile mill in Chemnitz in Saxony they duplicated some of the machinery (especially Dyers slubbing apparatus) that they had become familiar with at Rosendahl and elsewhere.[14] Hennig had been born in Saxony. Thus the entrepreneurs and the bearers of technological knowledge shuttled back and forth from one country to another in this formative period of industrial change.

The kind of knavery exhibited by Hummel, Strimberg and others, if such it can be called, was occurring all over the continent. The British were—naturally—trying to protect their secrets, and others were—naturally—trying to steal them. Exports of machinery had been forbidden and skilled workers not allowed to leave the country by the parliamentary acts of 1719 and 1750, a ban lasting until 1824–25 for the workers and until 1842 for machinery. The manufacturers had long been arguing that they might as well be allowed the profits from continental markets since similar machines were now available there anyway.[15]

In textiles the well-known fundamental inventions, after John Kay's flying shuttle, had been the spinning jenny of James Hargreaves, the water frame of Richard Arkwright, Samuel Crompton's spinning mule, and the power loom of Richard Cartwright; they all appeared between 1768 and 1785. (One other basic invention, the Jacquard loom, originated in France in about 1804.) Details of these innovations and others could not be indefinitely kept secret. The Swedes were merely being typical of the continental peoples when they went to Great Britain for a closer look. Some Europeans were resolutely barred from factories while others were courteously allowed a fairly thorough inspection, this largely depending upon the attitude of particular proprietors. Licenses were occasionally issued for the export of otherwise prohibited machines, and many others were smuggled out. Publications of professional societies sometimes conveyed information, and the Swedes were assiduous readers of such journals. Knowledgeable workmen in factories were tempted to profit from their knowledge by going abroad, especially in times of unemployment. In this fashion the ripples spread outward from the British "engine of growth" (Hartwell) to the continent.[16]

Among continental employers in various industries who were hiring British workers and using British machinery, smuggled or duplicated or licensed, were John Holker (Rouen), Lieven Bouwens (Ghent), John Cockerill (Seraing and Liége), Scipion Périer and Humphrey Edwards (Chaillot), and Friedrich Harkort (Wetter). John Milne had smuggled an Arkwright machine into France before the Revolution and became a leading cotton manufacturer. Textile machinery of British origin was being made in France by John Collier, William Douglas, and John Heywood. A German who had worked in Arkwright's Cromford cotton mill started an early mechanical spinning mill near Düsseldorf, even naming it after the original (1794). In Saxony someone began using Crompton's mule a few years later, and another proprietor installed Arkwright's water frame. John Cockerill set up an engineering works in Berlin in about 1819 for the purpose of constructing textile machinery, and his brother, James, was similarly engaged in Aachen. John Heywood and James Longworth installed cotton spinning mules at a mill in Switzerland in 1801, and four years later a firm in Zürich began making textile machinery.[17]

This brief list offers some orientation for Swedish developments within the context of the greater whole. Samuel Slater could be appropriately added to the list: apprenticed to a partner of Arkwright, he later constructed an Arkwright machine from memory in Pawtucket, Rhode Island (1790), and then went on to become "the founder of the American power textile industry."[18]

The Cockerills claimed that they knew about any new English invention within ten days after its appearance. William Cockerill, an unemployed "maker of jennies," migrated in 1797 and in 1799 was constructing textile machinery for a firm in Verviers. In 1807 he settled in Liége, making spinning machines and mechanized looms for the wool industry. His three sons continued to expand the family enterprise, including a large iron foundry and blast furnace at Seraing, and John long continued to manufacture British models of textile machinery in Liége. S. A. Cockerill at Seraing is still Belgium's largest steel producer.

It is not irrelevant to the Swedish struggle for modernization, however, to recall that even the land of the "engine of growth" did not adopt new methods overnight. A. E. Musson writes that steam power would drive out water wheels in the long run, "but it was a longer run than is generally realized" in England. Nor did the use of horses, for those without water power, vanish quickly. Wooden machinery, with metal fittings, remained common in the 1820s, and wooden spinning jennies, turned by hand, did not disappear from Lancashire mills until about 1830.[19]

Swedish manufacture of cloth was greatly encouraged by the postwar tariff of 1816, by the high tolls or outright ban on imported finished cotton goods and the deliberately low rates on imported raw cotton. Prohibitively high tariffs initially stimulated the existing handicraft spinning and weaving industry, but British goods in transit to the continent during the early years of the century had offered interested Swedes clear proof of the advantages of the new textile machinery and techniques. It quickly became a question of how to acquire and make use of them. Textiles never would approach the importance of iron or timber in the Swedish economy. Nevertheless, the timing of its industrialization corresponds roughly with that of iron and timber, it did employ a relatively large number of factory workers, and here, as in other countries, the inexorable advance of machinery destroyed the cottage handicraft livelihood of many people. In terms of general usage of industrial textile machinery, the sequence in Sweden as elsewhere tended to be first, cotton spinning, followed by cotton weaving, then mechanical spinning of wool, and, finally, the coming of the power loom in the wool industry.

Though textiles made up about 40 percent of Gothenburg's industrial production (including handicrafts) in 1820, it would not become Sweden's major textile center. A thriving industry did spring up to the east of the city in the Sjuhärad region and the nearby town of Borås. Malmö, Gävle, and several other cities had textile mills of some importance. It would, however, be Norrköping, with its excellent water power potential, which would become the country's greatest textile manufacturing center, the "Manchester of Sweden."

The Sjuhärad (Seven Districts) region around Borås had not been richly endowed by nature. Nor did it even bear that name until a professor so dubbed it in the source of a geographic study in 1919.[20] Located on the same rocky plateau as Småland farther east and suffering from excessive rainfall, only the river valleys offered much opportunity for productive farming. Perforce, the inhabitants had sought other means of support. Extensive meadows amidst forests and rain-induced swamps encouraged the raising of cattle in the sixteenth and seventeenth centuries, these cattle (especially oxen) then being sold in better farming areas and in Bergslagen. The making of wooden articles, another common pursuit, was gradually replaced by cottage spinning and weaving, which became the characteristic occupation of the region. Wadmal or rough wool cloth and, somewhat later, linen made up the bulk of the work. A growing number of entrepreneurs engaged in the putting-out system, acquiring the wool and flax elsewhere in southern Sweden and doling them out to the peasants to be finished with spinning wheels and hand weaving looms. "The spinning wheels hummed and the weaving looms thumped all over the Sjuhärad" (Sterner).[21]

This development would not have been possible without the assistance of a unique system of distribution, of the *gårdfarihandlare* (literally, "farm-traveling-traders") or peddlers who carried the goods all over the country and beyond. Starting in the early 1600s, they numbered well over two thousand by the beginning of the nineteenth century. Some were well-equipped merchants traveling with wagons and hired hands, but most of them were simple peddlers plodding along from house to house with their goods. They tended to have their regular rounds and customers, returning to the same area year after year. Independent spirits defiant of authority, they evoked mingled anticipation and apprehension upon arrival, and the authorities had learned from many brisk encounters that it was best to leave them alone. They even had their own private language, a mixture of local dialect, twisted Latin, Finnish and German, the latter from ex-soldiers formerly stationed in Germany.[22]

"Mor Kerstin" ("Mother Kerstin") was one of the twenty or more entrepreneurs in Mark, one of the seven districts. She had continued the business after the death of her husband, an entrepreneur in the weaving and selling of linen, and Mor Kerstin became one of the first, if not the first, to "put out" cotton yarn for weaving among the cottagers. She bought the yarn in Gothenburg and sold the finished product there and to the *gårdfarihandlare*. Yarn was available, so was the market, and cotton weaving quickly became a major activity in the area in the decades after 1815.

Her son, Sven Erikson (1801–1866), never did go to school; she taught him how to read, and for the rest he was mostly self-taught. At the age of eighteen he started his own entrepreneurial business, buying as much yarn in Gothenburg as he could carry on his back; in the early 1830s he may have had seven hundred weavers at work in their homes. By then he had a sufficiently certain income, a sales force in the peddlers, and enough business contacts to fulfill his long dream: the founding, with two associates, of the first cotton weaving mill in Sweden at Rydboholm (1834).[23]

The factory, placed along a stream about eight kilometers south of Borås, had 148 looms and perhaps 130 workers in 1837. Erikson encountered many problems, including heavy debts, incurred because the costs of building and equipment ran far beyond original calculations, and numerous complaints arising from the early unevenness of quality of the product. To provide more yarn for Rydboholm, he established a spinning mill at Rydal on the site of a former sawmill (1853), and ultimately moved the Rydboholm machinery to better water power at Viskafors (1854–56). In 1857 Viskafors had 790 weaving looms and about 470 workers. Much of the early machinery came from the Cockerills, and the Munktell machine shop in Eskilstuna constructed fifty-one textile machines for his mill, but the greater number later were purchased from Wolff, Hasche & Co. The yarn originally came from the same Manchester firm, afterward increasingly from Swedish spinning mills; subsequently, for Rydal, agents in Gothenburg and Borås arranged the import of cotton, mostly American.

Like other pioneers, Erikson had called in British foremen to train his workers in the factory system and the relevant textile techniques. Among these foremen, Charles Hill from Manchester served from 1843 until 1852 before moving to a new cotton weaving factory at Norrköping; in 1865 he started his own spinning mill at Alingsås, site of the former Alströmer textile manufactory. Another one, Edward Davies, founded a cotton weaving factory in Borås in 1870.[24]

In the Gothenburg area, where one cotton mill (Lerum) had been active in 1815–20, their number rose to eleven in 1840–45 and seventeen just before 1860, meanwhile growing in size and mechanization. Formerly a luxury, cotton became the cheapest textile, thanks to industrialization and the fall of prices for the raw material as American cotton arrived in quantity. Then came catastrophe. The American Civil War shut off two-thirds of the supplies, and even in 1870 the cotton exports from the United States remained at only two-thirds of that in 1860.[25] Compounding the difficulties, the series of bad crop years in the later 1860s reduced purchasing power. Many mills closed, and not until about 1870 did the Swedish cotton industry regain momentum and resume its expansion.

These years also saw the end of the cottager weaving of cotton. First, supplies were unavailable; then such mills as that of Charles Hill at Alingsås, copied by others and especially by entrepreneurs formerly in the putting-out system, drove out the cottagers. As for the Sjuhárad *gårdfarihandlare*, they ceased to make their rounds. At Rydboholm itself, Sven Erikson started using wholesale merchants for the most populated areas in about 1840. Small stores in towns and villages were beginning to replace the itinerant traders by midcentury, and many of the peddlers themselves opened permanent stores in the regions where they had formerly carried their wares.

Norrköping, an old community already in existence in the twelfth century, has historically been one of Sweden's largest and most important cities. It had grown up near the eastern end of the Motala River, which flows into a deep and protected harbor in the long Bråviken inlet of the Baltic. The rapidly flowing stream offered ample water power, and it was here that Louis De Geer presided over the Holmen cloth factory after 1627 while also founding a munitions works at Finspång, northwest of the city. Henceforth an industrial town of some repute, Norrköping suffered crippling blows early in the next century when a pestilence killed about 2,700 persons in 1710–11 and the Russians harried the vicinity near the conclusion of the Great Northern War. At that time the population had fallen to only about 2,600. Textile handicraft industry, largely wool, continued to be maintained throughout the century in the city and surrounding countryside.

About two-thirds of Swedish woolen textile production was still concentrated in the Stockholm area in 1800. A few of its manufactories that had some factory attributes merit mention. Lars Fresks Klädesfabrik, the enterprise with an original Edelcrantz steam engine, was housed, after a fire in 1807, in a large five-story, stone building on the island of Lidingö; axles and cogwheels transmitted power to fourteen spinning machines (688 spindles), a press, cutting and carding machines, and some other installations. The manufactured yarn was put out to cottagers for weaving, then finished for market in the mill.[26] Samuel Owen's first steam engine, made at Bergsund, ultimately was used at another mill, Zach. Tillanders Klädesfabrik. Both John Elvius at Bergsund and Charles Apelquist appear to have worked, at one time or another, on the mechanical installations of Daniel Asplund's Tvetaberg mill near Södertälje, and Apelquist naturally equipped his own Marieberg textile works.[27] Elvius also constructed similar machinery for a mill north of the city at Norrtälje, owned by Carl Christopher Arfwedson. Stockholm's first cotton spinning mill, Bergman & Bohnstedt, opened in 1834 with machines from Cockerill, including Sweden's first two mules, and a Samuel Owen steam engine. The mill burned down early in 1842 and was not restored.[28]

By 1830 over two-thirds of Swedish wool manufacturing was taking place in Norrköping, attracted there by its available water power and lower living costs. Increasing mechanization, coupled with the need for cheap power, made that city the natural center for textile industry. It also had relatively easy transportation and a long handicrafts tradition in spinning and weaving. Out of these circumstances would emerge several families who built up expertise and continuity as leaders in the industry over several generations.[29]

Johannes Swartz (1759–1812) is said to have brought the first British textile machine, probably a flying shuttle, to Norrköping (1799). He was the uncle of the John Swartz (1790–1853) who started a steamboat service to Stockholm with *Rosen* and who in popular parlance was known as the "King of Norrköping." The family, descended from Värmland miners, began with a snuff factory in 1753, then added a flour mill; in its completed form, Djurökvarnen (the animal-island-mill), resembled "a fairy castle risen out of the waves" of Bråviken, complete with tower and crenelated walls.[30] The family made many other contributions to the city, starting with Johannes' mother, who founded a first-rate school modeled on the famous Herrnhuter institution in Halle, and continuing with John's leadership in founding a savings bank, a gaslight works, and a firefighting corps after a big fire had devastated part of the city in 1822. He also contributed a cholera epidemic, dying of it on his birthday after returning from a journey; he had infected others, from whom it spread all over the community (1853).

His son, Janne (Johan Gustaf), devoted himself to agricultural innovations at Hovgården, an estate with antecedents going back to Birger Jarl (d. 1266), where he invented the "Swartzka ice-method" for use in creameries, brought in German ways of making sausage, and promoted the factory preparation of butter and cheese. His futile campaign in favor of home-grown beet sugar culminated in financial ruin and the loss of Hovgården. The family exported oats (later, imported grain from Russia and Germany) and purveyed flour, fodder, fertilizer, and peat. In 1905, still pioneering, they were transporting flour with a 12–16 hp Daimler truck.[31] With all these achievements, the career of Carl, nephew of Janne, as a Riksdagsman, finance minister and briefly prime minister (1917) may not have seemed so remarkable, and as for Edward Mauritz, an actor and Hamlet player in Stockholm, the family considered him to have disgraced the fair name of Swartz.

However, back to Norrköping textiles. Johannes Swartz by unknown means brought back a spinning jenny, if such it was, while serving in the Swedish legation in London. His interest derived from having set up a tannery and yarn spinnery at Smedjeholmen, an abandoned weapons factory; rebuilding it, Swartz called in Apelquist, whom he had been assisting financially, to construct the necessary machinery. The spinning jenny attracted a lot of attention, but Swartz never did use it and four years later sold it to the firm of Söderberg and Arosenius for Gryt, a newly opened textile mill.

A flour mill when purchased, Gryt for a time became one of the country's most important industrial establishments and briefly accounted for over 10 percent of Swedish wool manufacturing. Carl Arosenius (1778–1839), who had studied textile manufacturing in central Europe, mechanized the plant to the extent then possible, including flying shuttles and weaving looms "perhaps only partially mechanized"; also scrubbing, carding and napping machines, all driven by a water wheel transmitting power through iron axles and cogwheels. In addition to the continued milling of flour, Gryt made paper, and here Arosenius experimented with the use of straw. One of the genuine early innovators, he also founded the so-called Normalfabriken, intended to be a model weaving mill and as such to serve as a training school in textile techniques. Its foreman came from Saxony. Though lacking water power, it briefly had the second highest production in the city, but financial losses closed it in the mid-1830s.[32]

Several other proprietors introduced some mechanization around 1800, including Philip Jeremias, Laurentius Acharius, and Samuel Sorbon. In 1805 the various owners sent Jacob Eurenius to Aachen to study machines and techniques there. Too much must not be made of reports in these years of mechanization in the wool industry; the machines were mostly devices for washing, carding, cutting, and napping the woolen materials in manufactories where artisans otherwise worked by handicraft methods. Apelquist and Elvius were, to be sure, duplicating machinery seen and perhaps personally used in Great Britain, and a merchant in Karlskrona reportedly "invented" a spinning machine (1790), but these initiatives were not being followed up.[33]

From 1811 on, machinery in Norrköping was being made by Anders Ahlm, largely self-taught, who had worked for Swartz and Sorbon, after which he began to construct machinery on order in his own shop. With primitive tools and lacking water power, Ahlm and his men, in the years when Norrköping became Sweden's woolen textile center, helped to equip many of the "factories" of the time with machinery made mostly of wood. Lacking the proper equipment to do better, Ahlm's enterprise, which was employing about fifty-six workers in 1835 shortly before his death, was essentially an improvisation and a stopgap operation.[34]

It would seem as though Swedish textiles needed a Samuel Owen, a British expert like, say, William Cockerill, whose presence might have spared the Swedes many years of improvisation. Apelquist did have a British foreman at Marieberg in 1797. He had come to Sweden in the hope of making machinery for the carding and spinning of wool. The Swede wrote that he was "especially competent and must be kept here regardless of what it costs." The next year the man moved on to Hamburg and then to Verviers. His name? William Cockerill.[35]

Norrköping acquired a more respectable verkstad after the death of Ahlm (1835) when Alexander Malcolm, one of four brothers who had come to Sweden, began making machinery there. Failing to make the enterprise profitable, the Glasgow-born technician returned to Scotland, and Andrew Malcolm, who had moved from Motala in 1842, took over his brother's plant. On a trip to England Andrew had returned with a gear-cutting machine, two smaller lathes, and some screw-cutting apparatus; also some British machinists. More important, he came back with the idea of the improved mule, and its general adoption after 1840 seems to derive from Malcolm's initiative. (The automatic mule had been patented, in its successful version, by Richard Roberts, one of the greatest machine-tool inventors, in 1830). Andrew also helped to introduce the use of water turbines in Sweden. The machine shop manufactured water wheels, water turbines, and the shaftings and axles for connecting the motive power to machinery. Also becoming the principal maker of textile machinery in the kingdom, Malcolm often imported the most complex parts, manufactured the rest, and then assembled the machine. The national market, however, was not large enough; or if it was, too many owners, for Malcolm's welfare, bought machinery directly from the British Isles or the continent. He never did attain mass production, nor was Malcolm a good financier; he bitterly complained in a book in his old age that Swedish circumstances, especially the lack of a sufficiently high protective tariff, made a profit impossible.[36]

The spinning machines used in Sweden for both cotton and wool were based on the simple throstle device on the Arkwright water-frame principle, each carrying about fifty spindles; but after 1840 the mule, able to make finer and softer yarn, was replacing them. The automatic mule, however, did not come into use in Norrköping mills until the 1860s. The improved Cartwright loom began to give way in Swedish weaving to the Jacquard type, where particular patterns could be woven by means of "Instructions," holes punched in cards. Wallbergs in Halmstad, founded in 1823, became Sweden's first fully mechanical wool weaving mill. Of 746 wool looms in Norrköping, however, 196 were still run by hand in 1863.[37]

Imported Norrköping textile machines tended to come from Chemnitz (Schönherr und Seidler), Aachen and Seraing (the Cockerills), and Ghent (Phoenix), at least until the lifting of the British ban in 1842. D. H. Bagge, buyer on behalf of Hargs spinnery near Nyköping, happened to arrive in England just in time to hear that the ban had been abolished, and forthwith purchased machinery for it. This was some deserved good luck for August Bergman, just starting Hargs after his joint venture with Bohnstedt, the cotton spinnery in Stockholm, had gone up in flames. Bergman, incidentally, had come directly out of the cottage spinning industry, where his father and brother had long been entrepreneurs.[38]

Water power and mechanization had transformed Norrköping's wool spinning industry by the 1830s.[39] The mills became larger, though not big by British or French standards, and the proportionate work force lessened as machines took over the labor. Spinning, which had employed three-quarters of the workers under the handicraft system, now accounted for only about a fourth, the continued handicraft weaving absorbing the great majority. Not all the spinning-mill owners could find or afford space on the river, and oxen or human muscles had to suffice for them. Water power greatly enhanced productive capacities in enterprises like Gryt, Drag, Bergwall, and Wetterling. Gryt, for example, employed 77 workers in producing 42,000 rdr. worth of goods annually, whereas Stenhusfabriken, without it, used 315 persons to make goods of 26,000 rdr. value a year. Steam engines came into use only very slowly and even in 1865 were in operation at only five plants. Twelve mills completely filled the riverfront, of which three had gone from the water wheel to the water turbine.[40]

Small textile enterprises were constantly appearing or disappearing, due to overly optimistic founders and oscillating prices, during the first half-century of Norrköping's blossoming textile industry; thus, a number of them were founded in 1830–35, then, as textile prices dropped, fifteen small ones vanished in 1835–40.[41] At midcentury three important changes were underway: the factories became larger, often employing several hundred workers; the wool industry began to go to mechanical weaving; and the cotton industry invaded Norrköping. The Drag textile mill, directly across the Motala River from Gryt, exemplified the first two trends.

Drag had been making textiles ever since its founding by a former worker for Louis De Geer in 1642. Christian Lenning (1781–1854), having married an heiress, purchased the deteriorating plant and began a modernization that made it one of the city's most substantial during the following decades. He had inherited his interest in textiles from his family, which had acquired a wool weaving manufactory in Nyköping in 1777 and would continue to hold it until the 1860s. (Confusingly similar names for neighboring cities, Nyköping translates into Newmarket and Norrköping into North Market.) Christian had made his work-study tour in Germany in 1805–07; most individuals from this region who studied wool textiles abroad at this time went to Germany, the land that had long influenced the Swedish industry, and only later would they turn to the British.

A further modernization brought Malcolm's first mules to Drag, among other new installations (1840). Christian's repeated expenditures in trying to make Drag the city's leading textile mill had overstrained even his financial resources, however, and it was transformed into a joint-stock company with his son, Johan, as the new leader (1854). The names of the stockholders are revealing. The Söderberg and Arosenius families were originally (but briefly) represented. Reinhold Ramstedt, who had moved his textile mill interests from Stockholm in order to use water power, now merged his enterprise with Drag, and so did Fredrik Blombergh, who lacked a water wheel. C. G. Sundström was a Stockholm cloth merchant, and several others were wealthy textile manufacturers or merchants.[42]

Johan Lenning (1819–1879) was more abreast of current textile developments than anyone in the city since Carl Arosenius. After studying at the Institute of Technology in Stockholm and working at Drag for a while, he spent several years in England, France, and Belgium learning the trade before returning to Sweden in 1842. Backed by the ample capital of the new Drags AB, Lenning went over to mechanical wool weaving with looms purchased from Schönherr und Seidler in Chemnitz. In 1855 Drag had 30 mechanical and 32 hand looms, 280 workers, and two added water wheels. The wool was being purchased in Breslau, London, and Antwerp. Johan Lenning, like a couple of his forefathers, later went into politics, becoming known as a strong advocate of a protective tariff in the Riksdag.[43]

The State giveth, and the State taketh away. The Swedish government, which had protected industries in the tariff of 1816, had, as may be surmised from the plaint of Malcolm and Lenning, progressively lowered the tolls, from about 1830 on, achieving virtually free trade by 1865. Forced to compete with foreign imports, Swedish textile manufacturers had to go to large-scale production. As prices fell, only those completely mechanized could survive, and, according to Malcolm, the factory horsepower at work in Norrköping rose from 504 to 1842 to 1,799 in 1868. Norrköping's population also increased from 10,030 (1830) to 23,850 (1870).[44]

Mass production efficiency and costs demanded the use of larger mills, but mechanization was expensive, requiring the initial investment of much capital. The State taketh, and the State giveth. In 1848 it legalized the modern limited-liability stock company. (The Swedish word for a joint-stock company is *aktiebolag*, often shortened to AB; thus, Drags AB or Bergs AB.) About one-half of the capital invested in stock companies in Sweden during the next dozen years went into textile factories. In addition to Drag, the nature of the changeover can be clearly seen in four other Norrköping factories.

Bergs AB, a cotton mill, was founded in 1847 under another name by several associates, two of whom closed their mills in order to join this larger one; some of their spinning machines were made by Malcolm, and he bought others for them in England. A few years later it became a stock company, six of the largest shareholders in Drag also buying stock in Bergs AB. Lenning himself was excluded, despite his threat to start a competing cotton mill. Three other owners, originally from the west coast, combined their resources and switched from wool to cotton production (1850); their Norrköping Bomullsväveri AB attracted nine other manufacturers and investors. The twelve stockholders, using Rydboholm as a model, brought some workers from there as well as the knowledgeable Charles Hill. Needing a spinnery to complement their weaving, they bought the then run-down Gryt and brought in modern spinning machines (1856). This company would have the largest cotton production in the city for a time, followed by Bergs AB and Holmen, the latter also known, of course, as a paper-making firm.

After it became a company (1854), Holmen's owners bore names like Trozelli, Philipson (formerly Jeremias), and Bergwall and also included three Gothenburg investors. Smedjeholmen, the old Swartz workshop, was acquired by eight men, who in 1855 had shut down their six medium-sized mills to merge into the one large one. A woolen mill, it had a Belgian technical director from Verviers and the first water turbine in the city (1852), thanks to Malcolm. Bergsbro and Ströms followed in 1863 and 1866, both in the woolen sector and both industrial reincarnations of older firms.[45]

The very first Swedish stock company to be organized after the passage of the 1848 law was the Gefle Manufaktur AB, founded in 1849 in Gävle, with British help, as a cotton spinning and weaving mill. Its giant 13-meter water wheel came from Fairbairn in Manchester. Some of its leaders—Per Murén, G. F. Göransson, Robert Rettig—will reappear in other activities in one of Sweden's liveliest commercial towns. So will another participant in this enterpise, Lars Johan Hierta of Stockholm. A wool weaving mill was also started in that city in 1862. In Malmö, cotton spinning and cotton weaving mills were started in 1855 by two separate companies; several individuals held shares in both. The machinery for both plants came from England, an Englishman served as foreman in the spinning mill, and two Germans presided over the weavery. Another enterprise, Rosenlund (1847) of Gothenburg (to be distinguished from Francke's Rosendahl), became one of the largest mills in the country. Among those participating at one time or another were Alexander Barclay (exporter and owner of a sugar refinery); Brüsewitz & Röhss (a merchant house exporter of iron and timber and importer of cotton and coffee); and the real founder, C. D. Lundström, whose father had helped to loot the John Hall fortune.

After the triumphant 1850s came the disheartening 1860s when the Swedish cotton mills, deprived of American cotton, either closed down or went on exceedingly thin rations; all of Norrköping's cotton spinning mills closed in 1863. Recuperating when shipments resumed, the approximately forty Swedish cotton mills in 1870, comprising about twenty spinning mills and twenty weaving or combined spinning-weaving, employed approximately 6,000 workers. In the following decade several of Sweden's largest cotton mills would be established, some having ten to fifteen thousand spindles.[46] Though cotton had gained preeminence, wool products would begin to stage a recovery in the 1880s and once more passed cotton in total production by 1890.

Except for the omnipresent liquor distilleries, textiles must surely, by the 1870s, have been the most completely industralized branch of the economy.

Disregarding linen, silk, and other special branches for the sake of simplicity, the pattern of development differed little from those on the continent, though the tempo may have been somewhat slower. The Swedes served part of their apprenticeship in factory industry here, but, unlike a number of other sectors, they would not make any notable technical contributions to the textile mills; the basic transformation occurred before they were prepared, with a few individual exceptions, to do their own inventing.

The development of the textile industry does fully exhibit the dynamics of the nineteenth-century economic transformation, of the entrepreneurial spirit responding to, and in turn stimulating, the market demand. For businessmen, the innovations promised good profits for those alert enough to grasp the opportunity. Each advance forced others to follow or ultimately lose out. A history of individual business enterprises in its detailed manifestation, the composite story can be read as one of successive innovations, borrowed from abroad, at repeatedly higher technological levels leading to full industrialization.

The two-way traffic of Swedes going abroad to learn and of foreigners coming to Sweden to teach mechanical and industrial techniques is part of the general European scene at the time. The work-study travels of Munktell, Nydqvist, Arosenius, and the Lennings, reminiscent of the *Wanderjahre* of the handicraft apprentices, are typical. Throughout the century, this practice, wherein a young man would secure foreign employment for two or three years in enterprises using advanced techniques, would remain a major characteristic of Swedish development. By no means all of them returned, but their cumulative contribution to bringing and keeping the Swedes abreast of contemporary developments in successive industries was of crucial importance.

To some extent, obviously, industrial textiles rose out of the earlier handicraft spinning and weaving, but any generalization depends upon definitions and where one looks. Sven Erikson and August Bergman (and a few others) came directly out of handicrafts; several Norrköping families had begun with handicraft manufactories and a partial putting-out system. Other textile mills, however, were started by, especially, merchants with capital to invest who directly imported factory machines and techniques from abroad. In general, the persistence of strong continuity did characterize much of the Swedish economy in even its greatest period of change. Swedish industry is still embellished with numerous companies bearing centuries-old names, however much they may have transformed their methods of manufacture or switched from one industry to another. Holmen, Drag, and Klippan had many compeers. This continuity also helps to explain the geographically scattered distribution of industry, including the peculiarly Swedish persistence of sizable factories far out in the countryside. The textile industry did tend to concentrate in a few cities, especially in Norrköping, but Sweden never would have the large industrial cities so typical of other industrialized countries. Nor does the so-called Industrial Revolution seem very *revolutionary*, except in long-term impact, within the Swedish context; in fact its processes, viewed in detail, offer virtually a classic example of gradual, evolutionary change.

Though this narrative depicts individuals acting in free will to utilize economic realities and technical advances, the Swedish state was no passive onlooker during the early decades. The government still shared the paternalistic outlook of the continental regimes. Through its generally earnest and comparatively able bureaucracy, the state intermingled encouragement and restraints, the latter frequently vexatious to business proprietors with plans beyond the ordinary. It enforced guidelines, licensed enterprises, often set quotas of production, authorized or rejected proposed alterations, determined what could or could not be imported or exported, and granted loans or subsidies. Gradually the liberals, led largely by businessmen in the Riksdag, managed to wrest most of these powers away from the bureaucracy. By the 1850s the abstract picture of economic decisions freely made and implemented comes closer to the authentic reality of prevailing circumstances.

5. CRISIS IN IRON

Bengt Andersson Qvist (1726–1799) sounded the first alarm in 1767 after visiting the British iron works at Cyfarthfa and Penydoren (Pen-y-Daren). Sent to England to study Benjamin Huntsman's crucible process for making steel, he had also wandered down to South Wales where, at places that sound as though they belonged to the Britain of King Arthur, he found magic that would have astounded Merlin. In the red glow of the furnaces Qvist saw that Anthony Bacon and Samuel Homfray were successfully smelting iron by the use of *coal,* in the form of coke, in place of charcoal, the traditional fuel. Grasping the implications, he warned the Swedes that there might be "some reason to dread . . . injury to our iron trade."[1]

No one in Sweden paid much attention to him in this heyday of the proud iron industry, when the Swedes were able to export at will at prices essentially regulated by themselves. Swedish iron was relatively clean of impurities and possessed unique qualities of malleability. This high quality iron constituted about 30 percent of European iron production at this time, and iron made up about 75 percent of the total Swedish export. Well over one-half of this export went to Great Britain, which meant that any great technological advance in Britain's own iron production could spell disaster for the Swedes.

Abraham Darby of Coalbrookdale had in 1709 succeeded in smelting iron by the use of coal, and for a long time the Swedes kept a wary eye on British developments; nearly twenty Swedes visited British iron works between 1686 and 1772.[2] Others, however, were unable to repeat the Darby achievement: the iron was either too brittle to work when red hot because of sulfur from the coal, or too brittle when cooled because of an excess of phosphorus in the iron. The Swedes therefore had grounds for believing that coal posed no peril to their own abundant charcoal as a fuel, and ceased to worry about the British. Not that anyone could as yet explain the failures in these precise chemical terms, though Torbern Bergman (1735–1784), initiating the chemical analysis of iron, was finding that steel contained 0.3 percent to 0.8 percent carbon while cast iron ran from 1.0 percent to 3.3 percent. The Swedes thought, with good reason, that in Bergman, Sven Rinman (1720–1792) and others they had chemists/metallurgists second to none, and so an effective response to the growing peril would be long delayed by, among other reasons, an excessive reliance on theoretical chemistry for the answers.

Impelled by the urgent need for iron during the Seven Years War, John

69

Roebuck's Carron Ironworks in Scotland, started in 1759, succeeded in making coke-smelted iron in improved blast furnaces with the help of cylinder blowing engines. Cyfarthfa and Penydoren followed, as did John Wilkinson, the greatest ironmaster of his time, at Bersham and Broseley. The British continued using charcoal for the second phase of iron preparation, the conversion of cast iron into the purified and malleable wrought iron, until Henry Cort developed the puddling technique with a reverbatory furnace. The flames from the coal in the hearth were deflected into a second chamber onto the iron while the sulfur in the coal was safely retained in the hearth area; meantime, the metal was "puddled" by stirring with a long bar to permit the oxygen in the air to burn out the carbon.[3] It was now possible to fine the iron, to remove excess carbon, without contaminating it from the sulfur in the coal. To further remove impurities, Cort passed the iron through rollers, originally devised by Christopher Polhem (1745), who may have gotten the idea from the British in the first place.[4] The Swedish ironmasters, seemingly secure in their orderly, well-organized world, failed to take sufficient notice of these decisive developments; few Swedes visited the British iron works during the final crucial quarter-century.

The Swedish iron industry stretched primarily across the so-called Bergslagen, north of the big lakes, in the provinces of Värmland, Västmanland, Närke, and southern Dalarna. Much of it is a lovely rolling land of fir and birch trees interspersed with small lakes, clear flowing streams, and river valley farms. Värmland is (or was) Selma Lagerlöf country, suffused with nostalgic and highly romanticized memories of idyllic bygone days; its inhabitants still speak the lilting Swedish language at its brightly melodious best. This was the setting for the activities of the busy miners, a landscape, to paraphrase Birger Steckzén, of red flames from the small iron foundries, the sound of the hammer at the forges, the busy charcoal burners deep in the forest, the caravans of sleds transporting the iron across the snow to the lake ports, and the lively social life of the brukspatroner, the ironmasters.[5]

The brukspatroner, who owned most of the surrounding land and who included some of the most prestigious noble families in the kingdom, presided in paternal fashion over the miners and peasants. The work tended to be hereditary, the same proprietors and miners passing on their techniques of iron mining, smelting, and fining from generation to generation. Eight different markets brought the inhabitants of each district together for both business and recreation; the Hindersmässan at Örebro had existed far back in the Middle Ages, as had the Hedemora market, held at the oldest town in Dalarna.

Some of the iron works or bruk (pronounced "brük") had been started in later medieval times by peasants in order to make such tools as hammers, knives and axes. In the sixteenth century the Swedes imported the German method of using a blast furnace to smelt the ore into pig iron, then fining it by hammering at a forge in order to reduce the carbon content. The iron industry became centered in Bergslagen (the term means "the mining teams") because it had the necessary conjunction of iron ore, forests for fuel, and water power. Water power was needed to run the blowers or bellows that poured air into the blast furnace and to provide power for the hammers in the fining. The *bruk* were more likely to be located close to the fuel supply, difficult to transport in such quantities, than at the ore quarry. Pig iron was produced at the *hyttorna* (foundries), then taken to the scattered forges for the fining into bar iron.

In the seventeenth century the De Geer family brought the so-called Walloon type of iron handling to the Dannemora area of northern Uppland. By replacing the log furnace with one made of brick and using a special hammer on a separate forge for the fining, they produced a better quality of iron. About three hundred Walloon families from the area of present-day Belgium settled in Sweden at this time.

At the beginning of the seventeenth century the government limited the peasants to mining and smelting, thereby restricting the making of bar iron to burghers and nobles; the *brukspatron,* a type of aristocrat peculiar to Sweden, emerged as an important figure in the economic and social life of the country. The government, fearing that the wood for charcoal might become exhausted, rarely granted permission to set up new forges in Bergslagen after about 1600, thus effectively dispersing them to other parts of Sweden. Although the state forced the iron works to scatter in order to conserve the forests, it also resulted in keeping them small and in preventing any concentration of manufacturing. To prevent a higher production of iron from driving down the prices, the state maintained strict quotas on the *bruk,* rigidly fixing the amount of ore for each foundry and of bar iron for individual forges. In order to safeguard the supply and livelihood of the forges, the export of pig iron continued to be forbidden until 1857. With the output effectively curtailed, the export of bar iron rose from about 33,000 tons per year in the 1720s only to about 40,000 in 1780. High quality standards and subsidized metallurgical research were maintained by the state through the Board of Mines.

The *brukspatroner* themselves had organized an Association of Ironmasters (Brukssocietet), divided regionally into eight districts based on the prevailing eight markets. In 1747 they secured a royal charter for an Iron Office (Jernkontoret) as the executive office of the association; independent of control from the Riksdag after 1769, it possessed more autonomy from state control than any organization in Sweden at that time. Its creation, sponsored by the Hat political party, reflected the importance and influence of the ironmasters as a society in themselves, cohesive and powerful.

The Iron Office henceforth regulated the industry to keep prices high, to grant loans whenever needed, and to further metallurgical research. The Association of Ironmasters chose the directors, the votes being weighted according to the number and capacity of the foundries and forges each individual owned; a special levy on the foundries and forges ensured the financial health of the organization. The Iron Office maintained a permanent staff of technical and financial experts for research and for supervising the operation of the iron works. Granting loans on favorable terms remained the single most important purpose, but it also sponsored scientific and technical research and experimentation, a matter of the utmost urgency when the nineteenth-century crisis struck. It offered travel stipends, published journals, collected models of inventions, conducted geological surveys, gave medals for noteworthy contributions, and maintained a museum of minerals. The Iron Office also set up a Metallurgical Institute in Stockholm, supported students at such enterprises as Motala, and later gave assistance to mining students at schools in Falun and Filipstad.[6]

The eighteenth century was an age of prosperity for the Swedish ironmasters, of security and high prices in which even the small iron works showed good profits. In 1800 Sweden possessed about 510 officially recognized *bruk,* of which only 74 had quotas of any substantial size. Swedish exports had started to drop before the end of the century, but the Napoleonic wars postponed the full impact, and not until about 1820 did the competitive effects of the much less costly British production begin to be felt. In quantity if not quality, a threat had also emerged from the Russians, who, producing about 130,000 tons in 1790, were shipping more iron to Britain than the Swedes.[7] The Russians failed to modernize, however, until the much later arrival of John Hughes, a veteran of Cyfarthfa. It would be what J. D. Chambers has called the "new iron age" emerging in Great Britain that would confront Sweden with its greatest economic crisis in the very area in which it had formerly been supreme. Only the very highest quality bar iron made by the Walloon method seemed safe from competition; most of this exceptionally pure iron, extracted from the Dannemora mines, went to the specialized manufacturing in Sheffield.[8]

Whenever a group of people have succeeded in arranging their affairs to their entire satisfaction, someone else is altogether likely to come along and upset it. The British ironmasters, at long last succeeding in substituting their abundant coal for their depleted supply of wood, turned the tables on the Swedes, who had safeguarded their forests—and who lacked coal. It remained to be seen whether the Swedish ironmasters, wedded to generations-old practices, could respond to the deadly challenge from Cyfarthfa, Penydoren, and the other British iron works.

This time the Swedes could not vault into industrialization the easy way by buying machinery from Bryan Donkin, Pontifex & Wood, or the Cockerills. It was not really a question of installations, for the Swedes should have been able to reproduce, with some effort, the British blast and reverbatory furnaces, the rolling mill, and the technique of puddling iron. To copy the British, they must buy coal or coke, and that was a self-defeating proposition. The vast majority of the iron works lay deep in the interior of the country, and, before the building of railroads, the costs of transportation added to the purchase price of the coal would render the Swedish iron industry even less competitive on the international markets.

Quite aside from the cost of the coal, the ironmasters had a more positive reason for persisting with charcoal. The famed high-quality Swedish iron, relatively pure when mined, had been smelted with sulfur-free charcoal, derived from pine and spruce, slow-burning but leaving the pig iron comparatively free of gases and oxides. Given these "Swedish circumstances"—to use the oft-repeated phrase in the interminable discussions at the Iron Office and in meetings of the Association of Ironmasters—they would have to adapt British methods to the continued use of charcoal, *if* possible. For several decades they sought to solve this vexing and seemingly insuperable dilemma, rooted in the inability to generate a sufficiently high temperature.

Should they solve the problem of heat, they would still not be free of their quandary. Before railroads, the individual *bruk* necessarily depended upon nearby sources of wood. That Sweden had widespread forests capable of sustaining large-scale lumbering did not much help the mining and metal industry, which in 1854, to take a later date, devoured four to five times as much timber as the total export of sawn and unsawn wood.[9] The limited supply of local fuel seemed to doom Sweden's iron industry to continued reliance on small iron *bruk,* not likely to compete with large iron works abroad. Experimentation and ultimate reconstruction required capital far exceeding their financial resources, nor would credit, based almost exclusively on the large merchant houses in Stockholm and Gothenburg, normally suffice to finance major changes. In the long run, the "new iron age" necessitated a greater centralization of production and larger iron works, however this might be brought about.

Any process of change is likely to create a sense of insecurity and apprehension. More than the vested interests of the *brukspatroner* were involved, for the closure of the many small iron works would destroy the livelihood of the miners dependent upon them. Quite naturally, the great majority of proprietors and miners preferred to postpone the evil day. The inertia of tradition, now extending back two to three centuries, and the sheer momentum of practices long successful and not lightly abandoned, militated against a resolute response to the challenge.

Neither Sven Rinman, late in the century, nor Eric Thomas Svedenstierna

(1765–1825), shortly after 1800, conveyed any sense of urgency upon their return from visits to Britain. On the contrary, both believed that the Swedes should attempt to improve their quality of iron by traditional methods, rather than adopt those of the British. Svedenstierna's account of his journey, published in 1804, may be interesting for his description of the general British scene, but the Association of Ironmasters, which had paid his expenses, was not satisfied with it, and ultimately he had to write a more specific essay on the significance of the puddling process for the future of Swedish wrought iron. When his travel book was republished in England in 1971, Svedenstierna was called an "industrial spy," rather too flattering a term for his actual achievement.

Gustaf Broling (1766–1838) visited England in 1797–99 with the financial support of the Board of Mines and the Iron Office, but his primary interest lay in Huntsman's crucible steel. He established a workshop in Stockholm for the manufacture of surgical instruments and similar tools out of steel, and, rather than import it, he also made, with "mixed results," the crucible steel. His venture received financial assistance from Count Erik Ruuth, for whom Broling had set up a foundry and a shop for producing (not wholly successfully) fireproof clay goods. Like Qvist earlier, Broling needed fireproof bricks for his crucible, and they would be necessary for new-style iron industry furnaces generally. Broling also attempted to construct small steel rolling mills, of which Svedenstierna had brought back models from France.[10]

Of the endless discussions, the sundry experiments, and the persistent research by the Iron Office, only the salient episodes can be described here. It was A. F. Rosenborg of Kloster in Dalarna who first acted to meet the challenge. Though experimenting would long be hampered by the strict bureaucratic regulations, and "manufacturing" was not normally permitted in Bergslagen, Rosenborg did receive permission to set up a rolling mill at Kloster. Samuel Owen, then at Bergsund, made it, and Svedenstierna helped in mounting it, but it turned out to be too weak and had to be repeatedly improved. Despite stormy opposition at a meeting of the Association of Ironmasters, Rosenborg built a reverbatory furnace and tried to puddle iron, using charcoal. The result uncovered more problems than answers (1811–14). A high enough temperature for successful puddling could not be reached, nor could the furnace withstand even the heat that was achieved.[11]

Though unsuccessful, Carl David af Uhr (1770–1849), another metallurgist, thought the experiments sufficiently promising to be pursued. Son of a bruspatron, he had studied with Samuel Owen and Eric Nordewall, the latter renowned as an hydraulic engineer. Af Uhr, a man of many attainments who had also worked on fireproof bricks at Höganäs, was sent to England by the Iron Office in 1820, along with Broling, to undertake an intensive study of the puddling process. After publishing a complete description, he then, still supported by the Iron Office, conducted lengthy experiments at the Schebo iron works during the early 1820s.

Schebo was owned by the Arfwedsons. Carl Abraham Arfwedson had, in the course of his tour of Britain in 1796, visited Cyfarthfa and Coalbrookdale, shortly before Svedenstierna, and had apparently not forgotten the experience; this was the period when Richard Crawshay at Cyfarthfa, among others, was successfully introducing Cort's puddling process. Schebo already had an Owen rolling mill, and it was Owen who now constructed Sweden's first technically irreproachable reverbatory furnace. C. D. af Uhr, insisting on "Swedish fuel," used charcoal. They were fair enough tests, skillfully carried through, but the resultant iron was not as good as that produced by the traditional fining at the forges. He finally concluded that puddling "could not be used to advantage in our land," unless, indeed, some way could be found to create a more intense heat from charcoal.[12]

The Swedes were not alone in their reluctance to abandon charcoal and traditional methods. In France, Le Creusot, with nearby coal beds, began using coke in 1782, but it was still the only user in 1815. A British father and son, Aaron and Charles Manby, founded the coke-using Charenton iron works in 1822, using smuggled equipment and employing 200–250 British workers. In Germany, two Silesian coke-smelting iron works went into successful operation in the 1790s, following several visits to Britain by Prussian experts and the hiring of John Baildon, formerly at the Carron Ironworks. The puddling process was introduced into Prussia in 1824–25, led by two Germans who had studied it in Britain and who had brought back British puddlers. Friedrich Harkort, also employing English workers, adopted it at Wetter in 1826, followed by Jacob Meyer (who had worked in Sheffield) at Bochum.[13] The Germans and French had coal mines, of course.

By the late 1820s the situation looked grim for the Swedish ironmasters, and, after the impasse at Schebo, efforts to find a solution were being redoubled. Anyone in a position to do like the Prussians and use coke would be sorely tempted to try it. Carl Fredrik Waern had prospered as a Gothenburg agent for the sale of iron and timber abroad, and he had good contacts in Britain. In 1823 he purchased Bäckefors, where he soon received British complaints about the quality of the iron from his *bruk*. Failing in an attempt to improve the quality along traditional lines, Waern forthwith hired eight British workers to install South Wales iron techniques (1829). Bäckefors having rather less transport problems than most *bruk*, he also went over to the use of coke in the hollow fire blast furnace. The blast furnace, rolling mill, and coke eventually did produce better iron and higher production, but only after adding a welding furnace did he achieve bar iron of satisfactory quality. Waern had essentially gone to the Lancashire type of iron production. The name was a misnomer; his workers had apparently come from Pontypool in Monmouthshire, and the so-

75

called Lancashire hearth seems to have owed its name to the forges at Pontypool using pig iron from Lancashire.[14]

Emanuel Rothoff (1788–1832) agreed with Waern that they must go to coal and British methods.[15] Like Waern, he was directly on the firing line. His family owned the famous old Karl Gustafs Stad, a manufactory in Eskilstuna, and Rothoff was also part owner of Uddeholm, an old iron works in Värmland. Eskilstuna, on its way to becoming the Sheffield of Sweden by its specialized manufactories, needed the highest possible quality of iron and steel if its shops were to be competitive. An impatient exponent of discarding traditional methods for practical reasons, Rothoff also, as a student and coworker with Berzelius, knew his chemistry. In 1810–12 he was at the Göta Canal trying to develop more effective cement for the locks, and later he was experimenting, on behalf of the Iron Office, with the puddling process and rolling mills. Now, at the beginning of the 1830s, he was invited to participate in a promising experiment at the Nyby iron works.

Pehr Lagerhjelm (1787–1856) had instigated the Nyby tests. He also combined theoretical knowledge with the fruits of practical experience as a student of Berzelius and as owner of Bofors, where he laid the foundations for its future greatness. Twice he won gold medals from the Iron Office, the second time for a device that tested the density, strength, resiliency, and malleability of iron. By means of it, he demonstrated all too clearly that British methods produced much better iron (1825–27). Lagerhjelm insisted that the rolling mill must replace the traditional fining with the hammer; not only would better iron result, the milling enabled far greater capacity, and such mass production would be much cheaper. Lagerhjelm argued that rolling mills must be constructed at the centers of iron transport, that high standards of production there guarantee high-quality iron, and that the small *bruk* should forward much of their pig iron to the centers, instead of producing their own bar iron. The owners of small (and some not so small) iron works naturally became alarmed, and the battle between rolling mill and hammer adherents intensified. But Lagerhjelm in the 1820s and 1830s was visualizing the future inevitable centralization of the Swedish iron works.[16]

All this, of course, did not resolve the problem of the deficiency of charcoal as a fuel. Just then, near the end of the 1820s, came exciting reports that an Austrian at Wolfsberg had succeeded in developing a method of using wood for fuel. Erik Adolf Zethelius (1781–1864) bought the Swedish rights to the Wolfsberg patent for his Nyby iron works, then in the process of construction on a small canal near Eskilstuna. Though a Stockholm goldsmith originally, he had studied British iron processes on several trips abroad, and he equipped Nyby with reverbatory furnace and rolling mill, helped by Samuel Owen. He also hired some British workers.

Lagerhjelm, whose idea it had been in the first place, joined Zethelius, as did

Rothoff, to test whether wood could be used as a fuel by the Austrian method. The Iron Office loaned Zethelius 12,000 rdr., though begrudgingly and over the protests of the badly frightened proponents of the hammer. The test was made, the molten iron from the blast furnace went directly into the reverbatory furnace, and at the end of the puddling process the men found that it had worked—they had made reasonably good iron. Samuel Owen adopted it for his Kungsholmen machine shop the next year (1833).[17] Though hopes were buoyed, it was not a clear breakthrough: the iron had been especially good quality in the first place, and the process was too expensive to be generally competitive. As for Zethelius, he was so furious at Iron Office officiousness that, receiving the gold medal for his achievement, he promptly had the medal melted; later regretting his impulsive act, he secretly had the mint make him a replica.

Not yet, after some decades, had this tight little circle of men found a fully practical solution to the dilemma. These individuals, and others not here mentioned, made up a closely associated group in which everyone knew everyone else. Often members of *brukspatron* families, they had usually studied at Uppsala, with its excellent chemists and metallurgists, before taking the *bergsexamin*, the mining examination. Each one in turn went abroad, usually to Britain, to study new techniques. They gained experience in various *bruk*, within the same intimate network, and at times they worked directly in the service of the Iron Office. Familiar names and places occur and recur: Berzelius, Samuel Owen, Erik Ruuth, Motala, Höganäs, the Göta and Trollhätte canals. Grants from the Iron Office and the receipt of gold medals for achievement form part of the common pattern. They were working individually, or two or three together, in successive ventures, but nearly always within the framework of the larger organized group.

Experimenting one day in 1830 at Bäckefors, Waern looked up and saw an interested spectator, Gustaf Ekman of the Iron Office. Waern, an outsider who apparently had had his crawful of unpleasantness because of his "betrayal" of charcoal, did not welcome Iron Office representatives at his iron works and brusquely made his feelings known to Ekman. Though their versions of the encounter differed, Waern evidently told Ekman that he would be happy to see him whenever he severed his ties with officialdom and went to work, instead, at his father's Lesjöfors *bruk*.[18]

Gustaf Ekman (1804–1876) was certainly not unknown to Waern. The Ekmans, too, were major exporters of iron out of Gothenburg and had a vital stake in resolving the drawn-out crisis in the iron industry. Gustaf had, after attending Uppsala, taken the *bergsexamin* before reaching his twenty-first birthday and then served an apprenticeship under Count von Platen, his uncle, at the Göta Canal and Motala. Here he observed the practical application of theory, learned to see the hard reality of problems and how to go about solving them.[19] Next, as a student at the Falun School of Mines and at the Iron Office he must surely have become aware of the need for greater density and evenness of quality in Swedish iron and recognized that these depended upon higher heat in the furnace.

On his first of several visits to England (1828) he was stunned by the "revolutionary importance" of the British advances in both quality and quantity, but he still hoped that Swedish iron could be saved by a further development of the hearth method. At Ulverstone, particularly, he studied the Lancashire process, derived from the Walloon method, which was economical in fuel while resulting in first-rate bar iron. Its only major difference from the Swedish version of the Walloon originally had consisted in the use of a closed hearth, which saved on fuel, but the British had been going over to use of a welding furnace before the molten iron went into the rolling mill.[20] Here the Swedes could not follow unless they solved the problem of generating enough heat by means of charcoal.

Other options failing, one possible salvation for at least some iron works would be to expand the usage of the Walloon method, whose superior quality had kept it competitive. Ekman, on behalf of the Iron Office, attempted a variation of it at Dormsjö in Dalarna in 1830. Results were not good, because of the uneven quality of the iron, an inadequate blower, and workers not properly trained in this method. During the next few years he installed it at several iron works, where improved circumstances gave better results. However, Ekman at Dormsjö had seriously considered replacing the fining hearth with a welding furnace, but, ever cautious, he abstained. Having meanwhile learned about Waern's use of British methods, he journeyed to Bäckefors, only to be rebuffed.

He returned to Britain (1831), where at one point he had an illuminating discussion with James B. Neilson of Glasgow, inventor of a new blower for blast furnaces and hearths. Using Neilson's principles, he worked out his own blower, for which the Iron Office awarded him a gold medal. In 1836 he quit that organization to take over Lesjöfors, which as a small boy he had dreamed of running someday. Waern having relented long before this, Ekman had experimented with puddling at Bäckefors, and the two men were such good friends that at times they loaned each other the services of British workers. Nyby's relative success with puddling induced Ekman to try a Wolfsberg furnace; he did not like it, and, visiting Nyby, thought the Wolfsbergs there too awkward for practical iron handling.[21]

Prudently, step by step, Ekman was assembling the elements for adapting the Lancashire method to Swedish circumstances. His intellectual itinerary followed the usual pattern of inventing: a clear identification of the specific problem; repeated and seemingly unsatisfactory experiments with alternatives; a glimpse of the right answer, which was not yet followed up; and finally the perception of the hitherto missing key to a solution. M. Ebelman (France) and W. von Faber du Tour (Germany) published their new theories of gases, and Ekman saw that the attainment of high heat depended upon the hitherto not understood role of gases as a source of heat and their effective distribution from the burning charcoal. His instincts had been right at Dormsjö in 1830 when they had nudged him to try the welding furnace.

A visit to a gas puddling furnace in Württemberg confirmed his own deductions. He built a puddling furnace at Gammelskroppa, using the gas as a fuel. The resultant iron was still uneven in quality because the fuel was not evenly distributed. He remedied this by providing the puddling furnace with a special generator in which gas from the generator charcoal was blown onto the puddling process. In its final form, Ekman's so-called *koltornsvällugn* contained a tower or shaft into which was blown cold air, which pressed the gases below into the furnace itself and over the puddling iron. The flames of the charcoal did not reach the iron, would not contaminate it, and air blown into the furnace from other apertures ignited the carbonic oxide evenly over the iron.[22]

He then obtained money from the Iron Office to build one at Lesjöfors, and was promised additional support when at least two other proprietors had used the method successfully for three months (1843). By the spring of 1845 five owners had attested to its success. After a dozen years of work Ekman had made the Lancashire method practicable in Sweden, not forgetting Waern's prior use of coal, by using a welding furnace capable of intense heat with charcoal. Eli Heckscher called Ekman's achievement "the most glorious page in Swedish iron handling" and, in fact, in all of Swedish economic history. The Swedish iron industry could go on using charcoal (or wood or peat), and not as much fuel was required, thereby sparing on the forest supply. Making possible the effective installation of rolling mills, it implicitly required a greater concentration of iron works, but it also offered a reprieve for many smaller *bruk* if they adopted the Lancashire system.[23]

The Lancashire process was adopted by many iron works in the 1850s, though some, in these years, chose the Franche-Comté method, which used less fuel and was also derived from the Walloon. The Franche-Comté failed to survive the concentration of iron works and the rising cost of charcoal, but about forty iron works in 1893 were still using the Lancashire, producing the greater part of the 233,700 tons of iron made in that year.

Waern's original hostility to Ekman, not based on any personal dislike, sprang directly out of Waern's perception of him as a prying official, the momentary embodiment of the mass of regulations that he thought hobbled the industry. Parallel to the long struggle along technical lines another lengthy battle was being fought to liberate the iron works from the restrictive regulations. Very early in the century the dominant personality in the Iron Office,

Baron Lars August Mannerheim, repeatedly criticized these regulations from his position as an obdurate defender of aristocratic privileges; he had also been a leader in the deposition of Gustav IV Adolf. His family name would be made better known in the twentieth century by a relative, Carl Gustaf Mannerheim, field marshal and ultimately president of Finland. And, an odd coincidence, Bengt Andersson Qvist, he who sounded the alarm in 1767, belonged to a branch (*qvist*, now spelled *kvist*, means "twig" or "branch") of the Svinhufvud family, which also produced a president of Finland.[24]

Lagerhjelm and Rothoff led the attack on the restrictions, supported by such others as Johannes Noreus, who represented the Falun area of Bergslagen in the Riksdag. A nephew of the *brukspatron* of Bäckefors, Jonas Waern (1799–1868), the owner of Gullspångs *bruk* and managing director of Uddeholm, advocated the liberal program, especially the freeing of iron, in the parliament for many years. Loud, and sometimes counterproductive, was Thore Petré of Hofors, the *enfant terrible* of the industry and a passionate hater of bureaucracy and regulations.[25] Loose talk could be inflammatory with a public that had long suspected the ironmasters of exacting unnecessarily high prices and whose indignation added weight to the demands. Meantime, proprietors of iron works dependent upon the preservation of privileges naturally defended their interests in their association and in parliament to the limit of their ability.

Against their opposition and the bureaucratic mentality, deregulation could only take place piecemeal. First of any importance came the freeing of trade in pig iron within Sweden (1835) and the provisional suspension of regulations over the forges (1838); the latter were permanently liberated in 1846, as were the charcoal burners. The liberal political breakthrough in the 1850s brought deregulation in many areas, including the iron industry: the freeing of the mining of ore (1855), the right to export pig iron (1857), and the elimination of remaining restrictions in 1858. Thus did the industry, in the words of Arthur Montgomery, finish the long process of "laboriously freeing itself from the tutelage of public regulations and supervision."[26]

Viewed in retrospect, the long struggle to adapt more advanced technology to the circumstances of the Swedish iron industry, seemingly so central to Sweden's destiny at the time, is filled with irony, no pun intended. The innovators worked to resolve compelling problems within the exigencies of their existing situation. Then, the battle won, the circumstances shifted, as happens so often in the opaque and devious grooves of historical progression. The railroads made possible the much cheaper import of coal while the rapidly growing demand for charcoal drove up its prices until, with increasing concentration, the larger iron works began to go over to the use of coal. Furthermore, new technological advances brought the advent of steel in quantity (and, subsequently, the large-scale export of iron ore), thereby outdating and obscuring the achievements of Gustaf Ekman and his predecessors.

Göran Fredrik Göransson (1819–1900) went to England in the spring of 1857 to buy a steam engine for Daniel Elfstrand & Co. of Gävle and came back with partial rights to the Bessemer steel process. Göransson, never having attended Uppsala nor taken the *bergsexamin,* knew precious little about iron or steel. He was a businessman, a partner in the Elfstrand family enterprise, who had participated in founding the Gefle Manufaktur textile mill and in the start of a railroad from Gävle to Falun. Elfstrand, beginning as a merchant firm in 1738, had gradually expanded into landed property, forests, ships, and the sale of iron from inland *bruk.* In 1856 the firm acquired complete control of the Högbo iron works west of Gävle and put Göransson in charge of it.

To create steel, the carbon content in pig iron had to be reduced to an absolute minimum, at this time a slow and expensive process. In Sweden, Bengt Andersson Qvist had continued to make crucible steel by the Huntsman method in small quantities until his death at the end of the century, and Broling's shop produced it from 1808 until 1837. Carl Victor Heljestrand made crucible steel for his own manufacture of knives and razors in Eskilstuna, Ekman experimented with it for a time at Lesjöfors, and a number of iron works later included it in their manufacturing.[27]

At the 1856 meeting of the British Association for the Advancement of Science, Henry Bessemer created a sensation by announcing that he had found a way to mass-produce steel. He claimed to be able to make five tons of cast steel in thirty minutes, whereas it took fifteen days to make fifty pounds of the crucible variety. According to him, he accomplished it by blowing sufficient cold air on molten pig iron for the oxygen to eliminate the carbon by chemical reaction; later, he devised the "Bessemer converter," a huge pear-shaped container in which the pig iron was subjected to cold air by means of tubes in the bottom.[28]

Not everyone believed Bessemer's original announcement, nor did his background, lacking in metallurgy, inspire confidence. He had invented a rifled projectile during the Crimean War that interested Napoleon III, but, unfortunately, the iron in the guns cracked when shots were fired. He went back to London and experimented with iron for two years before emerging with his startling claim. The following spring Pontus Kleman, the Swedish agent in London for the Elfstrand firm, introduced Göransson to Henry Bessemer. No doubt Kleman, who had also represented Carnegie and Waern and who was now a well-known financier and speculator on the lookout for new ventures, helped the Gävle businessman to make his fast decision to buy one-fifth of the Swedish rights to the patent for £2000.

Göransson had British engineers set up two Bessemer furnaces, one at Dormsjö, the site of former Ekman experiments where Kleman now held part interest, and the other at Edske, a blast furnace belonging to Högbo. Attempts to make Bessemer steel at Dormsjö failed completely. So did experiments at Edske later in the year, and the British helpers were sent home. The Edske furnace was torn apart and rebuilt to conform exactly to Bessemer's own specifications, with results no more encouraging. At this point the Elfstrand firm collapsed, a victim of the 1857 financial crisis and losses on its ships. New funds had to be found, and Göransson managed to procure 50,000 rdr. from the Iron Office, although many ironmasters, fearing a new source of competition, wished him no good luck.[29]

Experiments at Edske continued, assisted by Johan Leffler, Victor Eggertz, and other knowledgeable Swedish metallurgists, but all to no avail. Their growing mood of frustrated desperation was not helped one whit by the flow of news from England, all bad. British ironmasters, using his converter, could not make Bessemer steel either; it fell apart under any impact. Iron works in the United States reported the same results. The newspapers were calling Henry Bessemer a charlatan and a cheat. The helplessly confused man, who *knew* that he had made good steel, sank into acutely embarrassed despair.[30]

Though Andreas Grill, another metallurgist, had by now given Göransson a cram course in the handling of iron, he still did not know enough chemistry to realize that, according to current chemical knowledge, further experimenting was hopeless. At the moment, the harassed amateur ironmaster thought the helpful, sympathetic Victor Eggertz, head of the Falun School of Mines, his only friend. Possibly Eggertz gave him the idea, or perhaps, all else failing, he acted on impulse—he widened the apertures through which flowed the cold air onto the molten iron. On July 18, 1858, at Edske, he produced good commercial Bessemer steel, the first in the world.[31]

Triumphantly, Göransson lugged a sample to England to show a baffled Henry Bessemer. The inventor finally had recourse to an eminent chemist, who duly explained to him that his process had eliminated carbon from his iron, but not the phosphorus. As little as four-tenths of one percent of phosphorus in the iron would cause the steel to disintegrate. In his own original experiments Bessemer had happened to get his iron from one of the very few mines in Great Britain that was virtually free of phosphorus. Hence his experiment had worked, but the ironmasters who tried to copy him were using less pure iron from other mines and therefore failed. It so happened that Göransson's Swedish iron had little or no phosphorus, hence he produced Bessemer steel, once he got his techniques straightened out, including stopping the blower when the carbon content had been sufficiently reduced. Bessemer never did give Göransson any credit, a perfectly natural human response under the circumstances, but he did start using Swedish iron in his own work.

The Sandviken iron and steel mill now erected by the Högbo company inaugurated a new chapter in the history of the Swedish iron industry for another reason than its Bessemer production. It was the first of the larger iron works that would emerge in the period of concentration; in fact Sandviken remained the country's largest until overtaken by Domnarvet at the end of the century. In a radical departure from former practice, Göransson and the company did not locate the steel mill near forests for fuel or near the mines; they placed it at Storsjön, a lake, within easy access of the harbor at Gävle and, even more significant, on the newly constructed railroad from Gävle to Falun and its abundant supply of iron and charcoal. For the first time a railroad emancipated a Swedish iron works from the inflexible costs of old-time transportation.[32]

Sandviken started pouring steel at the end of August 1863. And closed down again in March 1866 when financial distress forced liquidation of the Högbo company. This crisis makes up one episode in a series of events, one part of the entangled skein of financing of early Swedish industry, and can be better delineated later in terms of this larger picture. In short, it involved Pontus Kleman in London and Johan Holm, one of the most aggressive capitalists in Sweden. Holm went into bankruptcy at the beginning of 1865, and Kleman, still nursing ambitious projects of his own, vainly sought supporting capital in England. The company left large unpaid debts, mostly for the purchase of equipment, to Giles Loder, Hinde and Gladstone, I. Thomson, T. Bonar & Co., and the English-Swedish Bank in London.

Göransson managed to buy the Sandviken mill back at auction, through his family and associates, and production resumed in 1868. This time the company prospered, particularly with the manufacture of rims for railroad wheels and solid steel cylinders for the boring of cannon, and a new building soon had to be added. The original edifice housed one of the largest hammers in Europe, bought from the Kirkstall Forge Co. (Leeds), which the Swedes liked to compare to the gigantic "Old Fritz" at the Krupp works in Germany. Less than a fifth of the Sandviken production was sold in Scandinavia, the bulk of it being exported to Great Britain, Russia, France, and Germany. Göransson broke with traditional sales policy; rather than exporting through agents, he stationed permanent company representatives in London, Paris, Hamburg, St. Petersburg, and Copenhagen.[33] His son, Henrik, traveled abroad for some years, keeping in touch with the salesmen, learning local demand and discovering more sales opportunities.

Bessemer steel mills did not long hold the field unchallenged. Emile and Pierre Martin, with William Siemens, originated the Siemens-Martin process

(1864) in which more efficient use of the gases produced a more intense heat. A small Martin furnace began pouring steel at Munkfors in 1868, and two others were put up at Hellefors and Kilafors in 1869, the same year that Krupp adopted the method. It took another twenty years, however, before others followed these leads and adopted the coal-consuming Siemens-Martin; eventually its open-hearth process was producing more steel in Sweden than the Bessemer mills.

The phosphorus in iron, which bedeviled the British ironmaster contemporaries of Abraham Darby, had still baffled the unsuspecting Henry Bessemer in 1856–58. At long last this demon that had held so much iron in thrall was exorcised by the Thomas-Gilchrist method (basic process) in 1878, whereby limestone or dolomite, lining a converter, absorbed the phosphorus and so freed the iron for industrial use. The Thomas-Gilchrist process would unlock a treasure of hitherto unused iron ore in central and northern Sweden for large-scale export and thereby begin still another chapter in the history of the Swedish iron industry.

6. TIMBER FOR EXPORT

Robertsfors, its houses clustered along both sides of the rushing Rickleån, presents " . . . a tableau, full of idyllic peace. . . . The big new buildings are just completed around the lower falls and bridge . . . , a picturesque and changing view whose individuality is enhanced by the dwelling houses on the higher river bank. . . ." A little marketplace (*torget*), barns and sheds, bathing cabins, and some other buildings complete the scene. The new structures contain a blast furnace, hammer mill, manufacture works, smithy, sawmill, and carpenter shop. The flames rise from the blast furnace, and above the roar of the falls and rapids can be heard the thumping of the bar iron hammer and the pecking sounds from the hammers at the manufactory. As described by Bertil Boëthius, Robertsfors must have looked like a hundred other iron *bruk* and sawmill communities in the years shortly after 1800.[1]

About 200 persons were employed in the village, 178 of them at the iron *bruk,* some at the sawmill, and a few others in such capacities as charcoal burner, tailor, shoemaker, and watchman. A master smith with a journeyman (*sven*) worked at one hearth, and at a second one labored two other journeymen, these two couples being assisted by a number of hired hands. The sawmill employed a few permanent operators and additional seasonal laborers as occasion demanded. An inspector managed the enterprise on behalf of the absentee owner; he had a reasonably good, rent-free house and several other perquisites, but when the owner visited, he also moved in there. So did the Lutheran pastor. Only the inspector, pastor, and the poorly paid bookkeepers had a higher status, and they made up their own little social group, playing cards together and organizing hunts with hounds.

Here, near the land of the midnight sun, the crews worked long, hard days in summer. During the brief daylight hours of winter, things quieted down, though charcoal and ore had to be transported to the *bruk* over the snowy, frozen roads. The springtime melting of the river brought the floating of logs for the sawmill. Says Boëthius, a *brännvin* premium would sometimes speed up the logging work or reward those compelled to work late into the night. Along with the strong drink often came brisk fights.[2]

The village name, Robert's Rapids in English, honored its founder, Robert Finlay (1729–1773), met earlier as a leading figure in the Swedish East India Company. Born in Dublin of a Scottish noble family and banker father, Finlay, with John Jennings, had become a leading Stockholm exporter of iron, and as such had started the *bruk* in 1759. If it differed in any major respect from other small iron works, it was only in its remote location in Västerbotten, the northernmost province along the coast of the Gulf of Bothnia. Behind it, the dark green spruce of the virgin Norrland forest stretched westward up to the barren highlands along the mountainous Norwegian border. From Lapland's tundra in the far north, the vast forest covered Norrland, which makes up a good half of the kingdom, and spread southward beyond it to a line running approximately from Lake Vänern to Gävle. Twelve rivers, or fourteen if the largest tributaries are counted, flowed from the inland highlands through the forest to the sea. Along the coast lay small ports from whence in time would be exported huge quantities of Norrland timber: Söderhamn, Hudiksvall, Sundsvall, Härnösand, Örnsköldsvik, Umeå, and several others beyond these. Robertsfors lay some distance to the north of Umeå.

That Robertsfors combined sawmill operations with an iron works was nothing unusual. A *bruk* owner with ample reserves of forest often augmented his income by using part of its timber and some of the power from the water wheel to run a saw. Later, when the concentration of iron works forced the smaller ones out of iron smelting or forging, they frequently went over entirely to the sawmill industry.

Whether owned by an iron works, local businessmen, a merchant house, or a timber baron, a sawmill needed unobstructed waterways to float timber, a fine-bladed saw, and a water wheel for power. The work of cleaning the streams, starting in the mid-1700s in Norrland, would continue until near the end of the nineteenth century, when, at the peak of Swedish lumbering, the northernmost rivers were opened up. Sweden's total floatways (*flottledningar*) ultimately covered about 24,000 kilometers.[3] The work entailed cleaning out the fallen logs and other debris, eliminating obstructing sandbars, and building flumes to bypass falls and rapids; where small lakes were encountered, arrangements had to be made to form rafts of logs in order to tow them across to running water. The clearing and use of the floatways required the cooperative effort of all sawmill proprietors on that river; logs, each one bearing its owner's mark, were jointly escorted to the mills, where they were sorted out according to ownership. The journey of an individual log in Norrland in the later 1800s might be a long one. The sawmill owners often had to go far upstream to buy forest land or clearing rights, so far that floating the logs downstream often took two years, sometimes as much as five.

A fine-bladed saw had just been installed at the rebuilt Robertsfors. First introduced into Norrland soon after 1740, these greatly reduced the amount of sawdust and wasted wood, and commercial sawmills everywhere were adopting them in place of the older coarse saw by about the turn of the century. Finlay had established his enterprise some distance inland where Rickleån, rapidly descending from the plateau to the coastland over falls and rapids, enabled the efficient use of a water wheel. This, too, was typical; the sites of the earlier Norrland sawmills stretch in a jagged zone north and south precisely where the rivers enter the lowlands along the Bothnian gulf. Robertsfors had been started by a foreigner, a forerunner of several others who would contribute to the Swedish lumber industry, in a decade when a number of sawmills came into existence in Norrland, where the great development of the industry would occur in the second half of the nineteenth century. Typical in so many respects, Robertsfors ultimately earned its own small special distinction by keeping its large water wheel, the last to do so, until 1935.

Sweden, in the decades after 1840, built up capital by shipping raw materials, especially timber, to more industrially advanced nations. Wood products replaced iron as the principal export in the 1860s, and in this period the export industries expanded much more rapidly than those engaged in production for the domestic market. The exploitation of Swedish forests as a major source of national income in turn greatly stimulated the forces leading to full-scale industrialization.[4] It was singularly fortunate that as the need for capital for industrial transformation grew increasingly acute, the British demand for Swedish softwoods for the building of cities should become so great. (Grain exports also helped; the 150,000 horses pulling London omnibusses devoured huge quantities of Swedish-exported oats.)

Timber in the form of masts, spars, and logs had been exported in the 1600s from west coast sawmills to Holland, then the leading woodworking country. A substantial part of the industry in the following century consisted of making tar, much of it for export. Britain, becoming dependent upon foreign timber imports by the 1700s, replaced Holland in Swedish exports, but high import duties, imposed during the Napoleonic wars and retained afterward, virtually closed that market. Denmark and western Germany consequently absorbed much of the exports, especially boards from southern Sweden, but France was also importing sizable amounts of timber.[5]

Swedish sawmills grew up in the shadow of the iron industry and were as fettered by regulations as the iron works. Though the severe restraints had been imposed in order to conserve the forests as a source of fuel for the hearths and forges, the limitations, in accordance with mercantilist theories, were applied to areas far distant from iron works. Government policy, aside from the iron works, largely limited the use of wood to household needs, and even a household saw required a permit. Tree-cutting limitations were imposed on sawmills, and tolls were levied on exported timber. Until 1812, foreign ships were forbidden by the Swedish Navigation Laws (*Produktplakatet* of 1724) to enter the Bothnian ports. The abolition of restrictions, necessary if the timber industry was to meet foreign demand and the needs of domestic urbanization, parallel those in the iron industry: the right to set up a household saw at will (1828); the abolition of tolls on unsawed wood for export (1842) and for other forms of wood (1864); an end to limitations on the amount of sawing (1842); and the freedom to establish commercial sawmills without permission from the state (1864).

In the middle of the eighteenth century the government had begun to franchise "privileged sawmills," using fine-bladed saws, to cut an annual quota of trees from the Crown forests. This practice persisted officially until 1820, though some continued to be given this privilege until midcentury, when about forty sawmills seem to have enjoyed this largesse. Most of them kept the privilege until the 1880s and 1890s. Sawmill proprietors all too frequently also carried out lumbering activities on Crown forest land without permission. In the 1820s the state started to parcel out portions of the Crown forests to the peasants, unintentionally contributing to opening up the forests for commercial exploitation. This long-term project, continuing for about fifty years, put the greater portion of forested lands into the hands of the country people, who, however, derived little benefit from them except as grazing land.[6] As demand for wood products grew and prices rose, speculators bought the forests, or the right to cut the timber, from the peasants at prices that seemed high to the peasants, but were actually low in terms of the market. In this fashion, huge tracts of forest came under the control of sawmill entrepreneurs.

To supplement their Canadian supply, the British had been importing timber from Norway, but the more accessible Norwegian forests near the coast had been used up by the later 1840s. They then turned to Sweden, and from about 1850 into the 1880s it was the single largest exporter of wood to Great Britain, which had an "insatiable appetite for Scandinavian softwoods."[7] Swedish forests consist of 44 percent Norwegian spruce, 40 percent Scottish pine, some birch, and, in the far south, oak and beech.

West Sweden, which had exported about a third of Swedish sawn timber in the 1830s, accounted for over half of the deals and battens in the 1840s as the British market opened up. Most of the timber from the west coast went out through Gothenburg, where John Hall had dominated the export in 1800, and where the exporters now bore such familiar names as Jonas Anders Kjellberg, Olof Wijk, William Gibson, David Carnegie, Wilhelm Röhss, and Robert and James Dickson. These exporters and owners of sawmills, possessing investment capital and excellent commercial contacts, were the best organized to take quick advantage of the opportunity.

The larger water-driven sawmills of the 1850s belonged to Gothenburg exporters and the Stockholm merchant houses.[8] Other sawmills were being founded by Norrland merchants who, concentrating on timber exports, built up substantial forest and sawmill properties themselves. Outstanding examples were Johan Wikner & Co. (Härnösand), H. F. Postal (Sundsvall), and J. A. Enhörning (Sundsvall). Starting a modest sawmill required no great amount of capital, and men like these, austere and frugal, steadily plowed their profits back into their growing businesses.[9] Joint-stock companies also began to appear, more slowly than in textiles, but some twenty of them had been established by 1870. Out of these various sources sprang a number of good-sized timber empires.

The Dicksons led the assault on the forests, introducing lumbering practices common in North America, and earning both fabulous wealth and notoriety as robber barons. Robert, awkward and limping, and the stately, reserved James had, it may be recalled, engaged in transit trade out of Gothenburg. After the wars, James Dickson & Co. moved into the export of wood, buying up large tracts of forest in northern Värmland, where few iron works contested the ownership of natural resources. Lumber began to flow from the Dejefors sawmill on the Klarälv stream, and soon the Dicksons had control of its floatways.[10] Affairs in London, where Peter (the eldest brother) was making a fortune in East India trade and colonial goods, were handled by their Dickson Brothers company. Another Robert (grandson of the first), inheriting Peter's wealth and sharing, it was said, in the Rothschilds' fast news service from the Crimea, speculated in the London market to amass another fortune.[11]

Using British sawmill equipment, the Dicksons ruthlessly and rapidly cut down the Värmland forests, leaving a wasteland. Already in the 1820s they had the consummate foresight to begin purchasing land at low cost in Norrland. Envisioning the depletion of the Norwegian supply, they bought, in the 1830s and 1840s, forests or rights of clearance in four different localities near Söderhamn, Örnsköldsvik, Sundsvall, and Umeå. Water-driven sawmills at Askesta, Matfors, Husum, and Baggböle opened up Norrland timber for the world market.

As their operations stripped the countryside, the peasants who had sold or leased forest land became increasingly incensed. Two utterly different worlds collided: the careful Swedish husbanding of resources by strict government regulations and cheeseparing peasant economy, versus the North Atlantic rugged individualism nurtured by worldwide commerce and the subduing of wilderness. From the Dickson point of view the bureaucratic restrictions were ridiculously outdated, while the Swedes, muttering at the despoliation, mourned for their slow-growing spruce and pine, perched on the scanty humus over the granite rock. In the Crown forests, where they had clearance to take specific numbers of trees, the Dicksons obviously cut much more than that. At Baggböle on the Ume River, where they were privileged for 17,000 trees a year, they were loading wood from more like 150,000 trees annually, and, though this included the wood from their own holdings, the sum totals added up to flagrant illegal lumbering.

In the midst of the public outcry, the provincial authorities filed suit against James (1810–1873), son of the first Robert and head of the Norrland sawmills, who had a reputation as a hard-nosed and heedless, albeit skillful, lumberman.[12] Intimidated witnesses at the trial furnished little evidence, but James was declared guilty and fined (1843). He appealed the verdict, and, amidst maximum publicity, the highest Swedish court reversed the judgment. Olof Bjur, the provincial official (*länsman*) who had started the proceedings, thereupon appealed directly to King Oscar I. The king, caught between inflamed public opinion and the country's higher economic interests, dug deep into hallowed Scandinavian tradition and asked James Dickson to take a *värjemålsed,* an oath of innocence.

By now it was 1850. A large, hostile crowd gathered in the assembly hall of the *ting,* the court of the province, for the oath-taking. Dickson arrived in a splendid carriage, belonging to a Härnösand merchant, drawn by three horses. He strode to the front of the assembly, now totally silent, and took the oath, whereupon the crowd gave "one single deep sigh." When he left, the carriage was drawn by only two horses, prompting someone to say that only two were needed because Dickson, having lost his soul in the *ting* hall, was now much lighter.[13]

He was by no means the only unscrupulous operator in the timber industry, but he had become the most conspicuous. James thereafter absented himself from Norrland, and his son, Oscar (1823–1897), increasingly took over leadership of the Dickson timber empire. He, too, combined clearsighted business acumen with bold, sometimes amoral, practices. A "Second Baggböle War" broke out in 1867 when timber stolen from Crown forests turned up in Dickson possession. No Dickson volunteering for a repeat performance, two of the floatway chiefs had to swear innocence this time. Although the Dicksons successfully carried on their practices for many years, the word *Baggböleriet* permanently entered the Swedish language, meaning robber baron ruthlessness in exploiting the land in defiance of decency and legality. Undeniably there were two sides to the drama, viewpoints that more than a century later are still voiced, in various guises, by business interests and environmentally concerned groups. Whatever their respective merits, the Dicksons, historically, pioneered modern lumbering practices in Sweden, with all their accompanying social and ecological costs.

The early Dickson sawmills were placed inland, where rapids or falls drove the water wheels for the saws, the lumber then being floated to the loading places at the sea. Matfors, using water power, had the largest production of any Norrland sawmill in the early 1860s. With the arrival of steam-driven saws, the Dicksons illustrate the common pattern within the industry, the shift of sawmills to the coast where the beams and planks might be directly loaded onto the waiting ships. Thus, in the 1870s, the Dicksons moved production from Matfors to the loading area at Svartvik, where steam saws were then installed. Baggböle was eventually, in 1884–85, replaced by Holmsund, at the head of the estuary of the Ume, as the production center. In a third location, at Askesta on the Ljusnan, was placed one of the three largest early steam saws in Norrland; a short railroad brought its wood to the coast at Sandarna. The Dicksons, with their usual foresight, sold off their timber interests just as the industry was reaching its maximum production.

Other timber empires were built by Fredrik Bünsow, Carl and Henrik Kempe, and the Kjellbergs. Fredrik Bünsow (1824–1893), neighbor and rival of the Dicksons in the Sundsvall district, illustrates both the opportunities and vicissitudes in the lumber industry. Born in Kiel in Germany, he worked for a time at the Bonniers Book Company in Stockholm, then moved to Sundsvall, where H. F. Postal, his uncle, owned a small lumber and shipbuilding business. When the uncle died, the young man took over his enterprises (1847). Bünsow, like the Dicksons, bought land or clearing rights cheaply from the peasants in Medelpad province and also inland in Jämtland. He also purchased a glass works at Skönvik from Hew, Prescott & Co. of London and converted it into a sawmill with a large steam saw.

Then came the economic crisis of 1857, catching Bünsow with heavy debts incurred while establishing his business. He was forced to sell off part of his promising industry, including some to the rival Dicksons. Instead of giving up, he went to Hamburg and talked the Salomon Heine firm into providing the money for his creditors in return for half ownership in Skönvik. Organized as a stock company, Skönvik AB prospered under Bünsow's management; he bought out the Hamburg bank again, and when he died in 1897 he left a fortune of about ten million kronor.[14]

The Kempes, a merchant family in Greifswald and Stralsund, had been Swedish citizens in Pomerania since the time of the Thirty Years War. Early in the nineteenth century two of five brothers moved to Sweden, two went to Russia, and one stayed in Germany. The two who migrated to Sweden, Carl (1799–1872) and Henrik, began by working for their mother's brother in his Tanto sugar refinery in Stockholm. One day Carl, an athletic young man, went for a long swim, and his stiff and proper employer fussed about it. Carl indignantly quit his job and headed for home. While waiting for his ship to sail from Ystad, he received a letter from a Stockholm acquaintance, Olof Johan Wikner, offering him a position in his father's firm in Härnösand. Carl changed his mind, accepted the offer, and ultimately married his friend's sister.[15]

The brothers-in-law founded Johan Wikner & Co. after the death of the father, who had been a sea captain and owned a sawmill (1823). Once on his own feet, Carl began building ships and operating a fleet of vessels that by 1870 consisted of ten ships. As a partner in Johan Wikner & Co., he first shared in the operations of a water saw at Mo, inland from Örnsköldsvik. Becoming sole owner after a time, he installed an iron works and a manufacturing shop there; in 1865 he started another sawmill at Domsjö, downstream at the harbor near Örnsköldsvik. By now he was selling timber in England, Germany, and France through agencies. After his death the two sawmills were merged into Mo and Domsjö, which his son, Frans, greatly enlarged by adding chemical plants, sulphite mills, and other subsidiaries; Mo and Domsjö (MoDo) ultimately became one of the largest cellulose producers in the country.

In the dark forests of Norrland all sorts of weird stories circulated. Mo had earlier been owned by a legendary local figure, the district judge Johan Henning Tideman. Long after his death, it was said that he could sometimes be seen in the dusk of the forests dashing by in his carriage or sled, muttering "*Till tings! Till tings!*" ("To court! To court!").[16]

Carl's brother, Henrik (1807–1883), had become associated with the wealthy Wilhelm Röhss of Gothenburg in the acquisition of Voxna *bruk*. It possessed large forests in addition to its iron works, and here in 1860 a sawmill was established, along with blast furnace, foundry, and machine shop. When Kempe bought out the Röhss interests, the Ljusne-Voxna AB was founded with Henrik as managing director (1881). Another member of the family purchased Robertsfors in 1897 and, closing the iron works there, concentrated on the sawmill and cellulose. For Wilhelm Röhss, a sawmill with *bruk* was only one of many interests; originally a textile worker in Germany, he had passed on his knowledge about a secret dyeing process to Grönvall & Co. in return for a partnership in the firm, then parlayed that into a variety of ventures and a great fortune.[17]

The Kjellbergs, too, had many interests. Jonas Anders (1788–1877), exporting iron and timber from Gothenburg, purchased Lo sawmill in 1837 and Kramfors in 1848, both located south of Härnösand. Kramfors controlled forest areas clear up to the Norwegian border, and its steam saw (1852) greatly increased the already large Kjellberg flow of exports. Nor did timber deflect the Kjellbergs from their iron interests; by the later 1870s they held a controlling share in the Bofors-Gullspång iron works.

When the Swedish timber industry reached its peak of production just before 1900, the Kempes owned the largest holdings. Second was William Ohlsson (1862–1923), an agent or broker in the buying and selling of forests and sawmills. The Bergvik and Ala company ranked third; British creditors had acquired Bergvik in its second bankruptcy in ten years (1867), and it continued to be owned by a British consortium, successive major interest being held by Christopher Weguelin, by I. Thomson, T. Bonar & Co., and by Sir Ernest Cassel. The Hudiksvall company, the fifth largest, had been founded by British interests (1857), then sold to a local group (1868). Number four, Svartvik, was sold by Baron Oscar Dickson to a Norwegian group (1891); Norwegians also acquired Tunadal (1857) and some other Swedish timber tracts. Arend Nicolaus Versteegh (Dutch-born) dominated the sixth-ranking company. The following four in size included Skönvik (Bünsow), Enhörning, Vivstavarv, and Kramfors (Kjellberg).[18]

By no means all Norrland timber fell into the hands of the major timber barons or foreigners. A group of nearby businessmen owned Vivstavarv, the oldest timber goods enterprise in Norrland; here the relationship of sawmills to other economic activities along the coastal strip can be clearly observed. A sawmill near its future location, north of Sundsvall, had been using a fine-bladed saw by 1756, but this enterprise had been wiped out by an earthquake in 1782 and a great flood in the lower valley of the Indal River some years later.[19]

A mathematics teacher and rector of the Härnösand gymnasium, Pehr Hellzén, took the initiative shortly thereafter in founding Vivstavarv. It began in 1798 as a shipbuilding firm (a *varv* is a shipyard). About seventy sailing vessels, the exact number not known, were ultimately constructed there before 1870, by which time the steamship was beginning to threaten sailing vessel profits. Almost from the beginning, Vivstavarv became the owner of a fleet of ships, partly because they could not always be immediately sold. Two of its early vessels carried cargo to Virginia before 1807, and a couple of years later one went to Brazil, frequent destination for subsequent traffic. Some ships wandered remarkably. The *Helena* left its home port with a load of timber for southern France in July 1859; then it picked up coal at Liverpool for Gibraltar; then more coal, from Cardiff, to Barcelona; in Spain it loaded salt for transport to Riga; there it received lumber for London; once again coal, and it was unloading at Alexandria in Egypt in December 1860. Salt was the most usual commodity on homeward voyages.[20]

Timber from the Sundsvall area made up the bulk of the outgoing cargo on Vivstavarv ships. Naturally, the firm decided to acquire its own sawmill, and in 1827 it purchased Sillre, fifty kilometers up the Indal. The timber was sold through merchants in Stockholm, through foreign agents, and by ship captains carrying it to foreign ports where sales were likely; in the 1860s and later, agents in London and Paris usually arranged the sales. After the shipbuilding and shipping activities ceased, Vivstavarv continued as a lumbering enterprise, still owned by a group of families in Sundsvall and Härnösand until nearly the beginning of the twentieth century. As in so many places, "generation after generation of company officials, foremen, and workers . . . served the enterprise" (Althin). The village in midcentury numbered about 325 persons, living in two-story red houses with white trim along a dirt road.[21] In 1907 Marcus Wallenberg and Stockholms Enskilda Bank obtained control of Vivstavarv, and the new owners expanded it into a large cellulose industrial complex, including the then largest sulphite mill in Sweden.

A small group of Sundsvall businessmen installed the first Swedish steam saw at Tunadal in 1849. The idea originated with J. E. Söderberg, a merchant who intended to run a steam-driven flour mill and attach a sawmill to it; the flour mill would be operated in the winter, and his workers could be kept occupied with wood sawing during the summer. The application for permission to build by Söderberg and his partners met opposition from three different quarters: the Dicksons protested that their Matfors sawmill had exclusive right to the timber on the Ljungan River; the owners of an existing water wheel flour mill objected; and a man by the name of Parks in Liverpool claimed that the steam engine, constructed at Bolinders in Stockholm, infringed on his patent. Nevertheless, the governor approved the application. The sawmill equipment came from Jensen and Dahl in Oslo (then Christiania), which sold machinery to a number of Swedish sawmills.[22]

The next two steam saws, also in the Sundsvall area, were mounted at Bünsow's Mon on the outskirts of Sundsvall, and at Vivstavarv. Apparently the Vivstavarv owners had talked with Carlsund at Motala about buying a steam saw in the early 1840s; according to Althin, the first ones in Sweden had been made by Carlsund after he had seen them in England, though no market existed for them as yet in his own country. As it happened, the owners procured theirs cheaply when Dickson & Co. lost a court case to set one up at Gideå and then sold it to them. The remaining machinery had been manufactured at Bergsund and was in operation in the spring of 1852. A big fire destroyed the whole sawmill six years later, and a new steam saw had to be purchased, traditionally from Bolinders, though not mentioned in its records.[23]

The steam-driven apparatus had several advantages, the paramount being increased production and greater use of the equipment. A sawmill need no longer be located inland at a falls or rapids, it could be placed near the coastal loading place. Wood from a saw near the harbor tended to be of better quality, much less likely to sustain damage during transport to the ship. No longer were the operators at the mercy of high or low water, which formerly stopped the machinery, and the saw could now be run when the water was frozen. However, the mills usually shut down during the intense cold and short days of winter, not least because illumination of the working area, open flames near an abundance of combustibles, was always hazardous.[24]

Carl Anton Jensen (1817–1890) had supervised the installation of the saws at Tunadal and Vivstavarv. Each new branch of industry created its own kind of expertise, and Jensen became the best-known sawmill authority. (The Swedes benefited, of course, from the Norwegian experience with modern sawmills and their floatway techniques.) Jensen had worked at Motala and Bergsund, then served as machinist on the *Norrland* before settling in Sundsvall. He was also responsible for the next two Swedish steam saws at Sandö (1853) and Kramfors (1854), and many more after that, in addition to acquiring three patents on improved saws.[25] Shortly after 1870 the timber industry had more than 70 steam saws in use, compared to 211 water wheels.[26]

Bolinders, the Stockholm engineering works that had provided Tunadal with its controversial steam engine, delivered a complete steam power and sawing apparatus to Sandö. Founded in 1845 by Jean and Carl Bolinder, who had studied sawmill machinery in England, it came on the scene at just the right time to secure a head start in Norrland developments, and it would make by far the greatest contribution along mechanical lines in the timber industry.[27] Ernst Victor Stridsberg (1839–1925) became another pioneer in the mechanical aspects of the industry. He studied sawmill technology in Germany and England, then for a time made saw blades and planing apparatus in Sheffield. He returned to Sweden in 1867 to found a saw-blade factory near Eskilstuna (Torshälla), but later moved it to Tröllhattan and its good water power. A number of other machine shops also began making sawmill equipment.

Planing machinery, first devised in 1802 by Joseph Bramah for the Woolwich Arsenal and increasingly used by the British in the 1830s, was introduced into Sweden at Mon, the old Postal and Bünsow sawmill. Bünsow sold it to a new company, Mons Trävaru AB, whose leader, Nils Wikström, decided to install planing machinery after seeing it in operation in Norway (1870). Purchased from Jensen & Dahl, the planers were operated by Norwegian workers. Though a few others followed, not until the 1890s would there be a genuinely strong development in this branch of the industry, which, however, continued to expand after the actual quantity of exported timber began to decline.

That indispensable tool of the forests, the axe, had been much more in use than the saw in Swedish households. The axe underwent transformation in the 1870s, some imported from the United States and others made at Hult, near Norrköping. Hult was one of those fabulous little *bruk* so common in Sweden, of ancient origin (1698) and long held by the same (Ekelund) family. It still exists today, now owned by Holmen. Three-fourths of its axes are exported, and in New Guinea, according to a Stockholm newspaper, a Hult axe is as expensive as buying a wife.[28]

Swarms of "carpentry factories" (*snickerifabriker*) appeared in Sweden as an offshoot of the timber industry. A number of Swedish workers were paid by the state to attend the London Exposition of 1851, and while there they inspected the famous woodworking factory at Woolwich; here they saw a variety of machine tools, saws, lathes, planers, and boring machinery. In the same year Sweden's first similar factory was started in Gothenburg, a number of its foremen having worked in England.[29] The real breakthrough came in the early 1870s when a series of woodworking factories went into production. Gothenburg and Stockholm led the way, coastal cities followed, and in time a widespread growth of small industry woodworking ensued, stemming at least partially from the older handicraft tradition. Jönköping and Kalmar became important centers, and a multitude of small, almost family, shops began to proliferate in Småland.

The shipping of Norrland timber was necessarily seasonal, since the Gulf of Bothnia froze over for several winter and early spring months. The Norwegians, with many ships and long experience in the trade, were the most prominent carriers. For instance, in 1884 the Norwegians accounted for 543 of the nearly 1,500 shiploads; the Swedes carried 207, the Dutch (continuing their ancient Swedish ties) 160, the French 76, the British 75, followed by the Danes, Finns, and others. In that year 443 of the ships went to Great Britain, 302 to France and 266 to the Netherlands; Finland and Denmark took 152 and 123 respectively, over a hundred ships went to German ports, and others carried Swedish timber as far away as Australia and the Cape Colony.[30] The British were importing over half of the Swedish wood in the earlier years, and the French took about a fourth; in fact Sweden was France's largest supplier of wood products between 1875 and 1900.[31]

Wood exports rose fairly steadily from about 1840 until the maximum was reached in 1897, when Sweden was briefly the largest exporter in the world. They increased over 150 percent between 1862 and 1871, quadrupling in the Sundsvall area as the steam-driven saw came into use.[32] During the economic crisis at the end of the 1870s, prices were cut in half; when the sawmill owners tried to reduce wages accordingly, the workers started the famous Sundsvall strike of 1879, Sweden's first great confrontation between labor and employer. Renewed prosperity returned to the industry in the 1880s, and over a million standards of boards were exported in 1897, compared to 475,000 in 1870.[33] Though a relative decline followed, wood products of various kinds still accounted for about a fourth of industrial production.

While timber from Finland and Russia to some extent replaced the Swedish, the Swedish companies were busily building wood pulp mills in response to international market demand. Quite often an enterprise had started as a small iron *bruk*, then, during the centralization of iron works, gone over to exploiting its forest reserves at its sawmill; finally, sometimes, in a third transformation, it used its forests to manufacture cellulose. It was, to reiterate, typical of Swedish development that when, in the words of Althin, an enterprise could no longer "drive in the old wheel tracks" it switched to an alternative industry.[34] In this way a village of skilled laborers remained together as a group, the community survived, continuity was maintained, and Swedish industry continued to be scattered over the countryside.

7. THE GASLIGHT ERA

London's 385 gaslighters had long gone their rounds before Sweden's first permanent gaslights were turned on in Gothenburg on December 5, 1846. The Gas Light and Coke Co. of London started in 1812, and Glasgow and Edinburgh used the new form of illumination for street lighting before 1820. Across the Atlantic, where the industry would ultimately generate an income of about $150 million a year, it appeared in Boston and New York City in 1822 and 1823 respectively.[1] Gaslights came late to Sweden, but illumination by electricity would begin almost immediately after the invention of the light bulb, one indication of the rapid Swedish industrial and technological advances during the intervening years.

High fuel costs were also a factor. Gaslighting had emerged from the British iron industry and its use of coke; when coal was heated without contact with air to make coke, one byproduct was coal gas. William Murdock, connected with Boulton and Watt, made the first practical application of coal gas to lighting in England in the 1790s, and Philippe Lebon developed it in France.

A retired Swedish army officer, Carl Reuterskrona, did make an early attempt, using Lebon lamps. Receiving a *privilegium* in March 1803, he mounted some gaslights in Stockholm, including seventeen of them at the Opera House. Eric Ruuth, that eager adopter of modern devices and coal mine owner, placed one outside his Stockholm home. A few others tried it, but the lights required too much attention, the pipes leaked, the fuel was expensive, and the abortive effort failed. Berzelius, entranced by London gaslighting during an 1818 visit, sent home descriptions of the process, and Gustaf Magnus Schwartz, similarly excited during a stay in Paris, attempted to make small gas works that could use alternative fuels.[2]

In 1824 the Imperial Continental Gas Association, which brought gaslighting to Copenhagen, Berlin, and some other cities, unsuccessfully applied to build and operate a gas works in Stockholm to light the streets and official buildings. The story went around that Schwartz, a professor of physics who became head of the Institute of Technology in 1825, had influenced city officials to reject it in order to protect his own venture, but in fact the company itself had lost interest when it found that it would not be allowed a monopoly. Instead, the city began replacing the old, ineffective so-called *Vargögon* (wolf eyes) oil lamps with the much better Argand lamps, also using oil for fuel, which were made and supervised by Gustaf Klemming, a Stockholm entrepreneur.[3]

When Gothenburg did adopt gaslighting, it thought the project too financially risky to be undertaken by the municipality and awarded a contract to James Malan, then similarly engaged in Hamburg. Stockholm did it by public subscription to a company, the actual supervision being under Jules Danré, a French expert (1853). Two Englishmen, H. A. Milne and Henry Beatley, working separately, directed construction in eight other cities. Alexander Keiller, with his usual foresight, had already sent one of his men, J. Andersson, to England to study its techniques, and he came back in time to direct the installation of Sweden's second city project, at Norrköping in 1849–51. Keiller reaped his reward by building the actual gas works. Andersson was also called to Jönköping, which at that time had only 38 widely spaced oil lamps. The first illumination from its 114 street lights on November 27, 1862 brought celebrating crowds into the streets and even a poem suggesting that the old lamps be sent to the rival town of Värnamo so that the "peasants" there might get their first taste of culture.[4] Some industrial enterprises installed gaslighting in the 1850s: Motala, Höganäs, the Lundström match factory, Korsnäs sawmill, and Manufaktur Malmö, the latter two at the time of their original construction or soon thereafter.

Daguerrotype photography is associated in the public mind with the era of gaslighting, and Johan Wilhelm Bergström (1812–1881) combined both. The new form of illumination and the beginnings of municipal water systems in these same years created a virtually new industry, the making and installation of pipes for the city and for private housing. Bergström, the first to see the possibilities in this new development, started a workshop for the manufacture and repair of pipes. Earlier, however, he had won his small niche in fame by opening a daguerrotype studio and there taking the first photographs in Sweden (1844). In Gothenburg a man by the name of Hasselblad could scarcely have imagined that a century later the world-famous Hasselblad camera would emerge out of what was once his modest men's clothing affair.

The old and the new stood in sharp juxtaposition in this era: water wheel and steam engine, stagecoach and railroad train, sailing vessel and steamship. Therein lies much of its nostalgic charm for posterity. Far more sailing ships than steamboats lay anchored in Swedish harbors during the gaslight era. The sailing vessel was starting, worldwide, on its final golden years; in Sweden it passed through one period of prosperity at midcentury and would enjoy one last heyday in the years between 1866 and 1877. The Swedes in 1870 possessed 368 steamers, whereas 1,402 sailing vessels visited foreign ports and an additional 1,685 were in domestic service.[5] In 1894 Sweden still had 2,914 ships of various sizes under sail compared to 1,248 steamships, and only in 1899 did steamship tonnage forge ahead. Sweden's proportion of the world's merchant marine throughout the century normally amounted to between two to three percent, but its share of shipping to foreign ports dropped from two-thirds in 1800 to a little over one-third because so much of the timber and iron exports went out on foreign bottoms.

Despite their early start in steamboat construction, the Swedes abandoned sailing vessels reluctantly, due in part to the lack of domestic coal and sufficient capital. Swedish steamboats were geared to the relatively calm waters of lakes and canals and otherwise were limited to the Baltic and the North Sea. Sailing vessels everywhere continued to be more economical for oceanic freight traffic.

While the splendid New England clippers raced over the oceans, the seaports along the Gulf of Bothnia, building their small, sturdy, old-fashioned vessels, nourished their own seafaring tradition in the more modest Swedish maritime history. A greater number of ships were built in other parts of the country, but the Norrland tradition, seen in retrospect, has a special glamor of its own because small seaports, set on the edge of the great forests, responded to their milieu by sending out, with the most limited resources, their sailors and ships to seek cargoes in far distant ports.

Gävle, particularly, had a long seafaring background. In 1559 when Stockholm had 28 ships, and the predecessor of Gothenburg, Älvsborg, had 18, Gävle boasted 19. In 1783, 41 Gävle-owned vessels visited foreign ports, 11 to the Mediterranean. Early in the nineteenth century its ships often stopped first in England, usually Hull or London, with Swedish export goods, then went on to such western Mediterranean cities as Malaga, Barcelona, Marseilles, or Livorno. They carried out iron, timber, and tar and returned with salt, colonial wares, and other goods. At midcentury many of the ships might be gone for years, wandering about and picking up cargoes wherever they could be found. Elfstrand & Co. owned 15, and eight more firms each possessed at least 3, of the 75–80 Gävle-owned vessels. Many ships were still being constructed in the 1830s, though, out of date, they were frequently resold to Norwegians for rebuilding to suit their own purposes.[6] Then the Gävle shipyards fought back by introducing iron and steel sailing vessels with improved rigging, but, pressed by the inexorable advance of the steamship, they closed, one by one. By this time the city was fighting a losing battle to preserve its preeminence by means of the railroad.

In addition to Vivstavarv, shipyards farther up the coast at Sundsvall, Härnösand, and other towns built sailing vessels and maintained fleets of ships. Härnösand in the 1840s claimed to rank fifth in Sweden in terms of ship ownership. One shipyard, founded in 1781, produced a steady stream of vessels for over half a century, and Kempe's Nya Varvet built at least twenty-seven ships before it closed in 1860. The fleet of Johan Wikner & Co. in the 1840s consisted of four galleasses, four schooners, one bark, and one brig.[7]

Umeå, in the far north, enjoyed a boom period during the Crimean War because a heavy traffic in transit goods, evading the Anglo-French naval blockade by using the land route through Finland, passed through the town. Much of its income during the second half of the century derived from shipbuilding and Umeå-based merchant vessels. The Scharinska shipping company grew with the lumbering industry and also became wealthy by the transport of grain from southern Sweden. Scharinska vessels might turn up almost anywhere. In the year 1871 the *Bengal* carried timber to Bordeaux, then timber to Cardiff, where it loaded railroad rails for New York; the *Fanny* and the *Maria Augusta* sailed from Malaga to New York; the *Catharina* arrived in Montevideo; another ship was plying the coast of France.[8] This sailing tradition held on most tenaciously among the Swedish-speaking Åland Islanders, at the entrance to the Gulf of Bothnia, whose ships continued to participate in the famed Australian wheat races to England until the very end.

Two Stockholm-based ships made their mark in Swedish sailing history by going around the world in the early 1840s. Their energetic owner, Carl Fredrik Liljevalch (1796–1870), began his adventures, it was said, by being arrested in St. Petersburg after seeking an audience with the tsar to discuss a business affair. After considerable trepidation, he learned that it was customary to arrest persons awaiting an audience in order to have them available when the tsar could see them. Liljevalch, who must have misunderstood the procedure, was seventeen at the time. Back home in Stockholm, he started a mercantile establishment with a friend. One thing led to another, including advising King Karl XIV Johan on how to run His Majesty's iron works. In 1832 he received a royal contract to deliver grain to Norrland, after which he started a shipyard in Luleå and a woodworking shop in Skellefteå, both seaports in the far north.

Liljevalch's schooner, *May Ann*, first showed the Swedish flag in Australia (1839), then continued around the world, arriving home in May 1841. The second, *Bull*, a brigantine, was attacked by natives in the South Seas in the course of its voyage. In 1847 Liljevalch went out to Canton himself to negotiate rights of entry, and his ship, *Prins Oscar*, began trading along the Chinese coast. He spent his later years more quietly in trying to develop fodder beets on the island of Gotland.

Shipowners had always benefited from the parlous condition of Swedish roads. A journey by land from Stockholm to the southern port of Ystad in 1800 required five to six days—no wonder ships were preferred. The hard frozen roads of winter offered the best opportunity if heavy goods had to be transported. Poor transportation contributed to years of famine; a region with a surplus had difficulty disposing of it, whereas an area suffering a poor harvest might not be able to obtain the needed grain. Most prone to famine were inland

Norrland, northwestern Dalarna, and Värmland, an area that Malthus hastened to visit. However, poor roads were rather a universal condition in nearly all countries.

Mary Wollstonecroft in 1795 found the road from Gothenburg to the Norwegian border "uncommonly good and pleasant," and a few other decent carriage roads existed by that time. The government continued to improve the principal highways, using rocks broken into very small pieces, and the resultant throughways were "spacious and smooth." Henry Parnell in 1833 asserted that the Swedes had long been regarded as "excellent road engineers."[9] More good roads, however, were so necessary that in 1840–41 the state created a special authority, the *väg och vattenbyggnadskår,* the roads and waterways corps; a reorganization and extension of an earlier corps, it was based on the military reserve, and its director, a colonel, was directly responsible to the head of the army. Paul Du Chaillu, famous French explorer traveling in Sweden in 1871 and 1879, judged the King's Highways *(kungsvägar)* the best and most of the county roads *(häradsvägar)* very good; parish and village roads, on the contrary, often remained in poor shape.[10]

City streets evoked no praise whatsoever. Wollstonecroft declared those in Gothenburg to be "intolerably bad," and someone else wrote that the streets of Stockholm were "by far the worst . . . in Europe." Sixty years later Bayard Taylor reported that nearly all Stockholm's streets were still "narrow and badly paved." Du Chaillu described them as narrow, poorly drained, paved with cobblestones, and usually without sidewalks.[11] Stockholm's first sidewalk *(trottoar,* from the French) appeared in 1844 when a private individual, building a house, included a stone sidewalk in the project; the governor of the city considered it sufficiently important to offer a toast to the achievement at his next banquet. Norrbro Plaza, across from the royal place, had been paved with flat stones in 1806, and some had been laid later, but not until the late 1850s and the 1860s was a general effort made to use this material. Cobblestones continued to be the customary cover. A steam roller, developed into an effective machine in Britain in the early 1860s, was bought from Aveling & Porter in 1873 for macadamizing city streets. Cement was first attempted on a pedestrian walkway near Riddarhuset in 1892.[12]

Johan Ohlsson (1833–1910) introduced the use of asphalt. When Stockholm's first gaslight works opened, the residue from making coal gas was simply dumped into Klara Sjö, the inlet between the railroad station and the Eldkvarn. A graduate of the Institute of Technology, Ohlsson applied recently developed methods to this residue to extract useful substances, including asphalt. It was not yet sufficiently durable for street paving, but it could be employed for such household purposes as basement and shed floors.[13]

However wasteful or harmful the consumption of beer, *brännvin,* coffee, and tobacco may have seemed to some earnest bureaucrats and to a growing number of concerned reformers, they bulked large in the economic life of the country. They were very much part of the daily scene.

Swedish beer *(Svensköl)* in the 1700s consisted of three kinds, depending upon its strength. Two hundred years later Sweden had, glossing over minor variations, three kinds, depending upon its strength. Meantime, a revolution in beer making had occurred when the handicraft small-scale production of *Svensköl* had been replaced by Bavarian beer and its industrial type of brewery. In 1844 Fredrik Rosenquist af Åkershult (1805–1872) bought an abandoned brewery on Södermalm in southern Stockholm, and Beckmann, a German master brewer, rebuilt it to Bavarian specifications.

The name of Rosenquist af Åkershult was only too well known at the time because of an eccentric Oppositionist father who often provoked disturbances in the House of Nobles in the Riksdag. Some years after giving up his military career, Lieutenant Rosenquist, whose family owned breweries, went to Germany and spent a year studying beer production in Munich and Nuremberg. One well-meaning theory had it that Rosenquist hoped to wean the Swedes away from their prevailing addiction to hard liquor by attracting them to the much less harmful beer, but Samuel Bring, his biographer, doubted this, believing that such an effort several decades later had been wrongly attributed to Rosenquist.[14]

The other brewers, quite rightly fearful, launched barrages of criticism against his Tyska Bryggeri (German brewery). Rosenquist counterattacked with newspaper advertisements, including testimonials from doctors and chemists, and it no doubt helped that Queen Josephine, daughter of a Bavarian princess, became one of his early and best customers. Along with the beer, Rosenquist imported its well-known accounterments. A big horse-drawn wagon, flamboyantly labeled in Swedish "From the German Brewery" on both sides, went rolling over the streets, stopping whenever a thirsty customer stepped up. Barrels were brought to restaurants for sale as tap beer, distribution centers were opened all over the city, and he even arranged to sell it in grocery stores. Formerly sold in wooden containers, some was now bottled. A couple of years later Rosenquist added another attraction, a Tivoli copied from the original in Copenhagen, and special omnibuses circulated in the city to carry customers to and from his pleasure garden.[15]

His innovations had the same impact on breweries as the Bryan Donkin and the Pontifex & Wood machines on paper-making and sugar refining a few years earlier. *Svensköl* was virtually wiped out as other German breweries quickly appeared in various Swedish cities. Guild regulations no longer applied to breweries, and anyone with the necessary capital could hire a German brewing master and start production. Stockholm's gaslights and the drinking of the new-style beer spread simultaneously, the names of new breweries advertising their antecedents: Münchenbryggeri, Hamburger, Nürnberg, and (Beckman's) Bayerska. The Münchenbryggeri used a steam engine, and several others imitated it. In Gothenburg the big brewery names would be J. A. Pripp and J. W. Lyckholm, and, as a result of a series of mergers, the Swedish beer market is now dominated by Pripps Bryggerierna AB.

Ever since the state first levied a tax on the making of *brännvin* in 1638, the government has never quite ceased trying to legislate control of what at times has seemed an ungovernable elemental force. In the eighteenth century state policies were torn between righteousness, lust for revenue, grain shortages, and the dogged peasant defense of the right to maintain household stills. After one policy switch (1775) the state ran about 60 Crown distilleries and 3,000 official saloons, the latter bearing the royal blue and gold Three Crowns emblem and frequently placed near churches to augment sales. Several of the more clever minds in the kingdom (Broling, Edelcrantz, Gahn, Norberg) sooner or later were put to work improving the distilleries, and Johan Erik Norberg had more success with his invention of a cooling element than he ever did with his steam engine. It may be recalled that two of Edelcrantz's first engines were put to use in former Crown distilleries. Boilers, pumps, and sundry other equipment must surely have made the liquor industry the first industrialized line of production in the kingdom.

Even the king tried to take advantage of the situation. Trying to repair his personal battered finances, Gustav III had a big distillery, the largest in the country, built close to Gripsholm Palace and then proceeded to compete with the official network. It used so much wood, supplied by the elder Wahrendorff of Åkers Styckebruk, that Stockholm's supply of fuel became depleted. The ensuing public wrath, coupled with the not infrequent scarcity of grain, led to the ultimate closing of the Gripsholm monster and Crown distilleries were leased to private entrepreneurs.

Sweden had several hundred steam distilleries in the 1830s, and by the 1850s these had risen to well over six hundred. The number of household stills in the 1830s, when heavy drinking seems to have reached its peak, has been estimated at somewhere around 170,000. Industrial production, much cheaper, subsequently began to drive them out, and in 1860 the government forbade the maintenance of household *brännvin* stills altogether.

According to Torsten Gårdlund, the total liquor production value in the third quarter of the nineteenth century somewhat exceeded that of the country's timber exports. In the cities "the pubs stretched along the streets like strings of pearls" (Althin). Only against that background and the long, bitter temperance crusade against *brännvin* can the continuing, sometimes equally irrational, disapproval of hard liquor in wide circles be comprehended. The visiting Bayard Taylor complained that Swedish brandy was "a detestable beverage, resembling a mixture of turpentine, train oil, and bad molasses. . . ."[16] Most

103

Swedish liquor, grossly overpriced and almost literally the product of sawdust squeezings, still tastes like that to foreign palates.

Coffee drinking ultimately replaced hard liquor as a major recreational activity, though it had not always been looked upon so favorably. At the beginning of the nineteenth century the coffee houses were associated by high-minded people with such appalling vices as dice and card playing. The mercantilist-oriented government, regarding money sent abroad for coffee, tobacco, and tea as wasted (its list of such luxuries also included tropical fruits, chocolate, cacao, and spices), had taken the offensive against all three of them already in the 1740s, only about forty years after coffee first arrived in Sweden. Condemning the "misuse and extravagance," the state levied a special annual tax, ranging from two to twelve riksdaler in accordance with the wealth of the sinners, on coffee and tea drinkers. This had the added advantage that the state revenue lost to adroit smugglers would be recouped from the consumers. When the Riksdag during a grain shortage forbade the household making of *brännvin* in 1756, the representatives of the outraged peasantry in the Riksdag retaliated with a measure outlawing the use of coffee. Smugglers did such a thriving business that in 1769 the ban had to be lifted.

Coffee was again forbidden by the government during a fit of austerity, and January 1, 1794, when the edict went into effect, was treated as a day of sorrow. Public resentment flared so high that the regime felt constrained to give way in 1796, but it was again forbidden on two later occasions. After 1822 the authorities permitted coffee drinking without further interruptions, and at midcentury sugar and coffee were Sweden's two largest imports. Among Gothenburg importers, usually sending their own brigs and schooners to Brazil and Cuba, were Carnegie, Kjellberg, Wijk, and Grönvall & Co., the latter eventually owned by Wilhelm Röhss. Coffee imports rose from 712,023 kilograms in 1781 to over 29 million in 1908, and the Swedes, with the Danes, are now the champion coffee drinkers of Europe.

Tobacco was another colonial import subject to "misuse and extravagance." No one knows when it arrived in Sweden. Arne Munthe thought that it probably had come around 1600, though the first mention of it occurs in 1629 when some Uppsala university students held a formal disputation on the virtues and evils of tobacco.[17] The first Swedish edict designating smoking and nonsmoking sections in a public conveyance dates from the seventeenth century: passengers wishing to smoke on the Uppsala–Stockholm post coach were requested to ride on the roof. The New Sweden colony, founded in 1638, was expected to ship home tobacco and furs, and the first large tobacco consignment arrived in Gothenburg two years later. The trading company, the Southern Company, received a monopoly on the tobacco trade and duty-free import rights from America, but, smuggling persisting then and under later monopoly companies, the government abandoned the policy in the late 1680s and ordained free competition. Numerous tobacco spinneries sprang up all over Sweden.

When concerned with tobacco, as with liquor and coffee, the government, like all governments then and now, combined high morality with an avaricious eye on possible sources of state revenue. In the 1740s youth under the age of twenty-one were forbidden to smoke, while all citizens wishing to "enjoy this perverse and dangerous luxury" ("mistelige överflödsfara") had to pay a special annual tax. Here, too, the upper class miscreants were charged a much higher rate. The plebeian snuff, however, cost only sixteen öre a year.[18] Cigars, arriving early in the nineteenth century, were becoming the dominant mode of smoking during the gaslight era. Munthe suggested that their use might be considered symbolic of the increasing importance of the bourgeoisie, since only they had the time to enjoy cigars.[19] The first cigarettes arrived from Finland after the Crimean War, where they may have originated with the soldiers, but they were not made in Sweden until after 1870.

At midcentury the country had 86 tobacco "factories" (24 in Gothenburg) employing 1,129 handicraft workers. Growing larger as elements of industrialization were introduced, they averaged about 50 employees each by 1900.[20] Tobacco had a direct impact on industrialization to the extent that certain families accumulated sufficient capital over several generations to invest in industrial ventures. The Swartz family maintained their tobacco factory for five generations while expanding into various commercial and industrial enterprises. The Rettigs of Gävle, owning one of the larger tobacco establishments, were making crucible steel at Kilafors and were one of the first to introduce the Siemens-Martin process; Robert Rettig contributed financially to Göransson's Bessemer experiments. Thomas A. Aspelin bought a *privilegium* going back to 1688 and made so much money that his son was able to buy a major *bruk*, Fagersta, in 1852. Frans Henrik Kockum, one of the greatest Swedish industrialists of the age, had a century-long family background in the tobacco trade when he embarked on his career. And Jonas Alströmer, the early textile entrepreneur, grew tobacco and founded a tobacco spinnery at Alingsås that survived for 121 years.

The tobacco industry was taken over by the state, years before the Social Democrats came to power, with the establishment of AB Svenska Tobaksmonopolet in 1915. Big and small firms were all absorbed, including Prime Minister Carl Swartz's factory and little Reuters in Karlshamn, in existence since 1725. The sale of hard liquor, too, was centralized with the formation of a state corporation, AB Vin och Spritcentralen in 1917.

Most towns of any size possessed local handicrafts shops, so-called "chemical factories," for the preparation of such commercial commodities as soap, yeast, vinegar, and candles. Chemical products were also needed for bleaching and dyeing cloth and for use at glass works. The making of sulfuric acid in Great Britain, revolutionized in the 1740s, might soon thereafter be considered to have been on an industrial level. Later, by the Leblanc process (patented in 1791), soda was produced by the use of salt, sulfuric acid and calcium carbonate, usually in the same factories that were manufacturing the sulfuric acid.

One of Sweden's "chemical factories" in the first quarter of the nineteenth century, Gripsholm, achieved a stature to some extent corresponding to the level of the country's eminent chemists. A. F. Rosenborg, he who made the bold, premature attempt to use the new British iron techniques at Kloster, started it at Kummelnäs in about 1800, then it was moved to King Gustav III's old distillery near Gripsholm castle. Rosenborg soon left the enterprise, and a succession of owners followed. Gripsholm made sulfuric acid from sulfur and saltpeter; other products included white lead, paint, soap (from hempseed oil at first), and vinegar (from whiskey sugar and water in the early years). At least four competing firms appeared, one making glaubersalt and soda briefly, another producing soda by the old kelping method, and a third using a different process for white lead. The fourth one started the easy way when a man posing as a journalist extracted vital factory secrets at Gripsholm and passed them on to a consortium in Gävle.[21]

In 1816 three chemists—Berzelius, Johan Gottlieb Gahn (1745–1818), and H. P. Eggertz—and three others, including Carl Palmstedt (1785–1870), took over Gripsholm. Berzelius, from his knowledge and travels abroad, introduced new, successful methods, the competent Palmstedt directed the enterprise, and a period of prosperity followed. During the early 1820s Gripsholm had a sizable production of white lead, sulfuric acid, nitric acid, and hydrochloric acid. Catastrophe struck on August 3, 1825, when most of the buildings burned down. The enterprise transferred back to the old quarters at Kummelnäs, where it lingered on until 1851.[22] Berzelius soon sold his interest, and Palmstedt moved on to Gothenburg to lead the newly founded Chalmers school.

Kummelnäs did not make soap because of strong competition, nor sulfuric acid, bought more cheaply abroad. The production of white lead continued, and also of vinegar by the new Scheuzenbach method, brought from Germany by Palmstedt in 1825. Notably, when the match industry began, Sweden was not yet producing potassium chlorate, which had to be imported from England. Small shops for making soap and other commercial articles proliferated, and the Barnängen Tekniska Fabrik (1868) became well known for its superior brand of ink, so necessary for bureaucrats, industrial bookkeepers, journalists, and other scribblers.[23]

Liljeholmen candles, still being sold in Sweden, appeared in 1839. During a sojourn in Paris, Carl Palmstedt learned about stearine candles from Adolphe de Milly, who was operating factories for their manufacture in Paris and London by chemical formulas stemming from the work of Eugène Chevreul.Palmstedt wrote enthusiastically to Berzelius and the Board of Trade about them. Lars Johan Hierta may have been told about them by Palmstedt while on a visit to Paris in 1837, or the sight of stearine candles at an exposition may have been sufficient inspiration; not actually having seen a candle factory, he decided to start one in Stockholm.[24]

Ultimately known as the greatest manufacturer of chemical products during the gaslight era, Hierta had originally achieved prominence as the liberal editor of *Aftonbladet,* Sweden's first modern newspaper, in which he espoused a wide variety of reforms. One of the most influential voices in the kingdom in the 1830s and 1840s, no one could have been more completely representative of the midcentury bourgeois spirit (though a nobleman) than Hierta. Convinced by his travels that Sweden's economy was backward, he served as a gadfly in his satirical writings and polemics, all the more provocative because the Swedes preferred to take pride in their *cultural* achievements. An apostle of progress, modern science, free trade, a free enterprise system, and political liberalism, this many-sided personality, who had read his Bentham, will reappear in several different contexts.

He had business acumen in abundance, and the technical expertise he found in Johan Michaëlson, who almost certainly had obtained his knowledge of stearine from Palmstedt. Like the latter, Michaëlson had been at Gripsholm, where as a youthful stepson of one of the owners he had participated in its experimentation. Hierta and Michaëlson started Liljeholmens Stearinfabrik in a rented, wooden house at Liljeholmen in 1839, then moved to better quarters at Danvikstull a couple of years later. Though sales went slowly at first, the "chemical-technical factory" became a highly prosperous affair through the sale of stearine, stearine candles, paraffin, and similar wares. Hierta handed it over to a company in 1872, and in 1900 it was employing 239 workers. Michaëlson, who had become familiar with the preparation of sulfuric acid while at Gripsholm, discussed with Hierta the possibility of making it cheaply enough to compete with foreign imports. Sales to the early match industry seemed particularly tempting. After studying the process in Paris (1844) and experimenting at home, Michaëlson, with a patent, founded a successful sulfuric acid factory at Tegeviken in Stockholm in 1846.

Much levity had originally been evoked in Stockholm by Hierta, already trying to illuminate his readers through the columns of *Aftonbladet,* now resorting to illumination by candlelight also. The Swedes, suffering through their long dark winters, have always had an obsession about light. It can be witnessed at its most poignant in their simultaneously reverent and boisterous celebration of Midsummer Eve, its rites tracing far back into pagan generations. In a very real sense, the conquest of darkness may have been the most fundamental Swedish victory of the nineteenth century: the successive appearance of Argand lamps, stearine candles, matches, gaslight, kerosene lamps, and the electric light bulb. To apply the essentially Anglo-Saxon term "gaslight era" to Swedish circumstances may at first glance seem a bit forced, and yet, seen as a phase in the peaceful conquest of nature, it may also be entirely appropriate.

The humble match, that unappreciated miracle of daily life, originated in the exciting world of chemists and would-be chemists that spawned, among other things, sulfuric acid, nitric acid, soda, chlorine bleach, and new ways of manufacturing soap. The early Swedish contribution to the chemistry of matches came when Johan Gottlieb Gahn discovered the calcium phosphate ingredient in bones, and shortly thereafter, in 1775, Carl Scheele used sulfuric acid on bone-ash to release the phosphorus. Henceforth, phosphorus could easily be made in quantity.[25]

Match sticks first appeared in France in about 1805. In one version, the tip, dipped in potassium chlorate, ignited by chemical reaction when thrust into a bottle containing sulfuric acid absorbed in asbestos. In another, a stick with a yellow phosphorus head was used; it lit easily, too easily, hence became a fire hazard. It was also poisonous and might induce caries of the jaws in the factory workers. John Walker, an English apothecary, introduced the first successful friction matches in 1826–27. These contained no phosphorus; the stick had a head of potassium chlorate or antinomy sulphide and would ignite when scratched against sandpaper.[26] Soon such brands as the Lucifers and Congreves appeared on the market, the latter named for a rocket invented by Sir William Congreve. Bryant and May emerged as the first match company in the world, and in the 1830s a number of factories sprang up in England, Germany, Austria, France, and the United States.

In Sweden the impetus came from two scientists, Jonas Samuel Bagge and Gustaf Pasch, as strictly subsidiary sidelines to their main activities. An instructor at the Institute of Technology and later a professor at the Falun School of Mines, Bagge was led by his interest in chemistry to make Sweden's first matches (1836). These may have been Congreves, but J. S. Bagge & Co. was certainly putting out phosphorus matches before 1843. Matches were being made in 1844 in four different shops in Stockholm, two of them being one-man operations.

Gustaf Pasch invented a safety match, patented in 1844 and made at Bagge's shop. A student of Berzelius, he had served on the Göta Canal project as a chemist trying to find an effective cement for waterway masonry. Later, among other activities, he taught at the Karolinska Institute. Though obviously convenient, the early matches caused so many unintended conflagrations that they were forbidden in some countries, and the search was on for a true safety match, one that would burst into flame only when struck against a specially prepared surface. The discovery of how to make *red* phosphorus, nontoxic and much less chemically active, helped to solve the problem. Pasch had the bright idea of placing red phosphorus on the striking surface rather than on the match head, the latter containing potassium chlorate or antinomy sulphide. However, it was expensive to make, the phosphorus soon wore off the surface, and it failed to sell.[27]

One day a firm in Malmö, an offshoot of the Rohmell and Schüerer match company in Copehagen, had a visitor in the person of Carl Lundström. The two owners proudly showed him everything in the shop. Carl went back to his hotel, made drawings of the whole process, and sent them to his brother, Janne.[28] Carl (1823–1917) and Janne (1815–1888) Lundström, sons of a prosperous Jönköping newspaper publisher and businessman, were two young men in search of a vocation.

Johan ("Janne") had studied at Uppsala for about five years, wandering from one subject to another and never concentrating sufficiently on any one field to graduate. Carl had attended a trade school, worked in a business office for a while, and then studied technology abroad, mostly in England. According to one anecdote, Carl, hearing that the Earl of Derby needed grouse on his estate, collected a flock of them in Sweden and made a handsome profit by selling them to the lord. (A dubious tale: England had no dearth of grouse.) He did try to buy the Swedish rights to a mail envelope from a Frenchman, who lost interest when he discovered that he was dealing with a nineteen-year-old. Then Carl Lundström moved on to buttons, large quantities of which were being imported from England and Germany. His button factory opened in Jönköping in 1843, complete with the first steam engine in town. In the summer of the following year his interest in matches was aroused by a Lübeck merchant asking Carl to make small brass containers for his matches. Passing through Malmö on other business, he stopped off to inspect the Rohmell and Schüerer shop.

Janne, still more or less at loose ends, now devoted himself to experimenting with matches, which had in fact been one of his numerous interests at Uppsala. Reading foreign technical journals and procuring the help of a chemist (Clemens Ullgren), he ultimately discovered the correct chemical combination, and the first Lundström matches were sold on April 28, 1845. The town of Jönköping, which would someday take much pride in being called "the match capital of the world," possessed no particular advantages to make it the headquarters for Sweden's first *specialindustri*. Located on the southern end of Lake Vättern, it had no water power, no unusual raw materials, and no strong handicraft traditions; even though it had access to the inland waterways by means of the lake, Jönköping was distant from city markets. The Lundströms started their match industry in Jönköping because they were known there and could borrow money in their home town; very probably it never occurred to them to go elsewhere.[29] The personal factor here is reminiscent of Birmingham, England, which possessed few natural advantages either, and which owed its rise to Boulton and Watt choosing to found their industry there.

The brothers rented a house from a shoemaker, and, living in a couple of rooms, used the others for storing the material, cutting the sticks, mixing the chemical batches, and dipping the stick heads into the brew. Soon needing more room, they bought land and put up a wooden building, all that they could afford at the time. In 1856 they built and moved into a brick building and before long several more small structures became necessary. The original Lundström operation was strictly handicraft, copying the one in Malmö; an improved process in 1849 nearly doubled production per worker. The sticks were at first cut from a plank, then divided into match lengths; but by 1849 they had devised a machine powered by the muscles of two workers, later by a steam engine. Originally wrapping the matches in paper, the Lundströms started stuffing them into small boxes, cut in the shop out of cardboard or thin veneer and put together by families in their homes.[30]

Meanwhile, Janne experimented with the Pasch formula for safety matches, the use of nontoxic phosphorus for the rubbing surface of the box. He succeeded in developing a somewhat different chemical combination than the original, enough to get this version patented, and the Lundströms started manufacturing their own safety matches in 1852. Exhibiting them at the Paris Exhibition (1855), they won a medal as the best in the world, and after this triumph the firm grew rapidly.

Matches were soon being regarded as necessities. Once the new wooden shop opened, Carl made a long tour of Swedish cities to obtain orders, and almost lost his life in a big blizzard in which over two hundred persons perished. After some years they began exporting matches to England through the Bryant and May Company, and by 1857 two-thirds of the total output was being sold abroad. Transportation remained expensive and hazardous until the railroad arrived. Sleds were used in the winter. In the summer the loads would go out by small sailing vessels on the lake and then by the Göta or Trollhätte canals to the sea. In 1854 the sinking of the *Jupiter* carried large quantities of Jönköping matches to the bottom of the waters. Unable to interest local merchants in acquiring a steamboat, Carl rented one from Enhörning & Co., which worked so well that soon the company had three of them. Then the canal authorities obtusely raised the tolls at the locks to prohibitive levels. In 1863, however, a railroad connected the city to the new trunk line, and the following year another line to Falköping gave access to Gothenburg. Production promptly doubled.

In 1863 a total of 406 workers were being employed: 260 women, 68 girls,

29 boys, 46 men, and 3 foremen. That is, matchmaking became primarily a source of employment for women and children. An early photograph of a group reveals a fairly miserable looking lot, one small reminder that industrial success stories, though providing employment, might have a less happy side to them.

Janne and Carl complemented each other. *Stickgubben* Janne ("the stick man Janne") was the thinker and experimenter, Carl the organizer and businessman. Without Carl to arrange for purchases and sales the company would not have flourished, but without Janne there would have been no company. Janne was the "genial but restless pioneer type" who, once he had an enterprise running properly, would leave it to start another. In 1863 he sold his stock at three-fourths price to Bernhard Hay, the bookkeeper, and another man. Apparently he suspected that the company would collapse after he left, and suffered pangs of conscience from letting these men buy his stock. He found a new outlet for his driving spirits in the Munksjö paper mill, south of Jönköping, established with the financial participation of Hierta. By 1869 Munksjö was doing so well, and the visionary Janne and the hardheaded Hierta bickered so much, that he sold his part of the enterprise to the businessman.[31] He then bought the Katrinefors paper mill, transformed it from handicraft to machine manufacture, and, once successful, sold that also. A stint as state inspector of match factories quickly bored him, and he retired. Simple and unostentatious, he died without property, living on a pension from the company; Janne would receive much of the public acclaim in the Lundström saga, perhaps in part because he died poor.

Carl kept his 112 shares of stock, and became rich. Carl also pursued a career of enterprises started and (sometimes) relinquished. Among them was a gaslight works to illuminate the match factory and a few other buildings, after the city had balked at setting up a municipal plant.

Jönköpings Tändsticks Fabriks Aktiebolag prospered under the direction of Bernhard Hay, who held 113 shares of the 400 issued. Hay had joined the firm by pure chance; he was a student at a trade school in Gothenburg when Carl Lundström asked it to send him a bookkeeper, and the seventeen-year-old happened to be picked. The brothers being so often absent on purchasing and selling expeditions, he necessarily learned the business in a hurry.[32] Whether the company grew to the level of big industry *(storindustri)* because of Bernhard Hay must remain moot. He took over as managing director just in time to preside over the rapid rise in production and sales when the railroads arrived. It was Carl Lundström, however, who obtained the use of the Sebold method of mechanically setting sticks in frames for dipping, which facilitated production. Most fortunate of all, the company had the good luck to benefit from a second partnership of a good businessman and an inventor: of Hay and the truly inspired Alexander Lagerman (1836–1904).

111

Lagerman was a compulsive inventor, a genius at constructing automatic machinery. Motala, impressed by his early skills, had hired him as a draftsman, but a few years later he left the famous engineering works to devote himself entirely to working on inventions. In 1862 he unveiled a match machine that automatically cut the sticks, and sulfurized, dried, and packed them in containers, the entire series of steps in one successive mechanical operation. Impressed by it, Hay hired him to work full time at the factory. Despite innovations, much of the labor had remained at the handicraft level, but now Lagerman's step by step invention of automatic machinery led to complete industrialization of production. For example, one of his new machines could pack about 20,000 matchboxes a day (1877). Another one made the boxes by automatic mechanisms. Lagerman's greatest coup may have been machinery for the making of safety matches, still expensive because their manufacturing process was more complex than for simple phosphorus matches. His inventions were not patented until much later in order to prevent others from studying the details and devising similar types; consequently, Lagerman attained little public recognition until at an older age he began inventing improved printing presses and typesetting machines.[33]

The story of the Lundström match company previews the shape of things to come. Originating in the modest circumstances of the 1840s as a handicraft industry, the company was advancing toward full industrialization in the 1870s, the decade of industrial breakthrough. This transformation was spurred by the cooperation of a good businessman and an inventive genius, an arrangement that would be quite typical of Swedish developments in the last third of the century. The making of matches came quite naturally to a Sweden at that stage of evolution, hence it became the country's first special industry. Sweden possessed ample wood scattered over the country, it had (or would have) the chemicals, and, requiring no great outlay of capital, someone could start a matchmaking shop in almost any town in Sweden.

The Lundströms encountered dangerous rivals from the beginning. L. E. Nordenmalm in Stockholm took out a patent on a machine for making veneer wood for the boxes in 1851, and he also used a machine for cutting the match sticks. The Segelbergs of Örebro pirated their information from Nordenmalm. The wife took a job as a worker in Nordenmalm's shop, learned everything about it, and departed with a sample of the chemical mixture on the match head. Once this had been analyzed, Per Anton Segelberg was in business. He had children going around the marketplaces selling matches, and he sent his hired hands wandering around the countryside peddling them. His prices were low, though in fact much haggling took place with buyers. (The Lundströms sold only by set prices.) Segelberg may have been the first in Sweden to make matchboxes out of wood, and the lion sign on his boxes achieved such good repute that the symbol was later adopted in Jönköping.

Match factories quickly sprouted up in various towns all over Sweden, and by 1870 about 2,800 workers were employed in 34 factories. An estimated 152 shops and factories altogether were started at one time or another, though many soon failed.[34] Another inventor-entrepreneur partnership in the match industry, that of Frans Lundgren (1854–1928) and Gerhard Arehn (1849–1896), gave rise to the company later known as Arenco AB (1885,1896), which manufactured and exported matchmaking machinery and, after 1920, automatic cigarette packers. Like virtually everything else in Sweden, the match industry would be subject to forces leading to centralization. In 1903 Fredrik Löwenadler (1854–1915) engineered the merger of six of the largest factories into the Jönköping and Vulcan Match Co., and ten years later the merger of eleven smaller ones, the "Kalmar Trust," signaled the entrance on the scene of Ivar Kreuger (1880–1932), the Match King.

Ivar Kreuger, whose family owned a match factory in Kalmar, had gone off to America at the age of twenty, and, after trying to sell real estate in Chicago, worked in the New York office of the Fuller Construction Co., which in these years was putting up such structures as the Flatiron Building, Macy's, and the St. Regis Hotel. After brief stops in South Africa, India, London and the United States again, Kreuger, another young man in search of a vocation, founded, with Paul Toll, the Kreuger and Toll construction company in Stockholm (1908). As building contractors they then proceeded to annoy the sedate inhabitants of the city with the rapidity and racket of American methods of construction. The stadium, the tall Norra and Södra Kungstornen (now dwarfed by more recent skyscrapers), and the foundations of Stadshuset still recall the work of these two men.

Four years after the formation of the Kalmar Trust, it merged with Jönköping-Vulcan to create the Swedish Match Co. With this as base, Kreuger swiftly built up an incredible international match trust with 250 branch offices in 43 countries; two out of every three people in the world were using its matches. The meteorlike rise of the Swedish Match King seemed too sensational to be true, and in 1932 he plummeted back to earth. Even his genius for sleight-of-hand finances could not cope with the world depression, and on March 12 he committed suicide in Paris. The Swedes, long bemused by this adventurous mutation in their respectable midst, were left to sort out their share of the debris and to conclude, in the words of Per Albin Hansson, long-time socialist prime minister, that "private enterprise and private initiative [should not be] allowed to run wild in the economic sector without any social control."[35]

Despite the ultimate Krueger debacle, the emergence of the Swedish match industry should be seen in a broader perspective. Sweden's first special industry, strictly based on Swedish circumstances and growing rapidly during the gaslight era, ultimately assumed an important place in the international economy. The Swedes never tire of saying that they live in a small country, but their spectacular success with this vital, if humble, article of daily life has been repeated on a more prudent scale by L. M. Ericsson, ASEA, Bofors, Atlas Copco, Volvo, and others. Perhaps it was fitting that the Swedes, with their deep craving for light, should so dramatically seize control of the match industry in so much of the world. Thirty years after the death of the Match King, the Swedes still held majority or partial interest in match companies in some fifty countries, or about a quarter of the world's match business.[36]

This is looking far ahead into history writ large. The detailed picture of Sweden's peaceful conquest of nature's forces is one of personal striving within broad molding circumstances that helped, subject to the whimsical intrusion of chance, to shape success or failure. The cast was large, most of the many episodes in themselves seemingly insignificant, and in the kaleidoscopic whole flowed the historical currents of the time. During the 1850s the preparatory work for the breakthrough of industrialization was being largely completed. Norrland timber had begun to move to world markets, the iron industry was surmounting its long crisis, and the textile mills were approaching complete industrialization. Capital was being accumulated. The agrarian revolution was bringing increased production, the export of grain, and the introduction of farm machinery. Responding to new demands, a whole series of machine shops (not yet described) was being founded, some of which would grow into full-scale factories. Limited-liability joint-stock companies had been legalized, the weakened guild system was being abolished (1846, 1864), and the accelerating liberalization would eliminate the remaining restrictions in the following years. It was the end of the beginning.

2. BREAKTHROUGH

8. IRON CORD, IRON HORSE

The first electric telegraph communication in Sweden occurred on July 16, 1853, only nine years after the famous "What hath God wrought!" message from Washington, D.C. to Baltimore on May 24, 1844. By that time every country in Europe had the telegraph except Turkey, Spain, and Sweden.[1]

The American Congress having ignored Samuel Morse's recommendation that the government build and own a national telegraph system, a number of noisily competing private companies sprang up to profit from the "lightning lines." In Great Britain the railroads introduced the telegraph, along the different technical principles of Sir William Cooke and Sir Charles Wheatstone, and it was long regarded as largely a railway convenience. The Paris–Rouen optical telegraph route was replaced by electric lines in 1845. On the continent the governments invariably built and continued to own the lines, at first limiting their usage to military and official communications; by 1852 Prussia had 1,700 miles of lines, Austria 1,053 and France 750.[2] In Sweden the iron cord preceded the iron horse, the very absence of railroads to some extent explaining why the Swedes did not stir sooner.

Gustaf Svanberg, professor of astronomy at Uppsala, had brought back a Gauss-Weber needle telegraph machine after attending a series of lectures by Karl Friedrich Gauss at Göttingen on electromagnetism and the principles of telegraphy (1833). Nothing came of it, nor of two proposals in 1849–50 by Charles and William Robinson (Americans) to King Oscar I to build a line between Stockholm and Gothenburg. The Board of Trade, sounding out the merchants in the two cities, met a negative response, partly because they claimed to see no advantage in faster communications and partly because they did not want to participate in it financially.

The three men who did introduce the electric telegraph into Sweden all came to it quite naturally from the nature of their occupations. Captain Anton Fahnehjelm (1807–1875) as an officer in the naval mechanical corps had been engaged in experimenting with underwater explosions; working with detonating mines and blasting underwater rocks, he had become familiar with electricity. Lieutenant Isak Fredrik von Heland (1801–1890) was a member of the topographic corps, and the third man, General Carl Fredrik Akrell (1779–1868) had been head of that service since 1831. The topographic corps, among its duties, continued to run those fragments of the optical telegraphic system that were still operational. In Sweden private individuals were permitted to transmit messages over it, in contrast to other European countries, although private commercial routes had appeared in England. Slow, clumsy, and expensive in terms of equipment and personnel, optical telegraphy was also vulnerable to fog, snow, and storms. Its rapid expansion in some countries, despite its limitations, testified to an urgent need for speedier communications; now the simpler and more efficient electric telegraph quickly replaced it, much like the railroads taking over most of the canal traffic.

Fahnehjelm and von Heland constructed the country's first electric telegraph device without having seen a Morse machine.[3] Put on display in January 1846 and demonstrated for the king and queen, it evoked no popular demand whatsoever. Four years later Fahnehjelm, on a tour of the continent to study electrometallurgy, inspected the Hamburg–Cuxhaven line, built by Charles Robinson in 1848 using the Morse system. Fahnehjelm bought a Morse machine to serve as a model for Swedish construction, and he and von Heland, now joined by General Akrell, resumed their campaign for a Swedish telegraph system.

They mustered their arguments for adoption: the king could keep in better touch with Stockholm during his annual half-year residence in Norway, the other half of the dual monarchy; merchants could get information much more rapidly; farmers would receive weather reports; and fleeing criminals could be more rapidly apprehended. The British police had caught the Salt Hill murderer, John Tawell, by telegraphing ahead that he was fleeing by a certain train, and, the public mind being what it is, this feat had become the best advertisement of all in favor of the new invention (1845).[4] The Swedish promoters asked, as a clincher, if the Swedes actually wanted the Turks to go ahead of them in the adoption of the telegraph. Nevertheless, they still encountered much opposition in the Riksdag, some caused by apprehension over the encroachment on private property by telegraph poles.

Fahnehjelm and von Heland had hoped that Akrell would give them an influential voice with the king. Akrell had had a long, distinguished career in the building of the Trollhätte canal and locks, the construction of fortifications, and on the general staff in the Swedish 1813 campaign in Germany. It did turn out that way, but affairs took a queer twist in the process. Akrell was due to be promoted to the chairmanship of the royal military tribunal (*krigshovrätten*). However, the general had just inflicted excessive discipline on an army officer for some offense, at least the king considered it excessive, and, furious, he refused to give Akrell the anticipated promotion. Instead, he *punished* the aged general by ordering him to sketch out proposed routes for telegraph lines and railroad tracks. Akrell was punished by being awarded a job guaranteed to be in some measure remembered by posterity. So, at least, ran the contemporary embellishment of his appointment, though, as director of optical telegraphy and of the kingdom's corps of surveyors, he would seem to have been the logical choice for the position anyway.

His report at the end of 1852 recommended that the telegraph be used for the needs of industry as well as for official and military purposes. He sketched out a number of lines, usually following the railroad routes that he was also proposing. The poles for an experimental line along the Stockholm–Uppsala highway were put up in the spring of 1853, and on July 16 the builders, "with beating hearts," received the first message from Uppsala. The wires, galvanized iron thread, had been purchased in England, the guttaperch isolators made in Stockholm, and the Morse apparatus constructed by Sören Sörenson and Frans Johan Berg. It was opened to public use in November after the operators had practiced to a reasonable level of proficiency.[5]

Other lines followed. Stockholm and Gothenburg were linked a year later, and on July 5 the Gothenburg newspaper *Handelstidning* published telegraphed news from Stockholm; by the end of the month the newspaper was asking for a second line. Fahnehjelm directed the installation of Morse station apparatus and the training of operators, while von Heland supervised line construction, aided by army officers in charge of the soldiers doing the manual labor. At the completion of each section, the local townspeople celebrated, having obviously undergone a rapid change of heart about the new means of communication. Thus, at Hälsingborg the station opened on a sunny summer day amidst a crowd of people cheering and listening to speeches, band music, and choral singing, while champagne flowed. They then followed Akrell to his quarters, loudly cheering the much-embarrassed general. In Malmö, Akrell was again annoyed by the public attention, by the music, speeches, horseplay, and general merriment.[6] All three leaders were being promoted in military rank, and some officers from Major Fahnehjelm's Hussar regiment turned up to help him celebrate, thereby adding to Akrell's irritation. The man was getting a bit old; he was seventy-five years of age.

An underwater cable at the Öresund connected Sweden to the Danish system; it in turn had a line to Hamburg, thereby opening up telegraphic communications with much of Europe early in 1855. Norway and Sweden were joined by the iron cord that summer, and an east coast line reached Haparanda and the Finnish border in 1857. Not until 1873 was a cable laid from Gothenburg to England. An astonished Baron Palmstierna, accustomed to being the target of criticism for his spending of revenue as finance minister, discovered that the outlay of several hundreds of thousands of riksdaler this time brought little recrimination. Suddenly the telegraph was popular, its use was heavy, and the towns, egged on by the businessmen, became willing to pay, themselves, for the privilege of putting up the local stations.[7]

Of the several entrepreneurs who tried to manufacture telegraph equipment, only one, Anton Henric Öller (1812–1889), survived for any length of time. As chief of the Uppsala station, his had been the finger that had tapped out that first message to Stockholm in July 1853. Sending out telegrams thereafter turned out to be no sinecure, for pranksters near the university repeatedly cut the lines. Öller, who ventured into an amazing variety of technical innovations, busied himself with early electrical apparatus for several decades, but, a poor businessman, he never succeeded in enriching himself. Having made several improvements in the early state equipment, he founded his own workshop in Stockholm for the making and repair of telegraphic apparatus. Though he outlasted his rivals, he was compelled to request a subsidy from the telegraphic agency. In 1869 Öller & Co., called a *mekanisk fabrik*, was advertising the sale of telegraphic apparatus, galvanic batteries, railroad semaphores, electrical educational machines, electric alarm clocks, and electrotherapeutic devices. Some of his former students, like those of Samuel Owen, tended to drive their old master out of business, and he closed Sweden's first electro-industry shop in 1886. One of those students, L. M. Ericsson, will be met later as the giant figure in another form of communications, the telephone.[8]

The state railroad began by putting up its own telegraph lines, but it quickly agreed to a mutual sharing of poles and costs with the national *Telegrafverket* (henceforth referred to as the Telegraph Service). Undoubtedly the rapid construction of the telegraph network, a rudimentary sort of nervous system for the nation, helped condition Swedish public opinion for that much larger and expensive undertaking, the building of the state railroads.

Count Adolf Eugène von Rosen (1797–1886) would seem to have been the natural leader for the construction of Swedish railroads. Of a German Balt family noble since the seventeenth century, Rosen must have been as familiar with the outside world and with the manifestations of industrialization as any contemporary Swede. Successively an Uppsala student, cadet at the war academy, and officer at the Karlskrona naval base, he rose to the rank of major in the mechanical corps while simultaneously engaging in a series of other activities. As a companion of John Ericsson in 1826–28 and as his representative in England in 1837–45, he had every occasion to see from the inside the workings of the British economy and technology. At other times he was an assistant to Baltzar von Platen on the canal construction, managing director of Motala, and founder/proprietor of Nyköpings Mekaniska Verkstad. He had also, with a brother, tried to start a business in Latin America and helped to organize the Greek navy.[9] This was the widely traveled, experienced adventurer who returned to Sweden in 1845 to launch a vigorous campaign on behalf of railroads.

That some sectors of the Swedish economy urgently needed them can be readily demonstrated. To carry goods from the *bruk* and paper-making works at Lessebo to the port of Kalmar required five days for a round trip by oxen, or three by horses. Eighteen pairs of oxen were used to pull the loads of one such trip. The paper-making proprietor at Klippan, inland from Hälsingborg, experienced endless difficulties and expenses with horse-drawn transport of the raw materials and bales of finished paper, and in the 1870s put himself in bad financial straits by investing heavily in a privately owned railroad that would alleviate Klippan's problems. When Rydboholm was installing fifty-one textile machines made by Munktells, their completion was delayed so long that only a few could be dispatched from Eskilstuna by boat; the remainder had to be sent over frozen winter roads. In Bergslagen, transport often required frequent loading and unloading wherever roads and waterways alternated. Iron goods from Gustaf Ekman's Lesjöfors in the late 1860s were carried to vessels at Kristinehamn on Vänern by the following stages: horse-drawn wagon on rails to a lake, across it on a barge, by rail to another lake; then by boat, rail, boat, rail, boat, rail, and boat to a junction with a recently completed steam engine railroad, which carried the goods to Kristinehamn.

These examples suggest why Rosen secured his strongest support in the Riksdag's House of Burgesses. Carl Fredrik Waern the younger campaigned for the railroads so important for his iron works, sawmills and export-import trade. Per Murén of Gävle, who had or would have interests in the Strömsbro cotton spinnery, the Korsnäs sawmill, the Gävle-Dala privately owned railroad, and the Sandviken steel works, was equally vocal in and out of the Burgesses. Among other proprietors, Sven Erikson at Rydboholm had already been advocating railroads in the early 1840s. As the discussion intensified, a certain "railroad fever" began to manifest itself in some of the towns, a strong demand that the future railroad go through their communities.

Sweden's delay in entering the railroad age can be attributed to several quite diverse factors. Some people in slow-moving Sweden questioned, as they had with the telegraph, the compulsion to greater speed inherent in modern industry. The farmers, not yet comprehending the importance of railroads for themselves, feared the expected financial burden. The inland small towns were relatively self-sufficient in their surrounding countrysides. Opponents of railroads stressed the lack of domestic coal for the locomotives; four-fifths of the coal later did have to be imported and led to the early electrification of Swedish railroads. Nearly everyone feared the daunting financial requirements in a country with insufficient capital, banking, and credit for such a large undertaking. The expensive ordeal with the Göta Canal had not been forgotten.

It was not easy, psychologically, for a people oriented to water transportation to change its outlook quickly. Stockholm, Gothenburg, and the other five cities with over ten thousand inhabitants were all located on the water, and many of the smaller towns lay along the coast or on the lakes. The Swedes had already been experiencing one dramatic improvement in ease and convenience of transportation with the steamboat, which may well have militated against another revolutionary change so soon. Canal companies and some shipowners now had a vested interest in delaying a new form of competition. It is scarcely surprising that the initial plan envisioned only a linking up of existing waterways by railroads and that the ultimately constructed state railroad system looked, according to some people, like a canal builder's notion of a railroad.

Short railways for horse-drawn vehicles existed in several places. Höganäs had one in the early years of the century. Uddeholm used a railway to bypass waterfalls at Forsnäs. In the Grängesberg ore fields the owners built 4.2 kilometers of railway, where small ore-filled wagons coasted down the incline to Södra Hörken, a lake; horses drew the empty wagons back up for reloading.[10] The most ambitious and intricate of these projects, the Yngen–Dalagränsen, consisted of eleven short railways between small lakes for horse-drawn wagons (1849). In this case the *bruk* owners (including Ekman at Lesjöfors) in eastern Värmland combined their efforts to build the lines and to maintain a joint transportation service. Entailing interminable loading and unloading, it would be superseded in 1870 by the building of the Nora–Vänern railroad, connecting the Stora Kopparberg region in Dalarna with Vänern; other railroads eventually crisscrossed Bergslagen.

Count von Rosen's original plan, when he returned to Sweden, met two of the major objections to railroads. To satisfy the waterways advocates, his railroad would merely connect ship transport on the big lakes across central Sweden. The route would run from Köping on Mälaren through Örebro on Hjälmaren and on west to Hult, a loading place on Vänern. To solve the financial problem, a private company would be organized, bringing in British capital. As an eyewitness of the frenetic British railroad boom, Rosen had good reason to expect a hearty British response. On November 27, 1845, a concession was granted for the proposed company. Requested, in addition, to submit a plan for an entire railroad system to be built within twenty years, Rosen proposed lines between Stockholm and Gothenburg, Stockholm and the postal terminal at Ystad, and Stockholm to Uppsala and Gävle, plus several subsidiary routes.[11] In 1847 the government also granted a concession (never used) to an English consortium to construct a railroad in Lapland to exploit the Gällivare ore deposits.

Another railroad panic in Great Britain (the collapse of the George Hudson railroad empire) gave the British more immediate problems, and they lost interest temporarily in both projects. However, a license was granted the Royal Swedish and English Company in December 1848, and the 1850–51 Riksdag approved a line from Örebro to Köping. John Sadleir, M.P. from Sligo with presumed British cabinet connections, now headed the British effort and the stock sold readily. Construction started in January 1853 when forty workers, spades at the ready, marched to the site, singing "Friskt mod i gossar blå."[12]

A soldier song, but the government never did provide the anticipated soldiers for the work, and it proceeded slowly. At this point the Swedish accounts generally slide into incoherence and tend to drop the subject. Costs ran beyond expectations, bonds were floated to get more money, and then on February 17, 1856, Sadleir committed suicide on Hampstead Heath. Among his sundry misdeeds, he had embezzled most of the company money. The *Times*, which noted that he was involved in a Swiss (sic!) railroad, called him "a national calamity" and Charles Dickens made him the model for Mr. Mercle in *Little Dorrit*. The company, to recoup, issued preferential stock, which naturally did not sell at all well. The Örebro–Arboga stretch opened for traffic in 1857, the Arboga–Köping section was completed ten years later, and the third link, Örebro to Hult, never did get underway.[13]

Bringing in British capital had touched off a vehement debate in the Riksdag and among the public. Nationalist opponents denounced it in language that now sounds as though it were coming from a Third World country. Among other charges, the English, who already controlled the seas, were accused of wanting to control the land also. Johan August Gripenstedt, finance minister, declared that "a few gentlemen on a street in London could bring about a thousand troubles and difficulties for us." Many years later Claes Adelsköld, a noted railroad builder himself, would sum up the common fear at the time that foreign capitalists would become the owners of the Swedish railroad system for an unlimited period of time and "lords over our industrial future. Our country's autonomous and free development, yes our independence was perhaps never more threatened than then." Rosen responded to the flowing oratory by pointing out that if the state had started building railroads earlier the private sector would not be offering its services now.[14]

Despite continued opposition, the scales had been slowly tilting in favor of at least exploring the possibilities. Military considerations contributed. The building of railroads in other countries, possible future enemies, gave rise to the thought that they might be a military necessity. The Russians would soon learn that truth the hard way in the Crimean War where, for lack of a railroad to the Crimea, a war was lost. In October 1851 King Oscar I (1844–1859) appointed a committee to study the matter further, and Waern was chosen as chairman. The next year Akrell was requested to survey the routes, along with that for the telegraph, and in December he submitted recommendations for southern and central Sweden. The Riksdag of 1853–54 accepted the basic plan, but stipulated that the state would build the trunk lines and private enterprise could, with state approval, construct the lesser ones. Some objected to any private railroads as unworthy of the dignity of the state. The planners did make certain that private railroads would not be powerful enough to make up a potent political pressure group.

In January 1855 the king selected the man to direct the construction. He did *not* pick the obvious man, Count Adolf Eugène von Rosen. His Majesty's newly appointed ministers did not like Rosen. His original plan of a private company building the lines, his reliance on British capital, and his expectation of using British engineers all went against the grain of Swedish patriots and Stockholm authorities. Rosen was by now associated with altogether too much controversy, and, quite probably, his fundamental approach had become much too Anglo-American for acceptance by Swedish officialdom. The king appointed Nils Ericson.

When John Ericsson emigrated, Nils, his brother, stayed home. John behaved like a genius, forever working on new inventions: the screw propeller, a steam fire engine, the caloric engine, a sun motor, a locomotive that competed with Stephenson's *Rocket*, and the ironclad *Monitor.* He was always "being lured away by the will-o'-the-wisps of untested theories" (White).[15] Nils Ericson (he dropped the second "s" in his last name when ennobled in 1854) was stable, prudent, trustworthy, and punctual, and carefully conformed to contemporary social forms. One theory has it that he spent his life trying to be as great as his younger brother, and that he carefully cultivated "an ability to make the most of his chances."[16] All of which, one suspects, is quite unfair to Nils.

Nils stayed on at the Göta Canal when John, after the angry scene with Baltzar von Platen, enrolled in the Jämtland Field Chausseurs. John fell in love with Caroline Liliesköld, daughter of an army captain, who brusquely broke up the affair; not until several years later did John, in England, learn that he had an illegitimate son. Typically, it was Nils who gave the boy, Hjalmar Elworth, his training and responsible positions. Also typically, Nils married a countess.

He moved through a succession of assignments, gradually attaining positions of command as a captain in the mechanical corps, chief of the western canal building district, and chief engineer and director of the Trollhätte canal company. Completion of the Göta Canal had outmoded the smaller dimensions of the locks at Trollhättan, and it fell to Ericson to prepare plans for locks large enough to accommodate the bigger boats. Since traffic had to be maintained during construction, entirely new ones, skirting the old, had to be built. Directed by Ericson, work started in the spring of 1838, and at its height employed 1,280 workers, 900 of them soldiers.[17] Having grown up with the Göta Canal, Nils must have derived much satisfaction from occupying a position equivalent to that of von Platen himself earlier. It was finished in 1844 in less time and at less expense than originally anticipated.

In that year brother John was heard from when a faulty cannon blew up on his propeller-driven warship, the 600-ton iron frigate *Princeton*, killing the U. S.

secretaries of state and navy and endangering the life of the American president. It was no fault of John's, but the incident was not uncharacteristic of his career. Meantime, Nils had also supervised the work on the Säffle canal in southern Värmland, intended to ease transport problems for the iron works in the area. After completing the Trollhätte locks, he found a new challenge in Stockholm. The so-called Slussen (the lock and sluice), the perilous exit from Mälaren at the south end of Gamla Stan, often carried such a strong current that vessels entering the lake had to be pulled through it. No one cared to attempt a restoration of the old, delapidated lock. Nils Ericson accepted the challenge to build a new one for 422,000 riksdaler, and he did the work (1846–50) for 87,000 riksdaler less than his original bid. Between 1852 and 1854 he built the Skeppsbro and Kornhamn quais, abutting Slussen on the east and west sides. During these years, from 1845 until 1854, Ericson was also the technical and administrative leader in building the Saima canal in eastern Finland, a distance of fifty-nine kilometers and containing twenty-eight locks.

The Finns still use the Saima for transport to the Gulf of Finland, though a portion of it, in Soviet territory since the Second World War, is leased from the Russians. As for the Slussen lock and quais, they slumber quietly below the everlasting rumble from streams of motor cars on the bridges above. Manifestly, Ericson, a superb administrator of prudently planned enterprises, had built for the ages. Now a colonel, the title he most preferred, ennobled as a *friherre* (baron), and honored with several decorations, he retired to Nygård, his estate on Vänern.

Nils happily went home to the peace and quiet of his home in the spring of 1854. Shortly before Christmas, King Oscar I summoned him to Stockholm, entailing a cold six-day journey through the winter snows. Arrived at the palace, Colonel Ericson was requested by His Majesty to undertake the construction of the Swedish railroad system. The king admired him and especially, no doubt, his ability to hold the costs down. Ericson, however, was a canal man, had seen few railroads, and was one of those who did not particularly like the prospect of an industrialized Sweden. He considered the waterways Sweden's natural means of transportation, and railroads would therefore, in his opinion, be a costly luxury. According to some accounts, the conference with the king waxed quite stormy, but Nils Ericson left the palace committed to doing his duty. Ericson had also extracted full powers, more than any modern Swedish citizen had ever possessed, for complete control of the project.[18]

Rosen was named to a royal planning committee, but Ericson never did offer him an administrative position in the construction. Rosen wrote to John Ericsson that his brother "has shut me out completely from any participation in the work so that . . . he alone would get the honor and income." But Nils once said that as far as Rosen was concerned, he was worthy of only *one*

125

position, "and that one I, unfortunately, had myself, and which was not my fault."[19]

Contemporary reports of his reluctance to accept the appointment may have been overdrawn, judging by the comment of a family member, Carola Goldkuhl, that he welcomed the new opportunity.[20] Certainly he lost no time in preparing his plan. It called for trunk lines (*stambanor*) connecting Stockholm with Gothenburg and Malmö, one from the capital north into Norrland, and a few supplementary routes. The Norrland line would bypass the seaport cities entirely, running fifty kilometers inland. This was presumably far enough to escape naval bombardment or enemy forays, and it also avoided the difficult inlets and river mouths. Like all the trunk lines, it also fulfilled one of Ericson's premises, that the railroads should stimulate the growth of the relatively underdeveloped parts of the country. The Stockholm–Malmö route passed through the western, thinly populated part of Småland.

This kind of plan would never have been accepted in the commercially motivated Anglo-Saxon countries because, aside from the three major cities, the routes almost seemed designed to avoid the other larger communities. They never paralleled the canals, only crossed them. People said that Ericson was afraid of both cities and canals, and critics scoffed that his railroads looked like something that only a canal builder would propose.[21] (Ericson was still a director of the Trollhätte canal company.) It did, however, have the merits of being a complete, rational plan and of satisfying certain major considerations within the Swedish context.

If the Swedes were slow to start, they did have the benefit of hindsight, profiting from other peoples' mistakes. The British railroad mania in the mid-1830s, with duplicate, competing lines, led to a horrendous, long-enduring financial mess. In 1846 nineteen of the twenty-one French companies collapsed. The Belgians had avoided all this by building a completely planned, state-owned network in 1835–44.[22] Ericson's relatively straight railroad lines, regardless of populated areas, resembled Tsar Nicholas I's direct track between St. Petersburg and Moscow, which missed all major communities except nearby Tver. Nor were the Swedes the only ones to contemplate using railroads as links between waterways. In 1857 Baron Stiglitz proposed a Russian network to connect the principal rivers in central Russia, as well as the Baltic with the Black Sea. And, as another example, the New York Central Railroad in upstate New York was not at first permitted to carry freight because it would compete with the state-owned Erie Canal; later, in 1844–51, it was allowed to do so only when the canal was frozen in winter.[23] Although Ericson tried to minimize competition with canals and shipping interests, he had seen the difficulties in Värmland of mixing land and water transport, with its "time-consuming and costly" reloadings, and refused to limit his railroads to serving as "canals on dry land."[24]

Ericson's plan evoked violent quarrels with various towns and local interests that wanted the route to service them; backed by the government, which made little effort to compromise, Ericson's decisions prevailed. The king and Gripenstedt, strong advocate of state-owned railroads, gave him full support, and the Riksdag approved the plans. One fundamental compromise with Rosen and other supporters of privately owned railroads had, as noted earlier, been made in the Riksdag measure; while the trunk lines would be state built and owned, private enterprise could organize companies to construct other railways for towns and regions not included in the national network. It was assumed, and rightly, that the private sector would use its own resources at least in part to supplement the trunk lines.

The vexing issue of foreign capital and the Swedish fear of consequent foreign influence was resolved by the government itself borrowing the money, using current tax revenues to service these loans. British capital helped to finance the earlier construction of the trunk lines through seven bond issues in 1858–70. France became the major source after this, both for the continued building of the Norrland line and for conversion of the earlier debts. The state passed some of the foreign money on to help private railroads; sources of capital for these companies included stock issues, loans from the state, local governments and credit institutions, and bonds floated in Sweden and, indeed, "a few abroad."[25]

Not enough soldiers were available for labor, so Colonel Ericson advertised for civilian workers, offering them at least one riksdaler a day and warm room in the barracks; recruits were advised to bring along a spade, a bed cover, and a bag in which to pack food and supplies. Also a *prestbetyg*, a statement of good character from their church pastors. Within six months nearly 2,500 soldiers and workers were on the job. Nils Ericson, like Baltzar von Platen, might turn up anywhere on the project. Since "his temperament, like his brother's, was not of the tranquil kind," the workers put up signal flags to warn others along the line whenever he appeared. Construction out of Stockholm, directed by Hjalmar Elworth, was delayed by a long acrimonious debate over whether the road should go the direct way south of Mälaren or curve by the more populous communities on the north side. Ericson wanted it to go south, and it did, though a short line from Hallsberg on the trunk line did connect with Örebro and its railroad to Arboga. The first stretch completed out of Gothenburg went as far as Jonsered, fifteen kilometers away. Soon such swarms of people were taking the train to a noted drinking place there that temperance advocates demanded that no trains run on Sunday, the one day working class folks had free.[26]

Once the western trunk line had been completed, the Swedes celebrated in style. The dedicatory train, drawn by the locomotive *Södermanland*, contained twenty-one carriages, four for the royal family and eight more for the Riksdag. Every town along the route had its triumphal arch, flags, bands, and ceremonies. It took two days to get to Gothenburg on the evening of November 4, 1862, where the train was greeted by bonfires on the hills and lights in the house windows. The king came off the train to be ceremoniously greeted by the governor in front of a large, cheering crowd, cannon began booming, the band played, and the biggest ball in Gothenburg history followed.[27]

With nearly two-thirds of the southern trunk line to Malmö completed, Ericson resigned and, receiving the Grand Cross of the Order of Vasa, retired to Nygård. That same year, in March 1862, a spooky little saucer-shaped ironclad, "a can on a shingle," came drifting along at Hampton Roads in the United States. The performance of John Ericson's *Monitor* against the *Merrimac* doomed Confederate hopes of cutting the North's sea lanes. It had been given to John Ericsson to make one small, vitally imperative, move on the gigantic military chessboard of the American Civil War.

Construction on the trunk lines continued under the new head, Carl Gottreich Beijer, hitherto in charge of the route to Malmö. He, too, was a waterways expert, his major activity having been concentrated on the improvement of the Malmö harbor; he had, however worked on a Russian railroad and was the first person summoned by Ericsson back in 1855.[28] The southern railroad was completed at the end of 1864, a northeastern line from Kristinehamn in Bergslagen was connected to the trunk line at Laxå in 1871, and another one, Katrineholm–Norrköping– Nässjö was finished in 1874. The railroad north from Stockholm crept on, reaching Storvik in 1875, Sollefteå in 1886, Boden in 1893, and Narvik in Norway in 1902.

Despite the original remonstrances, some British advisors were brought in. Also, eighty of the first ninety-eight locomotives were purchased in England, and experts came along to train the first crews. Lauenstein of Hamburg provided much of the rolling stock until Swedish factories could supply them. Ericson spent some time in England, and Claes Adelsköld was there half a dozen times to buy material and to study technical problems. Christer Petter Sandberg (1832–1913) served as the inspector of rails purchased for the Swedish state network, in the course of which he invented new types of rails that were used in various parts of the world.[29]

However much Nils Erikson may have loved canals, the effect of the western trunk line on the Göta Canal proved lethal. As in the United States, the glamorous and graceful canal era, at least as seen by a nostalgic and regretful posterity, came to an abrupt end. By 1868 only the serene passage of two passenger ships, the *Vadstena* and *Karlstad*, still recalled those brief years of hopeful achievement.

In 1870 the state owned 1,118 of the total 1,727 kilometers of track. Ten years later the total figure had risen to 5,876, of which 1,956 kilometers belonged to the state. The 1870s became the big age of railroad building as privately owned companies responded to the foreseen necessity of supplementing the trunk lines. At the end of the century over two-thirds of the track was privately owned, though these companies ran much less traffic and operated with inferior equipment.

The railroads running from the landlocked Bergslagen to the sea perhaps best illustrate the private enterprise initiatives. This wealthy industrial region contained a potent array of iron works and mills: Stora Kopparberg, Uddeholm, Fagersta, Bofors, Munkfors, Lesjöfors, Degerfors, and Billerud, to which Domnarvet, Hagfors, Bångbro, and the Korsnäs sawmill would be added as a direct result of railroads. Business groups in Gävle and Gothenburg had every incentive to build railroads that would siphon the lucrative trade out through their cities.

For seafaring Gävle, hitherto dependent upon coastal traffic and other shipping, the construction of a railroad inland to Falun became a matter of life or death. Plans were being hatched as early as 1851, not least because the terrain had been too difficult to provide floatways for timber from that region. Per Murén became the driving force, supported by Georg de Laval (an official in the Falun area), Henrik Munktell at the Grycksbo paper mill, and Göransson. The state loaned about 1.6 million riksdaler, an estimated two-thirds of the cost of construction, to the company, this as a tacit part of the deal whereby Ericson's railroad plan, which bypassed Gävle, won Riksdag approval. Additional capital came from sale of company stock and, later, from Stockholm interests.[30]

Claes Adelsköld, the young head engineer, had to work economically on the Gävle–Dala railroad, for the costs exceeded the estimates. Not only that, he lacked competent assistants because the few existing experts were all in Ericson's project. The result was a second-rate railroad, but it served the purpose (1859). Adelsköld, who claimed to have taken the first spadeful of dirt in Swedish railroad construction as a surveyor on the horse-drawn Yngen-–Dalagränsen railway, became the country's premier builder of private railroads.[31]

Göransson placed his Bessemer steel works at Sandviken on the new line, and he, with de Laval and others, founded the Korsnäs sawmill along the route. Several other sawmills appeared nearby. The railroad opened new possibilities for older enterprises, such as Hofors, Hammarby and Forsbacka, and the whole area along the route developed rapidly. Between 1855 and 1880 Gävle's iron and wood export quadrupled. In the long run, however, Gävle's location was against it, once the railroad network approached completion. Despite the farsighted and valiant effort by the city leaders, its export trade would thereafter increasingly shift to more strategically located seaports.

Some of the business interests in central Sweden wanted a railroad to a port on the west coast, and one proposal for a route from Dalarna and Värmland to a harbor farther north raised a storm of protests in Gothenburg. The line ultimately built by Bergslagernas Järnvägs AB, after an English concession had been refused, ran from Falun through Ludvika and Kil to Gothenburg (1879). The list of its major shareholders reads like a Who's Who of central Sweden's industry and finance: K. H. Geijer (Degerfors), E. G. Danielsson (Uddeholm), James Jameson Dickson (timber), Wilhelm Röhss (import-export), Elias Delbanco (oil), Theodor Mannheimer (finance), Adolf Wilhelm Waern (Boldernäs), G. A. Lundhqvist (Stora Kopparberg), and Josef Gabriel Richert (engineer).[32] Of the 70,905 shares, 48,577 were held in Gothenburg. The Gothenburg Commercial Co. (Göteborgs Handelskompani), founded to finance industry and railroads, took half of the bond issue and Stockholms Enskilda Bank bought much of the rest.

The first thirty locomotives came from Beyer Peacock & Co. (1873–79) and the first passenger cars from Ashbury Railway Carriage and Iron Co., both of Manchester. Though export ore and imported coal for the bruk were expected to make up much of the freight, the main products turned out to be wood, paper, and wood pulp as the centralization of the iron industry drove the lesser bruk to shift from iron to other activities.[33]

One hundred years later, on September 1, 1979, a centennial train, drawn by three steam locomotives, carried 750 passengers, including 119 more or less inebriated Englishmen and one Australian (according to Swedish newspapers), on a Gothenburg to Falun anniversary tour. The minister of communications delivered an address, but something had gone wrong with the state railroad locomotive of her train from Stockholm, and she arrived in a taxi.[34]

The coastal towns of Nyköping, Västervik, Oskarshamn, and Kalmar had all vehemently protested Ericson's route through western Småland, and they suffered badly when the state line opened; customs revenue at Oskarshamn dropped by half. Lacking sufficient capital, they could not sponsor private lines without outside aid. Finally, after successive years of crop failures, the government gave financial help to build a railroad out of Oskarshamn in order to provide employment (1869). The remaining money came from railroad stock, some bought by the British. Morton & Sons built the line, the cars came from the Midland Waggon Co., and the locomotives were of the Fairlie (English) type. Twenty years of talk in Västervik preceded the building of a railway between it and Jönköping on the state line; again the British were involved in the construction, but cars and locomotives came from Munich and Nuremberg.[35] Over near the west coast, Sven Erikson of Rydboholm, one of the earliest proponents, died in 1866, years before a railroad arrived in his area. To which must be appended an ironic note: his son, Johannes, by then old and deaf, was walking on the railroad tracks one day in 1912 when he was hit and killed by a passing train.

Although the Swedes had hoped to avoid the railroad mania of some other countries, an immediate result of the rapid construction of the 1870s was a "boom and bust" era of no mean proportions. Other consequences soon manifested themselves, one of these being the changing fortunes of towns as settled areas near the tracks grew in size while those not so fortunate stagnated. Where the route passed some distance away, railroad stations would be built there and new settlements would spring up around them, making these "double towns" quite common. Several entirely new communities appeared along the routes, including Eslöv, Nässjö, Hallsberg, and Bollnäs.[36] In 1905 ten of the fifteen cities in the 10,000–15,000 population class were now inland.

Undoubtedly the railroads helped to keep Sweden a country of dispersed industry by providing the small industrial towns with easy transport of raw materials and finished products. The trunk lines, passing through the countryside, tapped these smaller communities by means of spurs, while industrial settlements sprang up in the emerging railroad settlements. Railroads were self-stimulating in creating more economic demand and traffic as formerly self-sufficient towns and villages discovered new expectancies.

No more years of famine occurred after 1867–68, once food could be easily transferred from one part of the kingdom to another. Retail stores, eliminating the peddlers, proliferated as they gained rapid access to multitudinous kinds of finished goods. The market itself expanded with the feasibility of transporting the perishable products of dairy and garden. Growing cities, which could now be fed more expeditiously, needed milk, butter, and cheese, and thereby helped to cause a shift in agriculture toward dairying.[37] Farm machinery could be delivered far more easily and cheaply, enhancing both farm productivity and the growth of factories making the implements.

Railroads made possible the transport of bulky, cheap articles; luxury items had formerly been, usually, the only ones worth sending. After the completion of Sweden's railroads, by 1904, ore made up 28.89 percent by weight of freight on the state lines and wood products 18.88, the two thus composing nearly one-half of all freight traffic; grain, about 15 percent in the 1860s, dropped to 4.69. Although only about a thirtieth of Norrland timber moved on the state trunk lines, the figure was much higher in central and southern Sweden, where floatways were often lacking.[38]

The cost of freighting iron fell to one-fourth or one-fifth of that of the earlier transport, and the movement of charcoal, which tended to disintegrate in the course of repeated loadings, was greatly facilitated. By easing the shipping of ore and cast iron, the railroads made possible the rapid centralization of iron works, while iron ore for export could be sent to the seaports with much less

131

labor and cost.[39] The construction of the Domnarvet iron works in the 1870s could scarcely have occurred without the railroads. Bofors and Degerfors, both dependent upon the Nora-Karlskoga railroad began their strong development just after its completion. Bångbro, on the Frövi–Ludvika railroad, became the site for an iron works in 1872–74.

Railroads were virtually a prerequisite for industrialization. They resolved the unending frustrations of difficult transport of raw materials and finished products, lowered the costs dramatically, and expanded the domestic market for both farm and industrial goods. In sum, the railroads, transforming the contours of Sweden over a period of a few decades, enormously accelerated the breakthrough of the long-gathering forces leading to full industrialization.

However significant these long-term consequences, the immediate impact, in terms of the purchase of equipment, was not, according to Hans Modig, as decisive as formerly thought. The state railroad procured its early locomotives in Great Britain, and so did several of the larger private lines (Beyer Peacock or Sharp & Stewart); the latter also bought their original rolling stock in England. Rails had to be imported until Swedish iron works could convert technologically to their manufacture, and most of the coal came from Great Britain. Modig estimates that in the 1870s the railroad construction needs accounted for about 15 percent of the output of the Swedish engineering works.[40]

In European dimensions, Sweden is a comparatively large country inhabited by a rather sparse population. Due largely to these circumstances, it possessed, in the middle of the twentieth century, the fifth highest per capita railroad mileage in the world, after Canada, Australia, New Zealand, and the United States. This same combination of factors, plus the scattered industry, also meant, however, that the building of the infrastructure—railroads, highways, harbors, schools, hospitals, etc.—required an unusually high outlay of money. The foreign loans greatly helped to defray these expenses, thereby leaving private capital relatively free to be mobilized for industrial purposes.

9. MOBILIZING CAPITAL AND TALENTS

Wide sectors of the populace suffered a final bitter taste of Old Sweden's "poverty and limited horizons" (Söderberg) in the 1860s when the pressures of rural overpopulation were at their worst.[1] The crop failures in 1867–68 brought back for the last time the old scourge, famine in the countryside. British markets were temporarily depressed, and the American Civil War shut down the cotton mills, bringing distress to the textile centers.

Despite these dismal circumstances, the 1860s were in many ways a turning point in Swedish development. The four-chambered Riksdag met for the last time on June 22, 1866, in one final enactment of centuries-old ritual, thereafter to be replaced by a bicameral parliament. This culminating moment had been preceded by such other reforms as the establishment of elected provincial and town councils. Though the modernized Riksdag, limited to men with substantial amounts of property or income, introduced no immediate major innovations, the parliamentary reform, in the words of Franklin Scott, "marked a watershed" between the old and new Swedish politics.[2]

The 1860s also marked a watershed in the Swedish economy. The some 30,000 industrial workers in 1860 grew to approximately 80,000 in 1870, of which about 26,000 were in the iron industry and an additional 15,000 in lumbering. Though the figure rose rapidly thereafter as the changeover to machine production picked up momentum, this should not obscure the developments of the 1860s, attested to by the recruitment of nearly 50,000 additional industrial workers. Arthur Montgomery thought the 1860s to be the landmark years in Swedish economic history because of the role of the railroads in drawing the countryside into the economy, the rapid growth in the timber industry, returning prosperity for the iron works, and the expansion of the factory system. To which should be added the repeal of the remaining restrictions, the improvement in technical skills, and the easing of credits for investments. Industry, which by now had won freedom of enterprise, had access to sufficient capital for the "transition to a genuine capitalistic industry" (Hovde) to be in full swing.[3]

The guilds, with their entangling privileges and restrictions, had been abolished in 1846, replaced by associations of workers, whose representatives in the Riksdag for some years defended their interests with dogged pertinacity. The number of craftsmen continued to rise, 17.7 percent between 1846 and 1860, but industrial workers increased by 40.8 percent in those years.[4] The final relics of the old system were swept away in 1864 by a law granting full freedom of occupation.

Swedish industry would stage its breakthrough in a period of virtually free trade, a policy vigorously pursued by finance minister Gripenstedt. Already lowered rates were further reduced, import duties on grain were entirely eliminated, and a commercial treaty with France effectively opened the gates to nearly unhindered commerce. Emulating the British, the three Scandinavian states adopted laissez-faire policies as completely as any continental European countries.[5] Not until the entrance of American grain on European markets and a higher German tariff did pressures mount seriously for renewed protective tariffs, reinstituted in 1888, especially on farm products, and raised higher on these in 1895. Manufactured goods received some protection in 1892. Imports continued to exceed exports clear down to 1914.

The more Swedish production became dependant upon exports, the greater the impact of financial crises and downswings of business abroad, though the Swedish business cycle tended to be milder than the international. Short, sharp financial crises did strike in 1857–58, 1865–66, and 1878–79. The economy reflected primarily the year-by-year situation in Great Britain, to which Sweden was shipping about one-half of its exports, and, to a lesser degree, conditions in Germany. Paralleling good times elsewhere, Sweden enjoyed periods of prosperity in the 1850s (much helped by the Crimean War), the early 1860s, and "the greatest business boom of the century" (Montgomery) at the beginning of the 1870s.[6] Other upswings occurred later in 1882–83, 1889–90, and around 1900.

In one important respect Swedish developments of the period resembled those of later developing countries in the Third World—the bulk of the exports consisted of raw materials or semifinished goods. Relatively poor in capital, Sweden was gathering from its timber, grain, and iron exports the necessary money for its own industrial transformation, hence for the time being was heavily dependent upon the oscillating market demand abroad.[7] No great amount of investment capital was needed until the 1850s, and during the earlier period earned profits accounted for much of the money for expansion. Credits were available from merchant houses, although these were normally extended to meet day-to-day expenses rather than for starting new developments. Loans or grants from the state made up the single most important source for larger sums. Some affluent citizens—members of the upper bourgeoisie, top-ranking officials in the civil service, high military officers, rich *brukspatroner*, and landed proprietors—did have some money for investment during the first half of the century. The legalization of joint-stock companies in 1848 opened up one means whereby this capital might be channeled into industry.

Prior to this, the family-owned enterprise had been customary, though some firms were owned by partners or held in joint ownership. Nor did the new law bring any widespread distribution of ownership, for the original founders of a company usually restricted the stock to their own group of business friends. Subscriptions for stock might be announced, but no general offering was made to the public, and if more capital was needed the same group would generally buy up the shares.[8] Rather than sell stock to outsiders, the owners normally preferred to use their profits for further expansion. The textile industry was the first to avail itself, overall, of the opportunity to mobilize capital for ventures while avoiding the former individual financial responsibility for the bankruptcy of a venture. Sawmill companies also emerged in respectable numbers after about 1865, but only about one-half of the sawmills had adopted company form by 1911. By that time four-fifths of the iron and steel works were owned by companies. Family-owned enterprises long remained common, though many of them were reorganized into stock companies at about the turn of the century.

Larger companies tended, in Sweden as elsewhere, to characterize the opening phase of industrialization. In 1872 over two-thirds of all industrial workers were in companies with over a hundred workers. After the founding period in any industry, a number of smaller firms sprang up to offer competition. Still later would come a merger of surviving companies into one or more ventures able to maintain large-scale production, a process especially evident in the decade before the First World War.[9]

Merchant houses were nearing the end of their role in providing some of the functions of banks, and several of the most prestigious succumbed in the successive financial crises of the period. They lost their sales agencies as transportation and communications improved, the larger enterprises setting up their own sales networks. Better sources of credit, especially with the growth of banks, eliminated the need for their services in that respect. After about 1865 the merchant houses would increasingly divert their resources to the acquisition of stocks and bonds in the emerging companies.

As industrialization took on momentum between 1860 and 1914 the Swedish appetite for investment capital from domestic sources would grow correspondingly. As far as Stockholm and Gothenburg firms were concerned, Gårdlund found that only about 5 percent of their bonds between 1870 and 1909 were sold abroad. Söderlund believes that the proportion would be rather higher for smaller and new firms not within the orbits of these urban companies, that is, for segments of the timber industry, for private railroads, and to some extent for the pulp industry.[10] However, the bulk of the foreign borrowing would be carried on by the state, communes, and mortgage institutions. With so much of the industrial expansion being financed by Swedish capital, the role of the banks would be of crucial importance during the coming decades.

Despite the series of bankruptcies and frequent complaints about inadequate capital resources, the Swedish financial system at midcentury, compared to prevailing institutions and practices in continental Europe, was relatively good; the merchant houses and brokerage services provided, in the words of Olle Gasslander, a "loosely organized and flexibly functioning credit system" closely linked to commerce and industry.[11] The real problem lay in the lack of sufficient capital for the long-term loans needed for founding and expanding industrial enterprises and building private railroads. For a number of continental countries, including Sweden, the mobilization of money for these purposes was becoming a matter of great urgency.

Private banks, legalized in 1824, should seemingly have served as an agency for injecting private savings into commerce and industry. The venerable Riksbank, dating back to 1668 and hence the oldest national bank in Europe, was of little use here. It acted as a bank of issue and regulator of currency, not as a business bank, and it was not particularly interested in receiving savings deposits. Though the Riksbank did give some long-term loans to safe borrowers, its credit facilities were strictly limited and its policies inflexible. No more helpful were the eight private joint-stock banks (more, later) that had been founded, without limited liability, in eight different provinces between 1830 and 1855. They were small and precariously financed, and, customarily putting their savings into government bonds for safekeeping, were of little assistance to business. Their total deposits in 1850 amounted to less than 8 million riksdaler. (One British pound sterling in 1850 was worth 18 to 18.25 riksdaler. The skilling, 40 to a riksdaler, was replaced by the öre when the decimal system was introduced in 1855; when Sweden went on the gold standard in 1873, the krona replaced the riksdaler.)

The French tried to resolve their own difficulties at midcentury by establishing a network of limited-liability banks and by creating the Société Générale de Crédit Mobilier, intended to accumulate capital in order to channel it into industrial development. This reorganized banking system quickly became a model for other countries. Already in 1853 a group of Swedes, including Johan Gustaf Schwan and Axel Bennich, began pressing the government for the right to set up a limited liability bank of the *crédit mobilier* type. Finance minister Palmstierna was quite favorable, but the conservative ministry rejected the proposal. When Gripenstedt replaced Palmstierna in 1856, he promptly secured approval for a much less ambitious plan by A. O. Wallenberg.

Johan August Gripenstedt (1813–1874), whose name in Swedish history is associated with free trade and the final dismantling of state controls, had risen to high influence as the spokesman for King Oscar I in the House of Nobles. Primarily an astute political manipulator, he stayed on as a royal advisor when the conservatives replaced the liberals in power in 1851. By 1854 Gripenstedt, impressed by the political strength of the businessmen and the railroad lobby as well as by his own experience as the manager of large properties at Nynäs, had swung over into an alliance with them, and during the following years he served as the chief political instrument for carrying out their programs. (His pragmatic statesmanship led King Karl XV [1859–1872] to say later that his finance minister changed his mind every couple of years.) Having earlier collaborated with Wallenberg, he quickly approved his charter for Stockholms Enskilda Bank (July 1, 1856).

André Oscar Wallenberg (1816–1886), the son of the bishop of Linköping and himself a mediocre gymnasium student, had gone off to sea, later took the naval officer examinations, and, among other assignments, captained the propeller-driven *Linköping* on the Göta Canal. He may have discovered his true vocation while a sailor on American ships in New York and Boston, where he was fascinated by the bank crash of 1837. After founding Stockholms Enskilda Bank, Wallenberg, leading it with valor and constant controversy, would eventually move into a central position in Swedish economic life, and the powerful Wallenberg family would thereafter continue to play a pivotal role in the business affairs of the kingdom.

To the frustration of the group interested in encouraging investment capital, Stockholms Enskilda Bank (SEB) was originally set up as merely one more of the private banks, authorized to issue notes but not possessing limited liability. It did have a managing director (Wallenberg), a new development, but this was not at first a powerful position. Wallenberg, one of 72 shareholders, held only 50 of the 1,000 shares, and not until after a dissident faction had broken away in 1871 to found another bank did he achieve full control. Scarcely as innovative as formerly believed, he did introduce bank money orders and the systematization of credit ratings for would-be borrowers; from the beginning the Stockholm bank became a clearinghouse for the notes issued by the provincial ones.[12] Though the SEB was founded in the conservative tradition of the earlier banks, two factors induced it, gradually and a bit reluctantly, to respond to the capital-hungry market of the time. It was able to attract much larger deposits than banks located in smaller cities, money that could then be invested in industry and railroads. This was particularly true after the government in 1863–64 began to relax the "usury laws," which meant that banks thereafter could adjust to the credit market and use their interest rates to encourage long-term deposits. The other factor was the domineering personality of Wallenberg himself.

Scarcely had the bank been started than he had to prove his mettle in the short, violent business crisis of 1857–58. The war-induced prosperity, partly the result of high prices for Swedish grain while Russian exports were cut off, had led some financiers to overextend their investments. The foreign credit for the speculative grain trade had come mainly from Ullberg & Cramér and other sources in Hamburg, while Hoare, Buxton & Co. and some other London firms had been particularly involved in the transoceanic Swedish commerce in colonial wares. When a liquidity crisis struck and interest rates shot up to 15 percent, these financial institutions stopped extending short-term credits to Swedish firms and several themselves went into bankruptcy. The larger ones in Sweden easily rode out the storm, but a number of medium-sized firms were caught in risky financing. Over forty of them were involved, and no less than twenty-six collapsed in Stockholm, though very few in Gothenburg.[13]

The consequences would have been much worse had not Gripenstedt, his own policies in jeopardy, secured Riksdag approval for a state loan of 12 million riksdaler, which he obtained from the Salomon Heine bank (Hamburg), Raphael von Erlanger (Frankfurt), and others. It was expensive—12 percent interest. With this money some of those in distress were rescued, including Kempe, Kockum, and Johan Holm. Meanwhile, people stampeded to cash in the bank notes of one of the provincial banks, the Skånska Enskilda, which had issued more of them than its resources warranted. Should it run out of money to redeem them and close its doors, Wallenberg's own fledgling institution might well also collapse. Wallenberg, telling Gripenstedt that the Riksbank itself would then be in danger, procured a large loan on his own security and passed it on to the bank in Skåne. It survived, the crisis was surmounted, and Wallenberg had won his first big success.

Wallenberg and the bank first extended credit to the Norrland sawmill owners, with whom the managing director had formerly had close contacts while in business for a while in Sundsvall; credit was also extended to Uddeholm and to the Petré family. In 1862 it loaned money to the Lesjöfors iron works and to the Petré-owned Hofors-Hammarby, the latter of which would subsequently turn out to have been a horrendous mistake. The bank also started acquiring the bonds of the new private railroad companies, which would also lead to serious problems. The accumulating savings deposits were thus being put to use for commercial and industrial purposes, though Wallenberg, virtually the first to do this on a larger scale, never was enthusiastic about it. The circumstances of the time, the need for investment capital that made *crédit mobilier* institutions seem desirable, demanded it. Then, having ventured the money, he had to protect the interests of his depositors, and, several times, when the borrowers fell into financial distress, he had to intervene far beyond his original intentions. One of his sons, Marcus, would make it a deliberate policy in the 1890s.

Unpopularity is an occupational hazard for a banker, and many stories circulated about this powerful man, some of them venomous. He was arrogant, and the public, neither understanding principles of finance nor comprehending the pressures upon the bank that dictated his conduct, saw him as a hardhearted ogre, unscrupulously taking advantage of his position to ruin many. Lazarus, gleefully relating the whole batch of stories, wrote that a visitor's first impression of Wallenberg was one of good-naturedness and joviality, but if crossed "his mouth would tighten and his eyes turn mean"; he lacked, Lazarus assured his readers, any sense of benevolence or nobility of character. According to him, the "temple of Mammon on Lilla Nygatan was a gold mine for its owners, but a terror" for its borrowers, from whom the last öre was extracted.[14]

During a bank panic someone rushed in and withdrew all his money; Wallenberg paid him off in Stockholms Enskilda bank notes, and the man went off happily, apparently not understanding that he was as much vulnerable to the fortunes of the bank as before. Another person sold his stock to escape any financial responsibility in the event of a crash, but Wallenberg would not approve the sale of the man's last share, saying that the name of a person worth 3 million kronor could not possibly be allowed to disappear from the public image of the bank. Once, Wallenberg packed the bank's board of directors with relatives, a son (Knut), a son-in-law, and a brother. Every editor in town had something to say about that, save one, and Wallenberg chanced to meet him on the street. The banker asked him if *he* had any comment about the bank election. The editor's Jewish sense of humor got the better of him, and he blurted out, "Why not *Mrs.* Wallenberg?"

Extremely sensitive to the power of the press, he tried repeatedly to obtain control over a newspaper. He bought enough stock from Johan Gustaf Schwan to control *Aftonbladet* (Hierta's old paper), but the hard-pressed editor rebelled and secured sufficient help from Alfred William Dufwa, banker and formidable Wallenberg-hater, to escape his grasp. *Dagens Nyheter* ignored overtures, but he finally managed to make the *Nya Dagligt Allehanda* his mouthpiece. Its editor had earlier written that Wallenberg's sole goal was to loan money for the shortest possible time at the highest possible interest, and he had an editorial tantrum when the banker received the rank of commander in the highly honorary Vasa order from the king; Wallenberg later rescued the same editor from financial embarrassment while simultaneously taking over the paper. Wallenberg and Sven Hedlund, the redoubtable editor of *Göteborgs Handelstidning*, carried on a long, memorable, and mutually entertaining feud stretching all the way back to 1847 when Wallenberg, then captain of the *Linköping*, had officiously demanded that Hedlund, a student at the time, stop drinking on board ship.

The Riksbank had feared the SEB from its inception, and the hostility reached its sharpest when Dufwa, a man as overbearing as Wallenberg himself, headed it (1870–1883). Dufwa had fought Wallenberg while chief of the Skandia insurance company, had thwarted him at *Aftonbladet*, and continued to make life as difficult as possible for his rival by his use of the extensive power of the Riksbank. Lazarus commented that Dufwa (Dove, in English) was no dove as far as Wallenberg was concerned.

Wallenberg wanted Big Names on his board of directors. He even had the gall to invite Louis De Geer, the prime minister who engineered the 1866 Riksdag reform, to join it, but the great statesman declined. He did induce Axel Bennich, an influential Riksdagsman, to serve, but once together, they commenced fighting. By 1870 the board of directors had split into two factions, and the disaffected group walked out when Bennich failed to be reelected to the board. Strictly speaking, Wallenberg locked *them* out, but they then founded a new bank, Stockholms Handelsbank; the wits, playing on the word *enskilda* (private), called it the *frånskilda*, the seceded, bank. Not until Louis Fraenckel took over its leadership (1893–1911), however, would it play an important part in Swedish economic life.[15]

Another major bank, this one emerging from the need for a *crédit mobilier* type of financial institution, was founded in Gothenburg in 1863 under the name of Skandinaviska Kreditaktiebolag, later to be known as Skandinaviska Banken. It had its origin in an ambitious project to create an international Scandinavian bank, based on Copenhagen, with branches in Gothenburg, Christiania (Oslo), Paris, and Amsterdam. It was intended to serve as a conduit for foreign capital to invest in Scandinavian industry, but the idea, promoted by the leading Danish banker, Carl Frederick Tietgen, lost its feasibility when a temporary wave of Pan-Scandinavianism swiftly ebbed. Nor did the bank stock sell well in London, Paris, or Amsterdam. Gothenburg, however, was enthusiastic because its own private bank was neither large enough nor sufficiently venturesome to finance commerce and industry, and it therefore became the headquarters when the bank was founded as a purely Swedish enterprise. The stockholders included, among others, Oscar Ekman (head of Ekman & Co.), Oscar Dickson, Röhss, Wijk, Waern, and Carnegie & Co. Wallenberg was in it briefly. Carl Benedicks of the Michaelson and Benedicks merchant house, realizing that the banking role of merchant houses was drawing to a close, joined it, as did several other Jewish merchants. From the latter ranks came the managing director, the young Theodor Mannheimer, who was, according to Sven Brisman, the ideal man for the position, and who would rank with Wallenberg in the early use of deposits for commercial and industrial investments. However, this development remained strictly limited in this period; both men had to move slowly because of the constraints of political antagonism and public disfavor.[16]

Consequently, in 1871 some Gothenburg merchants and industrialists established the Gothenburg Commercial Co. (Göteborgs Handelskompani) to function as a *crédit mobilier* kind of company, able to finance industrial projects and, especially, the building of railroads. It collapsed in the 1877–78 crisis, and an earlier, similarly oriented, London-based institution, The English and Swedish Bank Co., Ltd. (1863– 64), failed to survive the 1865–66 crash. Stockholm had five commercial banks by 1871, counting a branch office of the Skandinaviska Kreditaktiebolag and two special institutions founded by Eduard Heckscher and J. H. Palme. (Heckscher, like Mannheimer, was Jewish and so was Louis Fraenckel, and the Wallenbergs sometimes grumbled among themselves about the power of the Jewish contingent in Swedish financial circles.) In addition to the above, the Riksbank, in response to the demand in the countryside and to protect its own interests, was in the process of setting up a network of branch banks in various towns. One other financial institution should be mentioned, the Allmänna Hypoteksbank (General Mortgage Bank), founded by the state in 1861, which sold mortgages in Germany (mainly in Hamburg) and funneled money from the Swedish state loans from abroad to, particularly, agriculture; by the mid-1880s it had about 400 million kronor outstanding in the various sectors of the economy.[17]

The early Swedish entrepreneurs, who were as necessary for industrialization as capital, were notably men of "enthusiasm, boldness . . . ruthlessness" (Dahmen), often characterized by a painful devotion to work. Their ventures tended to have a high mortality rate due to a lack of caution, bad timing, insufficient capital and credit, and markets too small to sustain the businesses. The first one to enter any branch of industry in a given region did have advantages; the likeliest to have access to whatever sources of credit there were, he could dominate the local market in an era of poor transportation and plow profits back into the enterprise. To get the jump on others in technology was extremely important, and to neglect continuing new technological advances invited disaster. Companies often forced the technological developments for their business purposes. Erik Dahmen, contrasting this to the earlier stability, has described the process as a "continuing struggle between old and new."[18]

In their own line of development, entrepreneurs were often vulnerable to advances in other technological or industrial areas, hence might be forced to become involved in these areas also in order to protect their original investment. In addition, the firms tended to acquire plants in two or more lines of production in order to assure raw materials or an outlet for their products. Thus, a machine shop might purchase an iron works for a ready supply of iron, or an iron *bruk* acquire a machine shop for the disposal of its iron and steel.

Some of the more lurid pages in Swedish business history narrate the death throes of formerly great fortunes: John Hall, William Chalmers, Johan Holm, Pontus Kleman, Emil Broms, Gustaf de Laval. To suffer bankruptcy before adequate investment capital became available was not a serious disgrace—it happened to the best of them, including Samuel Owen and Alexander Keiller. Kempe, Bünsow, and Kockum skirted the edge of disaster, Kockum more than once.

Others were either lucky or more skillful. Lars Johan Hierta, gathering

141

sizable industrial holdings while simultaneously selling candles, cloth, salt, wine, copper, tobacco, and paper in his highly lucrative mercantile business, was one of them. First came Liljeholmens Stearinfabrik and Michaëlson's sulfuric acid factory. In 1849 he joined Per Murén and others in founding the successful Strömsbro textile mill in Gävle. Murén, busily reading his *Manchester Guardian*, was as adept as Hierta in choosing and organizing feasible industrial projects, and both men had British contacts. Hierta visited Manchester, the city that best reflected his own ideas of progress, and especially nosed around in Fairbairn's sacred precincts. He had the perspicacity to avoid buying shares in Rosen's Köping-Hult project, but jumped enthusiastically into the campaign to build the successful railroad from Gävle to Falun. Hierta stayed out of Göransson's Högbo steel mill company, where son-in-law Pontus Kleman was heavily engaged; once that debacle occurred, he quickly bought shares in the successor company. In 1861–63 he financed Janne Lundström at the Munksjö paper mill, later to become sole owner. Finally, in 1871, he invested in Stockholms Superfosfat, which proved to be eminently profitable.

It was often said that the tall, lanky, red-haired man had a lucky touch, that he seemed to carry a dowsing rod that pointed to possible successful enterprises. If so, it was of dubious value in two other affairs. Liljevalch interested him in the possibility of draining swamps to make more farmland available; when crops from such land turned out to be poor, Hierta hurriedly pulled out. Nor could a silk factory, equipped with the latest machinery, compete with imports, so he transformed it into a cotton spinning and weaving mill (1867).[19] He also lost some money in 1865–66 when Johan Holm's business empire disintegrated.

Pontus Kleman (1817–1903), whose father had been imprisoned for several years for financial malfeasance while serving as an official, had married Bertha Amalia Hierta, but Lars Hierta soon learned to stay away from projects initiated by his wheeler-dealer son-in-law. The London-based financier had started with the Huth firm, joined Hoare, Buxton & Co., and later became closely associated with Giles Loder. As a sales agent and broker he represented Dan Elfstrand & Co. of Gävle, D. Carnegie & Co., C. F. Waern & Co., Wilhelm Kempe and a number of Stockholm merchant houses. Gifted with an outgoing personality and aggressive to the point of folly, Kleman, "the most daring speculator of his time," made a fortune by his speculations during the Crimean War.

His reckless financing first caught up with him in the 1857 crisis, when he suffered some losses and much bitter criticism. (Hoare, Buxton & Co., creditor through Kleman to too many Swedish firms that left unpaid debts when they folded, went bankrupt.) Kleman held interests in the Bergvik sawmill, Garpenberg *bruk*, and iron works at Dormsjö, Forss and Högbo, and he helped to finance the Bessemer experiments. The Johan Holm collapse, coupled with a crisis on the London exchange, put Kleman into bankruptcy (1866). A born survivor, he resumed his career in international finance and would participate in earlier attempts to open up the iron mines in northern Sweden. According to his biographer, Alf. W. Axelson, Kleman made considerable contributions to Swedish industrialization, but this has been undervalued because of his financial misadventures.[20]

Johan Holm (1815–1896) had escaped disaster in 1857, but his turn came in 1864–65. He had begun as a broker in foreign currency, then increasingly became a money lender through his contacts with merchant houses and private individuals having money to invest. He was thus performing banking services, using money deposited with him to lend to those needing it. For years he provided the foreign exchange needed by the Tanto sugar refinery (Stockholm) for its import of raw sugar, at times over 2 million riksdaler annually. Holm also owned ships and exported iron and timber. Inevitably his credits to industrial enterprises drew him into part ownership of some of them, a paper mill, a copper works, and Nyköpings Mekaniska Verkstad. At Nyköping he built Scandinavia's largest steamship, the *Ernst Merck,* for transoceanic freight service, but, because sailing vessels could still do it more cheaply, the big ship turned out to be a liability.[21]

In 1861 he secured a quarter ownership in the Högbo iron and steel company, Göransson's first Bessemer venture, by merging the Nyköping works with it. Holm, Kleman, and Carl David Arfwedson, whose son had married Holm's daughter, then founded the English and Swedish Bank, Ltd. as a vehicle for bringing British credits to Sweden (1863–64). All of which made good sense, except that Holm and Kleman were trying to use short-term loans to finance long-term investments in industry, a thoroughly dubious procedure.

Ever since 1848 he had been acting as agent for the provincial bank in Småland by redeeming its bank notes. In December 1864 he lacked liquid funds to do so, and he went off to London to seek help; Wallenberg thereupon took over the servicing of the Småland bank, but wisely refused to aid Holm, who, returning empty-handed, had to declare bankruptcy at the beginning of 1865. It turned out to be one of Sweden's most spectacular, 17.5 million riksdaler, of which 7 were owed abroad—nearly 4 million to Giles Loder in London and another million to the English-Swedish bank, which spelled the end of that short-lived institution.[22] The Högbo company collapsed, the Nyköping works had to close, and the Holm connection brought such suspicion on the old Tottie and Arfwedson firm, which suffered large losses along with a most untimely embezzlement by a treasurer, that in 1867 it had to be dissolved. Nevertheless, the Nyköping and Högbo ventures had both been very promising, and even the *Ernst Merck* was only premature. Holm's biographer, Staffan Högberg, was disposed to blame the debacle more on the "weakly developed capital market" than on Holm's brash optimism.[23]

Few individuals contributed as much to Swedish industrialization as D. O.

143

Francke (1825–1892). Of a family apparently from England originally, the father, Johan, seems to have altered his name from Fränkel to Francke when baptized in 1816. The son bought the Rosendahl textile mill in Mölndal when he was twenty-three, then, when it burned down almost immediately, replaced it with a sugar refinery (1849). Five years later he started a new cotton spinning and weaving mill. In 1856 he organized Rosendahls Fabrikers AB, made up of six partners, including Edward, a brother. (Two other brothers had gone off to Cuba and London.)[24]

Rosendahls had a stock capital of 3 million riksdaler, the largest in the country at the time. With the added money, the company was able to purchase the Korndal paper mill, and in 1861 it completed the Mölndal complex by acquiring the Mariedahl cotton spinnery. The ownership of Korndal led directly to the building of Sweden's first pulp mill at Trollhättan (1857). In 1870 Francke also bought the Götafors paper mill. By this time Francke had "built up, for its time, a mighty industrial empire."[25]

Francke became very rich, built a magnificent villa in Mölndal, and maintained a lifestyle that grated on some people. His list of idiosyncracies and purported misdeeds rivals that of Wallenberg. He usually wore a black skullcap, but when he was in a vile mood he wore a red one, so we are told. Also that he paid low wages and that too many accidents happened in his factories. Over the gate of one of them stood his initials, D. O. F., which, it was said, stood for "Den Oförskämde," the unashamed. Sven Hedlund attacked him in his newspaper as a man who did not know the difference between right and wrong, and successive pastors publicly upbraided him for his evil ways. Francke responded to one of these, possibly as a silent *riposte* in those days of long and dreary sermons, by paying for the installation of more comfortable church pews. He even had the distinction of being the model for a novel, *Mölndalsflickan (The Mölndal Girl)*, in which he figures as a lustful lecherer always looking for new prey. All of which, and more, is narrated by Hans Gillingstam in the usually staid pages of the *Svenska Biografiska Lexikon*.[26]

He had imagination in industrial affairs, too. In the boom period at the beginning of the 1870s, Francke embarked upon an extraordinarily ambitious program of industrial expansion. With G. A. Lundhqvist, he obtained control of Stora Kopparbergs Bergslaget, then in the process of planning the giant Domnarvet iron works. Simultaneously he took the lead in the building of the Bergslagen railroad from Falun to Gothenburg. He was an enthusiastic sponsor for Atlas, a Stockholm company specializing in manufacturing railroad equipment. Francke was also one of the businessmen who set up the Gothenburg Commercial Co. to pump money into industry and railroads. The four farsighted projects, complementary with each other, made up a well-planned, integrated whole. Meantime, he was still running Rosendahls. A. O. Wallenberg, participating in some of the same ventures, greatly admired him, and Marcus long afterward would call him a man rich in industrial and financial ideas.[27]

Certainly Francke had planned well, but, failing to allow for the inevitable downswing of the business cycle, he had become greatly overextended when the depression years began, most especially because of the costs of railroad construction. He lost his leadership in Stora Kopparberg, and the great enterprise was itself strained by the costs of building Domnarvet. In 1879 Rosendahls and the Gothenburg Commercial Co. both went into bankruptcy, followed by Francke himself. Two of his directors shot themselves. Brisman, an authority on Swedish banking whose judgment deserves respect, has commented that Francke handled himself extremely well, optimistic and vigorous, when business was on the upswing, but when conditions turned downward, he, and others like him, tried "the most impossible . . . dishonest" measures in order to escape.[28] His brother, Edward (1824–1891), who held part interest in Gideå & Husum AB, the Hudiksvall Trävaru AB, and Hörnefors *bruk*, helped to rescue him from the worst consequences. Korndal, the paper mill, was reconstituted as a stock company after the collapse, D. O. Francke becoming its manager. Stockholms Enskilda Bank had lost heavily on Francke, but Wallenberg extended another large loan to Korndal, a relationship that ultimately contributed to the bank buying and restoring it under the name of Papyrus. Francke suffered a second financial disaster late in his career, and he died at the breakfast table after returning from a business trip (1892).

Excessive private railroad construction helped to bring on the crash of 1878–79, as overextended companies and businessmen were caught short. Among others, the financier Carl Gustaf Cervin (1815–1899) almost went down in 1875 after investing too much in them. He had gotten his start as one of those who handled Gripenstedt's emergency loan in 1857. Now in trouble himself, he was helped by the government, and Dufwa of the Riksbank solicitously extended aid, probably because Cervin had also been feuding with Wallenberg. Lazarus maliciously remarks that too many government officials and other bureaucrats had too much money deposited with him to permit *him* to close his doors. Perhaps this was the time when a common ordinary mortal met the arrogant, formal Cervin, who never doffed his hat to anyone, on the street one day. Cervin took off his hat, cordially shook hands, and spoke kindly to him, whereupon the terrified man, assuming that something must be terribly wrong at Cervin's establishment, hurried right over and withdrew his entire account.[29]

The N. M. Höglund merchant house, agent for some twenty *bruk*, went bankrupt in December 1878, followed four days later by Godenius & Co., an otherwise sound firm pulled down by its association with it. Losses at Nyköping when Holm collapsed had undermined an already weakened Höglund; then the unwise purchase of two *bruk* in Dalarna, with Godenius & Co., brought the downfall of both firms. Another company, Guilletmot & Weylandt, fell at the same time. Pehr Lagerhjelm at Bofors suffered calamitous financial losses. Eight enterprises in Norrköping had to shut down, and in Södertälje a glass works, an oil company, and an engineering works all closed, while the Atlas railroad-car plant there had few orders with which to employ its workers.

The most melodramatic episode of all involved the destruction of the Petré family domain at Hofors, a tragedy in which Wallenberg attained new heights of nationwide unpopularity, and a story better told in connection with the Hofors company. The pressures on the bank were enormous in 1878–79, aggravated by Dufwa's deliberate obstructions at the Riksbank. A run on Stockholms Enskilda Bank by depositors stopped only after the stately King Oscar II walked in, December 7, 1878, and ostentatiously deposited, it was said, 600,000 kronor, while the government loaned the bank an additional sum.

In addition to the mobilization of capital for use by eager entrepreneurs, the Swedes, if they were to catch up to the most advanced industry, needed to recruit talented scientists, technologists, and engineers. The Swedes have often been said to have a special aptitude for engineering and, among the sciences, for chemistry and biology. Their national characteristics, as commonly perceived and to whatever extent such generalizations reflect reality, do seem to offer a fertile source for the emergence of these particular proclivities.

"The most deeply-seated feature of the Swedish character, the key to all the rest," says one writer, "is *love of nature*." Another asserts that "the real driving force in [Swedish] scientific studies has been a primary, emotionally colored interest in nature . . . . "[30] The same strong trait that led to an emphasis on nature in their lyric poetry, songs, paintings, and cinema also seems to have been formative in the scientific investigation of the physical and living world. The long struggle with nature and not overly abundant resources created a hard-headed attention to the details of the environment. "The Swede is an extremely practical fellow, who knows how to reckon with the hard, cold facts of life," and he "may be slow and deliberate, but he is thorough, oh, how thorough!" According to Hudson Strode, the Swedes developed an uncommon aptitude for machines and for manual dexterity. "There is a common saying that every second Swede is an engineer."[31] Franklin Scott has written that the most obvious inherent characteristic of Scandinavians "is their pervasive practicality. They can dream, yes, but they are likely to dream of worldly things."[32]

Eli Heckscher stressed that the long training in metallurgy had fostered skills in engineering, as well as in chemistry.[33] Whether the appearance of intellectual giants like Polhem (engineering), Linnaeus (botany and biology), and Bergman and Berzelius (chemistry) reflects an innate proclivity among the Swedes can only be a matter of opinion, but obviously their presence strongly influenced the direction of development. The government of the Hats, sponsoring new industries in the formative period of the eighteenth century, placed emphasis on *practical* science, and the Swedish Academy of Science, founded in 1739, concentrated on encouraging improvements in agriculture, mining, and manufacturing. The early nineteenth-century role of the state, the Iron Office, and various machine shops and *bruk* in practical training scarcely needs more elaboration here.

A series of professors at Uppsala and Lund stimulated the beginning of successful careers for many of the individuals prominent in economic and technical development. Formal technical schools, however, were also needed. The only fully high-quality institution of the kind in Sweden until about 1870, aside from the universities, was the Marieberg artillery and engineering high school (*Högre artilleri och ingenjörläroverk*) on Kungsholmen in Stockholm. It had been founded in 1818 by General Carl von Cardell on the site of Apelquist's old textile mill as a school for artillery officers. In addition to serving as a war college, it began to train those officers who wished to specialize in engineering: the earlier two-year curriculum also included mathematics, mechanical arts, physics, chemistry, and topography. More than a thousand military men altogether (and some civilians) studied at Marieberg.[34]

Being largely maritime in nature, such public works as canals and harbor improvements had hitherto drawn their officer engineers primarily from the mechanical corps of the navy. The training at Marieberg accounts at least in part for the subsequent prevalence of military officers in the construction of canals, harbors, highways, railroads, floatways, and water systems. As communications in general began shifting from waterways to cross-country routes, the need for civil engineers in this sector became imperative. Axel Erik von Sydow (1791–1857) in 1840 published a convincing plea for their improved training, and a special course for this purpose was then inaugurated at Marieberg (1842).[35]

Von Sydow became the first chief of the roads and waterways corps (*väg och vattenbyggnadskår*), established in 1840–41 and reorganized under that specific name in 1851. Some officers on active duty joined it, an examination in civil engineering being necessary to qualify. The complete corps in 1851 had twenty-one officers, some coming from the mechanical corps and some from the course work at Marieberg. Those who joined it lost their positions of command in the armed forces but kept their titles and membership in the military.[36] It became quite customary to secure one's engineering skills at Marieberg and in military service before going to work on civil projects.

In 1869 the engineering courses at Marieberg were transferred to the Institute of Technology, which had begun to offer instruction in road and waterways construction in 1858; most of the remainder of the work was moved there in 1876. Founded in 1798 to teach mechanical arts, the institute had as its first director the Johan Erik Norberg who had tried and failed to invent Sweden's first steamboat. It became the Teknologiska Institut in 1825–26 and the Tekniska Högskola (High School) in 1877, these name changes reflecting major stages of development. It had originally offered work in metals and wood and elementary courses in mathematics, physics, chemistry, and draftsmanship. Mechanical and chemical technology were later added, but the school's deficiencies in the 1840s forced the addition of more courses in theory, stiffer entrance requirements, and, in 1851, the lengthening of the two-year course to three. Absorbing the Marieberg course work and the Falun School of Mines, it attained a respectable level of repute. In 1875 it had nearly 250 students, and in that year graduated six in the school of mechanics and machine building, twelve in roads and waterways, five in chemical technology, five in the school of mines, and an additional five special students. The curriculum was extended to four years in 1877 when it became the Tekniska Högskola.[37]

Chalmers in Gothenburg started as a *slöjdskola* (school for manual training) for the poor youth of the city, as stipulated by William Chalmers in the donation that made possible the founding of the institution. Carl Palmstedt, met earlier at the Gripsholm chemical factory, served as its director until 1852, during which time it grew into a technical school. It was graduating about 22 to 25 students a year in the 1850s and had an enrollment of about 150 in the 1870s.[38] Elementary technical schools were also being established in the 1850s, some organized with the help of Palmstedt, in Norrköping, Örebro, Borås, and Eskilstuna. More appeared later. Because lower class students were often able to attend these, they became important in facilitating upward mobility in industry and technology.

Students in mining and *bruk* work were originally trained at Uppsala and by the Board of Mines and the Iron Office. Falun's School of Mines started in 1822, with the temperamental Nils Gabriel Sefström at its head. The regular students were required to have passed the university *bergsexamin* before enrolling, hence it was highly selective with a maximum enrollment of twenty students. A few of these held stipendiums from the Board of Mines and a few—students *extraordinair*—were permitted to attend its studies without the preceding examination. The high quality two-year course included analytical chemistry, mineralogy, geology, and forge techniques. Victor Eggertz, its head after 1853, strongly urged that it be moved to the Institute of Technology, and this occurred in 1869.[39]

The Filipstad School of Mines started as virtually a one-man operation by Franz Adolf von Scheele, who began giving a two-month course in 1830 with the help of an assistant. This course gradually lengthened, until by 1847 it ran for a full year and usually enrolled sixteen students. It was largely supported at first by the *bruk* proprietors in the vicinity, later by the whole industry and by the

Iron Office. In 1865 the course was extended to two years. Scheele directed it for thirty years.[40]

According to Gårdlund, of 1,159 technicians employed in Swedish *verkstäder* up to 1908, 254 had attended the Institute of Technology, and Chalmers had educated 199, Falun and Filipstad 68, and the elementary technical schools 537. (Others had been educated abroad.) Of 524 in metallurgy, 265 came out of Falun or Filipstad, 132 from the Institute of Technology, and 78 from the elementary. The elementary technical schools had the greater number of graduates in timber (27 of 55), paper and cellulose (87 of 213), and textiles (81 of 167).[41]

One special form of mobilization of talents occurred in the creation of engineering consulting bureaus. These usually began when a number of enterprises successively sought the assistance of a particularly knowledgeable expert, who, as the demand for his services grew, would then organize a formal bureau. Wilhelm Wenström may have founded the earliest in about 1870 in Örebro; several engineers received additional training and experience while working in his bureau. Håkon Steffansson worked out of Falun and while employed at Stora Kopparbergs Bergslaget was responsible for so many varieties of construction—dams, water wheels and turbines, blowers, flour mills, sawmills, and iron works—that Althin termed him "a later-day successor of Christopher Polhem."[42] Qvist & Gyers, founded in 1876 in Arboga, installed water turbines and helped to rebuild a number of iron works in the various Scandinavian countries. C. J. Nilsson and Erik Jansson also maintained bureaus in the Bergslagen region. Johan Gustaf Richert (1857–1934) established the most prominent of the later ones (1897), the Aktiebolag Vattenbyggnadsbyrå (VBB), which during the next fifty years had assignments in thirty countries on about two hundred projects.

From the 1860s until 1914 Sweden would have the highest per capita rate of growth in gross national product (GNP) in Europe—even though it has been an article of faith reiterated by numerous writers that "Old Sweden" was a poverty-stricken land. The contrast of this bleak picture against the subsequent remarkable advance does raise questions. No doubt the relatively low earlier GNP helped to make possible such felicitous percentages of growth mathematically, and the reduction of the total potential population base by emigration may have somewhat biased upward the per capita percentages, although the loss of young and vigorous sectors of the population could, on the contrary, quite possibly have had an adverse effect on productivity. Whatever the case, it was nonetheless a notable achievement.

On the statistical evidence, Sweden in midcentury did have one of the lowest levels of per capita GNP in Europe.[43] Other factors have tended, however, to color the received version of history. Swedish folk memory, family remembrances of former conditions, has been deeply etched by recollections of the consequences of overpopulation. The appalling years of famine placed an indelible imprint on recalled history, and there has been a natural tendency to univeralize over several decades the most grim conditions of the worst years. Furthermore, posterity quite normally exaggerates the past as either the idyllic good old days, like Selma Lagerlöf describing life in *brukspatron* Värmland, or as a dark background for later advances. Posterity has its own uses for the past, including denigrating its predecessors in order to exalt its own achievements; capitalists and socialists alike have had their reasons for stressing the worst aspects of society during the earlier period.

This is not to deny the obvious reality, only to qualify it with a certain cautious skepticism about conditions in Old Sweden as compared to other lands *at that time.* Included in the picture must be the tenacious advances whose significance could not then be fully appreciated by the general public because their piecemeal, unobtrusive arrival so often made them appear to emerge out of the old and habitual. In some respects, but only in some, Sweden resembled the later developing countries. It was still largely agricultural. It suffered overpopulation, due to a high birth rate, declining infant mortality, and increasing length of life expectancy. Typically, the exports were very largely in raw materials and semifinished products.[44] However, Sweden possessed certain important advantages not often present in today's developing countries.

Its agrarian revolution had fortunately occurred *prior* to its industrial breakthrough, and its revitalized agriculture, grain especially, for a time supplied about a fourth of the total exports, which in turn helped to stimulate the domestic market; the more well-to-do landowning peasants, as well as the gentry, were becoming a stable, growing market for city wares and for such factory goods as farm machinery. Equally fortunately, the overpopulation problem, so characteristic of developing countries, could be alleviated by massive migration to America, thereby avoiding possible social and political upheavals. Its technology had remained close enough to the level of the most advanced countries to enable Swedish visitors, in most instances, to return home and duplicate the latest advances. Gårdlund's opinion bears reiterating here, that "in the founding and early development of Swedish industry in case after case the decisive impulse came from those technicians who returned from abroad."[45]

Some sectors of the economy had already become effectively a province of the West. These sectors consisted of a busy and relatively wealthy merchant class, of a group of entrepreneurs behaving much like those in the most advanced countries, and of technicians going abroad to acquire the skills needed for innovations at home. These groups were forging ahead, painfully and with heavy casualties, but the momentum had been underway for several decades before the 1860s and 1870s. Once capital had to some extent been accumulated, the equally essential entrepreneurs, with their "rational economic thought" and their good contacts with more advanced countries, would transform the country while pursuing their well-developed pattern of behavior. The subsequent rapid advance is in part explained by the lengthy preparation for it in these sectors.

Sweden also possessed the *sine qua non* of a well-organized state and society. Unlike most developing countries, Sweden had been a proudly independent country for centuries, and it had a long history of political, social, and cultural unity. The Swedes enjoyed the inestimable advantages of a mature state, an integrated society, smoothly functioning institutions, and a conscientious, honest, and well-trained civil service—at least to the extent that these can be expected in an imperfect world. Even the banking and finance system, so often blamed for entrepreneurial disasters, compared well with other countries. Lars G. Sandberg contends that by 1870 Sweden already had a financial system as sophisticated as most other European countries at a more advanced level of industrialization and per capita income.[46]

Had Old Sweden been as stagnant as reiterated dogma would have it, the breakthrough would have been far more difficult. The literacy rate, about 90 percent, was the highest in Europe. The relatively low infant mortality rate for the times and the gradual increase in life longevity of adults argue against an overly bleak appraisal of the scene. The paternalistic policies of the government and the church would seem to have been helping to create a better human stock, a success that may go far toward explaining the almost obsessive Swedish pursuit of such a goal in the twentieth century. A temperance society, founded in 1837, and the subsequent crusade against liquor gradually sobered portions of the populace. Active revivalist groups (Carl Olof Rosenius, the Janssonists, the Mission Friends, Methodists, and others) offered outlets for human qualities cramped by prevailing circumstances.

As far as the country people were concerned, there was another, a peculiarly Swedish, factor in the human equation. Swedish peasants had nearly always possessed a political influence virtually unparalleled elsewhere in Europe. Michael Roberts believed that the medieval Swedish free peasant, in a land with very little serfdom, was "altogether a more considerable person" than in any west European country.[47] Possessing their own estate in the Riksdag, the peasants were later able, even under the strongest kings, to enforce respect for their rights. They continued to be strongly influential in the nineteenth century, and in the remodeled parliament they maintained a powerful political party. The upward mobility of bright peasant sons into the clergy, almost the only way to secure a higher education in the eighteenth century, had in turn produced pastoral homes out of which came some leaders in science, technology, and industry. Once industrialization and an expanding business sphere opened up new avenues, the movement of talent from the lower classes took on increasing proportions.

Calling the Swede of 1850 "the Impoverished Sophisticate," Sandberg has asserted that the "Swedish human capital stocks . . . were wildly disproportionate to income levels . . . . "[48] That is, the *human* capital in a materially poor country was remarkably high and foreshadowed the future steep rise. Given the opportunity, the work ethic, firmly implanted, would create wonders. Rising expectancies (those America Letters!) made the frustrating constraints of economic circumstances seem even darker to a generation able to anticipate better things. It was an explosive combination of factors, leading to domestic mobility and to mass emigration overseas. The great migration reflected poor economic circumstances, but it also evidenced the quality of the human stock that took advantage of the new opportunity.

Until the 1880s the industrial and technological advances still remained largely peripheral, as far as public attention was concerned, to the mainstream of Swedish life. Virtually everyone had been affected, of course, but the changes came in such a piecemeal and peaceful manner, were so much a part of ordinary life, that the average citizen could scarcely grasp their wide dimensions or appreciate their full significance. Older Swedish cultural traditions tended to hang on. However, the industrial breakthrough of the 1870s and the arrival of electric lights, telephones, and new industries based on recent inventions now awakened public awareness of the irresistible march of technological progress. A fine arts and industrial exposition in Stockholm in 1866 was only moderately successful. By comparison, the triumph of the world of factories and machines would be fully affirmed in another exposition in the capital city in 1897, one which became a paean to modern progress and an occasion for measuring the achievements of the last thirty years in industry, technology, and improving standard of living.

Johan Gustaf Schwan, speaker of the House of Burgesses in 1862, told his chamber, with a play on Swedish words, that "the bourgeoisie (*borgerliga*) . . . is no longer alone and excluded" because now "the citizens' (*medborgerliga*) element, after long and tenacious resistance, has found its way to our benches. This constitutes the bourgeoisie's real triumph . . . . [49] That is, according to him, the party of the bourgeoisie was becoming the citizens' party. To the extent that the parliament after 1866 was based on wealth rather than on caste, Schwan's assertion was quickly confirmed, but when much of that human capital out of Old Sweden became industrial labor, its enfranchised citizens would reverse the political balance by voting for the Social Democrats.

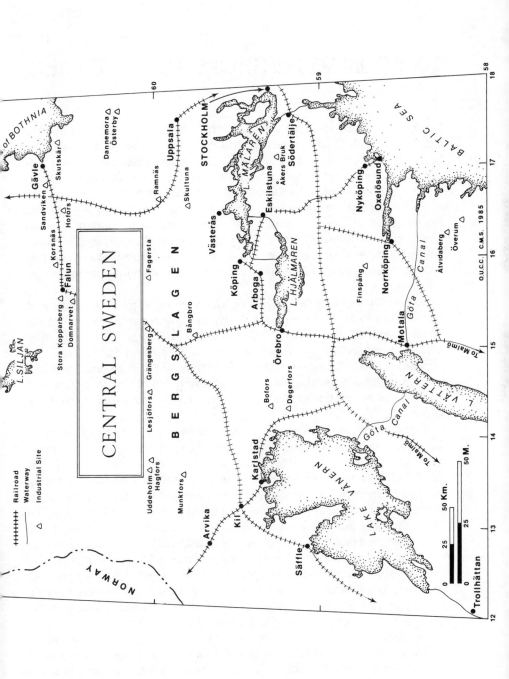

CENTRAL SWEDEN

Railroad
Waterway
△ Industrial Site

O.U.C.C. | C.M.S. 1985

GULF of BOTHNIA

Gävle
Sandviken
Skutskär △
Korsnäs △
Stora Kopparberg △
Domnarvet △
Falun
Hofors △
Dannemora △
Österby △
Ramnäs △
Skultuna △
Uppsala

L. SILJAN

Lesjöfors △
Grängesberg △
Fagersta △
Uddeholm △ △
Hagfors △
Munkfors △

B E R G S L A G E N

Bångbro △

STOCKHOLM

L. MÄLAREN

Västerås
Köping
Arboga
Örebro
Eskilstuna
Åkers Bruk △
Södertälje

L. HJÄLMAREN

Bofors △
Degerfors △

Arvika
Kil
Karlstad
Säffle

LAKE VÄNERN

Göta Canal
To Malmö

Nyköping
Oxelösund
Norrköping
Finspång △
Överum △
Åtvidaberg △
Överum

BALTIC SEA

L. VÄTTERN

Motala
Göta Canal
To Malmö

Trollhättan

50 Km.
0   25   50
0   25   50 M.

NORWAY

10. FROM WORKSHOPS TO FACTORIES

Nyköping, a small city in the 1850s, seemed destined to become a thriving industrial center. Then something went badly wrong. Situated on a Baltic harbor to the northeast of Norrköping, it had textile mills, a brass and iron works, and a shipyard. Attracted by the harbor, Count von Rosen, managing director (1828–30) of a Motala still lacking a shipyard for seagoing vessels, chose to establish an engineering works there. After becoming familiar with British factories while collaborating with John Ericsson, he thought Swedish machine shops outdated, still clinging too much to the eighteenth-century Polhem tradition. Once having assembled a modernized plant, Rosen sold it to Fredrik Morsing, owner of the brass and iron works, and hurried on to his next adventure.

Technically, in manufacturing boilers and steam engines for ships and factories as well as other iron goods, the Nyköping works fulfilled the purposes of the founder. It launched its first two ships in 1835, and, among other achievements, made the machinery for the *Norrland* (1837) and the *Gauthiod* (1840). Though it looked like an industrial factory, employed 372 workers, and had a production value surpassing that of Motala, its financial success did not match the technology, and in 1844 bankruptcy forced its closure.[1]

Twelve years passed. Then the obvious advantages of the place attracted some Stockholm merchants, led by Johan Holm; its new head, G. A. Lundhqvist, with the help of Carl Wittenström (an engineer), had it running again in 1857. This time the Nyköping works launched twelve steamships, including the *Ernst Merck*. It was also entirely appropriate that Rosen's former plant would receive the country's first order for full-scale Swedish locomotives; the state stipulated that these locomotives, some of their parts imported and assembled, be exact replicas of those purchased from Beyer Peacock & Co. An overly ambitious program, however, again sustained financial losses, and Lundhqvist moved on to Stora Kopparbergs Bergslaget while Holm merged the works in the Högbo Bruks AB. Högbo sent Håkon Steffansson, the able technician, to take charge, but its finances did not improve, and, with the collapse of Holm and Högbo, it had to shut down (1865).[2]

Motala bought it in 1869 in order to ensure that it *stayed* closed, a case of industrial murder, tempered, in a day of financial stringencies, by claims of justifiable self-defense. Nyköping's two flashes of greatness had frightened

Motala, and, indeed, the location did offer possibilities; within a dozen years a railroad from Grängesberg would be delivering iron ore to the nearby ice-free harbor at Oxelösund, and much later a large steel mill would be built at the latter port. The elimination of a dangerous competitor dealt a deadly blow to the future of the town and its embittered populace, though Rosen's industrial vision would be carried on elsewhere by such former Nyköping workers as William Lindberg, Jacques Lamm, and Otto Hallström in their own factories or shipyards. The railroad equipment men moved on to Surahammar *bruk,* which, benefiting from their learned skills, began making railroad car wheels and axles in 1865 and would still be doing so in the twentieth century.

Motala, owned by a consortium of investors and directed by Carlsund from 1843 until 1870, remained in a class by itself until fairly late in the century. In 1872 it was the country's largest industrial employer, with about 1,900 workers; the next four, in round numbers, were Rosendahl (1,300), Rosenlund (700), Jönköpings Tändsticks AB (700), and Bergsund (600). By 1892 it had launched 682 ships at Motala, at Lindholmen in Gothenburg, and at shipyards in Norrköping and Oskarshamn. It had manufactured 893 steam engines for marine purposes and 47 for use on land; also, more than 170 bridges. Among its many achievements, Motala became one of the two major Swedish manufacturers of locomotives, continuous production beginning in 1876.

The founding of Rosen's Nyköping venture had been followed the next year by the appearance of Munktell's workshop in Eskilstuna, and in 1835 Sweden had ten enterprises that might be considered *mekaniska verkstäder,* including Motala, Bergsund, and the Owen Machine Shop. Six more important ones were started in the 1840s: Kockums (1840), Keillers (1841), Ludwigsberg (1843), Bolinders (1845), William Lindberg (1845), and Nydqvist & Holm (1847).[3]

In the progression from small mechanical workshops to large industrial factories they assumed different forms. The variety of ways in which the term *mekaniska verkstad* has been translated into English when referring to specific enterprises in itself attests to the multiplicity of functions covered by the increasingly outdated term. At least a dozen variations occur, including mechanical workshop (the literal translation), machine shop, machine works, mechanical engineering works, engineering works, and factory.

Their founders, hungry for orders, were prepared to undertake almost anything that would bring in money, and many a later one, whose only assets when he started, in Gårdlund's phrase, were "two empty hands," tried to be a jack-of-all-trades.[4] In the 1850s they were making farm machinery, household articles, gaslights and pipes, dredges, bridges, boilers, steam engines, and self-propelling locomobiles (traction engines) to whatever extent their shop facilities made possible. The replacement of the old fireplaces by iron stoves between 1830 and 1865 created one lucrative market for sales. In the 1860s some men staked their future on supplying the growing sawmills and the railroads. When the combustion motor arrived in the 1890s, possibly as many as seventy entrepreneurs tried to enter that market. The more successful earlier ones had begun to concentrate on specialties by the 1860s, determined by particular regional needs, transport possibilities, access to capital, and technological advances of the moment. Plus, of course, by entrepreneurial boldness in seizing upon one or more lines of production at the earliest possible opportunity. A few of the mechanical workshops were going into genuine industrial production in the 1870s, mostly in the larger towns in central Sweden where they had access to iron, markets, and a good labor supply. A much more sweeping shift to specialization would occur in the 1890s.

One of the principal activities of the machine shops appearing in the 1830s and 1840s was making agricultural tools and machinery. A trickle of innovations from Great Britain, mostly from Scotland, had started in the 1790s. Several of Andrew Meikle's threshing machines, invented in 1784, arrived and were soon being copied. Scottish mechanics were brought in by estate owners to make threshing machines, plows, harrows, and grain drills, some of these being sold to other proprietors. Foreign models were also later imported and distributed by the Academy of Agriculture. The Scottish plow with share and mouldboard, developed by Small, was copied at several workshops and evolved into the Swedish swing-plow, the so-called Ultuna plow being one derivative of it.[5]

Swedish machine shops, adapting to local circumstances, freely imitated the foreign innovations. Samuel Owen manufactured over a thousand threshing machines; copied from British models, they were simple devices driven first by oxen, later by horses. Rothoff in Eskilstuna made grain drills and other farm equipment early in the century, but the drills became important in Sweden only after Garrett's model arrived in the 1850s. Johan Thermaenius at Torshälla (later at Hallsberg) imitated the Garrett machine, as did Brevens Bruk in Närke. Theofron Munktell (Eskilstuna) made the first Swedish reapers, turned out Clayton and Shuttleworth threshing machines, and introduced steam-powered farm machinery (1859). Överum, best known for its plow, imitated the Scottish harrows, which were replacing the earlier Swedish type in the 1840s. Keillers, Nyköping, Köpings and Kockums were among other early manufacturers. Drills, harrows, plows, and threshing machines dominated the early production at Kockums Mek. Verkstad in agriculturally rich Skåne, where the demand made such a plant imperative at this time. Kockums' later variety of offerings is evident from an 1858 price list of manufactured or imported machinery: a McCormick reaper (from Burgess and Key in England), threshing machines (Allerup, Herbot), winnowers (Hornsby), grain drills (Albans), the Ultuna plow, roller harrows, and others.[6]

Thanks to good prices for export grain, the years between 1850 and 1864 saw a rather extensive adoption of farm machinery by the larger landowners, mostly nobles and gentry, who owned 23.7 percent of the cultivated land in Sweden. About half of those in Skåne owned grain drills by 1860, and a fair number had recent models of plows, hay rakes, and mechanical threshing machines. In the area around Lake Mälaren many of the larger proprietors had acquired threshing machines because so much of the former harvest labor force had moved to the sawmill industry, and the owners of regional machine shops, seeing the opportunity, quickly furnished the needed labor-saving devices. A ready market for agricultural machinery was emerging on the estates and bigger farms in Sweden, and, according to Jan Kuuse, "the larger the size, the more advanced the equipment." The tillers of small farms, accounting for about four-fifths of the total acreage around 1900, still tended to retain old-fashioned homemade tools, mostly made of wood.[7]

Models from the United States gradually replaced the British. American reapers, which gained spectacular publicity at the London and Paris expositions, were soon being manufactured in Great Britain and arrived in Sweden from there. The first Hussey, made by Garrett, is said to have been imported in 1852, and a McCormick, from Burgess and Key, is first mentioned in 1857. Brevens Bruk, Överum, and the Västerås Mek. Verkstad were among those making American reapers.[8] Plows from the United States, light and cheap but not suitable for all Swedish soil, were copied at Åkers Styckebruk and long manufactured there. In the 1890s the new style steel cylindrical plows (Albion, Oliver, John Deere) were being imported and imitated. Smith's horse-drawn rake, used since the 1840s, gave way to American models in the 1870s, and U.S. and German grain drills pushed out the Garrett. As it happened, American machines, modified to fit Swedish circumstances, were usually admirably suited to the conditions of eastern Europe. The machine shops were exporting part of their output in the last decades of the century, and by 1910 about 80 percent of Swedish agricultural tools and machinery was being shipped out to Finland, Russia, and Asia.[9]

Successful enterprises like Kockums and Keillers would find their specialties in other areas. Among those that concentrated on farm machinery, Överum and Arvikaverken merit additional mention. Överum, in the northeast corner of Småland, began as a Walloon iron *bruk* in 1654–55, and, making cannon, functioned as a typical *brukspatron* barony under the Steen and Adelswärd families. To satisfy regional demand, it started putting out horseshoes, nails, spades, and axes in 1776. The owner took the next natural step, when its cannon were no longer in demand, of going on to the manufacture of farm machinery, hiring Carl Petter Spångberg (1822–1892), a skilled tool-maker at the Ultuna agricultural institute, for this purpose. His earliest plows (1851f.) were "virtually plagiarized copies" (Kuuse) of the imported British and American, but, in devising successive versions, he adapted them to Swedish tillage so well that Överum became their leading manufacturer in the country.[10] Överum made 2,669 plows in 1862, the annual production had risen to 5,685 by 1872, and it was the first Swedish machine shop to make them by industrial methods. More than half of them were being exported to Russia in the 1880s. The firm also made harrows and comparatively small numbers of reapers, grain drills, threshing machines, and other equipment; Cambridge, Woods, Hornsby, and Cornes were among the models borrowed from abroad.[11]

In 1872 Överum was purchased by H. A. Milne, resident gaslight man, for a group in England, whose attention had probably been attracted by its early sales in Russia in competition with the British. Six years later it passed to another British group, among them Daniel Sidney Hasluck, which continued to focus its sales endeavors on the Russian market. Meantime, Norrahammar, a rival started near Jönköping in 1877, steadily encroached upon its domestic sales, and by the turn of the century, as Överum's position deteriorated under Hasluck management, it became much the more important of the two makers of farm machinery.[12]

While other companies profited from domestic and foreign sales, Överum did not recover until acquired by the Swedish Match Co. (1918), whereupon Ivar Kreuger money made possible its renaissance. It produced the first tractor plows in Sweden, and, using steel from its own furnaces for its machinery, continued to export a portion of its output. In 1929 it even eliminated its rival by purchasing Norrahammar.

If Swedish industry became a blend of long-term institutional continuity and of the work of self-made men, Arvikaverken exemplified the latter. It sprang directly out of the personal achievement of Per Anderson (1861–1942) in the decades when the business climate and freedom of enterprise encouraged such careers. Anderson's father had died when he was four years old, and when he was thirteen, without benefit of child labor laws, he set up his own smithy. In 1885 at the ripe old age of twenty-four he moved it to Arvika (western Värmland) and the next year founded the enterprise soon to be known as Arvikaverken. Using American principles, he brought out successful models of reapers (Arvika's great specialty), binders, and cylindrical steel plows; the reapers sold briskly in competition with other Swedish makes and foreign imports, and by 1897 he was issuing about 2,000 a year, a figure that mounted to 10,000 by 1916. With such trademark names as Herkules, Viking, and Ava, Arvikaverken was turning out about 22,000 agricultural machines a year and grew into one of the largest factories of its kind in Europe. About two-thirds of its machinery was exported to Russia, Norway, and Finland. Also with an eye to prospective sales in northern and eastern Europe, International Harvester set up its first European plant in Norrköping in 1905.[13]

As for Per Anderson, he finally retired, presumably worn out by his arduous labors since childhood. Then he invented a new kind of stove and enthusiastically embarked upon a second career manufacturing *that.*

Eskilstuna owed its distinction as the "Sheffield of Sweden" to encouragement by the state and to its location on the main route between Mälaren and Hjälmaren, giving it easy access to Bergslagen iron by means of the lakes. Its manufacturing origins traced back to King Karl X Gustaf (1654–1660), who granted Reinhold Rademacher, a Dutchman (or German) from Livonia, the right to establish an iron goods manufactory in the town, and this so-called Karl Gustafs Stad, named for the king, remained a center of industry into the nineteenth century. In 1771 the government, trying to stimulate more manufacturing, made it a "free city," exempt from guild regulations and certain taxes. The war against Napoleon prompted the establishment of the Rifle Factory (*Gevärsfabrik*) in a building purchased from the Rothoffs, the most recent proprietors of Karl Gustafs Stad. In the 1820s it had forty to fifty workers making about six hundred infantry guns a year, a slow handicraft mode of production that continued until the 1860s.[14]

A small iron works at nearby Tunafors had started making knives, forks, scissors, and similar articles in the middle of the eighteenth century, and thereafter over the years one small workshop after another sprang up around Karl Gustafs Stad, some started by former workers at the manufactory. Eskilstuna became a city of small, specialized industry making cutlery and other iron-oriented wares. Olof Heljestrand (1781–1837), fairly representative, began turning out knives and razors in 1804, and this in turn forced him to set up a shop to make crucible steel; three of his sons, one of whom had worked for a time in Sheffield, in turn later led the enterprise. Christoffer Zetterberg, at the workshop later called Eskilstuna Jernmanufactur, was, among other things, forging sabers for the Swedish military. Among articles made in Eskilstuna were locks (by shops started in 1846 and 1849), files (1850), tiled stoves (1859), pliers (1856), and hinges and screws (1860).[15]

This was the community where Theofron Munktell (1805–1887) founded his machine shop. Though his father was a pastor, he had inherited the technical bent of a family with a background in the Falun iron industry and one branch of which owned the Grycksbo paper mill. Like so many others, he worked for Owen for a time, but essentially he learned the trade as a student and associate of Gustaf Broling in Stockholm. Once trained, Broling put him to work at the Mint; he was also tending Broling's crucible steel workshop, which Munktell later leased on his own behalf. During these years he made a variety of

159

things, ranging from a clarinet to a new printing press for Lars Hierta's *Aftonbladet,* not to mention a set of false teeth for the presiding officer of the Ironmasters Association. After seriously considering emigrating to the United States, he founded the Munktell Mekaniska Verkstad, with financial assistance from the Iron Office (1832). At first it served mainly as a repair shop for iron works and textile mills, but one of its first large orders came from the Rifle Factory.

Having visited England on a state stipend (1835), Munktell enlarged the shop in order to manufacture mechanical looms and steam engines. His close ties with the iron industry brought a request that he construct Sweden's first locomotive, *Förstlingen* (the First One), for use at the Norberg mine (1847). His second, *Fryckstad,* replaced horses at the Frycksta iron works railway in Värmland. Several more for the mining industry followed, and later he occasionally made similar narrow-gauge locomotives for small private railroad companies. An easy transition led from locomotives to the self-propelled locomobiles (1853), and, though there was no great demand during the early decades, Munktells had issued 2,269 of them by 1901. In reconstructing the workshop in order to make these traction engines, Munktell also made provision for the manufacture of reapers, winnowers, and threshing machines. In 1859 he combined the two lines of production, thereby bringing out Sweden's first threshing machines powered by steam engine. About 1,500 would be delivered by the end of the century. The growing factory also turned out dredges, warm water apparatus, and circle saws. Its 225 workers in 1879 had risen to about 800 by 1905, by which time it had four major specialties: traction engines, threshing machines, dredges, and machine tools.[16]

Munktells would merge with Bolinders in 1932, and AB Bolinder-Munktell would still later (1950) pass under the control of AB Volvo. The 1932 union was altogether appropriate, considering the similar origins of the two enterprises. Jean (1813–1899) and Carl (1818–1892) Bolinder also found technology more exciting than their parsonage home near Uppsala and a nearby smithy more interesting than the schoolhouse. Once Jean accompanied some hired hands delivering grain to the Dannemora mines and there saw all sorts of marvelous machinery, which "awakened my desire for mechanical studies."[17] A lady relative bragged so enthusiastically to Broling about Jean that the great metallurgist accepted him as a pupil, his last student, Theofron Munktell, having gone to work at the Mint. So the sixteen-year-old set out for Stockholm one November day in 1829, wearing a dark blue suit made by the parish tailor out of wadmal spun by Jean's mother. As Broling's pupil he lived in a small room filled with technical books, periodicals, tools, and a machine or two. He ate with the family, sometimes accompanied Broling on his errands, carried out work assignments, and studied chemistry, physics, mathematics, the mechanical arts, and foreign languages. In 1834 he took a job at the Mint, replacing, yes, Theofron Munktell.

Jean, whose name was actually just plain Johan until he expressed his rising social status by switching to "Jean," procured employment with Owen for his brother. Carl, liberated from school, happily went to work and did so well that he became a student at the Iron Office, then worked at Motala and Kockums. Using his savings plus grants from the Iron Office and the Board of Trade, Jean, accompanied by Carl, departed for England in 1841. Rosen helped them to locate employment, and they also met Carlsund and Holm, who happened to be there at the time. During the next two years they worked, one or both of them, in Birmingham, Manchester (Sharp, Roberts & Co.), Sheffield, and an iron works (Gladstone) in Scotland. All in all, a fairly characteristic beginning for the most promising young technicians in Sweden at this time.

Returned to Stockholm, they managed to find enough financial support, including a large loan from Zethelius (the Surahammer and Nyby ironmaster) and an interest-free loan from the Iron Office, to buy a suitable building on Kungsholmen and to furnish it with forges, hearths, and other necessities (1845). The edifice itself had formerly housed Edelcrantz's linen factory, and his steam engine was still in use. The lathes were acquired from Owen, whose famous machine shop, closed two years earlier, lay directly across the street. Quite literally, Bolinders Mek. Verkstad was built on Edelcrantz-Owen physical foundations, and part of the early production consisted of ornamental iron articles (railings, candelabras, fountains, garden seats, etc.) taken over directly from Samuel Owen. The brothers also repaired machinery in mills, breweries, tobacco factories, and printing shops. From the very beginning they made iron stoves in response to the rapidly growing demand; over the years, a wide variety of heating and cooking stoves for homes, restaurants, and hotels continued to flow from their factory.[18]

The Bolinders had started at the right time to cash in on the increasing market for several of their products, and they were especially fortunate with the Norrland sawmills. Between 1855 and 1859 they sold nineteen of their steam engines to sawmills, followed by many more later, and power-driven saws became a specialty of the Stockholm firm. Much of the later Swedish sawmill and forestry equipment came from Bolinders; when that demand tapered off, it sold British and American model woodworking machinery. Subsequently, it became a major manufacturer of internal combustion motors.

Bolinders was one of three larger mechanical workshops in Stockholm in the 1850s, the other two being Bergsund and W. Lindberg. Old Bergsund suffered the common financial problems of *mekaniska verkstäder* in the 1840s and 1850s, and its concentration on shipbuilding, peculiarly sensitive to the swings of the economic cycle, made it especially vulnerable. It had been closed in 1841–43 and it went bankrupt in 1858, terminating the half-century of Wilcke ownership. After its purchase by Anton Wilhelm Frestadius (1801–1867), a wealthy exporter of iron who had been helping to finance it earlier, Bergsund expanded into an important builder of ironclad steamships, especially after its acquisition of additional facilities at Finnboda in eastern Stockholm. By 1900 it was employing over a thousand workers and had launched over two hundred merchant ships, as well as a number of warships for the navy. In its second specialty, Bergsund had built over eight hundred highway and railroad bridges, including the country's first steel bridge in 1865.

William Lindberg (1818–1877), though starting slowly, competed with Bergsund in the building of ships. Lindberg was a "good technician, but better businessman, rich in initiative, daring and tenacity," qualities that enlisted support from Rosen, Carlsund, and Wallenberg at different stages in his career. Rosen made it possible for him to attend the Institute of Technology. A machinist on the *Norrland* under Captain Carlsund (1837), Lindberg worked at Nyköping for a time, then became foreman at a shipyard in Stockholm. After a precarious beginning, his own workshop, fully backed by Wallenberg, expanded rapidly once he had acquired Södra Varvet (the Southern Shipyard) on Tegelviken. His first vessel, an ironclad paddlewheeler, came off the ways in 1854, and by 1895 this enterprise had launched over two hundred iron and steel ships.[19]

Two other Rosen and Nyköping alumni, Jacques Lamm and Otto Hallström, also founded engineering works. Jacques Lamm (1817–1891) studied at the Institute of Technology, worked at Nyköping and at Motala, then was a draftsman in Paris for Count von Rosen, who was selling John Ericsson propellers there. Returned to Sweden, he helped to manage his father's shipyard on Långholmen, where the father also ran a textile mill and where Lindberg, through his Rosen and Lamm connections, had secured a position as a foreman. Jacques then started a shop for the manufacture of nails, the beginning of the ultimately large Ludwigsberg foundry and engineering works; it made Lamm one of the richest men in Stockholm.

Otto Hallström (1813–1880) went to work for Rosen at Nyköping in 1832 and remained there until 1840. After that he became a builder of bridges. He also proposed to lay a piped-water system on Södermalm, but the answer was no. Then he wanted to tear down and rebuild Gamla Stan, and the answer was still no, fortunately for the future Swedish tourist trade. By a strange turn of events, the 1851 London Exposition reawakened his original technical interests. Rosen, visiting it, took one horrified look at the botchy Swedish display there and minced no words in telling his countrymen about it. Others took up the cry that it was a national embarrassment; *Aftonbladet* asserted that Swedish industry was made to look as "naked as the Carpathian Mountains," and Hallström was dispatched with a more representative collection. The

British and American displays in turn made a deep impression on Hallström. After construction had started on Rosen's Örebro to Köping railroad, Hallström, borrowing money from Lindberg, established a machine shop in Köping to make equipment for the railroad. It was an astute decision—had the railroad arrived. Instead, construction stopped for years, leaving him stranded in a small town more redolent of hay and flour than of industrial activity. He survived by doing local repairs, finding customers in Eskilstuna, and manufacturing propellers and other articles for Lindberg's shipyard. It was a bleak beginning for what would years later become an ample fulfillment of Rosen's vision and one of the more scintillating pages in the history of Swedish industry.[20]

The circumstances in which these *mekaniska verkstäder* in central Sweden were founded underline the vital importance of the "old boy networks," of the master and student relationship, and of the continued collaboration of technicians who as young men had worked together in their training. By intelligence, drive, and luck, some members of the networks achieved a degree of national prominence, very much helped by masters who could procure stipends, employment, and loans at crucial moments, and also aided by a circle of colleagues functioning as a mutual assistance network. The history of Swedish technology and industry in this period is interwoven by the tenacious skeins of personal relationships around such figures as Owen, von Platen, Carlsund, Berzelius, Nils Ericson, Broling, and Rosen.

Having the right relatives and friends helped also, as witness the career of Frans Henrik Kockum (1802–1875). His mother's family had founded a tobacco spinnery in Malmö in 1726 and over the years acquired merchant ships, the Lomma clay works, the Limhamn lime plant, and the Svanen sugar refinery. Kockum at the age of twenty-three inherited all this, or, rather, would have inherited it had not the firm, hard hit by the postwar depression, just gone into bankruptcy. However, friends of the family rallied around with enough money to enable him to buy back the tobacco factory at the auction. These would not be the last financial perils of Frans Henrik Kockum, nor the last time that he would be rescued.

Skåne, a province of Denmark until 1660, still tended to look to Denmark and Germany for its trade, Copenhagen and Lübeck being its principal suppliers. Malmö, the third largest Swedish city in the twentieth century, had a population of only about 4,000 in 1800. This had risen to about 10,000 by 1840, but, aside from its location directly across from Copenhagen, the decisive step forward toward growth came when the terminal of the southern trunk line was placed in Malmö, rather than at Ystad. It was Akrell's decision, but apparently the Ystad leaders dawdled too long before frantically stating their case, whereas Carl Jöran Kock (grain dealer, soapmaker, Riksdagsman) and others in Malmö moved fast and effectively. Nor did it hurt their campaign that Beijer, brother-in-law of Kockum and the builder of the southern line, had been an engineer in the improvement of the Malmö harbor between 1839 and 1855.[21]

By 1841 Kockum's tobacco, sold under the label of "honest and good," had made him rich enough to found the workshop that became Malmö's largest industrial enterprise. It was a success from the start, selling farm machinery and household utensils to a populace now increasingly prosperous. Like Bolinders, Kockums found a strong market for stoves of all kinds, ornate heating stoves becoming an especially important sales item. Apparatus for distilling *brännvin* also sold well. The workshop turned out pots, pans, mirrors, fire engines, and much more, even a carousel. It received its first order from the state railroad in 1860, sixty cars for hauling gravel, and it began making passenger carriages a few years later, followed by sleeping and restaurant facilities. As one of the three major suppliers of rolling stock, Kockums would put out approximately 1,500 passenger and 10,000 freight cars over a 100-year period.[22]

To attempt to describe the career of Frans Henrik Kockum in detail would be to embark upon a survey of virtually everything of industrial importance in southern Sweden during his lifetime. His machine shop steadily expanded to factory proportions, and Kallinge *bruk*, acquired to ensure a ready supply of forged iron and steel, was equipped with modern furnaces. He became part owner of the sugar refinery at Landskrona, which was absorbed into the Skånska Sockerfabriks AB in 1853. The Lomma plant, sold to Skånska Cement AB in 1871, was transformed into a cement factory, in which Kockum also had a hand. He helped to start the Manufaktur Malmö spinning mill and had an interest in the Höganäs coal mines, a Malmö porcelain factory, the Phoenix safety match company, and the Malmö gasworks.

King Oscar I had to rescue him from a premature foray into Lapland and its Gällivare ore fields. The subsequent prosperity of the earlier 1850s encouraged him to further expansion, but he came through the 1857 crisis only with the help of loans from the state (the Gripenstedt emergency fund) and the Kredit und Versicherungsbank in Lübeck. Though Kockum was using credits from merchant or banking houses in Stockholm, Gothenburg, Copenhagen, Lübeck, Newcastle, and Hamburg (the ill-fated Ullberg & Cramér), Artur Attman, a biographer, blamed most of his problems on the absence of adequate financial institutions.[23] Again in 1866 his friends had to rush to his assistance, and this time it was thought best to reorganize into a joint-stock company, Kockums Mekaniska Verkstads AB.

In the 1960s and early 1970s Kockums would be a shipyard of world repute. This had been started in 1871–75, then greatly expanded with the hiring of A. Balthasar Munter, a Dane who had directed the building of ships at Burmeister

& Wain, Copenhagen's great engineering works. Munter's ambitious program, however, scared the board of directors, and Munter left at the end of 1882. Kockums did go on to build all sorts of commercial vessels and warships, including submarines and torpedo boats, for the Swedish navy. Munter thereafter represented Armstrong and Whitworth in China and Japan, in the process helping to develop the Japanese navy; it would be the Japanese, of course, who, by their competition, would help to put the quietus on the Kockum shipbuilding industry in the 1970s.

Three other *mekaniska verkstäder* of some importance sprang up in southern Sweden. The man originally in charge of the Kockum railroad manufacturing division, Carl Holmberg (1827–1890), later founded his own machine shop in the university city of Lund; it made steam engines, sawmill machinery, pumps, equipment for mills, and, after 1881, cream separators. A blacksmith forge in Landskrona grew into an engineering works largely making railroad equipment, then in the twentieth century became a major industrial factory manufacturing army tanks, earth-moving equipment, dump trucks, and cranes. Under the name of Landsverk, it ultimately became a part of the Kockum industrial complex. The earliest of the three had been started at Hälsingborg by Erik Ruuth (1798), a small machine shop that survived over the years and under various names to become Elektromekano, manufacturer of electric motors and transformers in the twentieth century.[24]

No, Count Sparre, head of the new Uddevalla–Vänersborg railroad, did not want to buy any locomotives from Antenor Nydqvist. When he saw Nydqvist entering the room he "immediately assumed his most aristocratic mien." Had not Beijer, *chef* of the state railroad, told him that no one in Sweden could make a good locomotive or supply the spare parts for them? He sharply informed Nydqvist that "I will not take the responsibility for ordering from you gentlemen!"[25]

Over a thousand locomotives had been delivered from Nydqvist & Holm (NOHAB) in Trollhättan by 1914 when the old man, father of the Swedish locomotive, died at the age of ninety-seven. The earlier ones were manufactured before Trollhättan even had a railroad through the town.

Antenor Nydqvist (1817–1914) and his older brother, sons of a Stockholm doctor, had attended the Institute of Technology, worked at Hennig's Rosendahl spinnery, and gone on the customary work-study tour, in the course of which the brother had died at Chemnitz. Antenor moved on to Neunkirchen in Austria, then to Escher, Wyss & Co. in Zürich, where he learned all about that new source of power, the water turbine. He completed his tour at the Köchlin locomotive works at Mülhausen in Alsace. Well-versed in water turbines and locomotives, he returned to Sweden to work at an iron *bruk*. In 1847 Nydqvist joined Olof Holm and another man to found the Trollhättan Mek. Verkstad, later successively known as Nydqvist & Holm and NOHAB. The cornerstone for the first building, on the west side of Gullöfallet, was laid on that sacred Swedish holiday, Midsummer Eve, in 1847.[26]

Trollhättan, a sawmill town, had gained added industrial possibilities with the completion of the new locks under the direction of Colonel Nils Ericson. The canal builder, who ran the community with an iron hand, responded favorably to Nydqvist's overtures, continued to give him good advice, and later even went security for his financial dealings. Some of the early capital came from Nydqvist's old grandmother, who sold her property in order to contribute to the enterprise, and from his half-brother, a doctor. Olof Holm, a "happy, jovial" type, attended to the finances until 1871. During the 1850s the machine works made steam saws, sawmill equipment, water turbines, traction engines, threshing machines, and other farm machinery, the same assortment that has been met at several other places.

When Major Claes Adelsköld, the noted builder of private railroads, was staking out the route for the Uddevalla–Vänersborg line, he chanced to see a locomobile from the Nydqvist factory. He liked it very much and commented that the quality of its construction resembled that of a locomotive; Nydqvist in fact had mentioned the possibility of making them in the application for a *privilegium* and had designed the first building large enough for the purpose. Adelsköld told Sparre, and they ordered a locomotive for hauling gravel, but then the count, recalling Beijer's warning, changed his mind. Nydqvist thereupon confronted Sparre, who, as related above, refused to take the responsibility.

To which Antenor quickly responded, "But the honorable count does not *need* to feel responsible, *I* will be responsible for it." Sparre liked the answer and the competent look of the man. "Oh, so, does the gentleman say that? Well, then, it might as well go ahead." Face to face with him, Sparre had reacted to one of the Sweden's greatest pioneering industrialists with complete confidence, much as Nils Ericson had done earlier. Antenor looks out from surviving photographs, broad-faced and sober, level-eyed, a practical man with his feet firmly planted on the ground. Noticeably, this was one machine shop that escaped the fluctuating fortunes that threatened some of the others.

Thus did Nydqvist get his first locomotive order (1865), followed some time later by a request for seven more from Sparre. The state railroad, its officials convinced, also began ordering locomotives from Nydqvist & Holm. In 1871, when twenty-four of them had been built, he made them the specialty of his factory. He did so at the cost of losing the aging Holm, who had held the company finances together during the early years, but who viewed this development with distrust and who may have "begun to feel the pace too swift." Locomotive No. 200 came out in 1884, No. 500 in 1897, and No. 1,000 in 1912, many of them exported. They were shipped out by barge until the railroad finally reached Trollhättan in 1877, though, oddly, the firm did not connect its works to it by a three-kilometer railway until 1894. Antenor, the venerable patriarch of Swedish industry, continued to make his daily rounds of his beloved enterprise even after passing his ninetieth birthday. Not until 1916 did the firm become a stock company, thereafter to be known as NOHAB.[27]

In 1920 NOHAB received the single largest locomotive order in history, 1,000 freight locomotives for Soviet Russia, of which about one-half were ultimately actually delivered. Payment was made in gold. In 1926–27 the Turkish government submitted an order for 100 locomotives and 1,500 freight and passenger cars as NOHAB's contribution to the work of a combined Danish-Swedish consortium that was building and equipping Turkish railroads. In 1933 the same consortium (Consortium Kampsax) cooperated in building and supplying the Iranian railroad from the Caspian Sea to the Persian Gulf.

Before becoming known for its locomotives, Nydqvist & Holm had gained its original reputation as a maker of water turbines. Having evolved out of the water wheel through the work of such men as John Smeaton and Claude Burdin, these had reached practical forms in the turbines of Fourneyron (by 1833), Poncelet (1838), and Jonval (1841). As noted previously, Andrew Malcolm in Norrköping introduced early models into Sweden, and by 1865 three of the textile mills there were using them. Jean Bolinder described water turbines in his account of his English travels in 1841–43. J. S. Bagge, who had made early matches, had the full support of the Iron Office during many years of experimentation with hydrodynamics and various types of turbines; as head of the mechanical staff of the Iron Office after 1853, he had ample resources for the purpose. Wilhelm Wenström, to be described later, also devised a series of turbines in the 1850s and 1860s.

By the time that Nydqvist & Holm began making them, Swedish enterprises dependent upon water power were clamoring to replace their old wooden water wheels with turbines.[28] Francke's pulp mill at Trollhättan used a 20-horsepower water turbine from the time of its founding. Each turbine made at Nydqvist & Holm, which Bagge regarded as the best in the country, was usually of new construction, as the workshop continued to improve and patent its models. Their production increased in the 1870s, but were replaced over the years by electric power and steam turbines made elsewhere.

Nydqvist & Holm sold a few of John Ericsson's caloric or hot air engines. Ericsson never did achieve his dream of creating one strong enough to replace the steam engine: it was too bulky, did not generate enough power, and, as mentioned earlier, technology could not yet produce iron sufficiently resistant to high-temperature radiant heat. At last giving up on the large engine, he devised a small model that served adequately for printing presses, sewing machines, small boats and pumps. Wenström, who had served in Ericsson's

New York bureau for a time, introduced it into Sweden while working at Finspång (1858–59). It was made in small quantities at Finspång, Breven, Bruzaholm, Hellefors, Åkers Styckebruk, and Nydqvist & Holm, mostly for printing presses and pumps, but maintenance was too expensive, they were noisy, and the heat continued to corrode the iron.[29] By no means all of the seemingly promising inventions of the century, eagerly seized upon by the owners of machine shops, actually caught on, and the caloric engine must be reckoned among the failures.

Another manufacturer of railroad equipment remains to be described. Atlas Copco, founded as Atlas in 1873, is today an international company employing 18,000 workers with worldwide distribution of mining and construction equipment, pneumatic and hydraulic tools, and electronics. Unlike nearly all the enterprises so far described in this chapter, Atlas did not grow from small workshop to industrial factory; it started as a planned factory for the specific purpose of supplying railroad equipment. Its founding is associated with the names of Eduard Fränckel, D. O. Francke, and Wallenberg.

Son of a Gothenburg merchant, Fränckel had been studying at technical schools in Hannover and Karlsruhe when he was summoned home by Nils Ericson, at the age of nineteen, to work as an engineer on railroad construction (1855). After some practical experience, Ericson sent him, at state expense, to Manchester for two years at Beyer Peacock & Co., which at the time was manufacturing locomotives for the Swedish state railroad. During the following years he served as superintendent of railroad machinery, advised Swedish factories attempting to make equipment, and went on several trips abroad, especially to Germany. He was also insisting that a *modern* railroad supply factory was necessary for Sweden.[30]

Fränckel, a very persuasive talker, had no trouble convincing Francke, who was deeply engaged in the Bergslagen railroad, and he in turn brought in the Gothenburg Commercial Co. An innovation at the time, the ownership was widely spread among nearly fifty stockholders, only one of whom (Wallenberg) held as much as 10 percent of the 3,150 shares. Wallenberg and Cervin headed the Stockholm contingent; though Wallenberg was not one of the initiators, contrary to formerly accepted dogma, it was he and his bank that eventually would have to take over the financing.[31] The spacious factory structures in Stockholm were quickly built in 1874, and Atlas also bought the former Ekenberg wagon factory in Södertälje. Here, railway cars had replaced horse-drawn wagons, a nice historical touch. David Joachim Ekenberg, foreseeing that the large transport wagons were doomed, had put up a big edifice for the construction of railroad freight cars (1866), and several hundred had been made before Atlas took it over.[32]

Though seemingly propitious in 1873–74, the timing of the founding of Atlas, which was employing over 600 men, had not been all that good. The

1875 value of production (nearly 3 million kronor, plus another million at Södertälje) made it the largest *mekaniska verkstad* in Sweden, but its production soon plummeted. The market had been saturated by the number of enterprises endeavoring to enter it, even allowing for continued prosperity. The state railroad, its suppliers already largely determined, never did order from it in the expected quantities, while the economic downswing drastically lowered orders from the private lines. Production in 1879 was less than a third of that in 1875, and the Södertälje factory, which had made 500 cars in 1873–75, built only 40 in 1879. The Gothenburg group began pulling out, its commercial company collapsed, and Wallenberg and the bank, by its financing, assumed control of Atlas.

With the decline of railroad construction in the 1880s, the company stagnated. Marcus Wallenberg would long afterward be disposed to put much of the blame on Fränckel, who, though adept in the technological aspects, lacked managerial abilities and still talked too much.[33] The bank learned from this experience that good leaders were necessary, leaders who would then receive long-term, effective financial support. Finally Fränckel was gently eased out of the enterprise he had started, Oscar Lamm (nephew of Jacques) replacing him (1887). The original company was liquidated, with heavy losses for the stockholders, and a new one was organized as Nya Atlas, in which the bank held a large portion of the stock. Manufacturing various products of steel, iron, and wood, Nya Atlas was at this time still a company in search of new lines of production.

Some of the original machine shops were on their way to becoming modern factories. One after another, the basic machine tools were being introduced, usually from Great Britain. Here the successors of the millwrights had been devising, amidst the clanging din of manufacturing, the tools and machinery for the dawning industrial age. Planing machines for wood and metals, the screw-cutting lathe, the slide-rest, a punching machine, the steam hammer, the facing lathe—these and others had been invented by Joseph Bramah, Henry Maudslay, Richard Roberts, James Nasmyth, Joseph Whitworth, and Joseph Clement. Others on this protean scene had helped to pioneer power-transmission systems. John Smeaton had written his germinal work on " . . .the Native Powers of Water and Wind to turn Mills and other Machines on a circular Motion," and John Rennie, William Murdock, and Sir William Fairbairn had made successive contributions to the technology of power transmission.

After the first two-thirds of the century the Americans took over the leadership in the development of machine tools and in the adoption of standard measures, interchangeable parts, and the assembly line. By the time the Swedes were ready to go to fully industrial production, the American influence was becoming paramount, and the Swedes tended to refer to the introduction of these manufacturing processes as "Americanization." (One step was distinctly not American: the metric system was adopted in 1878, to be fully implemented over the next decade.) Of the 1,423 *mekaniska verkstad* employees in 1900 who had at one time or another worked outside Sweden, almost half had been in one of the other Nordic countries. Only 47 had gone to Britain, whereas 176 had chosen Germany, now the scene of more exciting developments—and 437 had preferred the United States.[34]

Though the concept of interchangeable parts had been developed independently by Leblanc (a French gunsmith) and by Samuel Bentham and Marc Isambard Brunel (pulley-blocks for ships), it was Eli Whitney's firearms factory in Connecticut (1798) that became the prototype enterprise in the use of interchangeable parts and the division of labor on an assembly line. The manufacture of Colonel Samuel Colt's revolver followed (1835), then the manufacture of reapers and sewing machines. When "Americanization" began in Swedish factories, it started, quite naturally, with weapons, reapers, and sewing machines. From them it spread to industries based on new inventions whose apparatus demanded standardized parts: telephones, separators, electric motors, bicycles, and internal combustion engines.[35]

The Swedish military in about 1858 ordered a consignment of guns to be made by J. W. Bergström and W. Lindberg in their respective machine shops in Stockholm. Bergström made some parts of the gun, Lindberg made the others. When the parts were brought together for assembly, they did not fit![36] The contretemps generated a fair amount of excitement in military circles. Aside from evident carelessness in writing up the measurements for the order, the episode suggests that the age of interchangeable parts had definitely not yet arrived in Sweden.

It did begin in 1867 at the Rifle Factory when the military, which had gone over to rifled barrels in 1854 and to breechloaders in 1864, decided to rebuild the Eskilstuna weapons factory for the purpose of making Remingtons on license. Its director, Major Conrad Leonard Fries, and Theofron Boberg of Munktells spent half a year at the Remington plant; Boberg also visited some other factories. Two artillery officers were later sent over to watch Remingtons being made, and at the Rifle Factory an American instructed the Swedish workers in the new industrial methods.

American metalworking machinery, ordered by Fries, replaced outmoded types in the old and new buildings: milling, boring, punching, cutting, profile milling, and also steam hammer, eccentric-shaft press, and screw-cutting apparatus. The modernization continued under Captain Gustaf Blix, who had participated in the reorganization and who succeeded Fries as the director at the end of 1868. Soon the Rifle Factory was turning out 15,000 to 20,000 Remingtons a year.[37]

Its industrial method of manufacturing, with interchangeable parts and assembly line, quite naturally evoked a great deal of interest, and several persons who had worked there went on to install similar methods and machinery at other enterprises. Boberg, a nephew of Theofron Munktell and a partner in the firm after 1863, continued to improve the already relatively advanced forms of production at Munktells, and it made additional machinery, copied from the newly arrived American, for the Rifle Factory. His expert advice to other proprietors contributed to the industrialization of Eskilstuna during the next two decades. Eskil Lindblad wandered further afield. After studying at the Institute of Technology he became a foreman at the Rifle Factory, and his experiences during the reorganization turned him into an enthusiast. In 1870 he moved to Husqvarna, another weapons workshop, which now had to follow the Rifle Factory's example if it was to remain competitive. When the state, obtaining enough weapons from Eskilstuna, stopped ordering anyway, Lindblad assisted Husqvarna to go over to a technically allied field, the industrial manufacture of sewing machines. Later, in 1880–84, he served at the Palmcrantz factory on Kungsholmen where machine guns and reapers, invented by Helge Palmcrantz, were being made.[38]

Another man, Johan Henrik Fredholm (1838–1904), not directly connected with the Rifle Factory, had been manager at the Palmcrantz workshop in 1873–77 when the machine gun, of which more later, was first being manufactured. Studying farm machinery in Europe and the United States, he became an eager propagandist for the American machine tools. When he returned, Fredholm was wondering if Sweden would ever possess the economic resources to elevate itself to a comparable level of technology, and in a speech to the technological society in 1880 he urged the replacement of the "clumsy" (klumpiga) Swedish machines, based on the British and German, by the new model American ones. His enthusiasm would be echoed by other Swedes, former workers in the United States, who praised the efficient, beautifully polished machine tools there and the accompanying use of templates and gauges for precision work.[39]

Eskilstuna, with its many small handicraft workshops, was ripe for industrialization. The canalization of the stream that flowed through the city to Lake Mälaren had been completed in 1865, and a railroad arrived twelve years later. At least three former workers at the Rifle Factory during the modernization—Magnus Brunskog, August Stenman, and August Stålberg—subsequently introduced its methods in other Eskilstuna enterprises. The first two, who had also been in England and the United States, helped to mechanize the Eskilstuna Jernmanufaktur, especially Brunskog, who had visited several of the American machine tool factories and who now organized the industrial manufacture of its table knives (1877f.). This forced Lars Fredrik Ståhlberg, also making table knives, to reconstruct his shop for the use of similar

171

equipment. Several others, such as P. Liljeqvist (saw blades) and E. A. Naesman (locks), later taken over by August Stenman, were going to industrial drift in the late 1870s.[40]

Machine tools required stronger power than the water wheel or turbine, which were also, of course, vulnerable to conditions of low water and to the winter freeze. Munktells, though itself making steam engines, had relied primarily on a 25-hp water turbine, and only in 1866 did it begin to go over to steam power. When low water occurred in 1875, C. O. Öberg, who was making locks, installed an 8-hp steam engine. Other quickly followed, and by 1885, or soon thereafter, steam power predominated in the city. With the steam engine came the characteristic sound of the industrial era, a medley of various-toned factory whistles demarcating the working hours of the day. Knut Hellberg summarized his description of these developments by writing that Eskilstuna, nine of whose firms had won prizes at the Philadelphia exposition, went from workshops to modern industrial factories in the 1880s as though transformed by a *trollslag*—a wave of a magician's wand.[41]

Following its customary practice, the Swedish government awarded fifteen technicians grants to visit the industrial display at the Philadelphia World Exposition in 1876. Helge Palmcrantz (1842–1880), who may well have been one of Sweden's most brilliant inventors, was one of them. A lucky fluke had given him his first step up. The man with whom Helge was staying, while working as a student in a Stockholm machine shop, was so impressed by the boy's high intelligence that he persuaded a wealthy man to pay his way through the Institute of Technology. Failing thereafter to find a job, he returned to Jämtland, his home province, and there invented his own model of a rifle. When he took it to the military committee on weapons in Stockholm, they were sufficiently impressed to appoint him as a draftsman, and the next year, inspired by similar attempts in the United States and France, he invented a machine gun. After more work, an improved model, equipped with a cluster of six to ten barrels, was soon patented in several countries, and Thorsten Nordenfelt in London successfully introduced it on the international market. Meantime, the inventor was also busily working on a new kind of reaper, the first version completed in 1874 and a second one in 1877. His relative by marriage, Theodor Winborg (1832–1918), owner of a Stockholm company making vinegar, mustard, table salt, and sauces, financed the manufacture in Stockholm of his machine gun and reaper by Palmcrantz & Co., established for that purpose.

The long-bearded, narrow-faced Palmcrantz, eagerly peering through his glasses at the displays in the Philadelphia exposition, saw there the full realization of the kind of technological improvements that he himself had been visualizing. And Winborg, though he had studied in the chemical division of the

Institute of Technology and thereafter manufactured and sold "chemical" household wares, had also been a student at the Nyköping works in 1857; he would later manufacture electrical machinery and even undertake experiments with flying machines. Fredholm helped the inventor plan the original manufacturing in the modest quarters of a small machine shop on Södermalm. In 1879 Palmcrantz and Winborg moved into their newly built large factory at Karlsvik on Kungsholmen, a facility fully equipped with assembly lines and machinery for making interchangeable parts. Soon the company was employing about 400 workers. Suddenly, tragically, the 38-year-old Palmcrantz, a born inventor with a flair for visualizing possibilities and difficulties in a technical problem, died, cut down in the full momentum of his career. Winborg remained managing director for many years, assisted for a time by Eskil Lindblad. In 1890 the reaper division was moved to a new factory at Lövholmen, while the Kungsholmen plant continued to make armaments under the name of Stockholms Vapenfabrik.[42]

A few others were going to modernized industrial methods. From its inception in 1873 Atlas used an assembly line for its construction of railroad cars. The two rectangular buildings were divided into sections, each section attending to certain steps in the progressive building of a car. Another early, if small, assembly line came into existence at Uhrfors *bruk,* owned by Knut Wallenberg, for the making of horseshoes (1881f.). The six-meter iron bars were first cut into proper lengths by a mechanical axe, then the red hot pieces passed down an assembly line where six machines, in two parallel lines of three, each performed one simple task until the completed horseshoes emerged at the end of the series. Only after C. A. Rooswall's original invention had been revamped by K. T. Rennerfelt did the operation become profitable. Another early step toward standardization had occurred at the Bultfabrik at Hallstahammar (northeast of Köping), initiated by Nils Petersson and C. Gottfried Rystedt in 1873. The name means exactly what it sounds like, a factory for the making of bolts, nuts, rivets, railroad spikes, and similar items. Until now, such articles as bolts and nuts had either been imported or made with varying measurements by different workshops, an expensive and frustrating situation. Petersson installed machine tools, bought in England, for factory production, though a Swedish machine, patented by C. G. Gustafsson, began to be used a few years later. Demand immediately exceeded supply, and the Bultfabrik survived the later poor economic times with minimum strain.[43]

Köpings Mekaniska Verkstad, situated close enough to Eskilstuna and the Rifle Factory to be strongly influenced by the exciting developments there, quite possibly surpassed Munktells in its speedy adoption of machine tools. Though Otto Hallström died in 1880, he left five sons, some of whom carried on his work; equally important, the enterprise was supported by Wallenberg money. Ivar Hallström (1850–1897) had also been much impressed at the

173

Philadelphia exposition by American machine techniques, organization of work, and automatic machinery. After his return, Köpings started making transportable threshing machines, and, in order to compete with German imports, Ivar modernized the plant to use interchangeable parts, the assembly line, and series manufacture of a model. The resultant sales price was surprisingly low. Production started at the end of 1877, two years before Palmcrantz's second reaper. Ivar, after a visit to Germany, brought in the country's first foundry moulding machine and, interestingly, reported on N. A. Otto's gas engine, forerunner of the internal combustion engine.[44]

Gunnar, a brother, worked for two years in the pioneering American machine tool factory, William Sellers & Co. in Philadelphia, then installed lathes similar to those at Sellers (1886) and, copying American methods, set up a special machine tool room in the factory. (Köpings had adopted an earlier American lathe in 1871.) American-type horizontal boring machines began to be manufactured, drafted by engineer Sven Brunau according to Gunnar's instructions (1887–88). Brunau, who worked best when enveloped in a cloud of cigarette smoke, also devised a means to transmit electric power to the machine tools, and Köpings thereafter claimed to have been the first factory in the world to run machine tools directly by electricity.[45] In its standardization in the 1880s, Köpings acquired standard gauges from Smith & Coventry, micrometers from Brown & Sharpe, and precise die stocks from Pratt & Whitney; that is, Köpings was modeling itself on the leading Anglo-American machine tool companies. The purchase of a universal grinding machine from Geo. Richards (England) brought contact with John H. Newall, whose sheep-clipping machines were made by the factory for some years. This in turn required the use of the Newall system of tolerances. Köpings was furnishing machine tools to, among others, the Rifle Factory, Husqvarna, Bolinders, and Nydqvist & Holm, and in addition was making automatic machinery for the manufacture of horseshoes, nails, and pipes.[46]

Lower profits in the depressed 1880s stimulated mechanization, as companies tried to reduce labor costs, and the new inventions—L.M. Ericsson's telephone, Gustaf de Laval's cream separator, the turbines of de Laval and (later) the Ljungströms—entailed the use of interchangeable parts and the assembly line. Among others using precision tools were Ludwigsberg, Luth & Rosén (electrical machinery), and AB Centrator (another engineering works). Munktells over a period of three decades increased its manufacturing of machine tools for milling, planing, grinding, slotting, and screw and thread cutting. But even Munktells abandoned its specialized production for individual customers with extreme reluctance; in 1919 it was still making 98 kinds of motors and about 40 different kinds of locomobiles. Bolinders, the country's largest manufacturer of steam engines at the turn of the century, only began serial production of them in 1903. Similarly, it made only a few kerosene motors of any one type in the 1890s, hence production was limited to about 80 a year. Finally, in 1907, it installed milling machinery and turret lathes to make standardized models of compression ignition engines.[47]

The total number of *mekaniska verkstäder* had risen to 72 by 1860 and had passed 200 in the later 1870s, but in 1872 the 5 leading ones, all with over 500 laborers each, employed 45 percent of their workers. In 1912, when the full list contained 502 so-called *mekaniska verkstäder* and 23,864 workers, the 17 largest had 28 percent of the labor force. They ranged from those that were in every sense large modern factories to the great majority that were local, tiny, and still functioning mostly as handicraft repair shops.[48] In many of the small ones at the turn of the century, "the olden times foreman . . . went puttering about" (Gårdlund), still the obvious heir of the millwright from whom the modern engineer had so largely sprung. This bearded gentleman with his high collar "had often gone to some technical night school, but in knowledge he differed little from his subordinate workers."[49] Often of humble family background, the owners, like some of the pioneers, had frequently started their shops with their "two empty hands" as their only asset.

The founding of Stockholms Vapenfabrik had a sequel in the bold adventures of its part-owner, Thorsten Nordenfelt (1842–1920), whom an Englishman once referred to as "the handsomest old stout fellow ever seen." After attending Lund University and the Institute of Technology, where he first met Helge Palmcrantz, he worked for the state railroad before taking a position in London with the Waern family import-export firm (1862). A Waern himself on his mother's side, he shared the family's enthusiasm for railroads and for some years attempted to sell railroad equipment in Sweden, Russia, and the United States. However, his company fell into such financial distress that it had to be liquidated (1874).

At this point he saw the extremely promising possibilities in the improved version of Palmcrantz's machine gun and founded the Nordenfelt Guns and Ammunition Company, Ltd. for its manufacture and sale. Adopted by the military in several countries and by the British Admiralty, it sold briskly. Nordenfelt's munition works, its major factory at Gravesend, manufactured ammunition and various innovations developed by Nordenfelt and his staff, some of them Swedish engineers. They included a rapid firing cannon for light artillery, a new base fuse, the eccentric screw breach, a mechanical time fuse, and torpedoes. In 1885–88 Nordenfelt built four submarines of the Garratt type; these were driven by steam power both on the surface and underwater, enough steam being accumulated in the boilers for use while submerged. When underwater, however, they were difficult to control. The first one, sixty tons, was constructed at Bolinders and Stockholms Vapenfabrik, and sold to the Greeks (1886). The Turks naturally wanted anything military that the Greeks acquired, and they purchased the next two, somewhat larger submarines that were built at Chertsey in England. The fourth one was sold to Russia (1889), and the Germans constructed two similar ones in 1890.[50]

The Palmcrantz-Nordenfelt machine gun, like the earlier Gardner and Gatling, was based on the principle of a turning crank, and if it was revolved too fast it was likely to jam. It was rendered obsolete by Hiram Maxim's invention of a single-barreled machine gun in which the recoil of the gun moved the cartridge belt. Though the extraordinary salesmanship of the Nordenfelt agent in Athens, Basil Zaharoff, delayed the inevitable, Nordenfelt and Maxim merged their companies in the Maxim Nordenfelt Guns and Ammunition Co. in 1888, an arrangement in which Maxim, a Yankee from Maine turned British subject, soon gained control. Maxim had the support of Vickers Sons and Company, which in turn involved Rothschild money. Nordenfelt had originally also had Rothschild assistance, but the Swede managed to antagonize the great capitalist, who thereafter blocked his efforts. This, coupled with losses in some of his other enterprises, caused him to leave the company and move to Paris (1890).[51]

Here he opened a construction bureau for artillery in conjunction with the Société Cockerill, Seraing of Belgium. The British company protested that Nordenfelt was violating their separation agreement, and the legal case went all the way to the House of Lords, where Nordenfelt, defending his own case, lost. In 1903 he was back in Sweden, having ended his business career. "Like so many others who worked with inventions or other pioneering industrial development, he ultimately harvested no economic profits from his restless work." Or, as a biographer dryly summed up his career: "He seems to have been too bold, therefore on several occasions he encountered difficulties."[52] George Seldes, writing in the 1930s, listed him as one of the lesser figures in "the world-wide munitions racket," and invidiously misspelled his name, with implications of German militarism, as Nordenfeldt.[53]

Viewed in a broader perspective, Nordenfelt, as one of the first to sell the fruits of Swedish engineering abroad, foreshadowed the diffusion of its technology and the concomitant movement of its entrepreneurial activity into other countries. The signs were clear enough within Sweden. Between 1890 and 1912 the import of engineering products dropped from over a third to less than a quarter, according to Jan Kuuse, while their export, less than a fifth in 1890, shot up to 42 percent of the total manufactured.[54]

11. ANCIENT COMPANIES, MODERN INDUSTRY

The Great Copper Mountain—Stora Kopparberget—was discovered one day when a herder noticed that a white billy goat, butting the ground, had uncovered reddish earth. This, according to the legend, led to the extraction of copper, which pollen analysis and radioactive carbon tests indicate must have started around A.D. 1100.[1] The first documented evidence of its existence goes back to 1288 when Bishop Peter of Västerås exchanged an estate for a one-eighth interest in the mine at Falun. Sometime before 1347, when the king granted a charter, the miners organized the Stora Kopparbergs Bergslaget, often cited as the world's oldest industrial corporation.

Each of the joint owners had the right to quarry an annual share of copper ore out of the mine for smelting at his own hearth, which were scattered around the area wherever wood for fuel and water power for the hearth bellows were available. Nearly 200 small foundries ultimately dotted the Falun area. The shares, known as *fjärder* (fourths), had mounted to a maximum number of 1,200 in 1616, a single owner often possessing a number of them. For their own governance the early miners elected a council of fourteen and were organized in a guild that settled disputes, enforced the laws, and even mounted a troop of cavalry bearing the banner of St. George. The Crown naturally sought control, a pressure constantly resisted by the miners, and itself eventually began working a portion of the shafts.

It was dirty, dangerous work. Linnaeus, a visitor sometime in the 1720s, described the miners' working conditions: "Soot and darkness surrounded them from all sides; stones, gravel, corrosive drops of vitriol, smoke, fumes, heat and dust were everywhere."[2] The mine was often plagued by collapsing shafts and landslides. The greatest of these occurred in 1687, when the three large shafts or *stötar* collapsed simultaneously, leaving one immense hole thereafter known as *Stora Stöten*.

Export of copper buttressed Sweden's economic position in its days as a great power; peak production was reached in 1650 when some 3,000 tons were smelted. When the mining of copper ore declined, Stora Kopparbergs Bergslaget increased its smelting of iron; Svartnäs, the first iron *bruk*, was started in 1735. Stora Kopparbergs' total iron production, however, came to only about three percent of Sweden's total, about 4,000 tons of bar iron

177

annually. The council now consisted of twenty-four "eldest," and the head of Bergslaget was being called *bergshauptmann*, in imitation of German usage. In 1780 this governing body gained almost complete control over the operation of the various copper and iron works and of its other resources, which included large tracts of forest land. Additional minerals came, or would come, from this treasury of riches: some gold and silver, pyrite, sulphide of zinc, lead sulphide, ferric sulphate, and others. Its red earth would even contribute decisively to the characteristic rural scenery all over Sweden, as its hydrated iron oxide was used to make the famous Falu red paint for the omnipresent red and white houses of the Swedish countryside. Appearing in the middle of the 1600s, it was first used on the manor houses of the nobility, then later spread to the farmhouses.[3]

This was the most ancient of a number of enterprises with venerated names that have been active in the economic life of the country for the past three centuries. Among the other more prominent ones were Uddeholm, Hofors, Bofors, Finspång, Husqvarna, and Fagersta, but the list could justifiably be extended to include such others as Munkfors, Degerfors, Avesta, Ankarsrum, Iggesund, Ramnäs, and Österby. Unlike nearly all the mechanical workshops, which in their very founding were attuned to some phase of the new technology, these had usually originated as iron *bruk* and by now possessed proud traditions and generations-old techniques of work. In the middle of the nineteenth century they confronted the demands of a new industrial age: altered iron and steel techniques, forces leading to centralization of iron works, an awakening market for new wares, and the possibilities inherent in burgeoning new industries. In order to survive, each one needed advantageous location, natural resources, and competent management, had to respond to its own set of challenges in the most appropriate way during the coming of *storindustri*, big industry, in Sweden.

For Stora Kopparbergs Bergslaget, with its scattering of small *bruk*, centralization had become imperative if it was to retain any industrial significance. A start had been made in the 1850s when special assistance was given those *bruk* with the best access to ore, water, and transport. In 1862, at long last, its ancient form of management (and the office of *bergshauptmann*) came to an end in favor of a head director and three separate directors for its copper, iron, and timber divisions. The state relinquished any claim to ultimate control, and it became an entirely private enterprise.

Gustaf Adolf Lundhqvist, formerly at Nyköping, contributed the original ideas and impulse to action. Owner of a large number of *fjärder* by marriage, Lundhqvist possessed the appropriate attributes: rebellion against traditional methods, mingled acuteness and naiveté, a "majestic" appearance, and the ability to talk often and persuasively.[4] In June 1868 he carried a motion through the assembly of owners that a committee be appointed to study a proposed concentration of iron production, now first made practicable by the arrival of railroads. Much of the ore would come by railroad from the Grängesberg ore fields, 64 kilometers away, and the finished product could be dispatched by train to Gävle, Stockholm or, within a few years, to Gothenburg. After several committees and various changes of plan the firm decision emerged to build Domnarvet, one large iron works, at Tunaforsarna on the river Dalälven. Lundhqvist knew just the right man to put in charge of construction, Wittenström, the engineer who had rebuilt the Nyköping shops for him. Carl Gustaf Wittenström (1831–1911) had originally worked for Zethelius at Surahammar *bruk*; after the Nyköping assignment, he helped Immanuel Nobel install new equipment in his St. Petersburg factory. Then he built an iron works near Viborg and put in a rolling mill and puddle furnace at Dahls *bruk* for Wolter Ramsay in Finland; subsequently he participated in an ill-judged project (using charcoal) at an iron works (Dechourie) in India and served as an engineer for Carlsund at Motala. This was the experienced man who drafted the specific Domnarvet blueprints and supervised the construction.[5]

The plan, drawn up in the heady optimism of the early 1870s business boom, was an ambitious one. It called for four blast furnaces, two Bessemer converters, two Martin furnaces, rolling mills for plate iron and for railroad car wheels, and a total annual capacity of 43,000 tons a year, about a fourth of the annual iron production in Sweden. The surviving small iron works were to be closed, a decision not fully implemented later. The estimated cost ran to 3.1 million kronor. Lundhqvist and Bergslaget could not raise that kind of money. He persuaded Francke and his group, who were in the process of building the Bergslagernas railroad, to back Domnarvet as well. The Gothenburg Commercial Co. poured in large quantities of capital through purchase of *fjärder* and bond issues while also lending the railroad, through bond issues, a sum of 36 million kronor for the construction of the line from Falun to Gothenburg. Wallenberg, working with Francke, arranged a loan from his Stockholms Enskilda Bank.[6]

In the June 1873 meeting of the owners the Francke-Lundhqvist forces took full control and proceeded to revamp the management; a four-man directory would run the company from Stockholm, and a managing director and two intendants would be in charge in Falun and vicinity.[7] Though Francke became chairman and Lundhqvist the vice-chairman, neither one could entrench his position. Lundhqvist may have been the idea man, but he lacked the skills for practical construction and management; Francke spent his two-year term quarreling with the ironmasters while his own financial position deteriorated. The Gothenburg invasion collapsed as Francke and the commercial company headed toward bankruptcy.

Wittenström began building Domnarvet in 1872–73. Quite literally, the engineer had to direct the construction personally because no contractor

179

dared to bid on such a big project. First, a 7-meter tunnel had to be driven 300 meters through the rock for the water turbines that would power the plant. That alone cost over a million kronor, and the total expense had risen to nearly 4 million before the plant was completed in 1878. Rising costs coupled with the onset of depression forced the scaling down of the plans by Erik Johan Ljungberg, appointed managing director in November 1875. He cut out two blast furnaces and one of the Martin furnaces, while economizing where else he could. He also directed steady criticism at the "all too ambitious Wittenström," whose contract was not renewed upon its expiration near the end of 1877. On his departure he was given a silver snuff box, a Bible, and a rousing fireworks display.[8]

Professor A. Rickard Åkerman, a teacher at the Institute of Technology and a Stora Kopparberg director at the time, seems to have been largely responsible for the appointment of Ljungberg. Åkerman had been impressed by Ljungberg's work at Munkfors, where he had become manager at the age of twenty-five when J. F. Lundin, whom he was assisting, had suddenly died. Coming to Stora Kopparberg seven years later, he shouldered the arduous responsibility and would, during his four decades at the helm, become the very prototype of the factory managers who brought big industry to Sweden.

The story of the following decades "is Erik Johan Ljungberg's history."[9] An iron and steel production valued at 825,000 kronor in 1875 rose to over 13.2 million in 1913, while the total production in all branches of activity increased from 4.66 million to nearly 32 million kronor. At the beginning he had insisted on putting in six Lancashire hearths, with welding furnaces and hammers, because he knew that Lancashire iron would sell. Most of the construction men stayed on to become iron workers, but they were not properly trained, and somebody later said that during the first few years they made mostly junk. A large order of rails from the state railways tided Domnarvet over its most awkward years. Ljungberg moved slowly and carefully at an unruffled pace, never risking Stora Kopparberg's finances and largely disregarding the opinions of others. Domnarvet passed Sandviken as the largest Swedish iron and steel works at the end of the century.

In 1883 it made its first big purchase in the phosphorus-rich part of the Grängesberg deposits, henceforth a necessary source of ore if the company were to expand. This entailed more Martin furnaces and the conversion of the Bessemer furnaces to processing by the Thomas-Gilchrist method. As the price of charcoal mounted, Domnarvet attempted to make its own out of its wood debris, but ultimately it went over entirely to the use of coke. However, having ample water power, Stora Kopparberg began experimenting with electricity for the pig iron and smelted steel, and by 1913 this method was fully operative.

Stora Kopparberg's sawmills had been responsible for the biggest proportion of income in the years prior to the building of Domnarvet, and it continued to buy forests for fuel, for the sawmills, and for making wood pulp. In 1885 Stora Kopparberg purchased the Skutskär sawmill, which ultimately became one of the largest in the world. Skutskär and Kvarnsveden, the latter built at Borlänge in 1898–1900, became major producers of wood pulp.

In 1888 the complex enterprise became a full-fledged joint-stock company as Stora Kopparbergs Bergslags AB, each of the 1,200 *fjärder* being exchanged for eight shares of stock worth one thousand kronor each. The head office was returned to Falun. Some years later the company opened sales offices in London, Paris and Hamburg, but much of its iron—about one-eighth of all Swedish pig iron and one-fifth of the ingots by 1913—was going to the domestic market, contrary to the original plans. The company that centuries earlier had started mining copper ceased producing it in 1895.

The workers shared in the big general strike in 1909. Ljungberg had no love for labor unions, though he did not join the employers' association either until the workers started voting socialist. In one of his public utterances he warned the Swedes not to wait for the law or the state to perform miracles, "because a people cannot live off laws, regulations, inspections, etc. Productive labor is the only sure way to improve the common welfare." He then compared Swedish labor unfavorably with the American, which had 50 percent higher wages but produced five times as much.[10]

Stora Kopparbergs Bergslags AB continued to expand into a large industrial complex of iron mines, blast furnaces, forest reserves, sawmills, pulp and paper mills, and a large hydroelectric network; in 1960 it was employing 13,000 workers and had sales to the value of $137 million. In the 1980s it is primarily known, internationally, as an important exporter of wood pulp and paper.

A smith at old-time Uddeholm, so the story goes, was once asked his greatest wish. He is supposed to have retorted that when he arrived in heaven, he hoped to be seated between King Karl XII and the *brukspatron* of Uddeholm.[11] This small Bergslagen world, with its sense of *bruk* loyalty and pride of place and status, was transformed during the breakthrough of industrialization. Most of the some sixty small iron works in eastern Värmland would be closed, leaving the crumbling ruins of hearths and slag heaps, and also former manor houses now used for other purposes.

Founded in 1668 and after 1720 owned by the Geijer family and its Geijerstam offshoot, Uddeholm in north central Värmland survived. It lies on an *udde* or spit of land between a lake and a stream in a beautiful rural environment with blue hills in the distance. Having given its name to a giant corporation, it remains the administrative headquarters, but the industry has long since been dispersed to other locales. Farther down the Klarälv river, which bisects the province, Munkfors was founded in 1670 by an uncle of the first owner of Uddeholm. The rivalry between the two came to an end when Uddeholm purchased Munkfors after a series of vicissitudes had struck its recent owners (1829). Among other *bruk* that survived, Storfors and Nykroppa, both in existence before 1600, would become part of Uddeholm industrial empire in 1909, as would Degerfors (1654) in 1939.

Uddeholm's growth depended upon iron ore, water power, and timber, the same pattern as at Stora Kopparbergs Bergslaget in Dalarna to the northeast. Like Lesjöfors to the east, Uddeholm's most vexing problem had been its transportation; in desperation it tried canals, horse-drawn wagons on rails, and even self-propelled steam engines lumbering along the country roads. With the railroad came the concentration of iron works and sawmills, and Uddeholm became the first Swedish iron works to convert into a joint-stock company (1869) in order to acquire more capital for expansion.[12] Strong, farsighted leadership was required, and the Uddeholm-Munkfors duo undoubtedly owed their success to several unusually talented individuals who served the company during the crucial years.

Earlier, Emanuel Rothoff, inheriting a share in Uddeholm from his Geijerstam mother, had conducted a series of experiments in iron puddling and rolling mill techniques there. Jonas Waern (1799–1868), cousin of the younger Carl Fredrik Waern, served as managing director from 1831 until 1855 and presided over a great expansion of sawmill activity during the years when Värmland was temporarily the center of the lumbering industry. Elected to the Riksdag as the representative of the Värmland *brukspatroner,* he gained national prominence as a vocal exponent of liberating the iron industry from its straitjacket of regulations. He participated in the Köping-Hult railroad project, visualizing a future link to Uddeholm. His son-in-law and successor, E. G. Danielsson, led the company during the crucial years of decision from 1855 until 1880.

Eric Georg Danielsson (1815–1881) had become manager at Munkfors in 1840, long before he married Waern's daughter. Three years later he visited the United States on a stipend from the Iron Office to study American iron techniques and the American market potential for Munkfors exports. Three furnaces for the making of pre-Bessemer carburized steel, a long and expensive process, had been started at Munkfors after 1830. In England, where some of its export was used to make crucible steel and some was being shipped to the Orient, Danielsson discovered that Munkfors steel in transit was being stolen, replaced by inferior iron, and that its trademark was being falsified. His visits paid off in increased export to both countries.[13]

Johan Fredrik Lundin (1826–1868), who took over at Munkfors in 1856, set out to reduce the amount of charcoal and the length of time (over three weeks) required to make carburized steel, while also disposing of the huge piles of sawdust and debris accumulated at the Munkfors sawmill. In brief, he developed a hot air generator, employing the sawdust and gases as fuel, which blasted intensely heated air into a double furnace (1859). A system of pipes led directly to the bunkers containing the steel, ensuring an even hardness. The first time it was tried, two chunks of iron were used. The welder peeked in after a while and could see no trace of the iron. He rushed out to tell Lundin, shouting, "They're gone! They're gone!" Lundin, quietly jubilant, responded, "That's all right, that's all right, calm yourself, Karlgren." His sawdust generator had achieved a temperature high enough to melt the iron entirely, and the invention would reduce the fuel consumption while doubling the production. Lundin also patented a condenser for removing impurities from the gases (1865).

It so happened that (Sir) William Siemens in England just at this time had developed an open-hearth process for making steel, using preheated air. His tests failed, but the Martins, father and son, at Sireuil in France succeeded in 1864, using melting wrought iron and steel scrap with the pig iron to bring the carbon content down to the correct percentage. Years later, Pierre Emile Martin said that they had succeeded only after hearing about Lundin's hot air generator and how he had constructed his furnace. The Munkfors leaders, already partway to the Martin process themselves, were naturally interested in setting up a Martin furnace, but it would not be Lundin who would complete the work.

One day while fishing he made one cast too many and, long suffering from a heart condition, he fell over dead. Ljungberg, the future Stora Kopparberg leader, now directed the plant while Ludwig Rinman, a grandson of the eighteenth-century metallurgist, experimented with the Martin process at Munkfors after visiting Sireuil. The first Martin furnace went on stream at Munkfors in 1868–69. Siemens himself had one in successful operation in England in 1867. Much of the Munkfors steel was exported to the United States, though later the Russians would become the principal buyers.[14]

In the 1870s, under Danielsson's leadership, the Uddeholm company established a new iron and steel works at Hagfors near Uddeholm. Hagfors had water power and charcoal from company-owned forests, and, like Domnarvet in these same years, it rose directly out of the convenience of railroad transportation (1878). The building of the Nordmark–Klarälven railroad, mostly by the company, connected the ore fields to Hagfors, with its blast furnaces and steelworks. The ore fields, the production of pig iron, and the manufacture of steel and finished products could now be coordinated into one network of production. Gradually the small, now uneconomic, hearths and forges were closed. Their skilled workers, as necessary to the company as its vaunted metallurgists and managers, moved to Munkfors, Hagfors, and other larger iron works in the region.

Gustaf Jansson (1850–1934), who had learned American rolling mill techniques at the Washburn & Moen iron works in Worcester, Massachusetts, in 1876–80 and who became head engineer at Munkfors in 1884, introduced the cold rolling mill process. With the resultant band steel, Uddeholm embarked upon the manufacture of files, corsets, razor blades, springs, surgical instruments, clock works, saws, and wire.[15] (The steel for Gillette's early razor blades came from Uddeholm.) Well endowed with water power, the company built up a hydroelectric network sufficient for the entire province; an electric furnace was first installed at Hagfors in 1911. Concentrating its timber industry at Skoghall on Lake Vänern near the mouth of the Klarälv (1914–18), it added cellulose plants, a paper mill, and an electrochemical factory. After the Second World War the Uddeholm company employed over 15,000 and was in the process of building up a sizable international network of holdings.

Hofors, midway between Gävle and Falun, ranked third in its total annual iron production, after Uddeholm and Stora Kopparbergs Bergslaget, in the middle of the nineteenth century. Although its steel in the twentieth century has been exported all over the world, the name of Hofors has been obscured by its status as a subsidiary company of SKF, the ball-bearing corporation.

Robert Petré bought Hofors, where the villagers had probably been smelting iron by the beginning of the 1600s, in 1680. One of the three sons of George Petré, mayor of Montrose in Scotland, who migrated to Sweden, he was a merchant in Arboga before purchasing Hofors. In 1758 it had a blast furnace, a hammer with two hearths, a sawmill, and a brick works; a later engraving depicts a large water wheel and a number of low stone and wooden buildings.[16]

This *bruk* was the lair of the fiery Thore Petré (1793–1853), defiant leader of the radical liberal opposition in the Riksdag. As a skillful ironmaster, it was he who made Hofors, with its associated Hammarby, into one of the largest iron works in the country. Often frustrated in his modernization attempts by the "rigorous paragraphs and bureaucratic officials," he became convinced that the officials and their viewpoint, representing passivity and retrogression, must be eliminated before Swedish iron could regain its international competitiveness. Had he limited himself to fighting bureaucratic regulations and demanding free export of pig iron, he would have encountered less opposition in the Riksdag. However, he attacked not only the bureaucracy and conservative *bruk* owners, he also criticized the nobility, the clergy, the military officer class, the royal court, and even King Karl XIV Johan, thereby creating a host of sworn enemies.[17]

Shortly after his death Hofors went over to the Lancashire method, using its own pig iron (1855). Unfortunately, the sons of the mighty Thore lacked business sense. Hjalmar and Casimir not only lived in high style, which they could afford, they engaged in building projects and bought property far beyond even their means. Wallenberg first lent Hjalmar 75,000 riksdaler, then extended a large loan of about a million before he realized their incompetence. Already deeply in debt, the Petrés bought Avesta and Garpenberg at a low price as a speculation. As long as prices remained good in the early 1870s the Petrés kept afloat, but the deteriorating economy after 1874 spelled doom. By 1879 their debts had risen to an incredible 8 million kronor, of which over 3 million was to Wallenberg's Stockholms Enskilda Bank, and the family could no longer borrow more money to pay the interest on their current debt.

It will be recalled that the bank itself was in serious danger at this time; frightened depositors withdrew their accounts, and thirty-nine of its big borrowers would cease payments on their loans by the end of 1879. Wallenberg, quite aware that about a thousand workers and their families depended upon the several iron works and mines for their livelihood, demanded that the entire Petré property be put under administration to clear up the mess and avoid bankruptcy. He was one of the five appointed to the administration when it was established, along with Major Gustaf Lilliehöök, the manager and relative of the Petrés, and P. A. Cassel, representative of the Riksbank (and of Dufwa), which had also lent the Petrés money. Wallenberg and Cassel had fought before, and now they fought again, as Hofors became the scene for one more conflict in the long and bitter feud between Stockholms Enskilda Bank and the Riksbank. Losing patience when Cassel insisted that at least Avesta-Garpenberg be put into bankruptcy, Wallenberg had the entire property declared insolvent.[18] At the bankruptcy auction, Avesta-Garpenberg was bought by outside interests, while Wallenberg on behalf of his bank paid 3.5 million kronor for Hofors-Hammarby.

The Petré family, after two hundred years, had to leave Hofors in October 1880. Hjalmar and Casimir went into personal bankruptcy in November, Hjalmar's wife died on November 29, and on December 4 the sister of the brothers also died.[19] A great *brukspatron* family, well known for its aristocratic mode of living, departed under conditions of maximum melodrama. The bankruptcy and ensuing tragedy shocked the public, which felt that a part of traditional Sweden had been brutally and unnecessarily destroyed. The Riksbank, busily fighting Wallenberg, had actually precipitated the drama, but the public wanted a flesh and blood scapegoat, and Wallenberg, "who had few friends and many enemies," made an ideal target as the evil capitalist-banker. Mixing fact and fiction as usual, Lazarus would later describe it as the "Wallenberg plundering of the colossal Petré properties" and assert that the Wallenbergs made a fortune out of Hofors and Hammarby. The banker himself suspected that in buying them he was buying trouble. It went contrary to his own previous policy of being primarily a financier, not an owner of industrial enterprises. Wallenberg may have been too sharp-tongued and too personally involved in the affair, but, according to Steckzén, he "behaved like any responsible financier must behave in such an affair as that at Hofors." Whatever the case, the episode represented one of the most dramatic collisions between the old and the new Sweden.[20]

The fears of the workers that they would lose their jobs proved unjustified as the new stock company, controlled by Wallenberg, his sons, and the bank, expanded the enterprise. Lilliehöök remained as manager. The Lancashire iron, which was not drawing profitable prices, was replaced by a Bessemer furnace and blooming mill. For a time, however, they had trouble making good steel and the 1880s' prices were too low, so Hofors ran at a loss. Hammarby and Storvik were sold to a newly organized Storvik company, controlled by the Wallenbergs and the bank, which put up a large sulphite cellulose mill on the Hammarby grounds (1888). Knut Wallenberg liked to live, periodically, at the lovely and elegant Hofors manor house, and he got along well with Lilliehöök. Marcus, his half-brother, would much later say that Knut and Lilliehöök tended to avoid coming to grips with problems and continued to hope that things would straighten themselves out. That is, Knut supervised Hofors in the same manner as he did Atlas, where he continued to drift along with Eduard Fränckel. As in the days of the Petrés, Hofors was now having trouble paying interest on its debts. After Marcus assumed charge of industrial management for the bank in 1892, he reconstructed both companies, cutting down the value of the Hofors stock from a million kronor to only a hundred thousand and thereby reducing the cost of the dividends.[21]

Marcus had already shoved out Lilliehöök, and, following his customary strategy, he then appointed a strong man as leader, in this case Per Eriksson. A bald-headed, literal-minded, tough-looking gentleman who tolerated no nonsense, he had ample energy and broad, long-range vision. He closed the small mines, sold the outlying properties, and concentrated the ore, water power, and remaining forests on the Hofors production. Two Martin furnaces went into drift in 1896. Three new electrified rolling mills, the first in the world, were in operation by the middle of 1895. ASEA, a future international leader, gained one of its early laurels by using a waterfall 30 meters high and a 2.4 kilometers high-tension transmission line to generate and bring the electric power to Hofors.

Led by Per Eriksson, Hofors underwent continual improvements in the years before the First World War, when it was making about 50,000 tons of high-quality steel annually. Then suddenly in 1916 the whole direction of development of the growing, prosperous steel mill changed when SKF, looking for a mill where it could ensure the quality of steel necessary for its ball bearings, acquired the majority stock. In the future, Hofors would have, at least for a time, the second largest output of steel in Sweden, but it would largely lose its own identity in what has been described as the marriage of a noble lady of ancient lineage to a self-made young man.[22] Two generations later, in 1981, it would, as SKF Steel Hofors AB, be employing 2,760 workers and exporting about 70 percent of its production.

Bofors began to emerge in the 1880s as the great armament works of Sweden, replacing Finspång, which had occupied this position since the seventeenth century. Finspång failed to react in time to the rapidly changing technology of manufacturing cannon, whereas Bofors, originally a comparatively small *bruk,* geared itself at great expense and much travail for successful international competition.

Finspång (spelled Finspong until 1942) had been started as an iron works at a waterfall northwest of Norrköping in the middle of the sixteenth century. Under the successive direction of the de Wijks, William de Besche, and Louis De Geer, the advanced techniques of iron and cannon manufacture were imported from the Liège area of the Low Countries. Louis De Geer, who bought it from the Crown in 1641, received a monopoly on the making of cannon and the right to export them free of tolls. Finspång became a major European cannon manufactory, and for a time Sweden ranked as the largest exporter of cannon in Europe, greatly helped by the high quality of Swedish pig iron. In 1655–62, at its peak, 11,000 "pieces" were manufactured, of which 8,800 were exported.[23]

For two hundred years the De Geers, one of Sweden's most distinguished aristocratic families, presided over Finspång, but by the nineteenth century its facilities had deteriorated, neglected by a family now much more interested in political and cultural affairs. In 1848 Carl Edvard Ekman, aged twenty-two, became its administrator, and eight years later he bought the manufactory. His much older brother, Gustaf, had conducted the decisive Lancashire experiments at Lesjöfors, and he himself had access to capital from the family-owned Ekman & Co., large-scale exporters of iron. The transport of ore and finished cannon by road and wagon was replaced by a railed route to Norrköping, the cars being pulled by horses. Using the extensive forests, Ekman set up a modern sawmill and prepared better facilities for the chronic problem, the preparation of charcoal. A number of other iron works were acquired, and by the 1890s over 5,000 persons were employed in the extensive holdings of the Finspång company, which Ekman organized in 1884. He became one of the wealthiest men in the kingdom, and this "highly gifted and strong-willed man" served in the Riksdag for many years; in 1883 he refused the position of prime minister.[24] But in the struggle with Bofors, this otherwise highly successful industrialist lost out.

Bofors, east of Lake Vänern in the southeastern tip of Värmland, had been started in 1646, the third bar iron hearth in the area; nearby Degerfors became the fourth. These were the only two iron works in the region that managed, two centuries later, to survive foreign competition and the arrival of the new processes in the iron industry by renovating and centralizing their production. Bofors had been owned since 1812 by the Lagerhjelms, father and son. Pehr Lagerhjelm, it may be recalled, had strongly advocated the concentration of iron works into larger plants, and the son, Pehr Erland Lagerhjelm (1829–1890), fulfilled the father's vision at the family *bruk*. By installing a rolling mill in 1866–67 and a new blast furnace a few years later, Bofors attained the largest output of rolled iron in Sweden. Following the recent example of Uddeholm, the AB Bofors-Gullspång company was organized (1873), a number of owners merging their properties in it in return for shares of stock. The Kjellbergs of Gothenburg, the export and credit agents for the Lagerhjelms, injected a substantial amount of needed expansion capital by their purchase of stock. This growth would have been impossible without railroad transport, and Lagerhjelm invested large sums in the Nora–Karlskoga line that connected Bofors to Lake Vänern on the west and indirectly to the state railroad on the east. He also participated in the construction of three small private railroads. The burden of building the necessary railroads here also proved too heavy, and Lagerhjelm paid dearly for his long-term foresight; overextended when the depression hit, he had to sell his controlling interest in Bofors to the Kjellberg interests. (Wallenberg, having lent him money, again got most of the blame.) Lagerhjelm finished his career as managing director at the Kjellbergs' Kramfors sawmill.[25]

Meanwhile, Finspång, relying on Swedish pig iron, failed to improve its cannon to keep up with foreign development of projectiles traveling at a faster velocity and barrels resistant to greater explosive charges. Swedish attempts to utilize Bessemer steel had not been successful, nor did foreign companies do better at first with the Martin process. At the 1867 Paris Exhibition, the deteriorating Finspång position had been quite noticeable, and Swedish export of cannon declined. In some respects this was the crisis in the Swedish iron industry all over again, an ancient and proud armaments industry reluctantly forced to renovate or perish. Ekman failed to react in time, feared to undertake costly experimentation with uncertain results. Krupp, which now had its own secret process, defeated the Swedes in test trials in 1876. Krupp had only a slight advantage that time, but in 1878 the Swedish cannon soon burned out and the projectiles exploded in flight—"the sentence of death on Swedish field guns." The next year even the Swedish army was ordering Krupp artillery.

Now rumors were heard that Bofors had succeeded in producing steel of quality equal to Krupp's. Carl Danielsson, head engineer, had been given a brief look at the manufacture of an improved Martin steel in the Terre-noire mill in France. Danielsson, nephew of the Uddeholm leader and married to a Lagerhjelm, had been dispatched on a study trip to England and the United

States in 1875–76; Lagerhjelm, still managing director at this point, then performed his final service for his old *bruk* by sending him to Terre-noire, where, in the fall of 1876, they had produced a blister-free, strong, tenacious Martin steel suitable for cannon and relatively cheap to manufacture. With a license from Terre-noire, Danielsson directed the putting up of a Martin steel foundry for the new process (1879). The Swedish military had Finspång bore cannon barrels out of the new Bofors steel, they tested out extremely well, and so the Swedes had found an answer to Krupp.[26]

At Finspång, Ekman, having no Martin furnace, remained reluctant to modernize, and he hoped to force Bofors to deliver steel to him at a cheap price. As a prominent national figure, he had every expectation of being able to use his strong influence with the Stockholm government and its military leaders to compel such an arrangement. The military, however, was gaining confidence in Bofors while becoming increasingly exasperated with the low pace of the work at Finspång. Ekman then offered to enlarge his shop if the army and navy would guarantee him *all* artillery construction (1882). The military asked Bofors if it would provide the steel, and the men at Bofors, protesting the suggestion of a Finspång monopoly, began talking about putting up their own cannon factory. Ekman countered this by proposing to make his own steel. Since this kind of competition might ruin Bofors sales at home and abroad, this virtually forced it to go to the manufacture of cannon.

At the beginning of 1883 the army inquired if Bofors would deliver to Finspång the castings for forty-four artillery pieces. Danielsson responded that Bofors would deliver the *completed* artillery, not just the castings, by July 15, 1884. A new building for the manufacture of cannon hurriedly went up. Ekman, now alarmed, vainly proposed that Bofors be guaranteed the delivery of steel for some years, Finspång to have a monopoly on the cannon. Bofors duly delivered its first artillery pieces, and it has been an armaments works ever since. In 1885 Baron Arent Silfversparre (1856–1902) joined the staff and would direct the technical aspects of the armaments works for the next seventeen years. A graduate of the Institute of Technology (where he was a friend of Jonas Henrik Kjellberg), he had then worked in Thorsten Nordenfelt's Guns and Ammunition Company in England in 1880–85. An obvious aristocrat wearing a short, dark beard and sporting a twirled mustache, he had a brusque manner and the "look of an eagle," but this cofounder of the modern Bofors was also an extremely able technician. Among his innovations was a new method for calculating ballistics, one still used in the middle of the following century. He was one of the few Swedes of a peaceful century to be certifiably entitled to enter Valhalla, mortally wounded at the testing of a cannon not made at Bofors and one that he had advised against using (1902).[27]

AB Bofors-Gullspång paid its stockholders no dividends for twenty years while it was being transformed into a major European armaments works. The personnel had to be trained, mistakes were made, some customers lost confidence, and some Swedish military and state authorities thought the foreign manufacture superior. While attention continued to be focused on military production, its relative output of pig iron dropped; Uddeholm, Domnarvet and Degerfors were all ahead of it. As much as any Swedish company, says Steckzén, the Bofors staff tasted "both the bitterness of desperation and the happiness of progress."[28] Carl Ossian Kjellberg (1825–1891), whose steadfast financial support had kept the bold venture going, died in 1891, and Jonas, his son, took over control of a Bofors that continued to operate at a loss. Some of the debt to the Kjellbergs was written off by them, but manifestly the emerging armaments works required more capital than they could muster.

Although Alfred Nobel had been looking for an armaments factory to buy, he thought Finspång too old-fashioned; Ekman had, in fact, hoped to escape his own predicament by selling to Nobel, but "to Ekman's great disappointment no purchase took place."[29] Instead, Nobel bought up the Bofors stock and injected two and a half million kronor into it for additional modernization; he died two years after obtaining control (1896). The Kjellbergs returned, financially backed by Theodor Mannheimer and his Skandinaviska Kreditaktiebolag. Had this not occurred, it would have gone, very probably, to Palmer's Shipbuilding Co., which was eager to buy Nobel's shares in the liquidation of his estate. This was one of a number of attempted or actual takeovers by foreign interests in these years, and, now that they were approaching financial self-sufficiency, the Swedes were again becoming acutely perturbed about them.

As for Finspång, purchased by W. Beardmore of Glasgow in 1902, it passed under the control of its old arch-rival, Bofors, in 1905. War materiel production continued for a few years, but this work was then all transferred to Bofors. Refrigerators ("Loke," John Weyland's construction) were made for a time. In 1913 part of the plant was purchased for the manufacture of Ljungström steam turbines (STAL), and ancient Finspång thus regained a place in the mainstream of Swedish industrial life.

Husqvarna Vapenfabrik was another weapons factory, one of five in Sweden in the eighteenth century. In the 1870s it, too, faced a mortal crisis, of going over to new lines of production if it was to survive. Here also the personal element bulked large, the question being whether the leaders could move with the times rapidly and decisively enough in adapting to the new technology and industrial forms of manufacturing.

Husqvarna had been built beside the rushing rapids of a stream descending from the green, forested hills of the Småland plateau to the southern end of Lake Vättern (1689). Jönköping, the future center for the Swedish match industry, lay close by to the west. The sylvan peace of this rural landscape was repeatedly shattered by explosions at the gunpowder shop (1726, 1734, 1741, 1758, 1761, 1765, 1767, 1770, 1771, 1772, 1775!), and in 1792 the entire plant blew up, causing damage as far away as Jönköping. This last detonation so discouraged Göran Ehrenpreus, the owner, that he sought and received permission from the Crown to close the powder works. The gun factory, where somewhat over 200 laborers made about 2,000 guns a year, continued in operation at Husqvarna for another three-quarters of a century.[30]

Its venerable trademark consisted of an ornate "h" within a circle and surmounted by a crown, the latter derived from the days when it had been a state-owned enterprise. From 1820 until 1867, when it became a company, it was owned by the Sture family. Husqvarna had lustrous pretensions, as witness the aristocratic and notable industrialist names on the board of directors then or later: Ankarcrona, Reuterskiöld, Tham, Tamm, von Platen, Rosen, af Ugglas, Ekman, Gyllenstierna, Arvid Lindman. Its ancient antecedents and assertions of high status were, however, of little protection when the state stopped ordering guns from the newly organized company.

It had tried. It had responded with alacrity to the transformation of the Rifle Factory in Eskilstuna by summoning Lindblad to transform its handicraft manufacturing into the assembly line and interchangeable parts production of a modern factory. Nevertheless, the greatly increased output at the Rifle Factory rendered Husqvarna redundant, the state no longer needing its guns. Its last large order came in 1867, and the number of firearms delivered shrank each year thereafter until production ceased entirely in 1877. Husqvarna had learned, among other things, that having only one specialty could be dangerous.

Confronted by the utter necessity for change, the natural recourse is to make the minimum alterations by going to a related field. In this case, why not make sports guns for sale to the general public? In 1877 Husqvarna manufactured 1,635 hunting rifles and other weapons, a figure that rose to over 4,000 annually by 1885 and over 5,000 by 1900. Once burnt, the leaders cast about for a second article requiring a similar mode of manufacturing, the making of replaceable parts before assembling, and one that promised good profits. In the United States the original trio had been weapons, reapers, and sewing machines. In 1872 the Husqvarna directors decided to go into factory production of sewing machines, hoping to make about 6,000 a year.[31]

Victor Ankarcrona, managing director in 1867–76, sent an engineer to the United States to study their manufacture, choose a model, buy the necessary factory machinery, and recruit some skilled workers for Husqvarna. A new foundry was built to make the parts. But the new machine they called Nordstjernan (North Star), based on the chosen model (Weed), failed to sell in the Swedish market. (The Weed Sewing Machine Co. of Hartford, Connecticut, incidentally, followed the common pattern, stemming technologically from Sharps Rifle Works and later going on to manufacture bicycles.) Husqvarna, committed by its expensive reconstruction, had a major crisis on its hands.[32]

Hugo Tamm, taking over as managing director, consulted with Gustaf Wilhelm Tham, head engineer at Ankarsrum, and the latter agreed to move to Husqvarna as managing director in early 1877. The original model was dropped, and Husqvarna began manufacturing, on license, the ever-popular Singer sewing machine for both family and clothing factory use. Only 708 machines were made in 1877, but the figure had risen to nearly 5,000 annually by 1880 and had passed 10,000 before 1890. Husqvarna paid no dividends between 1877 and 1880, but by then Tham had turned the company around, and it had passed its crisis.

G. W. Tham and Hugo Tamm were actually both members of the same extended family, descendants of Sebastian Volrathson Tham (1666–1729), who as a son of an immigrant from Saxony had founded the family fortune. Several of his descendants were involved in the Swedish East India Company. Per Adolf Tham (1774–1856), one of several noblemen who renounced their noble titles in 1800 in protest against government policies, then changed his name to Tamm. The father of the new Husqvarna leader had served as the last *bergshauptmann* of Stora Kopparbergs Bergslaget, and a brother, Vollrath, will be met as an important figure in the development of the Swedish iron ore fields. Gustaf Wilhelm Tham (1839–1911) studied at Marieberg and Motala, worked as a draftsman in several shipyards in England and Scotland, and then became an engineer at Motala. From here he moved to Ankarsrum as head engineer and managing director. Harry Kolare wrote of the goateed, increasingly bald manager that "he was a whopper of a man (*baddare*) for ordaining and directing things." Under his long direction (1877–1911), Husqvarna became a large industrial company in which the number of workers rose from 181 to 1,517.[33]

In addition to pursuing the making of sports guns and putting sewing machine manufacturing on a successful basis, Tham initiated the production of various kinds of household goods, a list that would lengthen over the years: pots and pans, pressing irons, waffle irons, meat grinders, coffee grinders, kerosene stoves, cooking and heating stoves, radiators, lawn clippers. Today the Husqvarna emblem still appears on some of them. In order to compete with foreign-made goods, a series of retail outlets was opened for direct sales to the public; by 1914 its own exports, mostly to other Scandinavian countries and Russia, amounted to about a third of its production. After watching the growing demand for bicycles in England, Germany, and the United States, the management decided that this was more than a fad and began manufacturing them (1896). Bicycles, of course, fitted the Husqvarna factory system of interchangeable parts and assembly line, and hundreds of thousands of them would ultimately be sold; Husqvarna took another step forward by introducing motorcycles, at first based on foreign models, in 1908. Refrigerators would in time become another important part of its production. Husqvarna had successfully made the transition to a place in the modern economy and by the middle of the twentieth century was employing about 5,000 workers.

Fagersta, founded in 1662 in the heart of Bergslagen in the province of Västmanland, enjoyed a much less stormy entry into the industrial age than some of the foregoing. The digging of the Strömsholm canal in 1776–92, giving water access to Mälaren to the south, and the canal's further improvement in 1842–60 greatly assisted its revival and growth, particularly since no railroad reached it until 1900. Its modernization was the work of Thomas and Christian Aspelin, father and son, who took an unimportant and deteriorating bar iron works and raised it to a position of considerable repute as a maker of high-quality steel.

The Aspelins have been mentioned before as successful entrepreneurs in the tobacco industry, the revenue of which enabled Thomas, one of the richest men in Sweden, to purchase Fagersta and three small associated *bruk* in 1852. Thomas first installed a Franche-Comté furnace and five Lancashire hearths, but then Göransson's success with Bessemer steel prompted imitation, the more so since some of the experimentation took place at Västanfors, one of the Fagersta-owned *bruk*. After a few years of pioneering travail, the Aspelins could claim to own Sweden's second iron works, after Sandviken, to depend largely on the Bessemer process.[34] Once good-quality steel had been attained, a new rolling mill was added, and in 1870 Fagersta began making saw blades, circle saws, and gun barrels, and later also drawn wire and springs. Five large open-hearth Martin furnaces replaced the Bessemers in the 1880s and 1890s, and the earlier process was entirely dropped in 1897; three years later an electric rolling mill began production.

Christian Aspelin (1830–1919) found a novel way to advertise his steel. In 1873 he hired David Kirkaldy (London) to experiment with methods of testing steel; the results were sent to the 1876 Philadelphia exposition, with satisfactory attendant publicity for Fagersta. More testing followed, and Johan Brinell (1849–1925), coming to Fagersta from Lesjöfors as chief engineer in 1882, attained a world reputation with his studies of iron and steel, thereby adding luster to his firm. His device for measuring the hardness of a metal by means of a steel ball pressed into the metal received the Grand Prix at the Paris Exposition (1900) and went into worldwide usage.[35]

In 1907, after thirty-four years as *brukspatron*, Christian Aspelin sold Fagersta's 500 shares, each valued at 5,000 kronor, to Olof A. Söderberg of Söderberg & Haak. The financier shifted 152 of them to L. Possehl & Co. of Lübeck and 58 more to another man closely associated with that company.

That is, Fagersta passed under foreign control, and by 1914 Possehl owned nearly all the shares. The big attraction for the German company lay in Fagersta holding the majority stock in the Dannemora mines in northern Uppland, containing some of the purest iron in the world, and where Louis De Geer and his compatriots had introduced the Walloon method of iron handling in the seventeenth century. Possehl, which owned a blast furnace in Lübeck and a steel mill in Russia, had already acquired mines in Dalarna (including Idkerberget) and had bought up some shares of stock in Trafik AB Oxelösund, engaged in exporting iron ore from the Grängesberg ore fields to Germany.[36]

During the First World War, according to George Seldes in his sensationalized and by no means always accurate *Iron, Blood and Profits* (1934), the Possehl works in Lübeck made munitions for the Germans, the Possehl steel mill in Russia helped the Russian war effort, and Fagersta sold to both sides.[37] Afterward, however, Possehl was ruined by the postwar German inflation and lost its Swedish holdings (1923). Svenska Handelsbanken, which had been extending large credits, gained control of Fagersta and its related enterprises, and a big expansion would follow in the 1930s.

The list of ancient enterprises that survived the transition could be considerably augmented. The smelted copper from Stora Kopparbergs Bergslaget had been sent downstream to Avesta for refining and manufacture into copper ware; the Crown established its copper mint there (1644–1831). Louis De Geer, introducing the Walloon method, founded Österby in the Dannemora country (1643), and Hubert de Besche started Ankarsrum in 1655–59. Iggesund dated back to 1685, and Ramnäs had been founded in 1590. All except Avesta were typical *brukspatron* principalities until the formation of modern companies, owned for two or more generations by the De Geer, Grill, Tamm, Tersmeden, or de Maré families. In the eighteenth century Iggesund and Österby both belonged to Claes Grill (1705–1767), proprietor of Sweden's largest merchant house for a time.

Sometimes high drama hides behind the old names. Per Adolf Tamm, the man who renounced his noble title and changed his name from Tham, had been a war hero and his sloop had been shot out from under him in the battle of Svensksund (1790). When he discarded his noble title, the authorities stripped him of his military rank also. He rode home to Söderfors so furiously that he ruined his horse, which he then shot at the home gate as a gesture that he was leaving the military forever. Some years later his aunt, Anna Johanna Grill, turned "elegant Österby" over to him, and here he "ruled for fifty happy years over his kingdom." Karl XIV Johan restored him to the nobility in 1826, and he became a baron in 1843.[38] Österby had another distinction, in terms of personalities, as the birthplace of Arvid Lindman, the most prominent industrialist to become prime minister (1906–11); among his various positions, he succeeded his father as managing director of Iggesund (1892–1903).

All five enterprises made the transition to modern industry, though some of them were in serious financial difficulties for a time. Iggesund, possessing large forest tracts, was one of the numerous iron works to go over to sawmills, then to cellulose and paper-making, though it was still making saw blades, planing steel, and mining tools and did not close its charcoal hearth until 1953. At Avesta a bar iron works gradually replaced the refining of copper, and it survived the misadventures of Hjalmar Petré to become a substantial iron works; by 1914 it had two blast furnaces and three Martins. Stainless steel would be its later specialty. (A casual visitor today will be startled to see a herd of bison grazing in its northern meadows, but that is another story.) Österby, still extracting Dannemora ore, went over to the manufacture of various kinds of steel. At Ramnäs the Tersmedens put in a rolling mill in 1868 and in the 1870s began introducing a rather wide variety of engineering products. A chain factory was started in 1880. Ankarsrum gave up its iron works entirely in 1911, after 250 years, because of the long-distance transport of ore and the rising cost of charcoal. In a brave attempt to cope, the de Marés had installed Lundin and Martin furnaces and a rolling mill. However, by the 1880s they were also diversifying into what in time led to a great variety of wares: heating and cooking stoves ("Viking"), radiators, drinking fountains, milk cans, bathtubs, frying pans, and much more. In 1884 it also started an enameling shop, bringing in skilled German workers for the purpose; through its enameled signs for streets, railroads, and stores, Ankarsrum put its mark on every town and village in the country.

3. TOWARD AN INDUSTRIAL SWEDEN

12. NETWORKS: TELEPHONES AND ELECTRIC POWER

Another wave of innovations—telephone, chemical cellulose, electric lights, and generators—began to arrive in the 1870s. Hydroelectric installations would ultimately proliferate, as would sulphate and sulphite cellulose plants and a chemical industry. Sweden's phosphorus-rich iron ore became accessible with the introduction of the Thomas-Gilchrist process. A whole series of special industries would emerge out of Swedish inventions of telephones, separators, steam turbines, dynamite, and numerous other devices and processes.

Capital from the export of timber, iron, and grain had helped to accelerate the gathering momentum of industrialization. Farm products still made up about a quarter of the exports in 1881–90, but sank to 14.1 percent in 1901–10; grain virtually ceased to be exported, replaced largely by such dairy products as butter and cheese. About two-fifths of the exports in 1881–85 consisted of timber, then the proportion dropped to 26.1 percent by 1911–13, while iron and steel declined from 16.2 to 9.3. The appearance of new sources for export constitutes a major part of the story in these decades; iron ore (8 percent of the total by 1911–13), paper and cellulose (17.6) and, as a consequence of the inventions, products from the engineering works (10.5). Sweden's national income rose from an average of 781.4 million kronor in 1864–73 to about 3,300 million in 1914, the most rapid percentile expansion occurring in 1869–78 and after 1894. Real wages more than doubled; with 39 as the figure for 1860, they had risen to 87 by 1915. Even in the relatively depressed conditions of the 1880s, the total output continued to increase.[1]

Stockholm's *Dagens Nyheter,* reporting a speech by Lord Kelvin on September 30, 1876, seems to have made the first Swedish mention of the telephone. He had been a judge at the 1876 Philadelphia exposition, where it had competed for public attention with such other miracles of the miraculous 1870s as electric lights, the binder, musical and printing telegraphs, and novel machine tools. Now, addressing the British Association, Lord Kelvin lauded the newly invented Alexander Graham Bell telephone, though the London *Times* considered it "the latest American humbug."[2]

The Americans, once they grasped the financial possibilities, organized about 125 companies in three years, many of them by promoters much more interested in peddling humbug, in the form of shares of stock, than in offering service. In the summer of 1877 J.S.K. Hopstock, a Norwegian engineer who soon would become the Bell agent for Scandinavia, showed King Oscar II a model; one of those who probably talked into the apparatus was a man by the name of L.M. Ericsson, who would subsequently make millions of them. His first two were put together for Henrik Cedergren, who wished to communicate between his home and his jewelry store; a telegraph worker strung up Sweden's first telephone line between the two buildings (1877). That same year the indefatigable telegraph man, Henric Öller, made some Bell telephones and so did Hjalmar and Hakon Brunius, clients of his, in Jönköping.

Before the end of 1877 the firm of Numa Peterson had ordered and received a few Bell telephones from the United States on behalf of several Stockholm businessmen following Cedergren's example. By 1879 sufficient subscribers for telephones had been found in the city for two former commissioners of the Stockholm telegraph office and a third man, Gustaf Lybeck, to contact the International Bell Telephone Company in New York. Assuming the name of Stockholm Bell Telefonaktiebolag, it opened the first Swedish telephone station for 121 subscribers on September 1, 1880. Service cost 160 kronor "between the bridges" (most of the then downtown area) and 240 to 280 beyond this perimeter; the Bell-Blake apparatus was being used, the Blake half consisting of an improved transmitter by Francis Blake.[3]

Henrik Cedergren had been one of the first to subscribe to the telephone company, but he soon concluded that the charges were excessive. Receiving no response to his complaint from the Bell company, he invited others to join him in setting up the Stockholm General Telephone Co. (Stockholms Allmänna Telefon AB), hoping to reduce prices by securing large numbers of subscribers. Cedergren was an 1875 engineering graduate of the Institute of Technology, but, afflicted with heart trouble, he thought himself fated to run the jewelry store started by his father. Now, when no one else came forward to assume the leadership, he took the initiative himself and so was launched on a highly successful career as an industrial pioneer. Cedergren became managing director of the new company, whose first station went into operation at the end of October 1883. The next year it passed Bell in total subscribers, whereupon Bell lowered its rates.

Obviously the General company would not be able to buy Bell telephones. L. M. Ericsson, however, was delighted to furnish it with his model, an arrangement that led to a long association between Ericsson and Cedergren and that would bring Sweden an "honoring and advantageous" world industry.[4] Lars Magnus Ericsson (1846–1926) was a self-made, self-educated son of a poor peasant, one of the few in Sweden before 1900 to rise to the top without the advantage of a generation or two of family successes. His first job was sharpening boring tools at a silver mine, and later he worked in an iron *bruk* as a smith. At the age of twenty he got his big chance when he was taken on by Henric Öller, in whose telegraph shop over the next six years he learned the skills necessary for his future *métier.* Given a state *stipendium* to study abroad, he spent some of the time at exactly the right place—Siemens & Halske in Germany; Ericsson finished his European tour in Moscow at an electrical exhibition in a country where much later he would manufacture telephones.[5]

Back in Stockholm in the spring of 1876, he borrowed a thousand kronor to start a shop. Mostly engaged in making telegraph apparatus for police and fire departments, and also semaphores for the railroad, he was a man looking for something to manufacture, and here, in his own field of rapid communications, came the telephone.[6] In 1878–79 he persuaded friends to stake him to 10,000 kronor for the purpose of competing with Bell. He had married a lady as energetic as himself; she wrapped the spools for his early phones and for years headed this division of the firm. In January 1881 Ericsson offered for sale a micro-telephone apparatus he had been working on, and in May he sold a switchboard for fifty telephones to Norrköping. As orders flooded in, Ericsson opened a new plant on Tulegatan in Stockholm (1884) that later grew into a large complex of buildings. The first automatic switchboard appeared in 1886, developed by Ericsson and Cedergren.

The Telegraph Service (Telegrafverket) had assumed, like telegraph authorities everywhere, that the telephone was a "talking telegraph" and therefore fell within its realm of operations. Late in 1881 it installed a network of telephones for the government offices in the capital city, and two years later Bell and the Telegraph Service opened traffic between their respective lines. The appearance of Cedergren's company made three competing systems in the city. This lively rivalry contributed to Stockholm in 1885 having 4,832 phones, compared to London's 4,193 and Paris' 4,054.[7] At the end of 1887 General Telephone served 3,864 apparatus in the city, the telegraph agency operated 1,965, and Bell only 1,052, and soon thereafter Stockholm General absorbed Bell by procuring a majority of its stock.

Nor did Bell compete successfully in other Swedish cities. When the inventor visited Sweden in 1880 plans were made to furnish service to seven other towns, but the company managed to do so only in Gothenburg, Malmö, and Sundsvall. Its high rates, and very likely some antagonism to foreign ownership, doomed its ventures. Bell's price in Gothenburg, 160 kronor, soon brought the appearance of a rival, the General Telephone Society (Allmänna Telefonföreningen), which charged its members 50 kronor (later, 60) for the apparatus and telephone installations. Bell soon relinquished its holdings in Malmö to a cooperative society. A local company began operations in Norrköping, and cooperatives, providing its members service at the cheapest possible rates, were organized in Gävle, Örebro, Eskilstuna, Västerås, and

Linköping. Thirty-seven more local networks were set up during the next three years, most of them by cooperatives; 78 of the 93 towns and cities had telephone service by the end of 1887.[8] Bell had also invaded Norway in 1880, but had to yield to similar cooperatives, which quickly spread all over the country.

L. M. Ericsson delivered the apparatus to these Swedish groups. Gävle, in which the first of the societies organized, held a competition to see which phone to adopt. At first, in the contest, Ericsson's model would not function, but then it was discovered, so the story goes, that someone had sabotaged the instrument by putting the broken end of a pencil in the mechanism.[9] Ericsson's victory in Gävle quickly led to the adoption of his phone in the other cooperatives.

Public demand for long-distance service naturally followed. The General companies of Stockholm and Gothenburg connected clusters of neighboring towns into larger networks, as did the Gothenburg Bell while still in existence. The Örebro group provided long-distance lines for about twenty local telephone societies in the adjoining provinces. In 1888 Stockholm General sought state permission to set up service between Gothenburg, Malmö, Örebro, Sundsvall, and Stockholm. The state-owned Telegraph Service, however, remonstrated vigorously to this attempt by private enterprise to create, in probable result, a national system. The Telegraph Service had attempted from the beginning to start local branches, but its lack of funds and high rates persuaded numerous town or regional groups to organize their own. It did open in Härnösand and Uddevalla in 1882, and in the next two years it bought out two groups in southern Sweden, including the cooperative that had already bought out Bell in Malmö. Fifteen more local telephone systems, mostly in Bergslagen and in the northern Baltic seaports, had been established by the Telegraph Service by 1887. To protect its own interests, it had also created several interurban lines.[10]

When Stockholm General proposed long-distance lines in 1888, the Telegraph Service had compelling reasons for fighting back. The telegraph suffered increasing losses because its former customers now used interurban telephones. Where telephone and telegraph wires were close together, telegraph messages could sometimes be picked up by telephone, thereby jeopardizing security of communications. Telephone poles sometimes encroached upon space needed by the telegraph. No doubt the bureaucratic mentality contributed to the urge to absorb private lines and impose uniform regulations and technical standards on a national system, but the officials of the state-owned company believed that it could offer better service, better apparatus, more capital for improvements, and the advantage of connections over the entire kingdom.[11]

Policies varied somewhat among the major European countries in the establishment of telephone systems. The German postmaster-general made it a government monopoly from the start and ran it like the post office. The British postmaster-general assumed that the telephone was a variety of the telegraph and took over the fledgling private companies. Lawsuits followed, private companies were licensed, these were merged into one by competition, and in 1911 the post office annexed the whole system. The French government virtually expropriated the private companies in 1889; according to Herbert S. Casson, busily extolling the virtues of private enterprise in a biography of Alexander Graham Bell (1910), France then "assembled the most complete assortment of other nation's mistakes and invented several of its own."[12] In most countries the state ultimately took over privately owned networks. Though off to a successful start by private companies and cooperatives, the Swedes in time followed the trend.

Private enterprise in Sweden had not been tempted by the telegraph because it was not profitable; no law had been needed to keep it a state monopoly, which in turn made it legally more difficult to suppress private enterprises in the telephone sphere of communications. A royal order (1883) forbidding local private concerns to set up long-distance lines had been repeatedly ignored, and in 1888 the Telegraph Service took legal action against those who had violated the order. It also constructed a Stockholm—Gothenburg line, connected Stockholm and Malmö (with intervening cities), and within three years had installed long-distance service to the northern seaports.

Financial necessity now forced the Telegraph Service to coercive measures in order to take over private concerns in the towns and regions. The long-distance lines were expensive to put up and maintain, and their revenue by no means met expenses. Consequently, it needed to acquire the profitable local service in order to balance its finances and keep long-distance service relatively cheap. Money from the Riksdag was now forthcoming, enabling it to absorb most of the networks. Bell in Gothenburg sold out to the Telegraph Service in 1888, and in 1896 that city's General, having only 996 subscribers, also capitulated. The other private companies and cooperatives were mostly bought out in the years when, notably, the state was assuming control over private enterprises in a number of European countries. Stockholm's General held out until 1918, when the Telegraph Service purchased it for 47 million kronor, leaving only a few scattered companies still outside the national system.

Its early purchases of equipment came from Bell, then from L. M. Ericsson, but it started its own factory in 1891. Ericsson was too busy to meet the demand, and for a time Cedergren also ran a separate factory. In 1895 Ericsson patented a world novelty, a simplified telephone that combined the speaking and audio elements in one single instrument, which was subsequently adopted everywhere. The next year he established Aktiebolaget L. M. Ericsson & Co.; the inventor kept the majority of the stock, but he also distributed some shares to his foremen and older employees.

Stockholm General began placing its clutter of urban poles and wires underground in 1895, about a dozen years after Boston and New York. The cables came from a factory making copper telephone wires that had been started by the German-born Max Sievert in collaboration with the Max Vogel cable factory in Berlin. Another important contributor to the Swedish telephone was Ansgar Betulander (1872–1941), originally employed at the Telegraph Service, who obtained over 300 patents on his automatic telephones, switchboards, and relay stations.[13]

While the Telegraph Service conquered the Swedish telephone domain, Cedergren and Ericsson were being forced to invest abroad by its growing stranglehold on the Swedish market. Cedergren found his opportunity in Russia when the Bell franchise expired in five large cities. A contract for an eighteen year concession in Moscow and Warsaw was signed with the Swedish-Danish-Russian Telephone Co. on November 20, 1900, and that this happened to be the 200th anniversary of the Swedish victory over the Russians at Narva added relish to the occasion. Cedergren's General Telephone Co. held 40 percent of the shares, Stockholms Enskilda Bank owned 32.5, the Danes 12.5, and the French most of the remainder. (In Warsaw the Cedergren Tower, long the tallest structure in the city, became the center for heavy fighting during the Warsaw uprising in the Second World War.) In 1909 the Mexican government granted a similar company the telephone franchise; General Telephone held a fifth, Marcus Wallenberg a fifth, and AB L. M. Ericsson the other three-fifths. Other companies were founded in Spain, Turkey, and South American countries.

Still managing director of Stockholm General, Cedergren died in 1909, having, despite his bad heart, enjoyed phenomenal success. Casson, writing the year after his death, said that only one European country, Sweden, had properly "caught the telephone spirit," and much of this was due to having "a Man, a business-builder of remarkable force and ability, named Henry Cedergren." Oddly enough, Casson did not even mention L. M. Ericsson, much better known by posterity.[14]

L. M. Ericsson found another opportunity in St. Petersburg, where his company erected a six-story structure that stretched for a full city block (1900). Other factories were built in England (Beeston), Vienna, Budapest, and Paris. His company installed telephone stations in Riga, The Hague, Moscow, Singapore, Rotterdam, and Mexico City. By 1960 L. M. Ericsson & Co. headed sixty companies in eighty countries with annual sales of nearly $200 million a year. Meanwhile, Ivar Kreuger, the Match King, had gotten control of the gigantic enterprise; when his financial situation worsened, he sold 600,000 shares to IT&T, and it took the younger Marcus Wallenberg (1899–1982) twenty-nine years to regain full Swedish control of this company.[15] L. M. Ericsson, who began his "saga-like career" as a common laborer and ended up as the chief of a world industry, retired to a country estate in 1900 at the age of fifty, worn out by his labors. A silent, melancholy man, apparently suffering an inferiority complex and driven by a compulsion to work and to prove himself, he was totally absorbed in his work. Though his personality has been attributed to his harsh early beginnings, quite possibly he was just being very Swedish. A calm, patriarchal figure, decent almost to excess, he cared so little for honors or ceremonies that he did not even own an evening dress suit.[16] For the Swedes, moving toward becoming an industrialized nation, the telephone had particular significance. They had responded immediately to the new invention and then made their own contributions to its improvement. They were coming of age, were pulling abreast of the most advanced countries in technology and industry, and the consequences were or soon would be evident in several other developments. In the period between 1870 and 1914 the Swedes, formerly the recipients and adapters of imported technology, in turn began to export their own technological innovations and products from industrialized factories.

In approximately the same years as the arrival of the telephone, several individuals responded with alacrity to the invention of the light bulb, generator, and methods of long-distance transmission of electricity. Here, also, the Swedes would make innovative contributions. For the country as a whole, lacking much coal and having the potential for abundant hydroelectric power, the harnessing of electricity, the introduction of "white coal," helped to ease the vexing fuel problem during its great industrial expansion after 1890.

First came arc lights, in which two sticks of carbon, not quite touching, produced a bright light when current crossed the gap between them. The British staged an illumination in Trafalgar Square as early as 1845, but they did not become practicable until the development of a strong enough generator in the 1860s. Moses G. Farmer displayed three glaring arc lights at the Philadelphia exposition, and Paul Joblochkoff placed some arc lights on Parisian streets in 1877. The American Charles F. Brush began to make them commercially, and lower Broadway in New York was lit by his lights in the fall of 1878.

Korsnäs, which had been one of the earliest to use gaslights, put up Serrins arc lights (French) to illuminate the work area at its Näs sawmill in 1878, and a Stockholm café attracted attention and customers by using them.[17] The illumination was too glaring, however, to be comfortably enjoyed in a room, and they would be most often used at open-air public occasions. Hakon Brunius, the "little lively and alert" man who has sometimes been called Sweden's first electrician, put on a display in Jönköping in 1879, using Serrins arc lamps and a Gramme generator driven by a 4-hp steam engine. When he started a small power station there several years later, something went wrong with the machinery, and Jönköping, naturally encouraged by the local gaslight company, delayed installing electricity until 1905–07. Also in 1879 he linked a Gramme apparatus to a steam engine in Borås and shone lights from a factory roof.[18] His generator had come from France, invented by the Belgian, Théophile Gramme, in Paris in 1870.

The most conspicuous of these public displays, put on by enthusiasts to advertise electric lighting, occurred in Stockholm when King Oscar II departed for the marriage of Crown Prince Gustav in Karlsruhe (September 16, 1881). It was arranged by Ludvig Fredholm and Georg Wenström, the former just back from studying street lighting in England. They installed sixteen Brush arc lamps, with generators from Brush's Anglo-American company, on Gustav Adolfs Torg, Norrbro, and Mynttorget. These were kept in place for several months, and some incandescent light bulbs were also mounted, the first in Sweden. (Thomas Edison, adept at showmanship, staged spectacular displays in Paris in 1881 and in London at the beginning of 1882.) Soon some light bulbs of the Lane-Fox system were put up at the Strömparterre and in the government finance offices. Another advertising spectacle occurred in the autumn of 1882 when the first searchlight, mounted on the Mosebacke hill that overlooks central Stockholm from the south, began shooting its rays toward the city, this the work of Johan Erik Erikson.

Erikson represented Siemens & Halske, whose Werner von Siemens, brother of the inventor of the Siemens-Martin iron process, had greatly contributed to the development of a practicable generator. Schuckert & Co. of Nuremberg had John Luth as its agent, and J. W. T. Olán served on behalf of Edison. Ludvig Fredholm, as the above exploit indicates, had ties at the time with Brush and the Anglo-American Electric Light Company.[19] That is, behind the early rivalry of these men lay the competing interests of several foreign companies seeking to enter the potential Swedish market.

Johan Erik Erikson (1838–1883), another alumnus of Nyköpings Mek. Verkstad, seemed to have the early advantage. In 1882 he helped to set up Sweden's first hydroelectric project at the Rydal spinnery (founded, it may be recalled, by Sven Erikson), consisting of two large arc lamps and a generator powered by the big water turbine that also turned the textile machinery. In 1882 and 1883 J. E. Erikson's workers furnished lighting at Kockums, Boxholm bruk, and the Reymersholm cotton factory. They also put arc lights at the Slussen locks and vicinity. Apparently thanks to knowing the king, Erikson received the contract for lighting the royal palace (1883f.); in 1963 the wires and fixtures at the palace still dated, at the latest, from 1892, and it cost 600,000 kronor to replace one of Sweden's worst fire hazards. E. G. Beskow, who directed Erikson's projects, once installed lights in the royal yacht. Oscar II thought them very pretty until he bumped his head against one of the protruding mermaid light fixtures. He rubbed his head, glared at Beskow, then said, "Yes, I forgive you because you are so damned short. I am tall, and that one should take into consideration."

Erikson himself, never in good health, died in 1883, but his company, continuing the Siemens & Halske connection during the next years, placed lights in the parliament building and on a street leading to the palace, and it also built a power station (1887) to deliver electricity to the 4,000 light bulbs in Gamla Stan. At the time of Erikson's death he was having, as biographer Rune Kjellander delicately put it, such matrimonial problems that the Stockholmers tended to forget his very genuine technical contributions. He had, incidentally, been one of those who tried to invent the telephone, in Paris back in 1867 where he collaborated with Count Sparre of Söfdeborg in an unsuccessful effort.[20]

Although having some gaslighting until 1920, Gothenburg could also claim to have been the second city in Europe, after Milan, to possess a permanently electrified area supplied by a generator station (1884). An engineer with the state railroad, Edvard Bildt, rented a basement and there set up Sweden's first generating station, equipped with three small generators driven by three small engines, later replaced by a larger (120-hp) one. The luxury stores in the business area availed themselves of the novelty, but, with few customers, he gave up after a year. His creditors resumed the service as Göteborgs Elektriska AB, lighting about a thousand incandescent bulbs. Three rivals, including Brunius, appeared, and rates dropped so low that they were all in trouble; like the telephone, excessive competition did lead to a rapid increase in customers. Härnösand, however, became the first Swedish town, in 1885, to light its streets from a central generating station. In that year about one-half of the nearly one hundred electric light installations in Sweden were in the two largest cities and over four-fifths of the generators were being driven by small steam engines.[21]

Thomas Edison, after exhaustive search and experimenting, produced in 1879 a carbon filament lamp, using carbonized thread, that lasted for about forty hours, but more years would elapse before he had his incandescent light bulb perfected. Jonas Wenström in Sweden, when he heard of Edison's original feat, declared that the invention "by glowing carbon filaments is the same thing that I happened upon a year ago."[22] Several other persons in different countries thought that they had "invented" the light bulb. Joseph Swan (England) had by far the best claim, having worked on a glow bulb, using platinum or carbon, since 1860; his lamp gave a better light than Edison's, but it used more electricity and did not last as long.

Robert Wilhelm Strehlenert (1863–1935) started making carbon incandescent light bulbs in Södertälje in 1885, the filaments coming from the American Edison Co. Son of a Stockholm architect, he had graduated from the Institute of Technology before working in Taunton, Massachusetts, and New York for perhaps a year and a half. At one point he watched Edison light bulbs being made, and he also observed Edward Weston trying to make collodion out of cellulose and thus, by coagulation, getting thread. In Södertälje the neighbors complained about the danger of fire, and in 1887 Strehlenert moved his shop, then employing only ten workers, to Stockholm; for the next few years he fought to gain a foothold against keen German competition. He had originally used German glassblowers to make the bulbs, but then secured them from a Swedish glass works. He visited Germany at the beginning of the 1890s when cellulose collodion, which gave a more even thread, was coming into practical use, and he also attended the Chicago World Fair (1893) on a state *stipendium*. By 1892 Strehlenert had developed his own cellulose collodion filaments.[23] Although his plant was making two to three thousand bulbs a day, the hard competition reduced him to bankruptcy in 1895, and he thereafter turned his inventive skills to artificial silk (financed, briefly, by Alfred Nobel) and later to sulphite debris.

His two Swedish rivals entered the field from associated activities. The son and heir of the previously mentioned J. W. Bergström, photographer and manufacturer of pipes and sanitary conveniences, founded the factory that as Glödlampfabrik Svea, would be taken over by Gustaf de Laval and grow into one of the largest in Europe. The other rival, Wilhelm Wiklund (1832–1902), had been inspired to make the effort by the return of a Swede (C. A. Backström) from the United States with ideas for a somewhat different bulb (1891), but German imports, despite some protective tariff, were still too competitive, and Wiklund closed his factory in 1899.[24] He had originally been working with gaslights, but followed the fortunes of the time by going over to electricity (1883). One of his projects, at the Skutskär sawmill, is of interest because the direct current from a Schuckert generator had to be transmitted three and a half kilometers to the mill and because Svante Arrhenius, the great Swedish electrochemist, was involved in the project. Wiklund's attempt to manufacture a direct current generator, patented by Aron Thorins, failed by reason of too many defects. It would be ASEA that would produce the successful generators in Sweden.

At the age of fifty Ludvig Fredholm (1830–1891) was looking for a new career after serving for many years as the bookkeeper for the family's shipyard and fleet of sailing vessels. After the shipyard had been sold in 1863, he joined the Guilletmot & Weylandt merchant firm, but it had to close in the later 1870s. Fredholm, now at loose ends, would go from a shipping industry that was becoming obsolescent to, after a banking interlude, the most modern of industries.[25]

He saw the possibilities of electricity in England in 1880 and intended, originally, to serve as agent for the Anglo-American Electric Light Company in Scandinavia. The demonstration of electric lighting in Stockholm had been his idea, the actual installation being made by Georg Wenström. Another public spectacle was arranged for the Hindersmässan (the annual fair) in Örebro—illuminating the theater by electricity in the home town of the Wenströms—the idea being to attract the attention of the ironmasters in town for the festival. Here he met the brother of Georg, Jonas Wenström, for the first time and learned that he had just constructed a generator. Fredholm abandoned the Anglo-American agency and signed a contract with the inventor. The tests proving satisfactory, they founded the Elektriska AB, the beginning of ASEA, and its first workshop opened in the town of Arboga, where Fredholm had business contacts.[26]

The big international firms in electrical engineering were being founded in the 1880s and early 1890s: Oerlikon Maschinfabrik (Switzerland, 1882), AEG (Germany, 1883), Westinghouse (USA, 1886), General Electric, Ltd. (England, 1886), and General Electric (USA, 1892) as a merger of Thomson-Houston and Edison Electric. The Swedish equivalent, later customarily known as ASEA (Allmänna Svenska Elektriska Aktiebolag), appeared in 1883.

Its first equipment consisted of a lathe, a press, and a boring machine that had originally been a sewing machine. The transport system in the shop consisted of the strongest worker, a man known as "Big Lasse." (William Fairbairn's transport in his original machine shop in England in 1813 was "Murphy, a muscular Irishman.") A hand cart served for carrying goods to the railroad station; it was drawn by a worker named Broms, whose name aroused much hilarity because it means "brake" in Swedish.[27] One of the first projects involved replacing paraffin oil lamps, a fire hazard, with light bulbs and generator at the Viskafors textile mill, whose owner had earlier hired J. E. Erikson to put arc lights into the Rydal mill. By 1887 the company had manufactured 122 of Wenström's generators and mounted most of them for lighting purposes; quite often it was asked to illuminate a place for a special occasion, using a steam engine to drive the generator. By the end of the 1880s, however, the men were installing town lighting systems, and industry was becoming increasingly eager to use its services.

Georg Wenström, more interested in the problems of long-distance transmission of current than lighting, traveled in Germany, Switzerland, Italy, and France to study the several experimental approaches (1889), then founded, with Gustaf Granström (a mining expert who had accompanied him on the journey), a separate company to work on the generation and transmission of electricity. However, the Wenström and Fredholm companies soon merged as ASEA, having decided that they needed each other too much to maintain separate identities. The intense competition encountered from Siemens & Halske and from Schuckert & Co. in fact made it seem quite possible that these two might gain permanent control of the Swedish market. ASEA now moved its center of operations to Västerås, a city on Lake Mälaren with good railroad connections, where a project at the Västerås Mek. Verkstad had made O. F. Wijkman, its founder and owner, such an electrification enthusiast that he raised the money and secured the site for the new plant.[28]

Technologically, ASEA might well be said to have had an earlier background in the career of Wilhelm Wenström (1822–1901), the father of Georg and Jonas, whose work made up a quite respectable cross section of Swedish technological development during the crucial decades. Son of a pastor, he had served an apprenticeship with Gustaf Ekman at Lesjöfors and studied at the Falun School of Mines and the Institute of Technology. As a master builder and mechanic at various *bruk* he became thoroughly familiar with the problems of water power and devised a series of water turbine models to replace the water wheel. For a time, as noted earlier, he sponsored John Ericsson's caloric engine. At about the age of fifty he inaugurated his engineering consulting bureau at Örebro, conveniently near his Bergslagen clients, for whom he supervised the construction of various kinds of iron works furnaces.[29] Jonas and Georg had thus grown up in a home completely conducive to nurturing their technical interests, and they continued their father's long search for more efficient power for industry by helping to apply electricity as an alternative source. It may well be that Wilhelm made his greatest contribution by his encouragement and assistance with Jonas' inventions.

In his second year at Uppsala, Jonas was attempting to build a generator, using a spinning wheel for power. Unable to solve all the problems, he put it aside and tried to invent an incandescent light bulb, using bands of carbon; lacking the laboratory equipment to carry on, he heard of Edison's achievement with mixed feelings. A visit to a Paris exhibition in 1881, with its displays of generators and electric equipment, stimulated a renewed interest in them. Back in Örebro, where he was working on electrical techniques with his father, he quickly cleared up his old difficulties and in a week's time, with the help of his father, had a generator working. It was one of the first to have an effective magnetic circuit in the armature. Engelbrekt's Mill, where he did his experimenting, was for several weeks in February 1882 illuminated, to "the great wonder of the city's inhabitants." Now Fredholm entered the picture and secured the patent on his first generator, called *Sköldpaddan* (tortoise shell) because that was what it resembled. Later models included, among others, *Grytan* (kettle) and *Bikupan* (beehive), both named for their appearance. Another one was dubbed "Wenström's well-known."[30]

Direct current, using a generator on the premises or nearby, sufficed for lighting. It could not, however, be effectively transmitted any distance, nor did it lend itself to the large capacity necessary to power machinery. During the 1880s a number of men in different countries developed methods for generating alternating current, culminating in Nikola Tesla's use of an induction motor (1888). Alternating current could be transported at high tension over long distance, then be reduced at the place where it would be used; loss of energy during transmission, much too large in direct current, was minimized. Jonas Wenström was among those who had been working on the problem, and in 1890 he patented, and ASEA bought, his transformer for the "conversion and spread of the power through the use of three electrical alternating currents," the three-wire or three-phase system. In 1891 he visited Frankfurt to observe the epochal 175-kilometer transmission of alternating currency by a 100-kilowatt generator from Lauffen to Frankfurt. Filip Hjulström calls 1891 "the birth year for the white coal industry" because it now became practicable for industrial usage.[31]

Jonas Wenström (1855–1893) was not fated to complete his work; he had always been in poor health, and the "father of the Swedish high tension current" died in 1893 at the age of thirty-eight. It was up to another man, Ernst Danielson (1866–1907), to continue his work on alternating current. Other members of his family, it may be recalled, had made notable contributions to Swedish industry at Uddeholm and Bofors and his father had directed several enterprises. After Uppsala and the Institute of Technology, Danielson had made repeated trips to survey advances in the electrical industry in various countries; he was at Thomson-Houston, soon to become part of General Electric, in 1890–92. Having worked with Wenström off and on ever since 1883, Danielson had participated in the experimenting with alternating current. When Wenström became ill, he had to assume full responsibility, along with the problems of moving into the new quarters at Västerås. It was Danielson who improved Wenström's generator and transformer to make possible the early successes in long-distance transmission at Hällsjön, Boxholm, and Hofors.[32]

In the first of these projects ASEA put up transmission lines for power and lighting from Hällsjön, a lake, to the Grängesberg iron ore fields (1893). In over a century of effort, the miners, using rapids and waterfalls, ten dams, seven water wheels, and seven kilometers of canals, had fully exploited the possibilities of water power. The opening up of the phosphorus-laden iron ore areas put additional pressure on the facilities. The use of the steam engine of the 1880s and 1890s was still uneconomical for their purposes, and now electric power offered a solution to the increasingly desperate dilemma. ASEA built a power station where a stream dropped 45 meters in entering the lake; four water turbines powered generators of 100-hp each, which, with transformers, produced alternating electric current at 9500 volts. The double line of electric wires ran twelve kilometers to the Grängesberg terminus and functioned very well.

Boxholm *bruk* (Östergötland) had put in electric lights (Erikson, 1883), a short electric railway (Wenström & Granström, 1890), and now, its other sources of power potential exhausted, it attempted to use electricity for a rolling mill (1894). It was of modest size, but one at Hofors the next year was much larger; ASEA brought the power from the nearest suitable source, a 30-meter-high waterfall 2.4 kilometers away, by alternating current, and the electrified rolling mill went into production in the middle of 1895.[33]

Electricity came on the scene with perfect timing just as the big expansion in Swedish industry was getting underway, and without this new source of energy industrialization would have been much more difficult. Long-distance transmission of high-tension current now made possible the liberation of industry from the necessity of being placed alongside rapidly moving streams, an emancipation started by the steam engine. Other factors, such as good transportation and nearby markets, could now determine location. For an enterprise that had exhausted its water power potential, electricity also made it possible to expand production without moving from its old location. By making power available everywhere, electricity tended to *disperse* industry, including the encouragement of small industry in villages and towns.[34]

Stora Kopparberg began introducing hydroelectric power into its operations already in 1883, shortly after Rydal, by using a 60-hp water turbine and a generator to drive its sawmill at Domnarvet by direct current. The tearing down of an old dam in Svartån to restore a waterfall, capable of producing nearly 100-hp in energy, helped to persuade ASEA to move to Västerås. At the Grycksbo paper mill a kilometer-long canalization of water produced a 51-foot falls; a 200-hp turbine, installed by ASEA, produced 3,500 volts of high-tension current, transmitted to Grycksbo to drive a motor of 150-hp. Avesta Storfors had eight turbines for its generators in 1894–95, the largest in Sweden at the time. In 1894 Stockholm Superfosfat included a large turbine in the construction of the new Månsbo plant, the second chlorate factory in the world to go to electricity and the beginning of the Swedish electrochemical industry.

In 1900 the basic concentration of electricity still remained in the cities, with the addition of Bergslagen. The ironmasters rapidly took advantage of the new source of energy. Their long experience with water control through canals, dams, water wheels, and turbines made the development of hydroelectric installations both natural and practical. Machine shops and shipyards also tended to adopt electricity early, at least for lighting. Norrland sawmills, now located on the coast away from waterfalls and rapids, preferred to burn up their huge accumulation of lumber debris. In this region, steam engines were actually more economical at this time.

After rapid growth in the 1890s, the big electrical engineering firms all over the world, among them ASEA, experienced setbacks at the beginning of the new century. Stockholms Enskilda Bank poured money into it, including holding two million kronor's worth of bonds. In addition to suffering from competition within the temporarily depressed economy, the company apparently now lacked good financial leadership. Close cooperation with Gustav de Laval, who was heading toward bankruptcy, further complicated matters. ASEA was reconstructed in 1903, and Marcus Wallenberg of the bank appointed Sigfrid Edström to be its new head. Once again he was following his personal maxim: "No undertaking is so bad that it cannot be put on its feet by a competent man, and none is so good that it cannot be ruined by an incompetent man." As it happened, the reorganization was followed by a rapid growth of Scandinavian hydroelectric power, with consequent large orders for ASEA.[35]

Good times were needed, for competition was severe. Siemens & Halske merged with Schuckert & Co., both, of course, having had agencies in Sweden. In 1900 three other Swedish companies were active: Luth & Rosén AB, Elektriska AB Magnet, and Elektriska AB Holmia. The first of these had been started in 1883 as a consulting bureau by the Schuckert agent, John Luth (1857–1909), and, as a manufacturer of electrical machinery, it had workshops in Stockholm and Eskilstuna. It merged with the Ludwigsberg engineering works in 1904, adding pumps, compressors, and steam turbines to the list of products manufactured. The other two combined in 1906 and in turn were absorbed by ASEA in 1916, which also took over Luth & Rosén in 1930, thereby concentrating Sweden's electrical machine manufacturing.

In the first generation of pioneers in the electrical industry, Jonas Wenström and Danielson, and probably also Strehlenert, had made genuinely innovative contributions. Of the ten that happen to be mentioned here, six were trained engineers and five of them were completing their education just as the potential of electricity became apparent. Granström, older, was an established mining engineer. Though the commercial possibilities no doubt motivated all of them, this factor was most obvious in Fredholm, from the business world, and Erikson and Wiklund, owners of mechanical workshops.

The rapid development of hydroelectric power coupled with the need for power other than coal or charcoal by the Swedish iron works led to a series of important inventions in the next generation. Fredrik Adolf Kjellin (1872–1910), while director of the electrical steel works at Gysinge, constructed the first practical induction furnace for the smelting of steel (1900). Ivar Rennerfelt (1874–1949), after working at AEG in Berlin and for a number of years in the United States, made numerous technical improvements in electric furnaces. Axel Lindblad (1874–1944) experimented with the use of electricity in smelting pig iron, which led to the invention of the Swedish electric blast furnace; he also developed electric furnaces for steel, and for zinc and other metals. The first large-scale electric blast furnace went into operation at Trollhättan in 1910. In an area where the Swedes had long claimed European supremacy, they had now, thanks to electricity, regained, in technological quality if not in quantity, a position of equality with the world leaders.

In another kind of application of electricity, Oscar Kjellberg (1870–1931) developed a method of electric arc welding that led to the formation of a major company of international repute, ESAB (Elektriska Svetsnings AB). As a fireman and later as an engineer on board ships, Kjellberg became all too aware of the danger of leaks and the difficulty of repairing them. Experimenting in Gothenburg, he perfected a method that greatly expedited ship repairs and that led to the formation of ESAB in 1904. Kjellberg's feat was one more example of the innovations that rose directly out of day-by-day work and the sharp-eyed perception of a needed improvement, out of which emerged a new industrial enterprise.[36]

It has long since been forgotten that the triumph of electric lights was by no means as assured in the first decade of the century as it would seem later. Gaslights still had advocates. Kerosene glow lamps for street lighting were on the market. Some communities used acetylene street lights, "prettier and steadier . . . than electricity," and many hotels and stores had them.[37]

During the first decade of the new century the country was increasingly covered by electrical networks or grids from large power stations, and as this occurred hydroelectric power more and more preponderated over electricity from steam-driven plants. Not surprisingly, an Örebro company led the way (1898), obtaining its power from Svartälven by means of a 38-kilometer, 15,000-volt transmission. Communal power stations became common, including Stockholm, Norrköping, and Borås. In the case of Sydsvenska Kraft AB, founded in 1906 and covering southern Sweden, the controlling interest was held by the cities of Malmö, Lund, Landskrona, Hälsingborg, and Halmstad. Several private power companies sprang up. By 1914 a state-owned power company distributed electricity over wide areas of the kingdom, much of the north and a broad zone across central Sweden, and the state would continue to expand its sector of the industry. It should be added, however, that electricity would not provide more than a sixth of Sweden's future energy needs, whereas oil would ultimately account for nearly three-quarters.[38]

214

13. CELLULOSE AND CHEMICALS

Whatever derogatory comments might later be made about D. O. Francke and his financial dealings, he was, among other things, the founder of the wood pulp industry in Sweden. Briefly mentioned earlier, this important initiative merits a somewhat more detailed description. After purchasing the Korndal paper-making mill near Gothenburg in 1856, Francke immediately faced the problem of a scarcity of rags and scrap paper for the manufacture of new paper. Machinery for the mechanical grinding of wood into pulp had recently been invented by Friedrich Gottlob Keller in Germany, and this machinery was being manufactured by Heinrich Voelter, a paper-maker. Alert as usual, Francke bought the Swedish rights to the Voelter patent. His mill on Önan Island at Trollhättan became the first Swedish (and Scandinavian) wood pulping plant, using machinery, with its rotating grindstones, bought from Voelter (1857). The only partially dried pulp was put into barrels and shipped to Korndal, and some was also exported to England. About 40 to 45 percent of the pulp, usually, in the early years, consisted of wood, but rags or other content were also necessary to make good paper. By 1870 the Önan pulp mill had 14 machines and 126 workers.[1]

Klippan, where Sunnerdahl long ago had introduced the country's first paper-making machine, was now producing about 20 percent of all Swedish paper, and the scarcity of raw materials forced its new owner (C. A. Bock, a Dane) to set up the country's second mechanical wood pulping plant to fill the demand (1866). The third, Wärgon, is of interest because it was established by the sons of Nils Ericson; its machinery came from Voelter and its water turbine from Nydqvist & Holm. This was one of seven built in the early 1870s under the direction of G. Josephson, who, after meeting Voelter at the 1867 Paris Exhibition, established a pulp mill consulting bureau in Stockholm. Several more were built by Norwegians, who delivered machinery and provided foremen for the enterprises. Noticeably, the Swedes did not improve upon the Voelter machinery until after 1890, by which time chemical pulp mills were achieving preeminence.[2]

Chemical cellulose started with the soda method, whereby the wood chips were boiled in caustic soda; out of this, in turn, derived the sulphate method, the wood chips being subjected to sodium sulphate instead of caustic soda. Mixed with mechanically made pulp, it made good paper. A different chemical process, the sulphite method, produced finer, whiter paper; a solution of

215

sulphur dioxide in the form of sulphurous acid gas was used, to which was added magnesium or calcium. Here the Swedes would make important technical contributions.

Both the Houghton and Sinclair soda method were imported from Britain and installed by British engineers at the beginning of the 1870s before they had been properly tested. Count Sten Lewenhaupt (1819–1877), member of an aristocratic family going back to the sixteenth century, may well have ultimately regretted his purchase, through Thorsten Nordenfelt in England, of the apparatus for four Houghton chemical pulp mills. He had been rash before; in London in 1848 he had loaned Louis Napoleon Bonaparte his passport, to enable him to sneak into France to confer with his supporters, and thereby precipitated a minor diplomatic incident. Now the owner of cotton mills in Landskrona and Malmö, and apparently convinced by Nordenfelt, he started chemical pulp plants at Delary, Värmbol, Krontorp, and Bruzaholm. Meanwhile, four other ventures adopted the Sinclair type. However, neither kind had been fully developed, the boilers often leaked, and the actual percentage of wood utilized from a tree was not high until a good debarking machine could be devised. Several of the early mills had to close, and Värmbol did not become profitable until 1889.[3]

The introduction of sodium sulphate in place of caustic soda (1879) solved some problems. It was cheaper, brought a greater yield, and the resultant paper was stronger. Though it could not be properly bleached, it enabled the manufacture of strong wrapping paper, cardboard, newsprint, and paper for industrial uses. At Munksjö, the old Lundström and Hierta mill, Alvar Müntzing (1848–1917), a many-sided innovator in the industry, developed a process for making tough, cheap paper of this kind.

The sulphite method was independently formulated by Benjamin Tilghman (American) and Alexander Mitscherlich (German), the latter using calcium bisulphite, which became the most frequently used process. However, it was a Swede, Carl Daniel Ekman, boiling spruce with magnesium bisulphite, who first applied it industrially at British-owned Bergvik. Two other Swedes, Waldemar Flodquist and Victor Folin, also made significant contributions to the industry in this period.

Carl Daniel Ekman (1845–1904), not related to the Gothenburg family of the same name, had studied chemistry and mineralogy at the Institute of Technology before being hired as a chemist at Bergvik. Bankrupt a second time in 1867, the sawmill, one of Sweden's largest, had been acquired by its leading creditor, I. Thomson, T. Bonar & Co., of which Christopher Weguelin was now the head. Contemplating the huge amounts of debris at the sawmill, Weguelin decided to put up a chemical pulp mill, using a method developed by George Fry, the British company's chemist. Assigned the task of finding a bleaching agent, Ekman walked into the perfect setup, a project already underway and with ample financial resources to exploit his findings. Ekman was so sucessful with a process of boiling chips with magnesium bisulphite that the company hurriedly put up a special plant, which went into full production in October 1874. The first shipment to England, refined and made into paper, proved its feasibility; his process also permitted the extraction of much more pulp from the wood. Ekman later founded a pulp and paper company in England.[4] A dedicated inventor, he lived for his work, had few friends, exhibited little business sense, and died poor. He also had to endure a long controversy over the priority of sulphite inventions because the company, preferring secrecy, had not patented his original discovery.

In 1870 Francke's Korndal paper mill was manufacturing nearly one-half of all Swedish paper. Its prodigious appetite for wood pulp, surpassing even the capacities of the Önan pulp mill, led Francke to purchase Götafors, also a paper mill, and there establish one of the original Sinclair soda type of plants. Two years earlier he had hired Waldemar Flodquist (1847–1894), a Roads and Waterways graduate of the Institute of Technology, to head the Rosendahl industries' transport and machinery division. Later becoming its technical director, he apparently conducted some experiments, though not a chemist, with the sulphite method. Ekman, shortly before leaving Sweden, hired some facilities for his own work at the Korndal paper mill, and Flodquist became a most interested spectator. In 1880 Flodquist and Francke went to Germany and Austria to study the Mitscherlich system. Returned to Korndal, where Francke had started a sulphite mill in 1879, Flodquist, after more experiments, successfully made excellent sulphite cellulose by using white limestone chips instead of the magnesite layer of Ekman's. In the course of his experiments Flodquist went over to the direct system of boiling, and within a few years he was using a rotating boiler instead of Mitscherlich's stationary one. The irrepressible Francke filed for a patent in his own name, a lawsuit followed, and Flodquist parted company with the industrialist. Flodquist subsequently helped to build about twenty sulphite mills in Sweden, as well as several abroad.[5]

Billerud, located at Säffle on Lake Vänern, would grow into one of Sweden's major pulp companies. Founded in 1883 by Victor Folin (1856–1915), it was the first sulphite enterprise to make a profit. Folin had been or would be associated in some capacity with several of Sweden's most important paper mills and sulphite plants: Holmen (student), Jössefors (foreman), Munkedal (manager), Billerud (founder), and Storvik (managing director). At Billerud he worked out a system of combined direct and indirect boiling of the pulp, partially borrowing from Mitscherlich. His constructions there and at Storvik "became prototypes for a quite predominant portion" of Swedish sulphite mills, and Elis Boseaus considered his contribution easily the most important, in practical terms, of the three above men. The sulphite process in general did not require further rebuilding once installed, led to less financial problems, and, in Gårdlund's words, gave the victory to chemical cellulose. The break-through came in the 1890s when twenty-four plants were established, followed by thirty more between 1900 and 1910.[6]

Sweden possessed the resources to become an important producer of wood pulp. It had the forests, the rivers flowing to the sea (much water was necessary for pulp manufacturing), and it also soon developed the innovative talents to mature the possibilities. The earlier mills were established in the middle and southern parts of the country, especially in Värmland. Though a significant number remained in that province, near the end of the century the industry was moving into Norrland; ultimately the mills stretched from the Gävle area all the way to the Finnish border, with a particular concentration around Sundsvall. This new industry came as a blessing to the hard-pressed smaller iron works, which had forest reserves, were located conveniently on water, and had an available labor force; twelve of the eighteen earlier sulphite mills were former iron works; sawmill proprietors, on the contrary, rarely added wood pulp to their existing operations during the earlier period. They regarded it as a rival for timber resources, the same attitude the *bruk* owners had earlier entertained toward the sawmills. Later, when chemical pulp processes permitted the use of sawmill wastes, this attitude changed and companies occasionally added cellulose mills to their activities. Even in 1937, however, only four of the fifty-nine pulp mills in Norrland had sawmill connections.[7]

Paper mills very commonly started or acquired wood pulp facilities, as in the original case of Korndal, and by 1913 no less than fifty-four of the seventy-three active paper mills possessed them. Large companies like Svartvik and Munkedal maintained the full array of sawmill, paper mill, and mechanical, sulphate, and sulphite plants. Uddeholm's Skoghall on Lake Vänern had sawmills, sulphate and sulphite plants, paper mill, and electrochemical indus-try. Stora Kopparberg's Kvarnsveden at Borlänge became the giant of Swedish wood pulp mills, rather comparable in pulp industry to Domnarvet in iron; started as a mechanical pulp mill, it was later supplemented by a sulphite plant and paper mill. Holmen in Norrköping, in mid-twentieth century the largest producer of newsprint in the country, inaugurated a series of mechanical and sulphite mills at Hallsta, convenient to Stockholm newspapers (1913). As for the early pioneering paper-making firms—Klippan, Grycksbo, Lessebo, and Papyrus (Korndal)—they were now making high-quality fine paper.

Spurred by the increasing foreign demand, production increased rapidly from the mid-1890s until 1914, by which time Sweden had close to 140 mills in operation. The total output went up tenfold between 1893 and 1913, from approximately 112,000 to 1,187,000 dry tons. Mechanically produced wood pulp still made up slightly more than one-half in 1893, but by 1914 the breakthrough of the sulphite process is evident in the comparative figures: sulphite 719,000 tons to 269,200 by mechanical wood pulp and 134,000 for sulphate. In terms of actual use of timber resources, the growing industry in 1913 took 7,555,000 cubic meters of wood compared to the sawmills' 11,888,000, whereas in 1890 the respective figures had been 425,000 to 11,063,000.[8]

Just as dramatic as the production figures was the outburst of inventions within the industry, especially at the Skutskär laboratory.[9] Skutskär sawmill, founded by H. R. Astrup (Norwegian) in 1869–70, had been purchased by the forceful Erik Johan Ljungberg for Stora Kopparbergs Bergslaget in 1885, and here at the mouth of a river near Gävle, he concentrated, for a time, the company lumber activities. Sulphate (1894) and sulphite (1900) pulp mills were added, as was a well-equipped laboratory for further experimentation. The latter paid off handsomely in the work of such men as Ekström, Wallin, Rinman, and Sandberg.

While studying at the Technische Hochschule in Darmstadt, Gösta Ekström (1882–1949) had become interested in the possibility of making alcohol from the residue left by the manufacture of sulphite cellulose. Attempts in the 1880s and 1890s had not resulted in processes cheap enough to be commercially feasible, but after experimenting at Skutskär, Ekström patented a successful method for extracting alcohol from the waste lye. In May 1909 the first industrially produced alcohol from sulphite in the world was distilled in a plant designed by Ekström. A few months later a similar factory went into operation at Köpmanholmen, near Örnsköldsvik, which in 1907 had combined a sawmill, a sulphate mill, and hydroelectric power into one combined enterprise. This one had been developed by Hugo Wallin (1876–1956), also at Skutskär, working in parallel, though independent, experiments. Two other sulphite-derivative alcohol plants opened at Kvarnsveden and Bergvik in 1911, and many more would be established later, in what turned out to be a virtual industry in itself.

Sixten Sandberg (1880–1948) had been the first to use the Skutskär laboratory, primarily searching for uses for the byproducts from sulphate cellulose. Out of his work came new methods for dry distillation of the lye, the manufacture of turpentine and resin soap, an almost automatic debarking machine, and a new type of rotating boiler. When Ljungberg came to inspect the laboratory one day, he tipped his hat to Sandberg and said, "You have carried the message to Garcia!" Erik Ludvig Rinman (1874–1927) worked with Sandberg, and he himself experimented with acetone, ketones, and various oils.[10] The list of innovators could be greatly extended. Peter Klason (1848–1927), who must be mentioned, made an indispensable contribution as a professor in organic chemistry at Lund and at the Institute of Technology in both the training of students and the chemical analysis of cellulose. In fact, says Boseaus, his laboratory was originally *the* center for Swedish study of cellulose.[11] One of his students, Gunnar Sundblad, made notable improve-

219

ments in the apparatus while also constructing numerous sulphate and sulphite factories, including those at Skoghall and Iggesund.

Exporting about 72 percent of its output in 1914, Sweden now ranked first in the world as a supplier of wood pulp.[12]

Sweden's modern chemical industry largely originated in the same years as the rapid growth of chemical cellulose, in the 1890s under the impetus of the breakthrough of hydroelectric power. However, electricity was in too much demand by growing cities, the railroads, the pulp mills, and other industries for an unhampered expansion of electrochemical plants. Though developing simultaneously with those in other advanced countries, the electrochemical industry never would reach the proportions achieved in neighboring Norway.[13]

The earlier so-called chemical industry, as previously described, had included the making of soap, yeast, vinegar, candles, soda, and sulfuric acid. Shortly before midcentury artificial fertilizer began to develop into another prosperous chemical industry, buoyed by strong agricultural demand. In 1842 Sir John Bennett Lawes secured a patent on superphosphate, made by treating the phosphate of lime in bones, bone-ash or mineral apatite with sulfuric acid. His plant at Deptford (1842) was quickly followed by similar ones built by Edward Packard (1843) and T. Richardson (1844).[14]

Phosphorus-containing fertilizer had been made in England near the end of the eighteenth century out of bones ground into a sort of powder. Some of these bones came from the Danish island of Bornholm and from Kalmar, "dug up from ancient . . . mass graves of warriors." The shippers were careful not to send the skulls! By about 1840 the Swedes were themselves grinding up bones, these usually imported from Russia. Guano was first imported in 1844, and some shops began preparing ammonium sulphate from fish to serve as fertilizer. C. F. Waern & Co. started importing both guano (from Gibbs & Son) and superphosphate in 1852, selling most of it in agricultural Västergötland. A number of other firms moved quickly to satisfy the burgeoning demand, and in 1857 the Waerns built Sweden's first superphosphate factory at Klippan outside of Gothenburg. It was constructed according to German plans with German machinery, and the product was composed of 100 parts of bone charcoal, 18 of sulfuric acid (imported from Hamburg), 10 of guano, plus ammonium hydrate.[15]

Among other superphosphate firms that sprang up, the largest in 1870 was AB Fertilitas, owned by some landed proprietors near Gothenburg. However, they all had difficulty competing with imports because the necessary sulfuric acid was subject to high duties, whereas the imported superphosphate had no import tax whatsoever. To be successful, a plant needed to make its own sulfuric acid. Hierta's Tegelvik shop was producing more than it could sell, largely because it was too expensive, and in 1871 Hierta assisted Oscar

Carlson to start Stockholm Superfosfat, partly in order to have an outlet for his product.

Oscar (O. F.) Carlson (1844–1910), who would inherit Hierta's mantle as Sweden's greatest chemical manufacturer, was the son of a Norrköping textile family. After attending Uppsala, Carlson took his *bergsexamin,* attended the Falun School of Mines, and in 1866–70 studied chemistry and technology in Austria, Germany, and England; in the latter he also investigated superphosphate production. After briefly working in Hierta's office, Carlson went back to England in September 1870 to inspect Edward Packard's factories at Ipswich. He had found his calling, with the guiding help of Hierta.

Stockholm Superfosfat stock, worth 75,000 kronor in 1871, would mount to 12 million by 1916. Of the original twenty-five shares, each valued at 3,000 kronor, Hierta held five, Carlson eight; a few more were bought by members of the family, and most of the remainder were held by businessmen.[16] Carlson's factory, the first industrial-sized superphosphate plant in the country, obtained its machinery from Packard and the raw material in London, the trade in raw phosphates being concentrated in that city at the time. Although Hierta's business concern handled its early sales, the price of the Tegelvik sulfuric acid made successful competition with imports difficult, and already in February 1874 the company started making its own in a shop built for that purpose. Stockholm Superfosfat prospered thereafter. In 1884 it bought the Ceres superphosphate and sulfuric acid factory in Gothenburg. Ceres in turn had purchased another plant, founded by a son of Theodor Gullberg, a partner of Hierta (until they quarreled) at the Liljeholmen Stearinfabrik. Thus the usual pattern of centralization within Swedish industry was already asserting itself. The success of this enterprise, however, was only the foundation for the Carlson achievements in chemical industry.

Oscar Carlson's career over a period of nearly fifty years in some respects resembled that of Hierta, but Carlson followed a much straighter course within the chemical industry. He and his sons were always experimenting, and when something looked promising they took risks, usually successful, in manufacturing it. Swedish match factories were importing large quantities of potassium chlorate, and it was also used in fireworks and some kinds of gunpowder. Using Svante Arrhenius' theory of electrolysis, Carlson developed and patented a method for producing chlorates by electricity, a process subsequently adopted all over the world. A hydroelectric station constructed at Månsbo, near Avesta, served the second electric chlorate factory in the world (1894). Soon thereafter he patented a method for electric production of perchlorates, and in 1899 the company also began manufacturing calcium carbide at Månsbo.

Fredrik Carlson, son of Oscar, experimented with nitrogen, a problem that had frustrated many over the years. Its available sources were being fully used in the manufacture of fertilizers and explosives, and the only possible recourse was to capture it from the atmosphere, consisting of four-fifths nitrogen. Chr. Rinke had done it in 1845 and 1857, but it could not be used industrially. Gustaf de Laval worked on it for ten years without results, and an American factory at Niagara Falls closed after two years. The Norwegians, Kristian Birkeland and Samuel Eyde, ultimately solved the problem, out of which emerged Norsk Hydro and the famous Notoddon factory.

Meanwhile, Fredrik Carlson, after experimenting at Dresden, found that adding fluorspar (calcium fluoride) as a catalyst to carbon worked quite well, and he took out a patent for lime nitrogen. In 1907 it went into production at Månsbo. By now its capacity had reached its limits, and a new power station had to be constructed at a waterfall on Ljungan. Another electrochemical factory for chlorates and perchlorates was built at Trollhättan in 1915–16, using the father's patent for producing perchlorate ammonium, a substance employed in making explosives. By 1914 Stockholm Superfosfat was manufacturing iron vitriol (1891), zinc sulphite (1891), calcium chlorate (1892), sodium chlorate (1897), barium chlorate (1898), calcium carbide (1899), calcium perchlorate (1902), sodium perchlorate (1903), lime nitrogen (1907), sodium bisulphite (1911), and sodium nitrite (1914).[17]

Birger Carlson (1873–1928), the elder son of Oscar, had worked with electric furnaces and carbide products in Germany. He was responsible for the small calcium carbide factory at Månsbo and in time would have fifteen patents in carbides, nitrogen, and perchlorate explosives. A process for the manufacture of calcium carbide by heating a mixture of lime or carbon (coal or a derivative) in an electric furnace had been independently discovered by Th. L. Willson (Canadian) and Henri Moissan (French) in 1891–92. In 1895 a Swedish engineer at the superphosphate Ceres plant delivered an address before a technical society on the many possible uses of calcium carbide. The most promising, at first, seemed to be for the production of acetylene, formed by the interaction of calcium carbide with water. Gustaf de Laval, who was making acetylene and acetylene lamps in Stockholm, hastily put up a large plant on Önan Island at Trollhättan (1896–97).[18] Much of its production was exported to Germany, but demand did not reach the expected levels until other uses for carbide had been implemented; meanwhile, the spread of electric lighting undermined the market for acetylene lamps. Though the plant did well at first, he later had to shut it down, and by now his chemical complex at Trollhättan was in trouble for other reasons, including the premature launching of a zinc production unit.

A third venture into calcium carbide manufacturing occurred at Alby in conjunction with a potassium chlorate factory. Encouraged by the success at nearby Månsbo, Artur Leffler, who had worked in American industry, and a brother put up a hydroelectric station on a rapids in Ljungan for the manufacture of the potassium chlorate (1898). With power to spare, the Lefflers brought in C. J. Lundström, who had helped to build the de Laval plant, to add a calcium carbide factory. The Lefflers, like de Laval, had overestimated the demand and, heavily in debt, lost the Alby industries to a bank. After a succession of owners, including the Sun Gas Co. of London, it passed under the control of Stockholm Superfosfat, which acquired the majority stock in 1918. Soon after the Leffler collapse, demand picked up, and Alby began making excellent profits.

During the early discouraging years Alby had the services of Sweden's other calcium carbide expert, Albert Petersson (1870–1914). Having obtained his doctor's degree at Zürich, he had worked for the Compagnie de l'Industrie Electrochimique in Geneva and participated in building carbide factories at St. Michel and Briançon in France. The superintendent of the latter had worked with Henri Moissan on the original experiments. One of the Lefflers happened to visit Briançon, and apparently as a result of this encounter Petersson was invited to join the Alby group. After serving as an engineer and managing director in 1903–06, Petersson moved on to the extremely promising Norsk Hydro and Notodden project, where another Swede, Marcus Wallenberg, was involved in the financing. In August 1914 he boarded a Norwegian coastal steamer and vanished, apparently swept off the ship in high seas.[19]

Another company, Elektrokemiska AB, founded at Bengtsfors in Dalsland province in 1895 and financed by Alfred Nobel, made chloride lime, potassium hydrate, and sodium hydrate in the early years of the century and subsequently expanded its production. Ferrolegeringar ("Ferro") of Trollhättan was founded in 1913 and later would manufacture a number of ferro alloys.[20] Large companies like Stora Kopparbergs Bergslags AB and Uddeholm had also started electrochemical plants by 1914 or soon thereafter.

Swedish economic history is replete with the chameleonlike changes in lines of production by enterprises, but few have matched the record of the successive transformations of Reymersholm, bearing the name of a Stockholm island. It became the site for a very early oil refinery, then was converted into a liquor distillery by the Whiskey King, L. O. Smith. When, near the end of the First World War, the state took over the distribution of hard liquor, the Reymersholm company was left as a disembodied corporate being on the lookout for new industry. It so happened that Nils Persson (1836–1916), a founder of Skånska Superfosfat, had recently died. Persson had started as an importer of colonial wares and other goods, and in 1875, with a partner and without any technical training, began a superphosphate plant in Hälsingborg; three more factories were added to serve the agricultural south. Like Carlson and others, he needed sulfuric acid and began manufacturing his own. This led to the purchase of sulfur mines in Norway and to subsequent attacks on him by Norwegian nationalists when the dual monarchy broke up in 1905. The

Hälsingborg enterprise gradually broadened its production into other sectors of the chemical industry, such as the manufacture of aluminum sulphite. After Persson's death, his Skånska Superfosfat, needing new leadership, merged with Reymersholm, and so a company bearing the name of a Stockholm island would preside in Hälsingborg over the manufacture of a miscellany of chemical products.[21] In Sweden old companies rarely died, they reincarnated themselves in new forms.

14. IRON ORE AND HIGH FINANCE

A London police court clerk who had studied some chemistry set in motion a series of portentous developments of the utmost significance for the Swedish iron industry and for Sweden's position in the international community. Sidney Gilchrist Thomas determined that if a converter was lined with lime bricks, the bricks would absorb the phosphorus in iron ore, thereby freeing the iron for industrial use. Successfully tested by his metallurgist cousin, Percy Gilchrist, at the Blaenavon iron works, the Thomas-Gilchrist discovery (the basic process) was formally announced at a meeting of the Iron and Steel Institute in March 1878. The phosphorus-rich iron ore at Grängesberg, Gällivare, and Kirunavaara could now be exploited.[1] Soon thereafter, Carl Fredrik Liljevalch, in London for a meeting of the Swedish Association, had some urgent words in private with Ernest Cassel.

The phosphorus-free ore in the southern part of Grängesberg, which straddles the provincial border between Västmanland and Dalarna, had long been mined, but the ironmasters at landlocked Grängesberg, in addition to scarce water resources, had always had formidable transportation problems. A railroad would greatly simplify matters, making it possible to use imported coal and coke at the forges and thereby save the charcoal for the smelting hearths. British steel works, getting most of their phosphorus-free iron from Spain, were also eyeing the iron ore of central Sweden. This prospect of a railroad for iron ore export excited a group of British financiers, led by Christopher Weguelin; he had just taken over the leadership of I. Thompson, T. Bonar & Co. from his father and was, in these same years, starting the pulp mill at Bergvik. In 1869 his British consortium, originally called the Swedish Central Railway Company, Ltd., received a concession to build and operate a railroad between Frövi, on the British-owned Örebro-Köping line (Rosen's old project), to Ludvika in the Grängesberg area. Other members of the consortium included Bischoffsheim & Goldschmidt, and the railway builders George Wythes and J. A. Longridge.[2]

Three years later they secured another concession to construct a railroad southward from the Örebro–Köping line through Södermanland to the Baltic harbor at Oxelösund, the so-called Oxelösund–Flen–Västmanland railroad. Located about ninety kilometers south of Stockholm, Oxelösund, unlike harbors farther north, was not likely to become icebound in winter. Though

225

people along the route bought stock, over three-fourths of it was held by the consortium. Traffic to Ludvika opened in 1873, to the Baltic in 1876, and the harbor at Oxelösund was completed in 1879.

Meantime, the Weguelin consortium, its name shortened to the Swedish Association, also bought Kloten, a *bruk* situated near the Frövi–Ludvika railroad, from the Heijkenskjöld family. The transport of its ore and forest products on the company railroads would give them additional traffic, but, more important, Kloten held a large number of shares in the supervising body of the ore field, the Grängesberg Stora Konstbolag. This authority had emerged out of the long cooperation of the mine owners in building dams and water courses to provide additional water power, and its 225 *andelar* (shares) had been apportioned among the owners. That is, by the acquisition of Kloten the railroad consortium moved to take over control of the mines also. The Konstbolag was reorganized (1875), and additional shares began to pass into the hands of Liljevalch, Vollrath Tham, John Johnson (head of the Frövi–Ludvika railroad) and Ernest Cassel.

Liljevalch and Tham were the Swedish front men that made the British presence a bit more palatable. To get the foreign company properly registered, in fact, had required the skillful efforts of the influential Oscar Robert Themptander, future Swedish prime minister (1884–1888). Carl Fredrik Liljevalch (1837–1909) was the son of the shipowner of the same name whose vessels had adventured in the South Seas and the China trade a generation earlier. The son had worked for Hierta before completing his commercial education in the Thomson & Bonar office in London. Weguelin put him in charge of Bergvik, and it was Liljevalch who arranged for the purchase of Kloten, where he subsequently became managing director. Vollrath Tham (1837–1909), brother of the Husqvarna leader, joined him at Kloten, the beginning of a long association; oddly, the two men were born in the same year and died in the same year.

In 1878 the Thomas-Gilchrist process opened up for the consortium the tantalizing prospect of exploiting the phosphorus-rich part of the Grängesberg ore field. Out of the Liljevalch conversation with Cassel came orders that he and Tham buy up as many of the Grängesberg shares as possible. Working cautiously, lest the present owners be alerted to what was going on, they secured an appreciable additional number.[3] The accumulated shares and most of those belonging to Kloten were transferred to a new company, the Grängesberg Grufaktiebolag (Grängesberg Mining Co.), whose principal function would be the mining of the phosphorus-rich ore in what came to be called Exportfältet, the Export Field. Nominally owned by the members of the Swedish Association, the company was dominated by Cassel with the help of his Swedish confederates. Stora Kopparberg also purchased Grängesberg mines, and negotiations with Ljungberg over an exchange and alignment of their respective holdings went on for years.

Sir Ernest Cassel (1852–1921) had been born in Cologne, son of a Jewish financier. He began his career at the Anglo-Egyptian Bank in Paris, then joined Bischoffsheim & Goldschmidt in London. In 1874, at the age of twenty-two, he took over its leadership and soon absorbed that firm into his own affairs; after the death of Weguelin, he quickly added the Swedish Association to his financial domain. Cassel had first become interested in Sweden while handling several loans for the continued building of the state railroad, and he later helped to finance the Vickers takeover of the Maxim-Nordenfelt weapons company.

No dividends were paid from the mining or railroad stock in the early years. Though Weguelin had originally thought that he had the best railroad in Sweden, ore did not begin to roll over the line in any profitable quantity until 1887. The Grängesberg company took out an average of 73,500 tons a year in the 1880s, after which the figure rose rapidly to 480,000 tons in the 1890s. In 1904, 670,000 tons passed through Oxelösund in one year; much of it went to Germany, whose steel mills had converted to the Thomas-Gilchrist process much more thoroughly than the British.

In 1896 a further rationalization of structure took place when Trafik AB Grängesberg–Oxelösund was founded as a holding company for the several enterprises. Cassel may have considered attending the meeting himself, judging by a wired query that read: "When does the elk shooting begin?" The elk season, however, occurs in the fall, the founding session took place on July 30, and Liljevalch represented Cassel. Trafik AB now acquired the majority stock in Grängesberg Grufaktiebolag and the three railroads, Oxelösund–Flen––Västmanland, Frövi–Ludvika, and Örebro–Köping.[4] One stretch of the last had been used to connect with the other two routes, and its owners, put under heavy pressure, had been forced to sell out to the consortium.

Trafik AB began with a capital of about 19 million kronor. Cassel held 8,780 of the 19,090 shares, each valued at a thousand kronor. The Association, controlled by Cassel, owned 8,564 more. Liljevalch, Tham, and John Johnson also held shares. Two others who participated in the formation of Trafik AB were Fredrik Elias Warburg, whose Altona and Hamburg firm was a member of the chain of international finance houses with which Cassel had close working arrangements, and Theodor Mannheimer, head of the Skandinaviska Kreditaktiebolag. This bank had long been active in Cassel's Swedish affairs. The group chose Themptander, who had been useful before and who was now an ex-prime minister, as a politic front for the essentially foreign-owned company. When he died the following year, Vollrath Tham assumed the executive position.

THE SMALL GIANT

Sir Ernest Cassel's dominant role was nearing its end. Even his Swedish associates had begun to lose patience with his peremptory ways of doing business. In the face of strong nationalist hostility against foreign ownership in Swedish industry, Cassel very wisely and quietly started liquidating his holdings at good profit, and by 1903 had divested himself of six-sevenths of it.[5] His financial interests were virtually worldwide—Egypt, Ottoman Empire, Latin America, and the Far East—and he was one British citizen who had made money out of Swedish investments. In appearance the very model of a proper British capitalist in the glory days of Empire, he was a close confidant and financial advisor to Edward VII during the king's later years. A granddaughter, Edwina, married Lord Louis Mountbatten, whose sister became Queen Louise of Sweden. When Sir Ernest Cassel died, the London *Times* devoted more than two long columns to his obituary; it mentioned, among many other things, the Atchison, Topeka, and Santa Fe railroad and the names of some of his race horses, but not one word about his role in Sweden.[6]

Trafik AB rented the ore fields from the Grängesberg Grufaktiebolag in 1902 and thereafter managed the actual quarrying itself. In 1903–04 Vollrath Tham pulled off one of the greatest coups in Swedish industrial history when Trafik AB gained control of most of the Lapland mines. His dramatic move in gaining, for the moment, nearly a monopoly of Swedish export iron ore had been forced upon him by a series of increasingly crucial developments at the northern Swedish mines.

That iron ore existed at Gällivare in Lapland had been known since the early 1700s, and a Lapp discovered ore in the Kiruna region in 1736. Lieutenant Karl Tingvall secured a concession at Gällivare in 1735 and the right to set up a *bruk* near the coast, a concession passed on to Abraham Steinholtz, who, with Jonas Meldercreutz, founded Melderkreutz *bruk* and Strömsund's blast furnace (1742). The ore was transported from Gällivare by reindeer-drawn wagons.[7] Near the end of the century these properties passed to Baron Samuel Hermelin (1744–1820).

Hermelin had earlier been sent to the United States by King Gustav III, ostensibly to study the geology and metallurgy of North America, but in fact to look after Swedish trading interests (1782–84); he also bore a secret appointment as Swedish minister to the American government, which the continued war precluded him from activating. In Norrland he held large tracts of land in the region of the Kalix, Pite, and Rane rivers and ran several *bruk* and a sawmill near the coast. Living costs were high, labor difficult to find, transport with the south hard to maintain, and the so-called "King of Lapland" ultimately went bankrupt. He is best remembered as the founder of modern Swedish cartography because of his Hermelinska Kartoverket, a complete series of maps, in four parts, of Sweden and Finland. By sending out many young men to complete the survey for these maps, he also greatly contributed to the study of minerals in the far north.

Only with the coming of the railroad and hydroelectric power would any genuine development of the riches of northern Norrland become feasible. Lured by the manifest possibilities, a number of individuals would meanwhile lose money in the region. The senior Liljevalch, advisor to the king, reaped no financial reward from his grain ships, sawmill, and Luleå shipyard; his son, in more felicitous circumstances, would recoup magnificently. King Karl XIV Johan bought the Hermelin properties, but they distinctly failed to enrich the royal coffers. They did achieve one odd distinction, that of being, if only briefly and nominally, a principality. When Crown Prince Oscar was going to marry Princess Josephine of Leuchtenberg (she who liked Bavarian beer), the Pope requested that she be given a marriage present the equivalent of the principality bestowed upon her by Napoleon when she was baptized. The king conferred upon her the hastily fabricated "Principality Gellivare."[8]

King Oscar I (1844–1859), once he ascended the throne, tried to get rid of the unprofitable property. A British consortium secured a concession (1847) to build a railroad to the mines, but one of the periodic crises in railroad finances in England ended that possibility. The king then managed to sell it to Carl Wilhelm Hammarskjöld of Skultuna and two others. The brukspatron had bought the Skultuna iron works at a bankruptcy auction after his cousin, caught in a scandal, had fled to the United States (1844). In 1849 the second Hammarskjöld followed him to America, charged with unpaid debts and fraud. Their biographical notices are curtly scathing.[9] (Among others, F. H. Kockum, the Malmö industrialist, lost money, "only" 30,000 riksdaler, in the far north.) Dag Hammarskjöld, secretary-general of the United Nations in 1953–61, and his father, prime minister in 1914–17, were descended from another branch of the family.

The king, once again the reluctant possessor of the so-called Gellivare-verken, finally succeeded in disposing of it to a group of Norwegians for approximately a million riksdaler, the ubiquitous Pontus Kleman acting as intermediary (1855). Victor Kjellberg, who soon took over the leadership, had become rich fast by utilizing a loophole in the high Swedish protective tariff against foreign refined sugar, a stipulation that the tariffs would not apply to the Norwegian partner in the dual monarchy. He ran a lucrative sugar refinery at Fredrikshald on the Norse side of the border until the Norwegian Storting (parliament) closed the loophole and canceled the accompanying export premium (1852), whereupon Kjellberg shut down the refinery. Mostly from the Fredrikshald area, the Norwegians, who had become interested in Gällivare for its timber potential, chose Kjellberg as their managing director. Edvard Francke, brother of the Mölndal industrialist, became the administrator at Gällivare.[10]

THE SMALL GIANT

Nearly all the Norwegians, discouraged by the obvious difficulties, soon gave up, and Kjellberg, failing to enlist British capital, founded a new company, the Gällivare AB, along with Edvard Francke, A. O. Wallenberg, John West Wilson, and the remaining Norwegians. Wallenberg loaned the company a large sum, and the government, trying to provide sorely needed transportation, granted about 400,000 riksdaler more to begin a partial canalization of the Lule River. In 1864 the company sold its assets for £172,570 to the Gellivare Company, Ltd., organized as a speculative venture, and which in 1868, after bankruptcy, gave way to the New Gellivare Company, Ltd.

Giles Loder, who had made his original fortune in St. Petersburg and to whom the heavily indebted Kjellberg had by now lost his shares, held the largest interest. The other principal stockholders in The New Gellivare Co. included J. H. Johnson, A. H. Campbell, W. K. Gladstone, and E. Buxton. It was almost entirely British in makeup; the only Swede who held any substantial amount of stock was Wilhelm Röhss, importer and timber baron. The Gothenburg resident, John West Wilson (of a British shipowning family), also owned some shares. Both Buxton and Gladstone (of Hinde, Gladstone & Co.) had often handled Swedish financial affairs in London, and Gladstone, along with Loder, had lost large sums of money in the Johan Holm-Högbo collapse.[11]

The appointment of C. H. J. Matton, a Stockholm merchant closely associated with Kleman, as the Swedish front man and of J. A. Wikström, a competent timber man, as managing director, did little to appease hostile criticism of the New Gellivare Company. It concentrated its activities on the timber properties, mining only enough ore to satisfy the concession requirements; it operated seven water-driven saws and two sawmills newly equipped with steam engines, the timber being exported, usually on company ships, to England.[12]

In 1879 the New Gellivare Company, through three Englishmen, asked for a railway concession, though it was Kleman, still persevering, who lay back of the proposal. Emil Key, a member of the Riksdag, was using his considerable influence in political circles to forward the proposal, his own reward allegedly to be appointment as managing director of the railroad. However, Sven Hedlund, the redoubtable Gothenburg editor, who never hesitated to share his strong opinions with his readers, started such a heated newspaper campaign against it that Keys withdrew and Count Arvid Posse (prime minister, 1880–83) had to reject the application.[13]

Two other men, Robert Schough and Alrik Ljunggren, soon presented another proposal. An employee of the New Gellivare Company, Schough had been in charge of the Lule River canalization project, which never had made much progress. He had also staked claims to ore fields around Kirunavaara and Luossavaara. Ljunggren represented a consortium that included Louis Fraenckel of the Svenska Handelsbank and Stockholm financier Carl Cervin. Schough and Ljunggren petitioned for a concession to Wilkinson & Jarvis, a noted British railway building company, for the construction of a railroad from Haparanda on the Finland border to the Norwegian frontier. This application was rejected because King Oscar II feared that a line this close to Russian-dominated Finland might fall under Russian influence. They then offered an alternative, that the line begin farther down the coast at Luleå. This one was reluctantly accepted, and the Norwegians granted a concession to Wilkinson & Jarvis for their stretch of the route to Narvik on the Atlantic. The first section, to Gällivare, was completed by the end of 1887; it seems to have been a poor job, the crossties being of green wood and having to be replaced within a few years. In 1891 the Swedish state took over the railroad, for compensation, and the remainder of the route to the Norwegian border would be constructed in 1898–1902.[14]

Some elements of the resident population had always deplored the exasperating delay in opening up the north country. They were fully aware of the bonanza of riches awaiting bold, competent men prepared to take decisive action—and they deeply resented the continued presence of the obstructing British company. Conspicuous among their leaders was Colonel Carl Otto Bergman (1828–1901), who had returned to the region after a career as an army officer to build up his father's rather dilapidated sawmill properties. He had become a member of the provincial *landsting* (assembly) and of the Riksdag, a "strong voice" on behalf of railroad construction and a more rapid development of the mining industry. He had also been a partner in one of the larger local timber companies, Bergman, Hummel & Co., founded in 1850 by David Hummel (1820–1892), a member of the pioneering textile mill family at Lerum. In view of the strong competition from the New Gellivare Company, Hummel had wanted to merge with the British in the early 1880s, but other partners, disliking the hovering presence of the notorious Pontus Kleman in the background, had refused. In the ensuing quarrel the company was dissolved.[15]

A few years later Bergman took brusque action to break the mining impasse by hauling the British company into court on the grounds that they had not fulfilled the charter obligations. Wikström, the manager, had failed to extract, so it was claimed, the stipulated amount of ore per year at Gällivare, and Bergman and another man, Gustaf Broms, staked claims to most of its ore fields. Bergman won the court case (June 18, 1891), though, according to Bo Jonsson, the legal process "gave a strong impression of judicial bias."[16] In the same fateful year, 1891, the British were evicted from both their railroad and their mining concession in return for financial compensation.

Robert Loder, son and successor of Giles Loder, had died and his estate was being liquidated. The British had lost about a million pounds on the venture over the years. Their experience fully bore out an earlier statement by the British minister to Sweden; in a letter on May 11, 1873 to Lord Granville, foreign minister, he said that the Swedes believed that foreigners, especially the British, were carrying off large amounts of money from their profits, "whereas I am assured that . . . the very reverse has in most instances been the result of English capital in Sweden." In fact, he concluded, most English speculations in Sweden "have proved eminently disastrous."[17] Weguelin and Cassel, of course, were the big exceptions.

These events in the far north formed only a small, if characteristic, part of a rising mood of strong national feeling in the country. For the Swedes, these were years of mounting fears of foreign takeovers, stimulated especially by the strong British presence at Grängesberg and in the railroad to Oxelösund. They owned several other industrial enterprises and private railroads, and the death of Alfred Nobel in 1896 briefly raised the possibility that even Bofors might be acquired by the British. The Germans would move into Fagersta and the Dannemora mines in 1907. The sharpening Swedish hostility to foreign interests and the acute impatience of the Norrlanders at the slow development of their region were by no means the only manifestations of dissatisfaction on the nationwide scene. The farmers, threatened by the import of foreign grain, clamored for a protective tariff, and so did the owners of numerous industrial establishments, unable to compete effectively with cheaper foreign imports. In 1888 the Protectionists won a crucial election victory, signaling the end of the liberal, laissez-faire policies of the preceding decades. Prime Minister Themptander, advocate of free trade, had to resign.

The foundry owners made up a politically potent pressure group, who demanded that the state intervene in Lapland to keep out foreign interests. They feared that the export of its iron ore would lower world prices, a threat to their own iron works. They also hoped to reserve the the iron ore for their own use, perhaps by leasing the mines from state-owned companies. The successive prime ministers, Gillis Bildt (1888–89) and Gustaf Åkerhielm (1889–91), the latter with personal holdings in Kloster *bruk*, sympathized with the ironmasters. Although the railroad was nationalized, the government rejected state ownership over the ore fields, believing that control of the railroad and its freight charges offered sufficient leverage.

The northern mines would consequently be opened up by private enterprise. Gustaf Broms served as the managing director of the newly organized AB Gällivare Malmfelt (AGM), while Bergman led the work at the ore fields. Only 2200 tons had been extracted in 1887, but by 1895 the year's output had reached 518,614 tons. Originally helped by David Hummel, Broms purchased enough additional stock to hold majority control by 1894. A second company, Luossavaara-Kirunavaara AB (LKAB), had been set up to exploit the ore in these neighboring localities. Robert Schough and Knut Wallenberg, to whom Schough sold one-half of his interest, were the dominant owners. When Alrik Ljunggren died, Wallenberg also bought some of his shares. Seeing no prospect for profits until the railroad to Narvik had been completed, however, the two men sold much of their stock to Broms, who thus also gained control of LKAB[18]

Gustaf Emil Broms (1849–1903), the bold, competent operator that the region needed, had gone to work at Bergman, Hummel & Co. in 1869 and ultimately headed its Stockholm office. Once in charge in Lapland, he opened one mine after another, installed the necessary machinery, and constructed modern dock and loading facilities near Luleå. Unfortunately, Broms lacked the financial resources for such an ambitious undertaking. His fundamental problem lay in financing the development of the companies' mining facilities before the completion of the railroad in 1902. He received payment only during that part of the year when the ore ships could traverse the otherwise icebound upper Gulf of Bothnia, a major reason for placing loading docks at Narvik on the Atlantic. Forced to heavy borrowing, he became increasingly burdened by the payments of interest on the loans. According to Gårdlund, Broms' basic approach was both realistic and reasoned, though he was often regarded as reckless by his contemporaries; trapped in a financial quagmire, he would be compelled to contrive desperate and ultimately futile measures.[19]

In abbreviated summary, the issuance of more stock raised additional capital, and Broms secured credit from L. Possehl of Lübeck, to be repaid by ore deliveries. Two big bond issues by AMG and LKAB respectively, each worth 10 million kronor and to be amortized over the next twenty years, were bought up by the banks; the two principal lenders of money, as well as purchasers of bonds, were Stockholms Enskilda Bank and Ernest Thiel's Diskontbank (to use its later shorter name). Broms subsequently borrowed 2.2 million kronor from the Norddeutsche Bank (Hamburg), the representative of the German iron works. Altogether, he now personally owed over 6 million kronor.[20] AGM and LKAB had a combined debt of over 41 million kronor, of which about 28 million were in bond issues.

Trying to recover his bank's huge investments in the mining companies, Marcus Wallenberg started joint bank action against Broms at the beginning of 1901. He was not planning to take over the mines, which was impractical, anyway, in view of public hostility to the Wallenbergs. An agreement later in the year, however, conferred temporary control of the majority of LKAB stock on Knut Wallenberg and that of AGM on Knut Tillberg, representative of Stockholms Enskilda Bank, the shares to be returned in 1907, or earlier if the debts were paid. Broms twisted and turned, trying to find a way out. The Swedish press urged nationalization of the mines, but opinion was sharply divided on whether the state should lease the holdings to various iron works or itself operate them through contractors. The Erik Gustaf Boström ministry (the second: 1902–05) dithered. Broms could not turn to other banks; the Skandinaviska Kreditaktiebolag was financing the rival Trafik AB, and Louis

Fraenckel's Svenska Handelsbank was not on good terms with the Wallenbergs. Broms' ruthless and brusque way of managing his affairs further embittered the conflict, and, having given financial assistance to *Svenska Dagbladet*, the other newspapers handled Broms' affairs roughly. As his dilemma worsened, his actions became increasingly adventurous, and he now had no alternative except to seek aid abroad.[21]

He tried to secure 33 million francs by means of bond sales in France. This failed. Then he sought credit from his former sales agent, Jos de Poorter in Rotterdam, which worked only until the Dutch agent learned the true state of Broms' finances. After attempting to peddle Gällivare stock in London, Broms "sold" the majority stock of AGM to U.S. Steel; this automatically conferred control also over LKAB, in which AGM now had majority stock. However, as Broms knew perfectly well, he could not sell stock currently sequestered by the banks, and he was presumably merely maneuvering for better terms. L. Possehl & Co., which in 1907 would acquire Fagersta and control of the Dannemora mines, had been threatening to put Gällivare into bankruptcy and then acquire it for the consortium of German iron works that was importing the Swedish ore. Broms gave Possehl an option to buy the stock. August Thyssen, German iron manufacturer, turned up at the mines in the summer of 1902, planning a syndicate with Skandinaviska Kreditaktiebolag and Trafik AB to take over AGM and LKAB. Thyssen soon changed his mind, in view of Swedish nationalist feelings and the clear fact that the Swedish state, through the railroad, could throttle any foreign initiative. Broms then gave the Norddeutsche Bank the same option, but it too lost its nerve.[22]

At this point, like "a redeeming angel," Vollrath Tham of Trafik AB staged his *coup de théâtre* by taking an option on buying the majority stock in the two companies (February 1903). Trafik AB had compelling reasons. If the northern mines fell under German control, its own sale of ore to the Germans would be seriously jeopardized. With Louis Fraenckel handling the financial negotiations, the formal purchase, for 8.7 million kronor, took place on April 16, 1904. The money for the acquisition and for the repayment of debts, came from a bond issue of about 20 million kronor to be amortized in 1907–37; the Deutsche Bank in Berlin took one-half of it, and 2 million kronor's worth of bonds were each bought by the Skandinaviska Kreditaktiebolag, Stockholms Enskilda Bank, and the Svenska Handelsbank. Broms, who had gambled and lost, died of a heart attack in October 1903.

Though the direct foreign threat had been thwarted, Trafik AB, still under foreign influence, now had nearly a monopoly on export ore in Sweden. In 1902 the government had taken the Gällivare company to court on charges of irregularities in the original claim award, thereby challenging the ownership of the mines. The company won the case, but the state still had ways of exerting pressure through the freight rates or the threat of a direct takeover of the mines.

The Liberal Coalition party had favored the state assuming one-half ownership, and so had many in the Country (agrarian) party. However, opinion had begun to shift. The Conservatives, no longer certain of controlling the government as the electoral franchise broadened, now turned against state control, while numerous Liberals, following traditional liberal principles, also had second thoughts about enhancing the power of the state.[23] Prime Minister Karl Staaff (first ministry: 1905–06) tried and failed to get legislative action on an eventual nationalization of the mines.

Vollrath Tham, a Riksdagsman for many years and also influential in the Iron Office, negotiated with the government. By the final agreement in 1907, the state became half-owner of Gällivare and Luossavaara-Kirunavaara, with the provision that it could, if then desired, take over the mines entirely in 1932 or 1942. (It finally did so in 1957.) By the 1907 compromise, the state would receive royalties from one-half of the ore produced. The company agreed not to extract, between 1908 and 1932, more than 75 million tons in the Luossavaara-Kirunavaara mines or more than 18 million at Gällivare.

The railroad was subsequently electrified, using power from the Porjus hydroelectric station, built in 1910–14, on the Lule River. Later, the state constructed the huge Harsprånget (1946–51) and Stornorrfors (1959) power stations on the Lule and Ume. Large steel mills were built at the Swedish terminals of the two main export routes. A state-owned iron and steel works, Norrbottens Järnverk, went into operation at Luleå in the 1950's, using electric furnaces and the sponge-iron process, and another big steel plant, producing about 300,000 tons of medium-heavy plate annually, was opened at Oxelösund in 1961.

In the years after the First World War about 1.3 million tons were being mined annually at Gällivare, and Kirunavaara was yielding about 3 million tons. Mining at the phosphorus-rich Luossavaara field began in 1921. Another important ore field was found at Boliden in 1918, but Axel Lindblad made the real discovery in 1924–25, using an electric ore-searching instrument that he had invented. The Germans continued to take the bulk of the phosphorus-rich export. Some iron ore was being shipped to Belgium and North America. Virtually unnoticed in the nationalist fervor of the 1890s, the British had lost interest because of the careless mixing of the unacceptable phosphorus-rich ore with the phosphorus-free at the source of shipment. Once Narvik had been opened for traffic, however, the British resumed their imports, and by 1913 were getting 11.5 percent of their ore from Sweden. In the years just before the Second World War, Sweden had become their largest supplier (23.4 percent), and the stage had been set for the German-British confrontation in Scandinavia in 1939–40.

15. THE URBAN COMMUNITY: A MISCELLANY

Asiatic cholera, which had arrived in Russia in 1830 and spread all over Europe during the next four years, reached Sweden in July 1834. It first struck Gothenburg at suburban Majorna, inhabited largely by harbor workers and sailors, and about 4,000 persons died in the seaport. Stockholm, by no means known as a health spa, lost about 3,000 that September. It took a second major epidemic in 1853, however, to persuade the authorities that the eradication of cholera and some other pestilences required, among other measures, improved water systems. Central Stockholm's water pipes were in place by 1861, the plan drafted and construction supervised by Wilhelm Leijonancker, an officer in the roads and waterways corps who had studied urban water systems in England.

Jönköping had to be pushed into following the capital's example. The second great cholera epidemic alerted the city to the danger and Leijonancker's advice was sought, but the cost seemed too great. Soon, however, the railroad officials wanted to know where to get water for their locomotives, and apparently the railroad had more impact on the officials than citizens' health; water was pouring out of the iron pipes before the end of 1865. Leijonancker directed this one, too, and also a similar project at Karlskrona.[1]

Cholera epidemics and Jönköping's locomotives, writ large, forced many advances upon the country; that is, the needs of the growing urban community encouraged the introduction of modern conveniences. Although forging and laying pipes scarcely have the glamor of international finance and a struggle over rich iron ore beds, the creation of a community infrastructure, quite aside from its impulse to greater domestic industry, was a requisite for advances in other sectors. In addition to those described earlier (railroads, telegraph, telephone, etc.) these services would include, to select only a few, piped gas and water systems, sanitary facilities, fire departments, and city street cars. Urban construction and marine installations became avid consumers of cement and concrete, a whole new industry. Great cities, stimulating mobility of persons and goods, spurred the modernization of transoceanic shipping. To which should be added such other necessities as ready-made clothing, along with the extraordinarily useful sewing machine, and office equipment, ranging from furniture to calculating machines.

236

Watching in close detail the emergence of some of the new occupations, one is reminded of the natural world where each ecological niche nourishes some forms of life that find it congenial or have adapted to it. Industrial and technological innovations in the human community brought into existence a succession of occupational niches. Each innovation and discovered need quickly drew alert individuals, eager to colonize and exploit the new terrain, much like living organisms swarming into any new niche in the ecosystem that promises sustenance.

The rapidly growing demand for pipes for gaslights, water, and sewage gave rise to a distinct line of work, a type of *verkstad* entrepreneur sensitive to new industrial possibilities and new market demands.[2] They might reorient their work several times during their careers. Four Stockholm contemporaries, three met earlier in connection with gas or electric lights, exemplify the developments: J. W. Bergström, Wilhelm Wiklund, Johan Erik Erikson, and Gustaf Wikström (1818–1868). Pioneering in a not particularly august occupation, these men of humble origin foreshadow the later emergence from the ranks of numerous industrial leaders, especially after the First World War. Three of their fathers had been workers in industry, Bergström's as a carpenter for Samuel Owen, the other two as foundrymen at Skultuna and Avesta. Erikson's father was a farmer. Bergström went to work at the age of twelve for a glassblower, Wiklund at ten as a foundryman's assistant and then as a hand-yman, and Wikström in similar work in various *bruk* in Finland and Sweden. Erikson started as a student at the Nyköping engineering works.[3]

They produced an amazing variety of articles. Bergström, the man who had set up Sweden's first daguerrotype studio (1844), had earlier passed his guild examination in glass blowing and run his own shop until changes in customs duties rendered his glass works unprofitable. He maintained the studio for about ten years while also operating a little workshop for the manufacture and repair of pipes. When the city of Stockholm contracted with Smith & Outhwaite of London to install gas lighting, Bergström protested and invited such gas company leaders as Lars Hierta, Jean Bolinder and William Lindberg to an exhibition of his own gas pipe expertise (January 1854). He subsequently put in the gas pipes at the royal palace, Riddarhuset, the central railroad station, Storkyrkan in Stockholm, and the cathedral in Uppsala. By 1877 he was supplying water closets or toilets; he also manufactured glazed clay drainage pipes, warm water heaters, washing and bathing equipment, water hose nozzles, and stoves.[4]

Wikström started a small workshop in 1845, and in 1854 became the first Swede to "make" sewing machines. However, in 1859 he also began installing gas pipes, and this soon became his major activity; he also delivered machinery for Nordenmalm's match factory, for tobacco and instrument workshops, and for breweries. Erikson's machine shop made an improved version of

Ericsson's caloric engine, telegraph apparatus, meters and pipes before he concentrated on the new field of electric lighting. For Wiklund, the fourth man, bad luck led to good luck. Working at Skultana when the second Hammarskjöld bankruptcy occurred, he secured employment with Bergström, then began his own business, and in 1859 received permission to enter gas pipe work. A fifth man, Otto Fahnehjelm (1846–1911), had more exalted origins as the son of Anton Fahnehjelm, telegraph innovator, and as a graduate in chemistry of the Institute of Technology. After participating in preliminary work leading to the founding of the first Swedish cement works, he set himself up as a consulting engineer for cement, pipes, and lime works. Having devised a gas glow lamp in which small magnesium oxide pegs were mounted in the shape of a comb (1877), Fahnehjelm established a company to manufacture and install gaslights in private homes and to make pipes for gas, water, and sewers.[5]

Larger enterprises like Atlas, Storfors, and Bångbro also manufactured pipes. Höganäs, already producing fire-proof bricks, began making clay pipes in 1869, and Skånska Cementgjuteri, a big cement company in southern Sweden, pioneered the manufacture of cement pipes. Other accouterments of urban living were being introduced: radiators by Husqvarna; radiators, pumps, and spraying hoses by Ludwigsberg; a light steam-driven transportable water pump, invented by Gustav Flodman (1894) and manufactured by William Lindberg. When Ankarsrum ceased producing iron in 1911 after 250 years, it went over, among other things, to hot water heaters, articles for water and sewage usage, and other sanitation products.

The laying of water pipes made possible a very important advance in the security of urban life, the advent of modern fire-fighting equipment. Malmö began using piped water for this purpose in 1869. Swedish cities, like all others, had suffered from catastrophic conflagrations. The central section of Karlskrona burned down in 1790. Gothenburg was ravaged by its five successive fires around the turn of the century. Virtually all of Karlstad in Värmland was destroyed on July 2, 1865, and Gävle was hard hit on July 10–11, 1869. In Stockholm, in addition to the Riddarholm (1835) and Eldkvarn (1878) fires, big ones occured on Södermalm in 1857 and at Gustav Adolfs Torg in 1873.

All able-bodied men had earlier been legally obligated to help in fire fighting if needed, but in the nineteenth century special individuals were increasingly appointed to handle the equipment, and volunteers were permanently enrolled on fire department lists. Gothenburg set up an organized permanent fire-fighting corps in 1872. After the Gustav Adolfs Torg fire, Stockholm moved to establish a modern fire department, copying the Berlin corps, which had been organized by Scabell in 1851 along military lines. Endowed with a similar military structure and discipline by Commander Bruno Hallsten, the 130-man Stockholm department faced its first major challenge in the Eldkvarn fire.[6] Most of the Swedish cities replaced voluntary departments with permanent ones in the 1890s and early 1900s.

Sweden's first steam fire engine was purchased in England by Gothenburg in 1862, shortly after the British again began manufacturing them, but not until the cities established regular fire departments did they come into general use. The Ljusne Mek. Verkstad, better known for its extensive timber activities, became for a time the most important manufacturer of equipment. Ludwigsberg moved into the field later, making steam- and motor-driven pumps, compressors, and fire hose.[7]

Cement, like pipes, became a requisite for building the modern urban community, but it was the work on canals and harbors that originally stimulated a demand for it in Sweden. Gustaf Pasch, the inventor of the safety match, experimented with a cement for that purpose, made from limestone and burned clay. It hardened slowly and was expensive, however, hence the rapidly increasing import of Portland cement, invented by Joseph Aspdin and improved by Isaac Johnson. The growing demand helps to explain the motives for the founding of the Skånska Cementaktiebolag in 1871.[8]

A geological survey by Professor Otto Torell of Lund University and Otto Fahnehjelm found the clay and lime in Skåne suitable for the manufacture of Portland cement, and Wilhelm Michaëlis, a German expert, specifically approved using clay from Lomma and lime from Limhamn. These properties "happened" to belong to that skilled Malmö businessman and industrialist, Frans Henrik Kockum, who outmaneuvered a rich farmer, Hans Andersson, whose land also possessed the necessary components. During the negotiations, Kockum persisted in calling him "the *bonde*," (the peasant), though Andersson, too, had sat in the Riksdag. The Lomma and Limhamn properties were bought from Kockum, and, though the experts preferred Limhamn as the site for the factory, the buildings went up at Lomma, where a ready harbor and workers' quarters already existed. Michaëlis directed the construction, the Kockum factory made the machinery, and the steam engine came from Bolinders.

The new company found ready sales and was working at full capacity by 1875. The plant delivered cement for harbor construction at Hälsingborg (where cement blocks were being used in the 1860s), Malmö, Ystad, and other places, the railroads began buying it, and so did the farmers for new buildings. A big fire gave Rudolf Fredrik (Fritz) Berg (1846–1907), the managing director, an opportunity to introduce the production of *fine* cement, the coarser product not being suitable for some customers. In the same reconstruction he reorganized the manufacturing to reduce costs in order to meet the competition from Germany. In 1888 Berg rectified the original error by moving the factory to Limhamn, simultaneously installing ring kilns. A second plant was

239

inaugurated by other businessmen at Visby on the island of Gotland in 1883, a third at Degerhamn on Öland, and three others were in operation by 1900. Large imports from Britain ceased by 1890, and Germany remained the principal foreign supplier.

At the Paris World Exhibition of 1878 Berg studied a display of artistically created cement articles, such as mosaic tiles, steps, and decorative objects. Seeing the possibilities, he went home and, with Carl J. Åkerman, experimented in a cellar in Malmö until they had discovered the correct procedures for casting cement into various forms. A small factory was set up in the harbor area of Malmö, and in 1887 the Skånska Cementgjuteri (cement foundry), whose annual production value in the years after the Second World War would surpass 100 million kronor, was established as a separate enterprise. During the early years it made decorative articles (monuments and additions for churches), foundation work for buildings, and such accessories as pipes and sewer conduits. It also made fountains, cornices, urns, and decorations for balconies and terraces. Its first concrete reservoir was built at Västerås in 1887, and its first two cement bridges (in Skåne) permanently altered the art of bridge building in Sweden.[9]

Much public attention was attracted by its contribution to the building of the Johannes Church on Brunkeberget in Stockholm, where crowds, even including King Oscar II, came to watch the red cement being put into place. Many other churches were later modeled on it. Its decorative work was also used in renovating Uppsala cathedral and in the construction of the new opera house. Having purchased François Hennebique's Swedish patent on reinforced concrete (1902), the Cementgjuteri gained a dominant role in its use for buildings, hydroelectric works, harbors, piers, and bridges. In 1906 it was responsible for Sweden's first concrete street, in Malmö, but it would be the 1920s before these became common.

Stockholm and Gothenburg both began laying the rails for horse-drawn streetcars in the later 1870s, the decade of their rapid European expansion generally. Although a street railway had been laid down for a New York–Harlem line in 1832, its replacement, with better rails, under the direction of a French engineer, Alphonse Loubat, in 1852 is usually considered the first true street railway. Loubat constructed a similar line in Paris three years later. Among northern cities, Copenhagen followed in 1862, Berlin in 1865, and Christiania (Oslo) in 1875.

A Stockholm company, organized in 1872, had to wait for a committee report and then for royal approval until 1876. A new private company was then organized, the necessary stock subscriptions were soon in hand, and it received a 40-year concession. The laying of tracks started in three places in May 1877 in central and northern Stockholm, while a separate company built and operated the lines in the southern part of the city. The originally open streetcars were manufactured by the railroad equipment company, Atlas, which later also experimented with steam-driven cars. As elsewhere in Europe, the latter usage was strictly limited because of excessive pollution and uneconomical costs by comparison with horse-drawn traction. Electrification of tramways occurred with extreme rapidity in the United States in 1888–93 after the innovative breakthrough by Frank J. Sprague. European cities quickly followed in 1893–98. The two Stockholm companies went over to electric power in 1901 and 1904; they were preceded by the first Swedish electrified railroad, the Djursholm suburban Stockholm line (1895).[10]

Gothenburg's blue streetcars are still cherished by its inhabitants with much the same affection that the people of San Francisco retain for their cable cars. The original concession for a tramway was awarded to Captain C. J. Juel of Copenhagen in 1877, who began the construction. Two years later he turned it over to a British citizen who in turn relinquished it to a British-owned company, The Gothenburg Tramways Company, Ltd. The first horse-drawn cars rolled over the rails in September 1879.[11] On January 1, 1900, the municipality took over the system from the company, which, fearing loss of the franchise, had not kept it in good repair. Rather than restore it, the city decided to convert the tramway to electric power, and for this purpose summoned home J. S. Edström.

Sigfrid Edström (1870–1964) was the son of a Gothenburg sea captain. As a young boy he often accompanied the father on his voyages, and he once fell overboard in the English Channel, an exploit that may or may not have contributed to his life-long interest in sports. After graduating from Chalmers and studying at the Polytechnikum in Zürich, Edström worked in the United States for Westinghouse in Pittsburgh and at General Electric in Schenectady; both were involved in the electrification of streetcar lines. In 1897 he returned to Europe to participate in the conversion of the Zürich tramway to electricity, then went back to the United States, at which point his home town requested his services.

Edström was dispatching orders before he arrived personally, and this "dynamo of energy" who "worked 24 hours a day" had the job completed more cheaply and faster than anticipated. His exploit attracted the attention of Marcus Wallenberg, who was looking for a new managing director for ASEA, and suddenly Edström found himself holding one of the most important industrial positions in Sweden. He also became the driving spirit in the organization of the Swedish athletic association, played an important part in the staging of the Stockholm Olympics in 1912, and was long an international figure in sports, including serving on the Olympic committee.[12]

While directing ASEA, Edström also supervised the electrification of streetcar lines in Hälsingborg, Norrköping, Malmö and other cities. Seven municipalities, including Uppsala and Jönköping, had electric tramway systems by 1907, and five more by 1914. Beginning with the railroad to Narvik before 1914, the state would later convert the entire state system to electric power.

Another kind of transportation, this time vertical, became available to Stockholmers in 1883 when Kurt Lindmark (1838–1892) completed an elevator tower that gave easy access to the heights of Mosebacke. After graduating from the Marieberg engineering school, he worked as a surveyor for the state railroad, then became one of that increasingly numerous band of Swedish engineers who sought employment outside the country. Several had gone to Argentina, where the British held the railroad concession, and Lindmark in 1868 joined an engineering bureau in Buenos Aires that was drafting plans for the various railroad routes.

Having saved his money, he returned to Stockholm in 1876. He had become aware, during railroad work there, of the steep 35-meter ascent of Mosebacke, a thickly populated hill that rises abruptly from the waters of Saltsjön just southeast of Slussen. Here Lindmark erected Katarinahissen, the Katherine Elevator, and connected the tower to Mosebacke by a 151-meter pedestrian steel bridge. A restaurant, a "Schweizerei," perched on top of the tower. The two hydro-pneumatic elevators came from Weeks and Halsey of Brooklyn, and the power was provided by a steam engine. Traffic opened on March 19, 1883, and, at a cost of five öre up and three öre down, soon attracted over 4,500 passengers a day.[13] Stockholmers were disposed to regard it, with much exaggeration, as their Eiffel Tower after that more conspicuous Paris structure went up six years later. Though Katarinahissen had to be moved in the 1930s to clear the ground for a highway, the price remained the same until 1966. It now costs fifty öre to make the 18-second ascent.

Lindmark then solved a second traffic problem by digging a tunnel for pedestrians through Brunkeberget, a high esker lying between the city center and Östermalm to the east. When they started tunneling, the house above gave signs of restlessness. Lindmark rushed to England and bought a compressor cooling machine with which to freeze a third of a meter each night. It took four months to complete the first 35 meters. After that peril had been surmounted, things went faster, and the 231-meter tunnel was completed in March 1886. In financial distress from the cost of the project, Lindmark was named manager of Motala, only to lose the post soon thereafter when it changed owners. An attempt to start a combined shipyard and engineering works brought him to bankruptcy. His immediate family, whose savings had gone into it, was financially ruined, and on April 17, 1892, Knut Lindmark, distant relative of Berzelius and Sven Rinman, shot himself.

In the later years of the century about one-half of all Swedish steamships were based in Stockholm or Gothenburg and were almost exclusively engaged in Baltic, North Sea, and domestic traffic. Swedish transoceanic commerce was still largely by small (450-ton) sailing vessels, the greater number from provincial harbors.[14] Stockholm's proportion of exports had dropped from about 30 percent of the country's total in 1840 to about 11 percent by 1895. Its industries, aside from engineering and metal works, now tended to consist of breweries, bakeries, creameries, and tobacco factories for local consumption.[15]

The cities on the North Sea were Gothenburg's natural ports of destination throughout this period.[16] Swedish emigrants passed through its harbor in large numbers. Though some left by way of Copenhagen or Hamburg, most of them boarded ships in Gothenburg for Hull on the North Sea, from whence, in the 1880s, a four-hour train brought them to Liverpool for embarkation, usually on Cunard or Inman liners. The Wilson line, founded in Hull by Thomas Wilson (1835), had maintained a semiregular twice-a-month schedule between Gothenburg and Hull as far back as the later 1840s. A son, John West Wilson (1816–1889), moved to Gothenburg and handled the Swedish part of the firm's extensive business, which ultimately involved more than a hundred steamships. In addition to passengers, the Wilson line was shipping out oats, wood, paper, and pulp, hence John's interest in the New Gellivare Company and Norrland exports. Not even Lazarus could find anything bad to write about Wilson; according to him, his office possessed the best personnel in Sweden and John himself was one of the most popular men in the city's history.[17]

The Svenska Lloyd shipping company of Gothenburg was founded in 1869 for the purpose of maintaining regular steamship traffic with Hamburg, and the Svea Rederi of Stockholm took over the Stockholm–Lübeck route from Schön & Co. two years later.[18] Ludvig Fredholm, later business organizer of ASEA, participated in founding Svea, which was partially owned by the Samuel Godenius and N. M. Höglund firms. Although the merchant houses went bankrupt in 1878, the Svea shipping company survived and operated a number of steamships and sailing vessels, its old-fashioned sailing vessels often wandering from port to port in various parts of the world to pick up available cargo. In addition, Svea Rederi maintained some regular lines; one from Stockholm to Amsterdam often stopped at such other ports as Hull, London, or Calais.[19] Svenska Lloyd's first ship, built at Keillers, was wrecked, but it had four on the seas by 1872, and it soon extended its trading area to Bordeaux, Portugal, Spain, and the Mediterranean ports. In 1914 it owned fourteen steamers with a total tonnage of 26,832, and shortly thereafter, by the purchase of another company, it secured a sizable portion of the Swedish-British commerce.

These companies usually began by buying old ships, most often British, then using the profits from them to acquire more modern ones. Axel Broström (1838–1905) started with small freight sailing vessels on Lake Vänern, out of

243

which grew two companies, AB Ferm and AB Tirfing. The latter, founded in 1890, purchased a whole series of such British steamers with which to challenge the foreign-owned traffic of ore boats from Oxelösund; when the railroad to Narvik had been completed, the first load of Swedish iron ore went out on the Broström-owned *Uppland*.[20]

Under his son, Daniel Broström (1870–1925), the company built its own ships. Eriksberg shipyard was purchased in 1915, and the following year he secured majority control of AB Götaverken (old Keillers), which was then modernized. Meanwhile, in 1907 he had become the managing director of the Swedish East Asia Company, aimed at Swedish trade with China and Japan. This prospered so much that in 1911 two more companies, Broström leading in both, came into existence, the Swedish America-Mexico Line for traffic with Central America and the West Indies, and the Swedish Levant, later the Swedish Orient Company, to serve in the eastern Mediterranean. Finally, in 1914 Broström helped to found and became managing director of what later would be known as the Swedish-American Line. Obviously possessed of a keen sense of business, the bespectacled man with the "bird face" (Falk) built an empire without jeopardizing it by reckless speculative gambles. Politically active, he served in the Riksdag as a Liberal and was in the Hammarskjöld ministry of 1914–17. In love with ships and seafaring all his life, Broström was killed on dry land in an automobile accident in July 1925; Gothenburg had good reason to fly its flags at half mast that day.

Another ship-owning magnate, Axel Johnson (1844–1910), whose family name survives internationally in the far-flung ships of the Johnson Line, began life as the son of a saddler. The founder of one of Sweden's most powerful families went to work at the age of thirteen and by 1873 was able to start a company that imported coal and charcoal and exported iron, steel and timber. This in turn made it expedient to acquire a fleet of ships, leading to the organization of the Nordstjernan company (1890). Johnson, too, was drawn to the growing opportunities in the iron ore trade, and he had several special ships built in order to participate in the Oxelösund, Luleå and Narvik export. In 1904 he gained majority control of the Avesta iron and steel works. That same year he opened a transatlantic steamship route to South America, the Sweden–La Plata line, and this was followed in 1909 by a similar line to Brazil.[21]

His son, Axel Axelsson Johnson (1876–1958), built on this extremely promising foundation. In 1911, shortly after the death of his father, he decided to use motorships, a "brave resolve at this time," and ordered *six* of them, about 6,500 tons each, from Burmeister & Wain in Copenhagen. The first one delivered, the *Suecia*, was the first Swedish motorship and one of the earliest in the world. All launched by 1915, they were used on the Latin American routes. The Johnson business empire ultimately included a diverse group: Nordstjernan (also known as the Johnson Line), the Avesta steel works, Lindholmen shipyard, Nynäshamn petroleum refinery, the Linjebuss fleet of tourist busses, Karlstads Mek. Verkstad, and a part interest in Motala.

A third founder of shipping companies, Wilhelm Lundgren (1854–1914), began his career as a pilot and captain on ships based on Gothenburg. After an initial company largely engaged in transporting timber products to England, he organized, with Walter Dickson and Douglas Kennedy, the Nike Line for traffic with South Africa (1900), but, cargoes being difficult to find there, the Nike ships soon extended their range to Australia. In 1904 the Rederi AB Transatlantic was also formed, and the two were merged in 1909 under the latter name. Lundgren campaigned vigorously for a Swedish-American line, vainly seeking sufficient capital from both the state and private enterprise. Shortly before Lundgren's death in London, however, Daniel Broström joined a number of others in founding AB Sweden-North America. A Dutch ship, renamed the Stockholm, began transatlantic passenger service to New York in 1915; at 12,606 tons, it was Sweden's largest. In 1919, after the war years, the turbine-driven Drottningholm was purchased, and by the end of the 1920s the Swedish-American Line, as it was renamed in 1925, had three passenger ships in regular service.

Long afterward, in 1960, the Broström group (Swedish-American, Swedish East Asia, Swedish Orient, and AB Tirfing) possessed 89 ships, Svea owned 53, Transatlantic had 44, and Nordstjernan (Johnson) maintained 39. Other larger companies included the Salén group (44), Grängesberg-Oxelösund (32), and Wallenius (20). The Swedish-American passenger service dwindled away in the 1960s, its former customers now traveling on SAS (Scandinavian Airlines System). Swedish shipyards collapsed even more abruptly.

In the twentieth century about 90 percent of all Swedish shipbuilding was ultimately concentrated at three Gothenburg shipyards: Götaverken, Lindholmen, and Eriksberg Mek. Verkstad. After the bankruptcy of Alexander Keiller in 1867, the principal figures in the new company were Olof Wijk the younger, John West Wilson, and James Keiller (son of the founder), who remained managing director until 1906. The company was also making railroad cars, railroad switches, snowplows, and parts for bridges; the number of workers, varying greatly with the business cycles, averaged about 600 between 1870 and 1900. The company continued building smaller freight and passenger ships until 1911. In that year a contract for the Russian icebreaker, Peter the Great, inaugurated a new period of growth for the shipyard; between 1906 and 1947 it constructed 33 steamers and 285 motorships.[22]

Alexander Keiller had met fierce competition from Th. W. Tranchell, a merchant also trying to take advantage of the opportunities presented by the Gothenburg waterway traffic. Tranchell and colleagues founded Lindholmens Varv in 1844 and, after the completion of a dry dock (1855), its rivalry forced Keiller to more vigorous measures. Motala took over control of Lindholmen in

1858 and many Motala ships were launched there until 1893, when the Gothenburg shipyard again became a separate enterprise; it was subsequently owned by AB Lindholmen-Motala in 1920–36, by the Johnson interests in 1941–69, and by Eriksberg after 1969. Eriksbergs Mek. Verkstad had been started by C. G. Barchman (Norwegian) in 1853 as the first Swedish shop for galvanizing iron and steel. Also doing ship repair work, it began building them in 1871, and by the 1890s this had become its sole activity. By 1947–48 Eriksberg had constructed 126 steamers and 130 motorships.

Götaverken in the years around 1970 could briefly claim to rank as the second largest shipyard in the world, and Eriksberg and Kockums in Malmö were doing extremely well. Götaverken, Eriksberg, Lindholmen, and a fourth, Arendalsverken, had a combined total of over 12,000 workers in Gothenburg in 1974–75, after which, as happened in shipyards all over western Europe, they encountered almost insurmountable difficulties in competing on the international shipbuilding market.

Turning now to an entirely different sector of the urban economy, the arrival of the sewing machine (*symaskin*) made possible the emergence of a large-scale garment industry. The free sale of ready-made clothes had been legalized in Sweden in 1834, but the practice, arising naturally out of the handicraft putting-out system, had been covertly underway since well back in the eighteenth century. Though fought by the guilds, the making and secret sale of clothing out in the countryside was impossible to stop. Once legalized, the sale of clothing in booths and stores grew rapidly.[23]

In Stockholm, Julius Jacobsson seems to have been the first to use sewing machines in his own workshop to make shirts and collars (1861). In the following year, S. Berendt was advertising machine-made shirts in Stockholm newspapers. In 1873 he was employing 17 men, 193 women, and 6 children in his factory, plus an additional 230 women "outworking" in their own homes. Near the end of the century about 3,000 workers were employed in 54 factories, and by 1912 these figures had risen to 8,500 workers and 136 factories.[24]

Barthélemy Thimmonier in France invented a sewing machine in 1830, but his factory was later destroyed in Luddite rioting. Successive patents in the United States were obtained by Elias Howe (1846), A. B. Wilson (1848), and Isaac Singer (1851), and Singer's machine made possible the great growth of the garment industry. By 1860 no less than 110,000 sewing machines were made in that single year. The first manufactured ones in Europe appeared at the Deutsche Nähmaschinen-Fabrik in Frankfurt-am-Main in 1862 and Pollack, Schmidt & Co. of Hamburg, a German-American firm, followed in 1863. The Germans soon developed their own models, and in the 1870s were selling the least expensive sewing machines in the world.[25]

Moving with alacrity, Gustaf Wikström was attempting to make them by basically handicrafts methods in his small Stockholm shop in the 1850s. Having imported a model in 1854, he was already in July of that year claiming a patent on an "improved" model.[26] This kind of rapid improvement can normally be interpreted as alteration sufficient to escape buying patent rights on the original model. His few workers were still making them when Wikström died in 1868—that is, they were presumably assembling the parts, some bought abroad and others made in the shop. Wilhelm Wenström brought back a Wheeler & Wilson from the United States in 1858, but that many-sided Örebro engineer had too many other interests to do anything about it. Foreign-made models were being advertised for sale by 1861, the major demand coming from women who were making clothes in their homes for businessmen. Both Jacobsson and Berendt became sales agents for the Wheeler & Wilson machine, which they were also using in their own workshops. Herman Meeth began selling Singers in 1864, and five others were advertising foreign models in Stockholm before the end of the decade.[27]

Any foreign import was very likely to inspire a flock of aspiring entrepreneurs, always on the lookout for new opportunities. In this case they usually seem to have started by importing the parts and assembling them, then later, perhaps, introducing their own models. After Wikström, the second seems to have been Carl Gustaf Jachaeus, an ex-foreman for Bergström, who was making American-model machines between 1861 and 1866. Two neighboring shops, Öller & Co. and M. A. Rundlöf & Co., were producing them by 1863; Rundlöf was making instruments and Öller, of course, telegraph apparatus, both activities closely enough related to sewing machines to make the transition relatively easy. Arvid Böhlmark, who at this time was assembling the foreign-made parts for kerosene lamps and stoves, became the agent for the Elias Howe machine (1874). Several firms had appeared before 1870 in Gothenburg, Norrköping, Örebro, and Visby. An interesting variation occurred in Dalarna, then and now a center for Swedish home industries, where the Mora Mekaniska Fabriks AB had about fifty persons assembling American machines, probably the Wheeler & Wilson and called Svenska Symaskiner (1865).[28] After the small fry, however, came the industrial giant, Husqvarna Vapenfabrik, which, after initial problems, went into industrial production, forcing the smaller rivals to withdraw and giving imported sewing machines stiff competition.

Stockholm's concentration of factories on Kungsholmen, their chimneys belching thick smoke, may have spelled progress to industrialists and technologists, but for many others they seemed to threaten an evil future. The prospect of industrialization had evoked more apprehension than anticipation in wide circles. Factories and machinery seemed, according to Paul Lindblom, to be "something foreign, dangerous and hostile" that would "bind and enslave humanity."[29] Compared to outdoor work, the factory seemed degrading. Erik Gustaf Geijer, the great writer, had visited England in 1809–10, and, unlike the Swedish metallurgists and technicians, came away with a grim vision of its dark side. He returned home to write a description of the factory system in terms of poverty, unemployment, and abominable living conditions for the workers. Fredrika Bremer, in England in 1849, described child labor, young lives and happiness destroyed by the factories. Viktor Rydberg, in 1891, wrote a bitter criticism of the industrial community, Den Nya Grottesången (The New Treadmill Song). Swedish factories sometimes seemed to confirm such fears, including the widespread use of child labor in textile mills, garment factories, mines, and match-making.[30] The smallest workshops were usually the worst: longer hours, more overtime, poor protection against accidents. In most of them, twelve to thirteen hours of labor were customary.

Though bad enough in the early decades, the worst in terms of crowded housing and industrial cities never did happen as Swedish industry tended to stay in the countryside and the Swedes, starting later, learned to avoid the worst British circumstances. In Stockholm, those noxious factories on Kungsholmen were being moved to the outskirts of the city in the later years of the century. For that matter, conditions would have had to be very bad indeed to exceed the preindustrial crowding in the capital city and the overpopulation on the limited farming areas in the provinces.

One significant early reaction against industrialization took the form of organizing the Svenska Slöjdförening (Swedish Handicraft Association), aimed at the preservation and promotion of the peasant crafts (1845). It encouraged high quality, good taste, and beauty in the traditional crafts, and slöjd, meaning handicraft and especially woodworking, would retain an honored and typically Swedish place in the national culture. As it has continued to be practiced in Dalarna and Småland, the handicraft industry became the very antithesis of factory manufacturing in large urban communities.

In Dalarna, where the peasants had built up a handicraft tradition over several centuries, each parish developed a specialty: in Orsa they prepared grindstones, in Mora they made clocks, and others became known for leather goods, casks, baskets, bureaus, or other articles. Clock making, in which individual craftsmen made the different parts, was at its peak in about 1850, after which imports from Switzerland and the Schwarzwald (Black Forest, in Germany) destroyed their market. To provide new work for those who then lost their livelihood, a pastor suggested to an engineer at Furudal bruk that he initiate the Mora sewing machine project, with its rather similar kind of activity. When Husqvarna and imports eliminated that, the making of knives and other articles gradually took its place. Dalarna handicrafts persisted: perforation and boring tools, ladders, ticket punchers, and all manner of wooden articles, including the famous tourist item, a small, brightly colored wooden horse.[31]

Småland had sufficient woods and forests to undertake small wood products handicraft. For a long time some peasant families made spinning wheels, as long as they were in demand. Others made furniture, toys, doll houses, chess pieces, swings, skittles, and croquet sets. In the 1890s they were buying kerosene motors and machines for their village manufacturing and tending to specialize in furniture. Småland's glass works would become internationally famous. Kosta had been started as far back as 1742 by Baron Koskull, who brought in glassblowers from Bohemia. The best known of all, Orrefors (once a small foundry), began in 1898 and attained renown with the work of the designers Simon Gate and Edward Hald after the First World War. Not far from Kosta, the only active handicraft paper mill still survives at, of all places, Lessebo, where, in 1836, one of the first paper-making machines had been installed.

Small industry would continue to flourish in the province. By way of explanation, John Jansson quoted the head of a larger factory in the region in mid-twentieth century, who said that his best workers sooner or later quit his factory to work on their own. They seemed to prefer to work sixteen or seventeen hours a day for themselves by making "toys and other trash" for dubious profits rather than putting in an eight-hour day for secure and higher wages. "Soon there will be an electric motor in every woodshed hereabouts."[32] Things had obviously changed in Småland since the days of Dr. Aschan.

Office furniture, typewriters, and calculating machines are decidedly an important part of the modern urban community, and in Sweden these became associated with the name of Åtvidaberg, a former *bruk* situated in southeastern Södermanland. Dating back to the 1300s, its story, ranging from medieval trolls and sorcery to twentieth-century technological magic, in some respects even rivals that of Stora Kopparbergs Bergslaget.

The components of its original name are descriptive of the place: Åsvedher-berg—esker, woods, ore-bearing rock. Its first official notice occurred in a royal *privilegium* issued in 1413. In 1468 the king gave a new charter in which the miners received the right to choose their own bailiff (*fogde*), who would also represent the Crown. Another milestone was passed when, on January 3, 1500, ten persons met at Linköping and organized a company to exploit a silver mine at Åtvidaberg. They rented the accompanying copper mines to another group.[33]

According to the miners, a dreadful troll or witch, called *Mormor* or Grandmother, inhabited one of the shafts, and to keep on good terms with this apparition they named it for her, "Grandmother's mine." Swedish workers time and again had heard, in various mines, the mocking shrieks of trolls and caught glimpses of shadowy, lurking forms; Olaus Magnus (1490–1557), Sweden's great theologian and wise man, believed that six different kinds of trolls inhabited Swedish mines. Gösta Adelswärd, a member of the former owning family, related in his charming and humorously illustrated little book that Bishop Hans Brask of Linköping, who had to leave Sweden because he refused to accept Gustav Vasa's Lutheran church, may have put a curse on an Åtvidaberg copper mine. Tradition has it that he threw his episcopal ring into one of the mines and cursed it with the words, "Let no one find ore here before Brask's ring is again found!"—then had the mine filled in. It was reopened in the 1700s under such difficulties that the workers had abundant food for thought. In time the reluctant diggers discovered a ring, apparently episcopal, and soon thereafter they encountered ore. The ring is still in existence, but whether it once belonged to Brask remains very much moot. Adelswärd suspected that someone relieved the situation by pitching a ring into the mine for the laborers to find.[34]

The so-called "Barony Åtvidaberg," based on forests, farmland and the mining of about a hundred tons of copper a year, came into existence when Baron Johan Adelswärd (d. 1785) gained control of a company founded in 1761, and Gustav III then chartered the properties as an entailed estate (1783). Throughout the nineteenth century the Adelswårds maintained a virtual feudal lordship over their bucolic barony by their paternalistic management and strong caste system. Another member of the family owned nearby Överum (1816–1861). Paul Du Chaillu, who visited Åtvidaberg in 1879, saw in this "Arcadian spot" a street of red houses with tile roofs, a small market, and a bathhouse. From close by came the sound of splashing water going over the dam. The town still had a night watchman going his rounds with a *lur* (horn) and calling out the hours. Seemingly an attractive glimpse of the good old days, except that Du Chaillu noted that "the distant hills looked dark and desolate, for the sulfurous smoke, carried day after day with the wind, had destroyed the vegetation."[35] Copper production reached a peak of about a thousand tons in 1869. The Adelswärds had acquired one of Samuel Owen's steam engines, and in 1857 they opened their own railway, using two Munktell locomotives, between the town and the mines. Railroad connections north to Norrköping had to wait until 1879.[36]

Baron Theodor Adelswärd (1866–1929) at the age of twenty-three took over control from his father and continued to manage Åtvidaberg until 1913. The copper ore was running out; too many of the workers were migrating to the United States, and the ancient enterprise, like so many others at the time, would have to find a new industry or go under. It did have ample forest resources, and Adelswärd put the carpenters to work making wagon wheels by American industrial methods. Scarcely a promising solution, but who could know that at the time? Then chance intervened to propel Åtvidaberg in a new direction, into a future whose exciting possibilities could scarcely have been foreseen, either, in the early years.

Adelswärd attended the 1889 Paris Exposition, and there a display of American office furniture interested him. On his return train trip from Paris to Berlin he shared a coupé with an American who turned out to be the European agent for the sale of American machinery used for making office furniture. The agent altered his itinerary to visit Åtvidaberg, Adelswärd bought the machinery, and quite quickly the ancient barony, with its forest reserves and helped by the 1892 protective tariff, gained a national and even international reputation for its new lines of office furniture.[37] Most of its copper works burned down some years later, and some time after this, in 1911, the production of copper ceased entirely. No longer did sulfurous smoke desolate the landscape, and the town was attractively rebuilt into a veritable "Arcadian" garden city. In 1906 the various enterprises, including dairying, a mill, and a brewery, were combined into AB Åtvidabergs Förenade Industrier (United Industries). In 1917 the long Adelswärd regime came to an end when a majority of the stock was sold to a consortium, though the entailed estate itself was not abolished until 1963.

Adelswärd organized a hydroelectric company to provide electricity for the factories, and in time Åtvidaberg, like Stora Kopparbergs Bergslaget and Uddeholm, was generating the power for a regional network. The forward-looking baron displayed less foresight when he permitted a man returned from the United States to manufacture an automobile. It looked like a buggy and had the engine under the body, and nobody would buy an automobile already antiquated in 1910.[38] As for the doomed wagon wheels, the company once again had to find a new industry, and in the 1920s it began to make refrigerator cabinets for Electrolux and wooden elements for Volvo automobile chassis. Åtvidaberg's main development, however, would follow the direction inaugurated by the manufacture of office furniture: merging Åtvidaberg with companies making office machines and supplies—Halda, Odhner and Addo.

Halda and Odhner had their origins in the last quarter of the nineteenth century. Halda began as a pocket watch factory, for a time the only one in Scandinavia. It had been founded by Henning Hammarlund (1857–1922) in 1887 in a small town in the province of Blekinge after he had spent the preceding seven years traveling and working in cities stretching from Russia to Rockford, Illinois. Fascinated by watches since boyhood, he sought employment in watch factories and attended an instructional school in Geneva. One of his watches won a prize at the Chicago World Fair. Another one, given away in the United States, turned up, photographed, in a technical journal and credited to someone else's ingenuity. In 1892 his factory also started making the Telur, a device that he had invented for measuring the length of telephone calls. The first Halda typewriter, which would become one Swedish model, appeared in

251

1896. Another invention, taxameters, for use by taxis (horse-drawn at first) began to be made in 1902. In 1907 the Halda production consisted of 600 pocket watches, 1,300 Telurs, 190 taxameters, and 18 typewriters. Other devices, such as coin changers, followed in the small company that was catering to a whole array of new needs in the urban community.[39]

The Odhner calculating machines became internationally famous. The earliest in Sweden, however, had been devised by Georg Scheutz (1785–1873). Son of a Stockholm restaurant owner, he had attended Lund University and then served in the bureaucracy before becoming an editor and book publisher. He began working on a calculating machine in 1812 that would print out mathematical tables, a task that he continued for decades. In 1834 he read about Charles Babbage's so-called "difference machine" in the *Edinburgh Review,* forthwith decided that his own approach had been faulty, and between 1834 and 1853, helped by his son (Edvard), designed a successful one. Financed by the government and constructed by J. W. Bergström, the (primitive) automatic typesetting machine contained 4,320 different parts and was the size of a small piano. Scheutz received grants and a pension from the government, the machine earned a gold medal at the 1855 Paris Exposition, and it was purchased by the Dudley Observatory in Albany, New York. It now resides in the Smithsonian in Washington, D. C. Even that "irascible genius," the great Charles Babbage, treated Scheutz's brainchild most amiably. One more was constructed by Bryan Donkin in London for the General Register Office at Somerset House, but the £2000 price tag scared off any other buyers.[40]

Once Scheutz's first machine had been sold, the government discovered that it was needed to work out interest tables to be used in levying taxes. Whereupon Martin Wiberg (1826–1905) invented a calculating machine, based on different principles, which worked five times faster and was only a fourth as big (1859–60). The machine calculations were transmitted by lead on guttapercha, not durable enough for much printing, and it took Wiberg thirteen more years to develop a method using copper plate. This gave him an international reputation; the Academy of Science proposed to reward him with 3000 riksdaler, the king raised it to 5000, and the not usually generous Riksdag granted him 8000. Hoping to manufacture it in the United States, he wrote to John Ericsson. The disgruntled inventor advised him to forget about it because a Yankee capitalist was far more likely to invest in a new rat trap than "in your admirable calculating machine."

Martin Wiberg became one of Sweden's most gifted inventors, though some of the villagers in Viby (Skåne) had not expected the child to live long because his eyes "sparkled like stars so that one can scarcely look at him." His father put Martin and two brothers through Lund at the price of losing his farm. Offered a teaching position at the university, Martin refused, not able to resist his inventive compulsions. For half a century his fertile brain continued to produce new devices used in printing, railroad apparatus, the postal service, the match industry, dairying, and weapons. And—on paper—a jet airplane, patented in 1903![41]

The third man, Willgodt Odhner (1845–1905), spent his productive years in St. Petersburg, where, after studying at the Institute of Technology, he procured employment at the Ludwig Nobel factories. In his spare time he worked on calculating machines, possibly inspired by the mathematical problems resulting from the redistribution of land after the emancipation of the serfs. His first commercial calculator appeared in 1875, followed by a pinwheel adding machine a few years later. Ludwig Nobel helped defray some of the early expenses, but this particular inventor-entrepreneur relationship soon became strained and Odhner moved to the printing division of the Russian mint. His most significant contribution came with his multiplication machine in 1890, patented also in Germany and manufactured under the name of Brunsviga. His original aim had been to invent small, cheap models capable of being manufactured by industrial methods, and his type of compact machine with thin wheels was widely copied in other countries.[42]

A first little workshop, opened in 1880, was replaced in 1894 by a factory in which, in addition to the calculators, Odhner also made cigarette-packing machines, presses for multicolored currency, gramophones, and oil burners. After he died of a heart attack, a son and son-in-law carried on the firm, which became a company in 1912. Altogether, about 30,000 calculating machines were made, mostly sold in Russia, before 1917. When the Bolsheviks seized the factory, the relevant diagrams and documents had to be smuggled out to Gothenburg, where the leaders in the SKF ball-bearing company (Sven and Erik Winquist, Axel Carlander, Assar Gabrielsson, and others) furnished the capital for a resumption of production under the name of AB Original-Odhner.[43]

Competitors had appeared in Sweden, such as Merkur, invented by J. Hultman and A. M. Johansson in 1900–04. Most important was a ten-key calculating machine by Karl Rudin in the early 1930s and manufactured at Åtvidaberg. Sweden ranked second in the world in the export of calculating machines just before the Second World War, behind the United States and ahead of Germany and Switzerland. A series of mergers then and later have been intended to strengthen the industry's position in world markets. In 1938 Åtvidaberg Industrier acquired Halda, whose principal output during the preceding twenty years had been typewriters, and three years later Original-Odhner joined the group. The Addo company, based in Malmö (1918) and making calculating and bookkeeping machinery and also furniture, was added in 1966, the entire ensemble now being known as AB Facit. In 1971 Swedish Electrolux, with its abundant capital, gained control of the complex of companies and factories. In sum, Åtvidaberg and its cohorts have obviously, over the years, made an indispensable contribution, domestically, to the office work of commerce and industry, and to the arsenal of the proliferating state bureaucracy, within the increasingly urbanized Swedish community.

16. TECHNOLOGISTS TRIUMPHANT: THE INVENTORS

Sweden never would be able to compete with the great industrial powers in mass production. Beyond the export of raw materials, the most successful Swedish approach would be to specialize in certain highly developed industries and offer quality products in these. A series of "pioneering technical contributions and inventions during the greater part of the preceding decade prepared for . . . the industrial expansion" of the 1890s.[1] The so-called *intelligensindustrier* (intelligence industries), starting in the later nineteenth century, would greatly contribute to the Swedes carving out for themselves a profitable role in the world economy.

A number of inventors have been met in earlier contexts: John Ericsson, Lagerman, Palmcrantz, L. M. Ericsson, Jonas Wenström, Ernst Danielson, Scheutz, Wiberg, Odhner. They had emerged in the midst of the many innovators, some of the latter directly out of the old millwright tradition, that had been called forth by the struggle to catch up with the most advanced communities. Distinguishing between innovation and invention is not always easy, but Swedish biographers have tended to evade the problem by conferring the accolade of *uppfinnare* (inventor) on the lot of them. This predisposition, however, does reflect the milieu, helps to explain the *urge* to invent and the ensuing outburst of inventions in the 1880s and afterward.

Nineteen of the twenty-two individuals before 1914 who might be regarded as authentic inventors of mechanical devices (excluding, that is, inventors of processes, metallurgical and chemical) had been born in central Sweden.[2] Sixteen came from within about fifty English miles of one of the central lakes, and two more from the Kopparberg region. Their birthplaces were well scattered, ranging from larger cities like Stockholm (three) and Norrköping through towns (Uddevalla, Jönköping, Arboga) to completely rural areas; the Örebro region, with its ties to mining, produced three. Eight of the inventors had fathers in the professions, and six seem to have been exposed to technology by their father's occupations. Six were sons of farmers, eleven might be said to have come, broadly speaking, from middle-class families, and five were born into familes in poor circumstances.

Thirteen had university and/or technological training, and four more attended elementary technical schools. Disregarding the repeated (and suspect) tales of childhood precocity, at least nine of them started inventing when some aspect of an early job evoked their creative talents. Fourteen traveled abroad, but, in strong contrast to any similar group of innovators, the foreign experience rarely seems to have played much of a catalytic role. Ten of them spent long periods in their youth without outside financial support, while the others worked for an industrial enterprise or state agency. Nearly all of them seem to have been compulsive inventors, men who started early and persisted all their lives, regardless of successes or failures. Often transcending hopes for reward in the marketplace, their work seems to have emanated from a sheer need to fulfill their talents, to bring to tangible realization their tantalizing visions and to participate in technological developments beyond the narrow limitations of the home country.

Compulsive or not, these inventors had to have a market for their product. Sweden now possessed the entrepreneurs, the capital, and the growing market at home and abroad; central Sweden, with its metallurgical and mining tradition, had the technical schools to foster students in advanced technology and a number of strong engineering works for the manufacture of new devices. Right on schedule, the creative inventors emerged to fill the demand. Among the more prominent ones were Gustaf de Laval, the Ljungström brothers, Gustaf Dalén, C. E. Johansson, Sven Wingquist, and Alfred Nobel. Axel Wenner-Gren, much more promoter than inventor, appeared at the very end of this period.

One evening in 1877 the top personnel of Kloster in Dalarna were sitting at dinner, eating and talking. Fredrik Lagergren, the *brukspatron,* who happened to be glancing at a newspaper, reported an interesting item: a German had invented a machine that could separate the cream out of milk by rapid rotation of the milk. After some desultory conversation around the table, a young engineer, Gustaf de Laval, said, "Centrifugal power no doubt works the same in Sweden as in Germany. I hope to prove that soon." He borrowed the newspaper and took it to his room. The next morning he announced that not only could he do it, he could also make a machine that made skimming off the cream by hand unnecessary. A few days later he resigned his position at Kloster and went to Stockholm to work on such a machine.[3]

Many years later a biographer of George Westinghouse would write that Gustaf de Laval, "a distinguished French engineer, must not be overlooked," and in the process himself overlooked the inventor's correct nationality. Another writer had him descended from one of Napoleon's soldiers who supported Bernadotte.[4] The family name did derive from a French officer in the Swedish army who was ennobled in 1646. Gustaf attended Uppsala and the Institute of Technology, then, due to temporary poor economic conditions, could not find a job appropriate to his training. He finally went to work as an ordinary clerk in Falun for 75 kronor a month, plus a free sheepskin coat and gloves. After procuring a position at Wilhelm Wenström's engineering bureau, he found draftsmanship a bore, and, discovering that he needed more mathematics and physics, went back to Uppsala to earn his doctor's degree. Then followed successive assignments at Stora Kopparberg and Kloster.

His first impulse after making a model of a cream separator was to offer his improved model to W. Lefeld, the German inventor, in return for 5000 kronor or a royalty on each apparatus. Lefeld rebuffed him, claiming a Swedish patent. His conscience satisfied, de Laval went ahead on his own. In fact, two other Germans and a Dane had also invented cream separators; the centrifugal method had also long been used in the preparation of sugar. De Laval himself, while in Falun, had attempted to start a workshop in which glass bottles were made by fast rotation of the molten glass. He now borrowed a centrifuge from Liljeholmens Stearinfabrik, where they were used to extract stearine from oil and where a cousin, Tycho Robsahm, was technical director. A little later, de Laval, who had resorted to translation work in order to eat regularly, borrowed 3000 kronor from Robsahm and gave him a promissory note. The cousin remonstrated, "Ah, what is the use of that? You will not likely be able to pay it back!"[5]

Though he found that he could get more cream (9 percent) than expected by his separator, creameries objected that it would be necessary to stop the machine frequently in order to pour out the cream (the skim milk escaped through holes at the bottom). After one such discouraging interview, he went back to Stockholm and devised a rather small global container that rotated so rapidly that the cream spurted out through specially constructed pipes.[6] Perhaps this was the moment when he first conceived his favorite saying: "Speed is the gift of heaven!" De Laval now had his continually operating centrifugal separator, but he still had to sell it. In a letter to a friend he had alluded to a basic truth about the processes of invention: "Briefly put, it is the personal acquaintance who exclusively drives through the affairs; otherwise it is impossible, no matter how good the thing."[7] He was saying that the inventor is virtually helpless if he does not know competent entrepreneurs to market his discoveries. The inventor of the separator found his first business manager in Oscar Lamm, nephew of the founder of Ludwigsberg, with whom he signed an agreement in February 1878 that in 1883 led to the formation of AB Separator.

The cream separator might be said to have emerged out of the urbanization of the times. Growing cities needed milk, cream and butter, the railroads made rapid transport from country lanes to city streets possible, and the farmers, unable to compete with foreign grain imports, responded with a rapid increase in dairying. The mounting demand and de Laval's success inspired rivals, as patents permitted, including the Danish apparatus (by L.C. Nielsen) manufactured by Burmeister & Wain, the hand-driven Excelsior by Oscar and Carl Hult, and the Kronseparator, manufactured in the old Atlas buildings in Södertälje. At first, however, sales to creameries were inhibited by a not infrequent factor in the inventive process, the prior development of a less adequate but convenient and cheap method of solving the problem. This was the so-called "Swartz ice method" developed by Janne Swartz, a member of the Norrköping textile family. Soon after 1858 he had discovered that milk still warm from a cow would separate out the fatty substance when poured into a container and put into ice water.[8] This quickly went into general usage, and the fairly recently adopted innovation tended to hang on at most creameries for some time after the invention of the mechanical separator.

Nevertheless, AB Separator put out over 100,000 machines in its first fifteen yars by exporting more than four-fifths of them. De Laval and Lamm, however, parted company acrimoniously, Lamm soon being chosen by the Wallenbergs as the right man to straighten out the affairs of the Atlas company. The inventor was fortunate this time (and it would not always be so) in appointing John Bernström as managing director in 1887, a post he would hold until 1916. Bernström also had some straightening out to do in firing the incompetent, reorganizing the company, rationalizing production, and improving the sales department. An affiliate in the United States was doing so badly that Bernström visited it twice; the second time he cleaned out most of the original personnel, after which it did well.[9]

Most important, Bernström assured the success of AB Separator by acquiring the patent for the Alfa method (1890), invented in Germany by Baron Clemens von Bechtolsheim. Here, thin plates only a few millimeters apart divided the milk into thin layers, then the cream particles much more quickly and completely separated from the milk. By 1915 about 130,000 separators a year were being manufactured—dairy machinery had by far the highest production value among Swedish agricultural machinery—and daughter companies had been established in a number of countries, including Germany, France, Italy, Canada, Russia, and the United States. In Russia the Lavalka, under the aegis of the Nobels, long dominated the field, and in the United States the Alfa-Laval company controlled about 50 percent of the market. Alfa-Laval is still the leader in dairy equipment, with about 35 percent of the world market.

Less financially successful were his inventions of a device for determining fat content, an emulsifier for mixing cheap fats into skim milk, and a milking machine manufactured by AB de Lavals Laktator. Anyone who has ever milked a cow by hand will appreciate the value of the latter apparatus, but the cows protested vehemently and the farmers speedily agreed with their cattle; the machine, operated by pressure, was too "heavy-handed" on the udders. He had to abandon the project, though he did wryly say that there was nothing wrong with the machine, it was the cows who were wrongly constructed.[10]

Fredrik Ljungström, working at AB Separator after 1903, developed a more practicable one, and Gustaf Dalén, destined to become another famous inventor, improved upon that one. AB Separator successively manufactured both machines, eventually basing its models, however, upon the suction method that became standard.

Gustaf de Laval also found that speed is the gift of heaven in a second area—steam turbines, which he helped to invent and develop independently of the better known Sir Charles A. Parsons. A very early advertisement for the separator contained a picture of a harnessed horse plodding round and round a pole and thereby providing power for the separator; this undoubtedly illustrated a compelling reason for his interest in turbines. After working on them for some years, he patented an impulse steam turbine in 1883, a simple "windmill" version in which the motive power was provided by two bent "pipes" in the form of an S; it wasted too much steam to be economical, but it served the intended purpose of power for his separator. After more years of work (during which time Parsons invented his pressure-compounding turbine) he developed, by 1888, a reaction turbine in which the fixed nozzles ejected the steam onto moving blades eventually arranged in two rows. It took many constructions before he obtained fast enough velocity, reduced the resultant vibration by means of a long flexible axle, and successfully synchronized the separator's electric generator to the proper speed of the turbine.[11]

Some of the parts for his earliest turbines were made at AB Separator, others at Ludwigsberg. By 1890 he was delivering reaction turbines from his own factory on Kungsholmen, three years later the AB de Lavals Ångturbin was organized, and in 1896 the manufacturing was moved to a new factory at Järla on the outskirts of Stockholm. It turned out interchangeable parts, assembled as orders came in. His early single-wheel-geared steam turbines were quite small, produced in nine sizes ranging from 3 or 5 up to 100 hp but by 1900 a larger one led to the development of the De Laval Multiple, and the single-wheel turbine lost its importance.[12] By this time, too, the Ljungström turbines were appearing on the scene, and after about 1910 the diesel motor, which could start faster, offered serious competition to the smaller turbines.

Approximately 1,400 had been issued by 1898, all except about 300 exported. In the 1890s most of them, using much less steam than the steam engine and giving a better and steadier light, were being used to generate electricity. Turbines and electric generators evolved more or less simultaneously, two separate technological developments complementing and influencing one another. For a time, de Laval worked with the idea of block lighting, of providing illumination by means of turbine and generator for blocks of houses. This idea was also being tried elsewhere, especially in the United States, but advancing techniques of underground cables soon outmoded it by making feasible long-distance connections from one centralized power station.[13]

Gustaf de Laval resembled Thomas Edison in the breadth of his vision, the variety of interrelated fields that he explored, and, perhaps, in his gift for self-advertisement. The acquisition of Olofström's *bruk* and AB Bångbro were natural enough, intended to supplement the manufacture of separators and turbines. He bought out the Bergström light bulb firm (1894), and AB Glödlampfabrik Svea was soon making 3,000 light bulbs a day, the second largest in Europe. It also made arc lights, and, as noted earlier, acetylene lighting equipment was being manufactured in another of his enterprises. He carried on many other projects. As a youth he had tried to extract nitrogen from the air, a premature effort he abandoned after a decade. De Laval and John Schmidt installed a turbine in a boat in 1893 and sailed it around Lake Mälaren; Parsons did the same in a ship, *Turbinia*, in 1897, with efforts that would come to fruition a couple decades later. In about 1885 de Laval was experimenting with the possibility of spraying compressed air from the hull of a vessel to create a frictionless layer of air between boat and water, an early attempt at a hydrofoil.[14]

Torsten Althin, carefully illustrating the processes of invention as displayed in the career of Gustaf de Laval, quoted with approval one of the great man's maxims; "No construction, invention or machine is *one* man's work, but *one* man can take the first daring step."[15] In accordance with this dictum, the development of the turbine became a joint effort by a number of his men, the most conspicuous being John Schmidt, who made valuable modifications, and Daniel Norrman, who planned and managed the new Järla factory. De Laval hired bright young engineers and scientists to work in his laboratories on Kungsholmen, where the tradition of Polhem, Edelcrantz, Owen, the Bolinders, and Palmcrantz as a cradle or focal point of Swedish technological progress was thus still being carried on. Like Edison at Menlo Park, the men in these technological hothouses (*drivbänkar*) were assigned tasks by "the Doctor," as they always called him, and then permitted much freedom in finding solutions. Sometimes his instructions would be much too vague. Possessed of a lively and captivating personality, the Doctor could also on occasion be a difficult person to work with. Gårdlund called him *besvärlig,* thorny or vexatious.[16]

Some of this may be regarded as the forgivable prerogative of genius. For four decades he generated a "whirlwind of ideas"—and increasingly he lost his sense of proportions and ability to concentrate on any one of them. He justified himself by saying that one must always have alternatives, "have two galoshes to walk in." Much too often he put too many inadequately tested components together into a machine where any one failure wrecked the whole project. In consequence, as he himself said, "One must go forward over the junk heaps."[17]

By 1897 the little man, his eyes alert behind glasses perched near the end of his nose, who was constantly darting about in the laboratory, or office, or on the street, had achieved three successes: separator, turbine, and light bulbs, each one enough to satisfy most individuals. AB de Lavals Ångturbin and ASEA cooperated that year in providing the lighting for the big Stockholm Arts and Industrial Exposition on Djurgården. It was good publicity, and it was also the zenith of his career. After that, his original fortune melted away as he tried to develop his later ideas. In retrospect, he would have been much better off if he had avoided further ventures.

Such, however, was not the nature of the man. This "restless soul" who was a compulsive inventor and doer could not stop. Perhaps inebriated by successes and by his broad syncretic vision of a rapidly advancing technology, he plunged on. Acutely aware of opportunities at the pioneering edge of technology, he was also vulnerable to its perils, of moving too fast, in order to get the early advantage, or of losing out in the relay race of progress when one advance was quickly superseded by the next.

By 1899–1900 his financial position had rapidly worsened because of his overly ambitious expansion of sundry industrial enterprises. It would be, however, the heavy expenses and failure of immediate profits at his Trollhättan metallurgical and chemical plants that destroyed him. De Laval had already envisioned, as a young man, the industrial possibilities at the Trollhättan falls. By 1895 he was implementing big plans there for the production of zinc and carbide. He attempted to extract zinc (and some lead) from poor ore by electrothermal methods, the first person to attempt this; he invented an electric arc furnace for the purpose and also a method for blowing pulverized zinc ore into a furnace to make zinc oxide, which would then be reduced to zinc by blowing in carbon monoxide. Betrayed by his maxim that speed is the gift of heaven, he went into production long before he had completed the experiments, and the otherwise technically feasible project turned into a financial disaster. Meanwhile, he put up a big factory on Önan Island to produce calcium carbide. One of the two electric furnaces, bought in Germany, *melted* when excessive electric power was run into it. Supply exceeded demand after a few years, as more plants opened, and it had to be closed down.[18]

For his successive ventures he obtained capital in Germany, Belgium, England, and France, and he also borrowed 4 million kronor from Stockholms Enskilda Bank, the security being based on his separator profits and his stock company holdings. By 1902 his debts, personal and corporate, were approaching 3 million kronor. Knut Wallenberg had already written in early 1898 that "the pitcher is going to the well until it cracks" and "even de Laval is a human being."[19] Marcus Wallenberg was disposed to blame Ernest Thiel, banker, who had become the inventor's principal business collaborator in the early 1890s. De Laval's own business sense was limited at best, and Thiel was well known for his imaginative and daring financial dealings. In the rapid proliferation of companies, their mutual taste for risky ventures proved lethal.

Undoubtedly Gustaf de Laval was doomed anyway, but judicial processes over the ownership of water rights at Trollhättan irrevocably sealed his fate. The old sawmills at the falls had been replaced by industrial enterprises using power from a special water channel drawing water from the stream: Nydqvist and Holm (1847), the Francke wood pulp mill (1857), Stridsberg's saw blade factory (1878–79), and others. The proprietors assumed that ownership of a slice of the shore entitled them to the use of the water. The Crown and the canal company, increasingly uneasy over the encroachment, went to court against Stridsberg, claiming Crown ownership of the water and some of the land. De Laval had had ample warning, but nevertheless bought up more of the shoreline on the west side of the stream, founded a power company, and built his carbide and zinc works. Court proceedings against him dragged on for some time, but Sweden's highest court then ruled on August 19, 1901, that the water, including the falls, belonged by ancient rights to the Crown, and private companies held only such rights as the Crown might confer upon them. (The debate over water rights here and on the other streams paralleled, of course, the reassertion of Crown rights in the case of the Norrland iron ore.) In 1906 the Riksdag approved the construction of a state-owned hydroelectric power station at Trollhättan; dedicated in 1910, its 40,000 turbine horsepower made it easily the largest in the country at the time.[20]

De Laval emerged from the debacle a poor man, even his AB Separator stock lost. Although the eternal optimist and incurable inventor attempted to recoup in England, he could no longer secure credit. He came home to attend a demonstration of a new milking machine, then underwent an operation and died on February 2, 1913.

His manufactured inventions had been the first in Sweden "to make inroads upon world markets" (Kuuse). "De Laval's life has been rightfully called a drama by many. Few persons have lived a life so intensively as he, had such successes and so severely felt the bitterness of setbacks." Beyond his separator and steam turbine, according to Tore J. Lindmark, lies his significance as an inspiration, in the period of genuine industrial breakthrough, in giving the Swedes faith in their own resources and energies and in earning public respect for technological work.[21]

The quarters at Fabriksgränd on Kungsholmen, where de Laval had done most of his experimenting, also became the site for the development of the Ljungström turbines. Birger and Fredrik Ljungström had both become engineers at AB Separator in 1903, and some year thereafter Birger began experimenting with a novel and ingenious model that would become the Ljungström compound-reaction turbine. Like several of the other inventors, the brothers had been nurtured on mechanical devices in their parental home. Their father had run a workshop in Stockholm for the manufacture of surveying instruments, including a number of his own invention; some of them were displayed at the 1876 Philadelphia exposition. Birger and Fredrik as small boys were put to work helping the father in the shop, "where they seemed to thrive best."[22]

At the age of sixteen Birger invented a bicycle with an adjustable gear shift, a free-moving front wheel, and a foot brake on the back wheel, but, in contrast to most models, it was pedaled up and down, not round and round. After further improvements, it looked promising enough for Alfred Nobel to contribute £40,000 for its manufacture in Great Britain, a venture that failed through faulty sales organization. Birger Ljungström (1872–1948) worked for a time in the drafting bureau of the New Cycle Co. in London, then developed a reciprocating engine and a carbonic acid heat engine while working at Dunford and Elliot in Newcastle-upon-Tyne. Fredrik joined him there after being employed by Nobel for a time; he had devised a light steam generator, but, like Birger, lacked the capital after Nobel's death to put them into production. Fredrik Ljungström (1875–1964) improved the milking machine while at AB Separator and secured a patent on a die casting method, which, however, was premature because sufficiently heat-resistant materials were not yet available for its use.

After seeing de Laval's turbine, Birger had begun thinking about a new type, a double-rotation, radial flow, compound-reacting engine; he began work on it in 1906 and had it far enough along for the brothers to found AB Ljungströms Ångturbin in 1908. It took another four years for the two to solve its remaining problems, and in 1913 they founded STAL (Svenska Turbinfabrik AB Ljungström), later Stal-Laval. A portion of the factory facilities at Finspång were purchased for its manufacture. This turbine was immediately successful. The first big foreign sale occurred in 1914, a 1000-kilowatt, turbo-alternator, with an efficiency of 77 percent, ordered by the London street car company. The British patent was bought for £20,000, plus royalties; General Electric in the United States paid $1,000,000 for the American rights, but did not use it, presumably acquiring it to prevent competition.[23] Most of the Ljungström inventions would occur after 1914. Birger worked on plans for a monoplane, on parts for automobiles, and apparatus for cellulose production. Fredrik developed a turbine-driven locomotive, an automatic shift for automobiles, engine cooling devices, and an electrothermal process for extracting oil from shale.

Elma, who swore that she would never be a farmer's wife, had to wait fourteen years before Gustaf Dalén (1869–1937) was ready to marry her. He was not a good student in school, unlike his brothers and sister, and this coupled with the boy's obvious preference for working in the carpenter shed, caused his parents to choose him to take over the family farm. He had, however, given early evidence of his inventive talents by using the works of a discarded wall clock to make a device that would automatically start heating up his morning coffee fifteen minutes before the alarm went off. He also devised a bean-shelling machine, the power coming from a spinning wheel. Dalén seems to have been a born inventor.[24]

Noticing how much the fat content in milk varied from time to time, he invented a butyrometer. Then young Dalén had the nerve to take it to de Laval, not knowing that the great man had already invented one much like it, and to ask for a position in his laboratory. At first abrupt and discouraging to the youth, de Laval then softened and advised him to go to technical school, after which he would be welcome. Dalén enrolled at Chalmers after having hurriedly crammed in order to enter its second class. After Chalmers, he studied at the Zürich Polytechnikum in 1896–97, where he and another man devised a warm air turbine that de Laval found inadequate.

Dalén went to work for Svenska Karbid och Acetylen AB at Järla. He invented a gas pressure regulator, the patent being purchased and used by a Berlin company; then, moving to De Lavals Ångturbin in 1903, he developed a model of a milling machine. Dalén continued as a consulting engineer for Svenska Karbid, which changed its name to AGA (AB Gasaccumulator), and in 1906 he returned, first as chief engineer and then as managing director until his death in 1937. It was acetylene that lured Dalén back. The commercial manufacture of calcium carbide, as noted earlier, made feasible the production of acetylene from the interaction of calcium carbide with water. Svenska Karbid had bought the Scandinavian rights to a (French) patent by G. Claude and A. Hess on so-called "dissolved acetylene," a process whereby acetylene could be stored in cylinders and thus made useful for, especially, mobile lighting. Acetylene seemed attractive as a fuel for maritime beacons, lighted buoys, and lighthouses, which since the middle of the century had been illuminated by gas oil and later by kerosene. Their maintenance was expensive, and the lighting itself scarcely strong enough. Acetylene, however, was much too apt to explode when subjected to shock or heat, and it also required much attention because of the checking and refueling.[25]

These problems fascinated Gustaf Dalén. Most of the business of the Järla shop consisted in filling the gas accumulators, but the rather frequent detonations did not encourage customers. Dalén remedied the situation by his first famous invention, his Agamassan. This was an inert porous mixture of charcoal, asbestos, wool, and kieselguhr (diatomaceous earth) put into steel-cylinder gas accumulators, the interstices being too small for the acetylene to explode.

In the autumn of 1905 he invented a "flasher" (Klippljusapparat), the light turning on momentarily at regular intervals. The acetylene would enter a small chamber where its pressure, pushing on a membrane, would activate a spring that in turn opened the valve to a pilot light. A sharp flash of burning acetylene, the membrane relaxed, and the spring closed the valve. In opening this valve, the spring had closed a second valve, this one to the cylinder of fuel acetylene; now the spring opened this second valve as it closed the first one, gas entered the chamber, and the process repeated itself. The mechanism could be regulated for the desired interval between flashes.

Leaving lights on in daylight wasted gas. Next, in 1907, Dalén discovered how to turn them off automatically at dawn and turn them on at dusk. His Solventil, which has been called his most ingenious invention, functioned by means of a tiny black rod that, absorbing sunlight, would lengthen slightly (.0016 mm.) and thereby activate a delicate lever that in turn closed the gas valve. At dusk the rod would shrink and the lever would open the valve. The flasher and Solventil together reduced the expenditure of fuel by 93–94 percent. Formerly filled every third week, a cylinder would now last for a full year. The Dalén light (Dalénljuset) followed in 1909. He invented a mechanism for mixing 10 percent gas and 90 percent air, which then flowed down through extremely fine apertures onto a netting or mantle. The incandescent mantle gave an extremely bright light. To this, Dalén added an automatic device that instantly switched in a new mantle whenever the old one burned out.[26] AGA largely concentrated on manufacturing and selling Dalén's inventions. They were soon also adapted for railroad and street signals and later for airport lighting.

On September 27, 1912, he was in a quarry testing the safety of an acetylene cylinder in a fire. A malfunctioning manometer (an instrument for testing gas pressures) failed to give warning, and Dalén walked up to the cylinder to see what was wrong. Liquid that had spilled on the ground caught fire and blew up. Dalén was badly burned and lost his eyesight. "He, who had lighted the way . . . for so many, must himself go in eternal darkness until the end of his days" (Falk).

That December he was awarded a Nobel prize, though he was still too sick to attend the ceremonies. Some protested that his work had not been in pure science, and it was even said that he was only a glorified clockmaker. No doubt the tragedy had influenced the committee. Others, however, pointed out that Nobel's bequest stipulated contributions to the welfare of humanity and that Dalén's inventions had immeasureably enhanced human safety in sea and land traffic.

Friends persuaded him, after a long travail, that he still had work to do, and he resumed it, in total darkness, for another twenty-five years. Among other projects, he devised a new system for automatic signaling on the railroads. Ultimately employing about 10,000 workers, AGA became a company with a world reputation. In the 1970s it was still producing industrial gases and welding systems and had moved into medical and hospital equipment, precision engineering, batteries, central heating apparatuses and electronics.

Carl Edvard Johansson (1864–1943) also displayed an early aptitude for mechanics and carpentry, but his parents, disregarding his manifest talent, apprenticed him to a shoemaker. At the age of eighteen he escaped that by following a brother to Duluth, Minnesota. They attended Gustavus Adolphus College for a term and worked in a sawmill until it burned down, whereupon Carl went back to Sweden.

Obtaining work at the Beronius Mek. Verkstad in Eskilstuna, he also attended classes in a technical school, and after two years was able to transfer to the Rifle Factory. In 1890 he passed the state armorer inspection examinations, which required a complete knowledge of the manufacture of rifles and of the use of interchangeable parts. As an inspector, he soon became aware that, although standardization had been introduced, each workshop still had its own modified measurements, its own set of gauges, templates, calipers, and steel measuring rods. In the Rifle Factory each worker, once he had measuring devices that fitted the requirements, kept his own set. Each dimension required a separate gauge, and a shop would have thousands of them.

Matters came to a head when the Rifle Factory, which had been rebuilt to make Remingtons at the end of the 1860s, contracted to manufacture the German Mauser rifle on license (1896). Johansson, accompanying the group that inspected the German plant, was disappointed in its gauges, "stored in the thousands" according to size. Before the Swedish factory could begin production, it must first make a large number of these. On the train home, Johansson, considering how this arduous time-consuming work might be avoided, started jotting down notes. By the time he arrived in Eskilstuna he had the answer: the combination gauge block set. "[A] relatively small number of gauge blocks might possibly be made so that in combination with each other they could provide all the measurements required." With a set of 102 blocks, arranged in three series, he could make 20,000 measurements. One series of 49 blocks measured from 1.01 to 1.49 mm., the second ranged from 0.50, 1.00, 1.50 and so forth up to 24.50, and the third consisted of four blocks, 25, 50, 75 and 100 mm. Another block measuring 1.005 mm. was added later.[27]

Near the end of 1896 he had the 102 flat, rectangular blocks made in the factory tool shop, then finished them at home. When specially treated, the iron-surfaced blocks would adhere to one another, and he smoothed them to virtually total contact. He converted a sewing machine for the purpose, holding a block against a grinding wheel while tramping. His wife, married in April 1896 shortly after the return from the German trip, was drafted into giving them their final polishing. It was also necessary to heat the steel blocks to 100 degrees Celsius on the stove and then let them cool slowly, to "age and become stable," because the grinding and polishing, setting up stresses, threw the measurements off. Since different temperatures in the factory using them would also alter the dimensions, he tempered the blocks to give correct measurements at 20 degrees centigrade, which he considered the mean figure for the usual shop temperature.

Set No. 1 went, of course, to the Rifle Factory. Set No. 2 was sold to Stockholms Vapenfabrik. Johansson took his blocks to L. M. Ericsson, Atlas, Ludwigsberg, Luth and Rosén, and AB Centrator; in three days he received orders for four gauge block sets (1899). Munktells also ordered one. The five sets were delivered within a year at 700 kronor per set. The first ones were by no means perfect. Later he had the measurements checked by the Bureau International, based on the standard meter in Paris, until the blocks *were* scientifically perfect.[28]

The Patent Office refused his application (1898): his invention "could not be regarded as an industrial product or a pattern for the manufacture of such a product." He applied again in 1901, only to be told that his series of flat gauge blocks had been "previously known and employed. . . ." Finally the Patent Office personnel grasped that it was *an idea* that was being offered, and on January 30, 1904 he did receive his patent.[29]

Not until 1911 could he begin genuine factory manufacture. The French bought the greatest number. The U. S. War Department purchased thirty sets of his "Jo-blocks" in 1915 and made his system the norm in the manufacture of war materiel in the United States; Henry Ford invited "Precision Johansson" back to America, where he became one of Ford's close associates. Althin summed up his career: "In his life, one after the other, bit was fitted to bit with great care and accuracy—smooth, shining and hard as Swedish steel. Not a fraction of a millimetre did he deviate in his life and his work from the road he had decided to tread."[30]

By coincidence, an adjustable wrench was invented in these same years by another Johansson, Johan Petter (1853–1943), commonly called "Johansson i [in] Fanna."[31] A crofter's son, he was working as a manual laborer in railroad construction when an instrument maker at Munktells chanced to see some of his repair work on the house where he was staying. Advised to apply for a job at Munktells, Johansson was accepted on about his tenth try, mostly because of his obstinate persistence. Having acquired an on-the-job technical education there, he started his own workshop in Enköping, northwest of Stockholm; a few years later he moved to nearby Fanna, which had available water power.

The aged Theofron Munktell came by shortly after he had started his first shop, looked at it, and said, "This isn't so bad. . . . I didn't have much either when I started."[32]

For his own use, Johansson devised a pipe wrench that could be tightened to provide a firm grip. He made them in many sizes to fit a wide range of pipes. Lugging them all along on a job one day, he suddenly realized that by using a spiraling groove he could have *one* wrench that could be adjusted to any size pipe. The next year he developed an all-purpose adjustable wrench (1899). He would later secure many other patents, including a lamp on an adjustable, flexible arm. When Johansson retired, his company was taken over by Berndt Hjorth (1862–1937), his sales agent. B. A. Hjorth & Co., or BAHCO for short, made fans, ventilating equipment, and wrenches. It would be for a time the largest manufacturer of adjustable wrenches in the world, outside of the United States.

Sven Wingquist (1876–1953) was the inventor of another device that looked simple once it was in use. After studying at John Lenning's weaving school in Norrköping and spending about half a year in the United States, he became an engineer at Gamlestaden's textile mill in Gothenburg. Out of this company and his work would spring SKF (Svenska Kullagerfabriken).

Gamlestaden had been founded in 1854 as a cotton spinning mill near the original site of Sahlgren's early sugar refinery on the east side of the city. It was purchased in 1880 by Johannes Johansson and Christoffer Carlander, partners in a mercantile firm, and by 1900 Gamlestaden was the largest cotton mill in Scandinavia, employing about 1,500 workers.[33] Put in charge of the textile machinery, Wingquist was dismally impressed by the frequency of breakdowns of the ball-bearing installations. They were being imported from a factory in Schweinfurt in Germany that had prospered because the emerging bicycle industry used them. In heavy machinery they often jammed. When one too many breakdowns occurred and new ball bearings had to be ordered, the answer came back that the order could not be filled for a year. Wingquist is reported to have said that they could not wait that long, they would make the ball bearings themselves. Having apparently already given the problem considerable thought, he made the outer of the two bearings spherical in form, which permitted those in the inner circle to be self-aligning because they could now rotate freely. "So simple was it—but all ingenious constructions are simple when one sees them completed" (Modin).[34]

The later renowned SKF was founded in 1907 to exploit the invention. Financial backing came from the owners of Gamelstaden, two of the Carlander family and two sons of Johansson (who had taken the name of Mark), though the total amount was only 110,000 kronor for what was considered a risky investment. Wingquist had only a single 30-horsepower motor for this work, and a twelve-man labor force was hand-picked by Wingquist, the workers not at all certain that they ought to be pleased by their selection. As it turned out, the outlook was "particularly good, not to say tempting," in the words of Wingquist later.[35] The early balls were imported until 1910, when SKF started making its own. After further experimentation with steel, SKF bought Hofors in 1916 in order to control completely the quality of the steel. SKF began exporting ball bearings during the first year, and affiliates would soon be started in Great Britain (1911), Germany (1913), the United States, France, Russia, and Denmark. The total stock capital of 110,000 kronor in 1907 had risen to 84 million when Wingquist stepped out as managing director in 1919. By the 1970s SKF was employing 62,000 workers in various countries.

In 1914 Axel Wenner-Gren (1881–1961), the very model of a successful traveling salesman, was still busily laying the foundations for his career as a world citizen. He had almost failed to survive the age of twelve. Three Americans, carrying greetings from a relative in Chicago, had come to call at the large family farm in Västergöland. Then Axel had to hitch the horses to a sleigh and take them to their next stop; on the way back, he lost his way in a blizzard and very nearly froze to death.[36]

Three years later he went to work as a bookkeeper for a relative in Gothenburg, but he learned more about business by starting, with a friend, a stamp dealer affair. With admirable foresight, he took Berlitz courses in German, English, and French. After briefly attending Greifswald University and the Berlin School of Business, he applied for a job at AB Separator in Berlin. Told to try again later, he came back, much like Johansson i Fanna, every Wednesday. On the ninth visit the boss swore at him, told him that he was remarkably stubborn, and gave him a job. His success as a traveling salesman was marked by his improving transportation; starting with a bicycle, he graduated to a motorcycle and then to an automobile, meanwhile building up a network of acquaintances useful in his later career.[37] In early 1908 he arrived in New York, working for a short time as a laborer in a separator factory for fifteen cents an hour. He tried his luck as a chauffeur, but immediately lost that position when he drove the car out the gate, taking the gate with him.

Soon he was back in Europe. Walking up Kärntnerstrasse, Vienna's leading shopping street, one day, he looked into a window and saw Fate beckoning him. There was the perfect sales article, something everyone needed and cheap enough to be purchased—a vacuum cleaner.[38] It was a Santo, made in Philadelphia, and Wenner-Gren, procuring a job as a salesman for it, set up a German network, only to quarrel with the Santo general agent in Berlin. He returned to Sweden, still with vacuum cleaners on his mind.

In Stockholm, Eberhard Seger, who had once invented a turbine that foreshadowed the ones later developed by the Ljungströms, had brought out a vacuum cleaner modeled on Santo. In 1912 its motors were being manufactured by Elektromekaniska AB, while AB Lux, originally founded to make incandescent kerosene lamps, was providing the covers and suction tubes. Wenner-Gren suggested that they develop an improved, cheaper, and lighter model. AB Lux agreed to manufacture his second model if he could find 5,000 orders for it. He went to Hamburg, organized an agency using his old sales organization, and returned to Stockholm with the required number. Soon Lux was getting so many orders that it could scarcely fill the demand. The First World War totally frustrated the super-salesman, his carefully laid plans shattered by the battle lines.

By the end of the war Wenner-Gren had finished his fifth model, one that became his finished apparatus. When Lux balked again, he left the company and organized a new one, Svenska Elektron AB; he also reorganized Elektromekaniska AB into AB Elektrolux, containing the names of Elektron and Lux. Henceforth the vacuum cleaner bore the name of Elektrolux, spelled Electrolux since 1957. Borrowing a large sum of money from the Svenska Handelsbank and in the process risking everything that he owned, Wenner-Gren signed a very large contract with Lux for the manufacture of his machine. No one expected him to survive—Lux, AGA (part owner of Lux since before the war), or the bank. Certainly Arvid Lindman hoped that he would not. Member of the board of directors of the bank, of AGA, and of Lux, the former prime minister had manifestly had more than enough of this pushy salesman who seemed to appropriate most of the profits for himself. Their feud simmered on for several years. Expecting to deliver the *coup de grâce*, Lindman, as chairman of the bank board, demanded repayment of the debt; Wenner-Gren, with virtually a worldwide sales organization, emerged triumphant (1923).

The next year he invaded the United State in force. He acquired the patent for the Platen-Munters refrigerator (invented by Baltzar Carl von Platen and Carl Munters, two students at the Institute of Technology) and Elektrolux began manufacturing it in Sweden; in the United States it was called the Servel. Wenner-Gren was also buying much stock in the Swedish cellulose industry and in Bofors. Unlike Ivar Kreuger, another international figure in the 1920s, nothing could stop Axel Wenner-Gren except another big war.

He saw it coming. Twice he met Hermann Göring, in 1936 and 1939. Wenner-Gren was not the only one under the delusion that Fat Hermann was sufficiently normal and influential to brake the momentum toward war. Nor was he the only Swede who tried to bridge the widening chasm. In the summer of 1939, Wenner-Gren, recognizing the inevitable, moved his headquarters to the Bahamas, then, when he was put on the Allied Black List of alleged Nazi sympathizers, he moved on to Mexico. Walter Winchell and Drew Pearson, U. S. journalists, both found the Swedish industrialist peculiarly irritating, for some reason, and fabricated many columns of newspaper copy about him. Wenner-Gren was, of course, guilty of doing business in Germany ever since the early years of the century. (He was also guilty of having married an American, a girl from Kansas City.) Harry Truman, trying to make later amends, invited him to his 1949 presidential inauguration, but, if memory serves, he did not attend the ceremony. Large amounts of his fortune, said to approach a billion dollars, were distributed to foundations, and the tall Wenner-Gren Center in Stockholm still recalls the memory of one of Sweden's world citizens.

Though the Nobel family is now mostly remembered for the Nobel prizes, they devoted much of their work over three generations to pioneering industrial development in Russia. Above all, they opened up the great petroleum fields at Baku. This work has been obscured by the spectacular career of Alfred Nobel and his Nobel prizes and, even more, by the Orwellian suppression by the Communist regime of pre-1917 achievements in Tsarist Russia.

The family's founder, Petrus Olavi (c. 1660–1707), took the name of Nobelius as a student at Uppsala, adapting it from the name of his parish in southern Sweden. He married the daughter of Olof Rudbeck the elder (1630–1702), Sweden's first scientist, and it has been suggested that Rudbeck's genes strongly affected the later generations. Subsequently, another member of the family shortened the name to Nobel while in the military.

Immanuel Nobel (1801–1872), who would become the father of three conspicuously successful sons, went to sea at the age of thirteen on a Gävle vessel. After four years abroad, mostly in Egypt, he became a shipbuilding apprentice in Gävle. A sketch of a triumphal arch for a royal visit attracted sufficient attention for him to become a student at the Academy of Art's school of architecture, while also attending a school for mechanics. Going into business, he was forced into bankruptcy by a fire, whereupon he moved to Finland, then to St. Petersburg. For a time, two of his boys, Robert and Ludvig, were even selling matches on the Stockholm streets to help eke out the family livelihood.[39]

In St. Petersburg he experimented with land and sea mines, the military becoming interested when he successfully blew up a sailing vessel; his armaments factory, started in 1842, thereafter secured good government orders. The sea mines were used at Kronstadt and Sveaborg (Suomenlinna) during the Crimean War, and as long as the war lasted he was prosperous enough to pay off his debts in Sweden. The British fished up one of the mines, which exploded and killed a man, and they were even more impressed when a Russian sea captain ignored warnings and hit a mine off Sveaborg, with spectacular results. There was, naturally, a certain amount of irony in Swedish-devised mines protecting Sveaborg, a Russian fortress that had formerly been a Swedish bastion against the Russians. Immanuel was also manufacturing

271

marine steam engines, pipes, window sashes, and lathes at his factory, and altogether employing about a thousand workers.[40]

After the end of the conflict, Immanuel Nobel received no more government orders; the tsar awarded him a gold medal, but he never did get properly paid for the munitions delivered. In 1859 he lost his factory to creditors and returned, a ruined man, to Sweden. Alfred, the third brother, had resumed experimenting with nitroglycerin, started by his father, and in 1862 they began manufacturing it in their home in Stockholm. On September 3, 1864 an explosion killed several persons, including Emil Oskar, the youngest brother. The old man never recovered from this; he soon suffered a stroke and never regained his health. Suffering crushing defeats, this tragic figure had been born one generation too early.

Three years after his father's bankruptcy, Ludvig (1831–1888) started an engineering works at Ichervod on the Viborg road out of St. Petersburg, where he manufactured rifles (both muzzle and breech loaders), gun carriages, submarine mines, boring and drilling tools, hydraulic presses, and wheels. In 1867–70 he altered 100,000 guns from muzzle to breech loaders on orders from the government. Then he and Captain Peter A. Bilderling, a Russian, were asked to organize the manufacture of rifles at Izhevsk, east of Kazan, in a state-owned factory, where about 450,000 rifles were made in the next eight years.[41]

His brother, Robert (1829–1896), after two years at sea worked at his father's old factory in St. Petersburg for a time. Then he moved to Helsingfors (Helsinki), where he, with a partner, started a petroleum business, the Aurora Lamp Oil firm; he had to learn how to refine kerosene in just those years when it was coming on world markets, and, not yet realizing it, Robert had launched the family on a far-reaching adventure in the petroleum industry. He also set up a factory in the Finnish capital to make nitroglycerin, using Alfred's patent.

Ludvig asked Robert to go to the Caucasus to look for walnut wood, needed for the butts of the rifles that were being manufactured. The walnut trees turned out to be too scattered to be of any commercial use, but around Baku he encountered the familiar and exciting smell of petroleum. Sundry Russians, Armenians, and Azerbaijani Turks were leasing plots of ground from the state monopoly and taking out the oil, "Baku Sludge," from shallow wells, putting it into leather bottles and carrying them into Baku on carts. Ludvig promptly put the walnut money into buying plots of oil-bearing ground, then went back to St. Petersburg to explain the possibilities to the initially wrathful Ludvig.[42] By 1875 the Robert Nobel Refinery was putting out Russia's best petroleum, good enough to drive out the imported American oil.

It was Ludvig who took charge of the enterprise and who would become a formidable captain of industry in Russia. He organized the Nobel Brothers Petroleum Co., Ludvig and Bilderling holding the greater part of the stock, Alfred and Robert additional amounts; six other Russian, German, and Swedish shareholders were involved. Robert, not in good health, returned to Sweden in 1879, disgruntled at his brother muscling in so completely on what had been his project originally. Meantime, Ludvig purchased more land, installed boring machinery driven by steam engines, erected refineries and reservoir tanks near Baku, and ran pipelines from the fields to the refineries. The Nobels were making kerosene, paraffin, and lubricating oil and using the residue to run locomotives and marine engines in place of coal. Their oil company enjoyed, in European terms, an almost unparalleled growth and by 1884 was employing over 5,000 people.[43]

Ludvig copied American oil drilling techniques while pioneering the construction of Swedish ship tankers, which in turn were copied by Americans, British, Dutch, and others. The world's first, *Zoroaster*, was built at Motala-Lindholmen according to Ludwig's design, its name recalling, with fine historical sense, the ancient Zoroastrian sacred fires that had burned at oil seepages in Azerbaijan. When the oil arrived at Astrakhan it was moved by barges up the Volga to reservoir tanks at Tsaritsyn (Stalingrad, later Volgograd) for further distribution. The building of the Baku-to-Batum railroad by Nobel competitors with Rothschild money (1883), and of a Transcaucasian railroad, made possible the introduction of tank cars, imitating the Americans, of which the Nobels in time had about 1,500. A 560-mile pipeline was subsequently laid to the Black Sea port of Batum.[44]

A long international oil war, called "Europe's Second Thirty Years War" by Robert Tolf, took place during these years.[45] The competitors included Ludvig and Alfred Nobel, John D. Rockefeller and Standard Oil, the French branch of the Rothschilds and their so-called Bnita company, and Marcus Samuel leading Royal Dutch Shell. By the mid-1890s a division of the world petroleum market among the contenders had been completed, though the competition and maneuvering continued among the giant companies. The Baku oil wells were producing over one-half of the world's crude oil at the turn of the century, of which the Nobels controlled about 18 percent.

The short, broad-shouldered Ludvig, extroverted and dynamic, sought "the struggle, and the constant search for new methods." The Oil King of Baku said that "I need not only money, I need work."[46] And overwork killed him; he died at Cannes in 1888. His eldest son, Emanuel (he spelled his name differently than his grandfather), took over the Nobel Brothers petroleum business while a younger brother of Emanuel, Carl, ran the Nobel enterprises in St. Petersburg. Carl bought de Laval's patent on the separator for Russia and began making them; he was also the first in Russia to manufacture a safe kerosene motor, and had just started them when he suddenly died in 1893. Emanuel then became head of this enterprise also. The St. Petersburg factory began producing diesel motors and motor-driven ships, and twelve of the first sixteen larger motorships in the world were launched from here. The tsar strongly hinted that

273

Emanuel ought to become a Russian citizen, which he did. In 1916 the Nobel enterprises in Russia, including those in which it shared ownership, employed about 50,000 workers, refined 40 percent of Russian oil, controlled a major portion of the Volga petroleum transport, and produced about two-thirds of the oil consumed in the country.[47] All this was lost with the 1917 Bolshevik revolution; Emanuel escaped to Sweden, where he died in 1932.

The Nobels were not the only Swedes to suffer big losses. About 6,000 Swedes were living in St. Petersburg in 1914. Russia had become a highly lucrative market for Swedish engineering goods in the thirty years before the revolution: farm machinery, separators, electric motors and generators, machine tools, and steam engines. Nearly all its separators were Alfa-Laval; large quantities of Swedish threshing machines and reapers were imported. When the outbreak of war in 1914 shut off German exports, the Russians became heavily dependent upon Swedish engineering factories, whose production expanded rapidly to meet the demand.[48] The revolution cut off that trade for some years, and Russian subsidiaries of Swedish companies were expropriated. The diesel factory of the Nobels became Russkiy Diesel. The L. M. Ericsson telephone factory in St. Petersburg (Petrograd after 1914), the partly Swedish-owned Moscow telephone company, the Ryska Elektriska ASEA (founded in 1914), and the SKF subsidiary (started during the war) were all nationalized.

When Ludvig Nobel died in 1888, a French journalist mistakenly published the obituary of the dynamite king, Alfred Nobel, better known in the West. Reading his own obituary greatly disturbed Alfred, the more so because he was referred to as "the merchant of death." He, too, had begun in his father's factory in St. Petersburg before doing some extensive traveling and spending perhaps as much as two years in the United States (1850–52). For a short time, "possibly" a few months, he lived in New York at 95 Franklin Street, the residence of John Ericsson.[49] It was as obligatory for any Swedish engineer or scientist in America to meet John Ericsson as it was for a tourist to visit Niagara Falls, and any claim to a closer relationship must always be treated with reserve. Nevertheless, the idea of these two men living in the same house, however briefly, is a fascinating one: the mature, rather tragic, older inventor and the tight-lipped, silent young man just starting his career, both equally driven—and afflicted—by the demon of inventive genius.

After the father's return from Russia, the two of them experimented with nitroglycerin. Two chemists, one in Basel and one in Frankfurt, had independently discovered that cotton with a mixture of saltpeter or nitre and sulfuric acid resulted in "cotton powder," but this, when dry, soon fell apart. An Italian, Ascanio Sobrero, produced nitroglycerin in 1846–47, and Alfred had first learned about this from Nikolai Zinin, his Russian tutor. Alfred exploded nitroglycerin in 1862, and his invention of a detonating capsule (mercury

274

fulminate) to set off the nitroglycerin was perhaps the most important of his many inventions. A company was organized for its manufacture and sale, the shares of stock originally being held by Alfred, his father, and two other men (1864). After the calamitous explosion at Heleneborg on Södermalm, the police insisted that the work be transferred to a less populated area, and in 1865 Alfred moved to Hamburg, where he also founded a nitroglycerin company. Alfred thereafter paid little attention to his Swedish enterprise.[50]

Nitroglycerin was, in fact, much too dangerous. An oil liquid, it sometimes seeped out, with devastating effects. One consignment exploded in a Wells, Fargo & Co. warehouse, and a docked steamer, with some on board, blew up; the Krümmel nitroglycerin plant outside of Hamburg was badly damaged by an accident, and a fourth disaster occurred in Australia. A more stable substitute had to be found. According to a story that seems more myth than truth, Alfred one day noticed that some of the oily liquid had leaked out and soaked into the ground. He experimented with it: a knock, and it blew up. After more experimentation Nobel chose kieselguhr as the best inert absorbent.[51] The result, called dynamite by the inventor, brought a rapid proliferation of companies in various countries for its manufacture. In the United States these soon escaped any real Nobel control amidst a confusing issuance of company stock, transfers of ownership, and legal or illegal hanky-panky. In France the allegedly devious activities of the "sinister" Paul Barbe, a Nobel associate, highlighted the scene.

Alfred still wanted to find a stronger explosive by absorbing the nitroglycerin in a substance that was itself explosive. This time the story, almost certainly true, has it that Alfred, having accidentally cut his finger in the laboratory, put some collodion on the wound; this started him wondering whether collodion might be used with nitroglycerin and guncotton. When he combined these, the result was a transparent, jellylike mixture, blasting gelatin.[52] It contained, in its fully developed form, about 75 percent nitroglycerin, plus sodium or potassium nitrate, nitro-cellulose, and a little wood meal and chalk. Being waterproof, it could be used in underwater blasting. In 1889 he invented ballistite, a nitroglycerin smokeless powder, a much more powerful explosive; when others invented the rather similar cordite, Nobel claimed an infringement of his patent, but the courts ruled otherwise. One of his factories was now at Sévran-Livry, outside of Paris, where he was also considered a most uncomfortable neighbor; the newspapers worried about it being too close to a state-owned powder works, and they also had much to say about his unscrupulous French business partners. He then took himself off to San Remo in Italy, where he set up a new laboratory.[53]

August Strindberg would sneer that the Nobel Prize fund came from "dynamite money," by which, with a side glance at Nobel's purchase of Bofors, he meant armaments, but the inventions had many peaceful uses. The St.

Gotthard tunnel, built in 1872–80, was finished several years ahead of schedule and more cheaply because of his blasting gelatin. The digging of the Corinth canal in Greece and the removal of underwater rocks in New York harbor were aided by his inventions, while railroad construction and the mining industry benefited greatly from his work. Altogether, Alfred Nobel sought 355 patents and obtained 85 of them. His first had been a gasometer. He worked on gas motors, welding of iron and steel, and developing artificial forms of silk, rubber, and leather.[54]

This citizen of the world never did have a real home after his parents left St. Petersburg in 1859; his home was his laboratory, "where he would spend the whole day, engaged upon new discoveries, on which his brain was ceaselessly working."[55] Unlike some of the other inventors, he combined imaginative inventing with a sober sense of business, and in fact Alfred repeatedly pestered Ludvig with unwanted financial advice. An introspective, shy dreamer who in his youth had been sorely tempted to become a poet, he lived a solitary, lonely life. Herta Pauli has described him as a "shy, suspicious, sickly, grey little man," and his assistant said that he was alternately melancholy and facetious, his voice customarily sad or satirical.[56]

Birger Steckzén found him "a bold optimist in his experiments and markedly pessimistic in his perception of human beings.[57] He was a complex man of many paradoxes, quite suited to be "a passionate devotee of peace and a pioneer in war materials." In many respects Swedish to the very depths of his being, Alfred Nobel, resident in several nations but willfully not member of any national tribe, countered his cynicism with dreams of a better world; one day he sat down in the Swedish Club in Paris and wrote the last will and testament that would establish the Nobel prizes.

He always had been frail, and in 1896 he was consulting a doctor about heart trouble. At San Remo on December 7 of that year he wrote a letter to Ragnar Sohlman, head of his Bofors laboratory, and a few hours later suffered a heart attack. He died on December 10. Nathan Söderblom, future illustrious archbishop of Uppsala and a Nobel laureate himself in 1930, spoke at his bier in San Remo. His body was brought home to the land of his ancestors and, after a funeral service in Storkyrkan, he was buried in the family plot in a Stockholm cemetery.[58]

By his testament he left his money to be put into a fund from whose income would be distributed five annual prizes in physics, chemistry, literature, physiology or medicine, and efforts on behalf of peace. They were to be awarded to those who had done the most for *"mänsklighetens gagn och folkens förbrödring,"* for the benefit of humanity and for the encouragement of the brotherhood of nations. Ragnar Sohlman was named executor of the will. He had to fight litigating relatives, tax collectors of various countries, and distinguished academies reluctant to assume the burden of selecting Nobel nominees. Robert's two sons and son-in-law were particularly unhappy, having the least money in their branch of the family, and even King Oscar II opposed the will.[59] Emanuel Nobel thought that his uncle's wishes should be respected, and with his help Sohlman won the battle.

On every December 10, the anniversary of his death, the Swedish establishment gathers to celebrate their annual intellectual Olympiad, the distribution of all except the peace prize, awarded in Oslo. In a scene of immaculate elegance, the distinguished winning candidates file in and take their places on red chairs, across from the royal family and Academy members, to listen to laudatory speeches and to be handed their scrolls by His Majesty. Above and behind them, rows of red roses lead up to an effulgently lighted bust of Alfred Nobel, the native son whom few Swedes—or anyone else—had known very well.

17. THE PETROLEUM AGE BEGINS

Immanuel Nobel was responsible, many years before the work of his oil-rich sons, for an early harbinger of the petroleum age, with its internal combustion engines, rubber tires, batteries, automobiles, airplanes, and motorboats. Nobel started Sweden's first India rubber factory in the 1830s, this in the same years that a temporary flurry of interest in the new substance brought premature founding of rubber-making enterprises in Great Britain and the United States; the elder Fahnehjelm took over the workshop, which had been making surgical appliances and collapsible rubber sacks for the army, when Nobel moved to Russia. Other harbingers also appeared. An "automobile," propelled by steam engine, was constructed at the Nyköping works in the 1840s, designed by an Åtvidaberg smith by the name of J. A. Nordberg. It held ten persons and some goods, moved at twelve (English) miles an hour, and covered the distance from Nyköping to Stockholm in about six hours. Petroleum, in the form of kerosene, arrived from the United States in the autumn of 1861. Some velocipedes, with iron rims, wooden spokes, and a front wheel somewhat larger than the back one, were made in 1869 at Hultby *bruk* in Småland.[1]

A third wave of innovations, bringing with it some of the most conspicuous aspects of the twentieth century, was about to enter the country. Once again the well-known pattern would repeat itself as eager entrepreneurs tried to get an early edge in the market with imported wares, innovators and businessmen combined their talents to found new enterprises, and larger companies emerged out of the competition to win the national market and to seek international sales. The bulk of these developments occurred after 1914, and only some of the beginnings will be sketched here.

The bicycle, precursor of motor power transport, evolved over a thirty-year period in France and Great Britain, from front-wheel-drive velocipedes to essentially the form it has retained ever since. Harry Lawson invented a safety bicycle with a geared-up transmission (1876), ball bearings began to be used (1877), John Boyd Dunlop invented pneumatic rubber tires (1889), and soon thereafter "free wheels," enabling coasting, came into use. In the ensuing bicycle craze one man pedaled a bicycle from London to Constantinople (Istanbul), and the following year he went from London to Moscow and back again (4,281 miles in 47 days); another enthusiast cycled, more or less, around the world.[2] In a larger sense its rapid adoption reflected a growing need for individual transportation as contrasted to such public forms as trains and streetcars, a need that the automobile would later satisfy.

Continuing production of bicycles in Sweden began in 1884 at the Per Froms Mek. Verkstad, which at first imported parts and assembled them. Per Froms (1856–1931) had served at Bolinders and other machine shops, then at a Philadelphia locomotive works, before he and a partner started putting out the then-typical large front-wheel type. The company survived British and Swedish competition and was still manufacturing them after the death of the founder. Among the British companies, Humber, Ltd., founded in 1890 and incorporating the Dunlop pneumatic tire, organized a Swedish affiliate. Several small Swedish firms entered the market, assembling foreign parts. Swedish newspapers indignantly reported that small children and old ladies were being run over by their crazed drivers. About 10,000 bicycles were being produced annually at the turn of the century, of which 4,662 were factory-made in 1900 at Husqvarna.[3]

Two larger companies in time absorbed the others. One came out of an instrument workshop in Uppsala, where Anders Nyman had constructed a bicycle as early as 1882. His two sons transformed it into a major industrial enterprise, employing about 1,100 factory workers making, in addition to other articles, the Crescent, Hermes, and Nordstjernan; the last had originated earlier at another company (A. Wiklund) in Stockholm. The second company, Monark, rose out of the "rags to riches" career of Birger Svensson (1883–1944) of Varberg, who started, as a boy, with a store along a country road. At the age of eighteen he saw his first bicycle, an instant love affair; he bought it and promptly scared the neighborhood horses. Buying imported parts, he put them together for sale (1904). Within a few years Svensson was manufacturing the parts in his machine shop at Varberg and sending out mail-order catalogs advertising his bicycle and also sewing machines, musical instruments, guns, and other items. In time, the Monark bicycle crowded out everything else at the company except motorcycles, which were also made at Husqvarna (1908), Nyman, and two other places.[4] In this industry, too, the almost inevitable concentration of ownership and production occurred, not least because the sale of foreign models was again increasing. Monark secured majority control of Nymanbolagan AB in 1960, and in 1962 the combined firm took over the manufacture and sale of the Husqvarna bicycles and mopeds. Husqvarna continued to make internationally well-known models of motorcycles.

A wild oil boom struck in the United States after petroleum had been discovered at Titusville in Pennsylvania (1859). It cost twenty dollars a barrel at the beginning, but within two years had dropped to ten cents. In the refining process the raw gasoline (*bensin* in Swedish) emerges at 150 degrees Celsius and the kerosene (*fotogen*) and lighting oils at between 150 and 300, the remaining heavy oil being used for grease and "raw oil" motors. Production in the first decades, before the introduction of the gasoline combustion motor, was aimed primarily at the kerosene market for use as fuel in lamps and stoves.

Though some kerosene of poor quality had arrived from Germany earlier, two Americans, H. (Henry) O. Jones and Captain Charles G. Lundborg, imported kerosene lamps and fuel into Sweden in 1861. Obviously they must have been encouraged by the rapid development in America and hoped to cash in on a coming oil boom in Sweden. Obtaining Swedish patents on the production of kerosene and other oils and on paraffin, they put up a refinery on Reymersholm island outside Stockholm (1862–63). Though they seem to have planned originally to extract oil from coal, they apparently in fact imported crude oil. About 200,000 litres of kerosene were produced annually for a few years, but H. O. Jones & Co., could not compete with imported refined oil, and the refinery was sold at auction in 1868. L. O. Smith, the Whiskey King, bought it, as mentioned earlier, and thereafter distilled the fuel for a very different kind of illumination. Over 9,000 barrels of oil were being imported annually in the mid-1870s; gasoline for lighting purposes was also attempted, but so many explosions ensued that its household use had to be abandoned.[5]

Lundborg also started production of kerosene at a refinery at nearby Södertälje in 1865, making it out of coal. Not profitable either, it closed five years later. The former sea captain tried drilling for oil, but Sweden had even less oil than it did coal. A new company then refined imported American crude, but a drop in prices ran that one out of business. A third owner, Bengt Ohlsson, took over, and by making wagon grease and by being the first in Sweden to make machine oil he kept the enterprise going until his retirement in 1906.

Another small enterprise, Engelsberg Oljefabriks AB, founded in 1875, managed a reasonably profitable operation.[6] It did so in spite of, or perhaps because of, its odd location at Lake Åminningen some distance north of Mälaren. Per Ågren thinks that the oil works may have been placed there by August Ålund, its founder, in order to keep the processes secret, but it found a ready market in the iron works and mines of the region. It was making gas oil, machine oil, paraffin, and cart grease from American crude oil, Galician coal tar, and fats and tallows from Russia. A successor company maintained operations from 1905 until 1927; it is now a museum.

Swedish gasoline imports rose from 1,600 barrels in 1907 to 16,000 in 1914 and to 574,000 by 1939, when it was selling at 30 öre a liter. Svenska Petroleum AB, founded in 1896, became Svenska Esso AB, the AB Svenska Shell came into being in 1912, and the Svenska BP Olje AB in 1927. A large refinery was started south of Stockholm in 1928 by AB Nynäs-Petroleum, one of the companies in the Johnson group of industries. It later added refineries in Malmö and Gothenburg, and Shell and BP also set up refineries near the latter city. Petroleum would, it may be recalled, ultimately account for nearly three-quarters of the country's energy needs.

Another component of the petroleum age, the rubber (*gummi*) industry, emerged in the 1890s in Sweden, the first two factories appearing almost simultaneously in Hälsingborg and at Viskafors (1890). The Hälsingborg venture, first making galoshes, branched out into such other goods as rubber gloves and its still well-known sports shoes, bearing the trade name of Tretorn (Three Towers). The Viskafors factory, owned by the Skandinaviska Gummi AB, would subsequently make Firestone tires. A third, at Gislaved, appeared in 1895, supplying bicycle and, later, automobile tires; operated by Svenska Gummifabriks AB of Stockholm, it would be acquired in 1926 by KF, the huge Swedish cooperative. A fourth was founded in Trelleborg in 1896, and, among the later ones, a Goodyear factory opened in Norrköping in 1939.[7]

Most of the early storage batteries (*ackumulators*) at the turn of the century were imported from a factory in Westphalia. However, as in almost any technological field, the inevitable Swedish inventor had already appeared in the person of Waldemar Jungner (1869–1924). He invented his first battery in 1888 while still a student, when, working at a mill in the summer, he tried to make a fire alarm apparatus. He devised his famous alkaline battery NIFE in 1896: nickel oxide, iron sponge, and a solution of potash serving as the electrolyte. Ackumulator AB Jungner was founded in 1900 for its manufacture, and when Thomas Edison in that year invented a similar battery, the company sued the American inventor. Jungner won the case, but at such expense that the original company had to be liquidated and a new one founded, based on an improved battery (1910). (Edison was so often involved in patent infringement lawsuits, usually against those trying to profit from his ideas, that the Jungner episode does not usually rate a mention in the American's biographies.) In time the Jungner company became one of Sweden's major international fims, selling NIFE, SAAJ (lead battery), SATO (dry battery), and the accompanying apparatus. Like Edison, Jungner was interested in electric cars; in 1900, using a lead battery, he drove an "automobile" about a hundred English miles in twelve hours.[8]

Kerosene lamps sold briskly during the later decades of the century. Before their arrival, portable lamps in the home had customarily been fueled by vegetable oils. These were being processed industrially by Delbanco in Gothenburg and by G. Sommelius and J. Sundblad in Stockholm, though many small presses existed in the countryside; once the oil for lighting purposes (and linseed oil) had been extracted, the residue of seeds was pressed into cakes to feed the cattle.[9] The new kerosene lamps were directly copied from the vegetable oil ones and closely resembled them in function and appearance. The earliest in Sweden seem to have come from Germany, closely followed by the imports from the United States. Among those who were buying parts for lamps and kerosene stoves from abroad in order to assemble and sell them in Stockholm were Öller, trying to ride the wave of technological advances as usual, and his student, Johan August Buchau.

Another man, Arvid Böhlmark (1841–1897), was getting his lamp parts from a Christiania (Oslo) company and assembling them, but by the end of the 1870s he was also buying some of the parts from Brevens *bruk* in Närke, better known for its farm machinery. The burners were usually imported from Germany. His early quarters were too small for his business, so he dumped the boxes on the street until used. When a policeman came up and gave him still another citation, Bölmark queried, "Oh, so, have you come to collect the rent again?" It had scarcely been practicable to manufacture lamps because foreign models were cheaper, but the protective tariff of 1892 changed that situation. Whether by foresight or luck, Böhlmark had begun to make most of the parts in a new factory in 1888. By now, however, the electric lights had become a threat, and he soon also started putting out electric armatures. The firm would survive and is still in the lamp business in Stockholm.[10]

Böhlmark's brother-in-law, Carl Östlund, had patented a kerosene oil stove, consisting of two burners with flat wicks, in 1869. In 1885 he also invented the Excelsior stove, in which, the wick no longer needed, air pressure gasified the oil. Two similar inventions by other men, however, would be much more successful. Carl Nyberg (1858–1939), born in Arboga in working-class circumstances, had impressed an influential lady with his models of airplanes and submarines; this led to employment at a workshop where gas oil stoves were being manufactured. Quickly grasping the principle of the gasification of gasoline or light oils by air pressure, he adapted it to a new function by inventing a blowtorch (1881–82). It looked sufficiently promising for Max Sievert, German-born manufacturer of telephone wires and cables, to take over its sales, and Nyberg's blowtorch, fueled by gasoline, subsequently achieved a worldwide market.[11]

The other invention, the cheap and handy Primus kerosene stove, would become one of the best known of all Swedish products. Karl Modin attributed its success to the work of four poor young men, all of them former metal workers: the two Lindqvist brothers, Johan Victor Svenson, and Berndt Hjorth. One version of the invention has it that the Lindqvist brothers grew up in a family living in a single room, where food was prepared on a kerosene stove of the wick type. Detesting its pungent odor and its soot, the boys determined to invent something better. Another version has a fellow worker at AB Separator, Ludvig Holm, making the original model for such a stove, which Frans Lindqvist then improved. It operated essentially the same way as Nyberg's already invented blowtorch, using kerosene as a fuel instead of gasoline.

Johan Victor Svenson (1863–1938), going out to buy a kerosene stove for a friend, found the Lindqvists laboriously making them in their hours off from their regular work at AB Separator. He had grown up in an orphanage, and at the age of eleven became a sheet metal worker. Once old enough, he joined the navy and served as a fireman on the *Vanadis* on its cruise around the world (1883–85). After having bought the sheet metal shop where he had formerly worked, he discovered the Lindqvists' Primus and promptly suggested that he take over the sales. Svenson took the financial risk, guaranteeing them sufficient income if they would quit their separator jobs and work full time on the stoves; soon he was selling them so fast that the Lindqvists could not keep up. Needing more capital for expansion, Svenson brought in a fourth former metal worker, Berndt Hjorth, who then took over the sales rights (1892). When a company was organized in 1898, Hjorth was excluded, but in 1918 he bought AB Primus, having in the meantime become sales agent for J. P. Johansson's adjustable wrenches and the managing director of BAHCO. It was, essentially, Hjorth's salesmanship and contacts that turned Primus into an article in worldwide use.[12] When it celebrated its centennial in 1982, the firm, now known as Primus-Sievert and owned by Esso, was selling its stoves in over a hundred countries.

AB Lux, whose name became incorporated in Electrolux, had rather similar origins. Its founder, Sven Carlson (1847–1924), who had a doctor's degree from Uppsala and had studied at the Institute of Technology, was a veteran of the Nobel enterprises. After three years at the Demidoff iron works in the Urals, he had spent a decade in Nobel service at Baku and Warsaw, becoming thoroughly familiar with petroleum. After his return to Sweden, he invented, with H. Rustige, an incandescent lamp, using the Auer mantle (Auerstrumpa) and kerosene as fuel. The so-called Luxlampa found a ready international market for a few years, especially for use in railroad yards and farmsteads, until the spread of electric lights greatly reduced its sales.

The internal combustion engine in a relatively practical form arrived in Sweden in 1891, brought by Sjunne (Sune) Amilone (1847–1920). Partner in a Stockholm firm that sold machinery, he acquired a boat motor, a gasoline-powered Daimler engine, after visiting Karl Benz and Gottlieb Daimler in Germany. Benz had constructed his first land vehicle in 1885, a tricycle driven by a one-cylinder gasoline engine, and in the same year Daimler completed the high-speed engine that is commonly considered the true beginning of the automobile. Amilone also obtained an automobile in Paris, of which more later. He persuaded Vulcans Mek. Verkstad in Norrköping to make small gasoline motors for boats, but, unfortunately, they exploded much too frequently. The insurance companies balked, the authorities consulted the law books, and the customers became exceedingly uneasy. The name was changed, but this fooled nobody, and the experiment had to be terminated.[13]

Others soon followed, however, and the coming of petroleum-powered motors would greatly stimulate the growth of the Swedish engineering works as they moved to exploit the various possibilities. Bolinders, much of its manufacturing still in sawmill equipment, began to make oil engines in 1894. This major Stockholm company was now being run by Erik August Bolinder (1863–1930), who had recently returned from a lengthy study-tour of American factories. As the expansion of Swedish sawmill companies drew to a close, the company, casting about for alternatives, would gradually concentrate on the new automotive industry. During the first decade, Bolinders made 791 motors, including a model devised by John Weyland.[14] Finspång, still searching for a new identity after its loss of weapons orders, also began making Weyland's model, but this motor was soon driven out by superior engines.

J. V. Svenson, busily selling the little Primus cooking stove, became a combustion engine enthusiast. At an exhibit in Copenhagen he bought an American motor, dismantled it to study how it functioned, and in due course built the Augustendal factory in Nacka, Stockholm suburb, intending to manufacture automobiles. An engineer, dispatched to Germany to study auto manufacturing, also brought back a two-cycle boat motor. Svenson's wife had come from a family of fishermen, living on an island off the coast of Östergötland, and the uses for a cheap motor were quite clear to him. He hired Eric Anton Rundlöf, a former participant in de Laval's laboratories on Kungsholmen who had just returned from working at Campbell's motor factory in Great Britain. Here he had become acquainted with the pioneering work of Dugald Clark on two-cycle engines. Though Rundölf moved over to Bolinders in 1901, another engineer, Johan Kruse (1876–1934), at Augustendal from 1900 until 1905, developed a two-cycle motor that used kerosene or crude oil. The so-called Avancemotor went into production in 1907 and sold extremely well. AB Avancemotor would later, in 1932, become part of the Bolinder-Munktell group of companies.[15]

Meanwhile, Bolinders, abandoning Weyland's engine, began manufacturing a Rundlöf model, a two-cycle motor, using heavy oil. E. A. Bolinder now of necessity introduced the use of interchangeable parts, increasingly automatic machinery, and full-scale serial production. Demand for motors rose rapidly, and the big production of motors, with a newly built modern factory, started in 1907. A two-stroke vertical "E" type direct-reversible engine went into production in 1908 and an air-cooled "M" type in 1914.[16] Among others who devised kerosene motors were Oscar and Carl Hult, with their Archimedes outboard motor. After their return from working in American factories in 1887–90, they had invented a hand-driven cream separator, the Excelsior. They followed this by developing a rotary steam engine and also a friction-gearing mechanism; to manufacture the latter, AB Centrator was organized.

The invention of the diesel engine by Rudolf Diesel in the early 1890s quickly attracted the attention of Marcus Wallenberg. Oscar Lamm and several engineers at Nya Atlas, controlled by the Wallenbergs, attended the testing of the diesel motor at Augsburg in 1897. The next year Wallenberg met the inventor and procured the Swedish rights to the engine, Burmeister & Wain receiving the Danish and Emanuel Nobel the Russian franchise to build them. AB Diesels Motorer was founded in April 1898 by Marcus and Knut Wallenberg, Oscar Lamm, and John Schmidt (de Laval associate). Though its long-term prospects were excellent, its early difficulties gave Marcus Wallenberg more problems than any other company.[17]

The real breakthrough came with the adaptation of diesel engines to ships, particularly important for Sweden because the use of coal for steam engines had always been an expensive proposition. At Diesels Motorer, K. Jonas Hesselman (1877–1957) worked out a series of engines for marine navigation. His first effort went into the *Vandal*, used by Nobel Brothers in the petroleum transport on the Volga, and involved three four-cycle motors of 120-hp each, built by Diesels Motorer. However, the engines could not be quickly reversed between forward and backward by direct use of the diesel engines, and good maneuverability was a necessity in the Russian network of rivers, lakes, and canals. Hesselman soon, however, succeeded in constructing a directly reversible two-cycle motor. One was installed in the schooner *Orion* in 1907; two sister ships (1908) became the first that relied entirely upon the new engine. A four-cycle reversible engine followed in 1909, and in 1911 the *Toiler,* with two 180-hp motors crossed the Atlantic. That same year Roald Amundsen was using a 180-hp motor from Diesels Motorer on his Antarctic expedition.[18] Burmeister & Wain launched the first large transatlantic ship, the *Selandia*, for the Danish East Asiatic Co. (1912), and it was also, as noted earlier, responsible for six motorships of the Nordstjernan line.

Diesels Motorer merged with Atlas in 1917, then in 1948 was sold to NOHAB. Atlas, known as Atlas Copco since 1955, underwent a great transformation in the years before 1914, one that would result in it becoming, especially after the Second World War, a world leader in the manufacture of pneumatic tools, drills, and compressors. This started innocently enough when Atlas bought a British pneumatic riveting machine and an air compressor for its own use. Gustaf Ryd, an Atlas engineer, worked in the United States in 1892–93 and while there purchased a similar riveting machine, made by James MacCay in Brooklyn. He also bought pneumatic caulking apparatus and a caulking hammer in Glasgow (Greenhead Engine Works, MacEvan Ross construction). Returned to Atlas, Ryd made more riveting machines for use in the factory. Motala asked to buy one. So did others. Opportunity—a market for the machines—existed.

Gunnar Jacobsson, who would later replace Oscar Lamm as managing director of Atlas (1909–1940), returned from the United States in 1898, after four years there, as an advocate of compressed air tools. Ryd went to England that year to study the techniques. A new American type of compressor was acquired shortly thereafter. Atlas, the old railroad equipment company that had for so many years been in search of a new destiny, had at last found its specialty, spurred on, naturally, by Marcus Wallenberg. In 1901 Atlas began manufacturing riveters and chisel hammers, and soon thereafter reciprocating compressors and boring machines for use in the mines. Smaller ones were powered by electricity, bigger ones by steam engines. In 1907 the company started using kerosene internal combustion engines, later went on to gasoline motors and ultimately to diesels. By 1910 the manufacture of compressed air tools had become the predominant business of the company, and it was exporting about two-thirds of its production, the Russians being the best customers.[19]

Another company that would later become part of the Atlas group was the Svenska Diamantbergsborrning AB, founded in 1885-86. The first drilling in Sweden by use of machine power had occurred in Skåne in 1871–72 when American-type machinery from the Continental Diamond Rock Boring Co. (England) was used in exploring for more coal beds. A steam engine provided the power. Another company hired a German firm to do similar work. Captain Lundborg, drilling for oil in Östergötland, brought in American machinery. Costs ran high in each case, too high to permit prolonged use. At this point, as usual, a Swede with experience abroad entered the picture. Per Anton Craelius (1854–1905), a former student at Uppsala and the Institute of Technology, had worked for four years in Colorado mines, where he had become familiar with diamond-head drilling tools. Obtaining employment with the Norberg-Risberg mining company, he found a partner in its managing director, Gustaf Granström, who had not yet become associated with the work of Georg Wenström at ASEA. Craelius and Granström interested the dynamic Erik Johan Ljunberg of Stora Kopparbergs Bergslaget in the new drilling devices, and in 1885–86 they founded the Svenska Diamantbergsborrning AB.[20]

But what kind of power could they use for the drilling machinery? Steam power was expensive and not easily transportable. It was a bit early for electric power, though Granström would continue to have interests in both electric companies and mines. Craelius devised a hand-driven drill, made at Köpings Mek. Verkstad (1887), which was both light and cheap; it was also slow, hence offered only a temporary solution. The internal combustion motor, now arriving on the scene, seemed the obvious answer. Craelius, testing several possibilities, began using gas oil motors, but he soon found that gas oil was not always available. Kerosene, however, could always be obtained, and by the end of the 1890s, the company had gone over to kerosene motors. It soon had large contracts exploring for ore abroad, particularly in Russia before the 1917 revolution.

In addition to the boat motor, Sjunne Amilone had brought a Daimler-type automobile to Sweden, obtained from Panhard and Levassor in Paris in return for displaying it, as well as motors and motorboats, in an exhibit in Gothenburg in 1891.[21] Hoping to sell automobiles, he advertised them in his firm's motor catalog, claiming that the 2-hp, four-wheeled vehicle, costing 3200 kronor, could climb hills and would not scare the horses. (By 1894 the Panhard had its vertical engine in front and rather resembled later automobiles.) It didn't sell, and "Sweden's first motorist" took a position as a manager at the Bultfabrik. At his suggestion, Vulcan Mek. Verkstad imported a Daimler in 1895, but it had no more luck with this than the gasoline motor. Founded in 1877, Vulcan had in recent years been primarily engaged in making small kerosene motors, but it went out of business in 1905; its premises were then occupied by International Harvester.

A few other automobiles were brought in. A three-wheeled, single-cylinder Leon-Bollée was exhibited at the 1897 Stockholm exposition. Pellerin, a Gothenburg firm that sold margarine, came up with the idea of advertising its product by means of an automobile spectacular. A French car was driven from Gothenburg to Stockholm through all the intervening towns, though rumor circulated that it had in fact been shipped by train as far as Örebro (1898). The ornately uniformed chauffeur then took it on a tour of southern Sweden and, later, up into Norrland. In 1899 Viktor Wallenberg purchased an automobile in France and drove it home.[22]

The crown prince, the future King Gustav V (1907–1950), bought a Daimler in 1899. At least it made good copy for the newspapermen. It chugged and groaned, and when shifted into second made loud *krssch* sounds. Tested on a fairly steep hill one day, it made noises like a pig being slaughtered, went into convulsions, and stopped altogether. The passengers tried to push it up the hill, followed by the crown prince shouting exhortations. He thereafter refused to set foot in it, and the next year he purchased a much better behaved Peugeot. The Daimler was acquired by an outfit that rented droshky meters, to be leased out by the day to common folks who wanted to "ride as royally as the crown prince." Whenever it appeared in the streets it tended to be accompanied by a swarm of shouting small boys, some of the horses reared back on their hind legs, and "old folks climbed the lamp posts and spat three times. . . ."[23]

Two brothers in Ystad, Jons and Anders Cederholm, built two automobiles, powered by a small steam engine, in the early 1890s. The first one hit a wall, damaging car and wall; they then made a second one, reusing the original engine. Its speed was not much faster than a wagon, it had to be stopped every few kilometers for the engine to cool off, and it aroused much merriment among the spectators.[24]

Gustaf Erikson (1859–1922) made Sweden's first genuine automobile in 1897–98. Originally an engineer at the Skutskär sawmill and then at Domnarvet, he had read everything available about them. After traveling in Germany, France, and England to study their construction, he took a position with Surahammar *bruk*, which by now owned the old Ekenberg Vagnfabrik property in Södertälje. Surahammar, a part of ASEA's industries since 1916, has antecedents going back to the time of Gustav Vasa and had been owned for a time by Gustav II Adolf's great chancellor, Axel Oxenstierna; held in the middle of the nineteenth century by the ill-fated Hammarskjölds of Skultuna, it had passed into the hands of one of their big creditors, E. V. Zethelius, also owner of Nyby *bruk* and patron of experiments in the iron industry. Already making railroad car wheels, rims, and axles before it became a company in 1872, Surahammar's management thought that it made good sense to take over the Ekenberg industrial plant, where Atlas had stopped making railroad cars in 1887. Philip Wersén, son-in-law of Johan Ekenberg and a former Atlas director, was appointed manager in Södertälje and a new factory put up (1892).

Surahammar's manager, encouraging Gustaf Erikson to make an automobile engine, placed the Surahammar and Södertälje facilities at his disposal. His first venture, a four-cylinder, started up with much racket, stopped, and would not run again. He then made a two-cylinder kerosene motor and mounted it on a carriage. He and three passengers climbed in, the engine emitted "frightful explosions," women and children fled the place, and the vehicle continued to move until it hit the wall. Erikson eagerly proposed that they make more automobiles, but the manager indulgently suggested that he better improve this one first. After rebuilding it, Erikson invited the manager to go for a ride. Having surreptitiously arranged to be followed by a horse-drawn droshky, so that he would not have to walk home, the manager went along. They traveled 18 kilometers, including going up some hills and always trailing "clouds of vile-smelling smoke." Returned to the factory, the manager got out, took some deep drags on a cigarette to eliminate the kerosene odor from his nostrils, and announced, "I sure as Hell cannot exactly understand the good qualities of this automobile, but it certainly does smoke real damned good!" Erikson's next automobile, constructed amidst the clatter of workmen making railroad car wheels, had the motor underneath and was adorned with big rubber tires. Its four-cylinder engine was still fueled by kerosene because the insurance companies continued to frown on the use of gasoline, but when he substituted gasoline he obtained a much better performance. Thereafter he put out increasingly improved automobiles at the Vagnfabrik. The first truck appeared in 1903.[25]

The old Vagnfabrik had gone from wagons to railroad cars to automobiles, and the first two letters in the word for wagon (*vagn*) now survived in Vabis as the name of a gasoline-powered vehicle. A rival company had already appeared in 1897 after Wersén left Vabis to found Södertälje Vekstäder, also making railroad equipment and even a few automobiles. In 1911 Vabis merged with its strongest competitor, Scania, located in Malmö. The latter had originated as an offshoot of Humber, Ltd., the British bicycle company. Its first cars had their engines underneath, made by Fridolf Thorssin, who, without practical experience in their manufacture, dreamed up his model. When the wiser counsels of another man, Anton Svensson, prevailed, Thorssin stomped off to another infant auto company in Gothenburg. Svensson then made cars with the engine in front and two-cylinder German motors. One of them was driven to Stockholm in 1903 for the country's first real auto exhibit, and the crown prince added a Scania to his collection. Soon the company was turning out several each month, sales were good, and Scania and Vabis briskly competed for the available business until the two companies merged. Thereafter, passenger cars were manufactured in Södertälje and trucks in Malmö; it was putting out about two hundred automobiles a year by 1914.[26] AB Scania-Vabis would continue to be the Swedish manufacturer of trucks during the following decades.

Several others tried to make automobiles. C. A. Engström, owner of a wagon factory in Eskilstuna, constructed one in 1900 with a one-cylinder, 3½ hp gasoline motor that he claimed could go 35 kilometers an hour. Pity wagon and carriage manufacturers like Engström! Scarcely had they gone to industrial production in the 1880s when the appearance of the internal combustion engine foreshadowed their end. The largest, founded in Arvika in 1885, was turning out about 4,000 horse-drawn vehicles a year in the first decade of this century.

Knut Söderblom (1846–1913) in Eskilstuna had relative success with the manufacture of automobiles and trucks. Already making stoves, milling equipment, and other goods in his factory, he first tried to move with the times by making small 1½ hp crude-oil motors. In 1901 Söderblom produced his first passenger car, and two years later he made a van for the post office, one of the first in the world. Söderblom went about it quite professionally, hiring an expert German engineer (Bruno Büchner) to direct the works, which made only trucks after 1909. The Telegraph Service bought one of the earliest, an oil company purchased two or more for its deliveries, and the Hamburger brewery in Stockholm used his trucks for distribution of beer. Production ceased after Söderblom's death and the acquisition of his factory by Luth & Rosén. A small operation at Tidaholms *bruk*, started by a man who had worked in a bicycle factory in the United States, survived until the early 1930s.[27] Another former worker in America made a few automobiles for Baron Theodor Adelswärd at

Åtvidaberg, but, as mentioned earlier, they looked like carriages and no one would buy them.

Another venture, directed by Thorssin at AB Motorfabriken in Gothenburg was largely an assembly plant: two-cylinder motors from Aachen Stahlwaaren-fabrik, Michelin tires, parts of the vehicle from Nydqvist & Holm and other factories. The company ultimately went bankrupt. Gothenburg's successful automobile manufacturer would bear another name. In 1916 Sweden had 3,036 registered cars, and 8,506 at the end of 1919. About 12,000 automobiles, mostly American, were being imported annually in the early 1920s.[28] Obviously there was room for one or two Swedish manufacturers.

Meantime, the internal combustion engine had taken to the air. In 1910–11 Baron Carl Cederström was flying his airplane, *Nordstjernan*, around Sweden with maximum publicity; in October 1910 he flew over Stockholm and circled the Royal Palace. The first long-distance Swedish air flight, however, had ended in tragedy when an attempt to fly over the North Pole in a balloon failed. Salomon August Andrée, with Nils Strindberg and Knut Fraenckel, took off from Spitzbergen on July 11, 1897—then silence. Their remains were found on White Island east of Spitzbergen in 1930.

Carl Nyberg, the inventor of a blowtorch, became known all over Sweden as "Flyg-Nyberg" (Flying-Nyberg) because of his ridiculous notion that heavier-than-air machines could actually be made to fly. Already in 1875 he was planning a helicopter and soon thereafter was making models of airplanes. He carried on long experiments in a wind tunnel on the behavior of wings and propellers in a strong air current, perhaps the first in the world to do so. Nyberg developed a small high-pressure kerosene-powered engine in the hope that it would generate sufficient power to lift an airplane into the air. Attaching a monoplane to a wire, he ran it round and round on a track, trying vainly to pick up sufficient velocity for it to take off (1897). Max Sievert, business partner, worried that Nyberg might actually succeed and get himself killed in the process. Nyberg had the right principles fully in hand, but it would be a lighter and more powerful gasoline combustion engine that would solve the problem.[29] Two other Swedes also experimented with airplanes, Gustaf de Laval and Theodor Winborg, the partner earlier of Helge Palmcrantz.

Another inventor born too early, incidentally, was Captain Wilhelm Unge (1845–1915), who invented a "flying torpedo" or rocket that could travel 7,000 meters; though financed by Alfred Nobel, patented in several countries, and sponsored by a company (AB Mars) organized for its manufacture, in the long run it came to nothing.

Cederström, who had trained at Blèriot's flying school near Paris (1910) and secured Sweden's first international flying license, became director of the aviation division at AB Södertälje Verkstäder, which turned out airplanes (the Farman model at first) for the Swedish army and navy during the First World

War.[30] The first Swedish-built airplane, a Blèriot monoplane, had already been constructed in 1908 by Oscar Ask (1883–1916) in a small machine shop in Landskrona. In 1912 he founded the first airplane factory in Scandinavia at Landskrona, calling it "Aeroplansvarvet Avis." At this point the real founder of the Swedish industry, Enoch Thulin (1881–1919), appeared on the scene.

Thulin had received his doctor's degree at Lund University on a dissertation dealing with wind resistance, a subject some of the academic community did not consider an appropriate field for a degree. He had worked with Eiffel in France on it, Eiffel then being considered the leading aerodynamic expert, and he had also passed his flying tests in France. In the meantime, eight other Swedes, in addition to Cederström, had obtained their flying licenses. In 1914 Thulin took over Ask's factory and gradually moved it to the Landskrona harbor area, where it became known as Thulinverken. During the war his orders mounted rapidly; he was making airplanes on license for Blèriot and other French companies, and in 1915–18 he delivered over 700 motors and 101 planes of 15 different types. He was killed in May 1919 when an aileron fell off and his plane crashed quite close to the factory.[31] Baron Cederström had died in the preceding year in a crash off the Åland Islands while surveying the route for Sweden–Finland commercial flights.

Otherwise off to a good start, Sweden ultimately would become relatively self-sufficient in the aviation industry, no minor achievement for a smaller country. The big manufacturer would be Saab (Svenska Aeroplan AB), founded in 1937, which would also begin making the Saab automobile in 1949. The Volvo had gone into production in 1927.

The name Volvo, from the Latin for "I roll," derived from a ball-bearing company of that name, which had been founded as a subsidiary of SKF. In 1924 Assar Gabrielsson (1891–1962), sales manager of SKF, and Gustaf Larson (1887–1968), who in 1911–13 had worked at White & Poppe in Coventry in England, began planning the manufacture of motor cars by a reorganized AB Volvo in the old, abandoned SKF plant on Hisingen in Gothenburg. The early cars were assembled there with parts manufactured elsewhere according to SKF specifications. In appearance it was modeled on the French Voisin,and the motor resembled the six-cylinder engine being developed at the Pontiac division of General Motors. The founders considered naming the car the Larson, but then settled on Volvo.[32]

The first one was completed on April 14, 1927. The leaders planned to ride it ceremoniously out of the factory while the crowd cheered. The driver shifted into low, and the car backed up. After thinking that over a bit, the driver put the gear shift into reverse—the car moved forward. The automobile had three shifts backward and one forward! Somebody on the assembly line by the name of Fingal, a foreigner, had put the rear axle on in reverse. The crowd had to wait while the back of the car was hoisted and the axle was properly mounted; only then could the No. 1 Volvo, which would in time become one of the world's best-made automobiles, emerge triumphantly from the shop. Assar Gabrielsson hoped that "everybody would forget the whole thing."

18. IN SUMMARY (1914)

By 1914 Sweden could be said, without much exaggeration, to have reached the rank of an advanced industrial society. The structure of the industrial community, though far from completed, had by then emerged, and thereafter a rather different set of circumstances would mold future developments.[1]

Over the preceding fifty years the Swedes had averaged the most rapid per capita increase in gross national product in Europe, 26 percent per decade, compared to the Japanese, the world leader, with 33.7 and the United States with 27.5; Canada had 24.7 and Germany 21.6. Sweden's national income rose from an annual average of 781.4 million kronor in 1864–73 to 3300 million in 1914.[2] The population was now about a quarter urban, compared to about 11 percent in 1860. Agricultural pursuits, still occupying 72.4 percent of the inhabitants in 1870, had dropped to 62 percent in 1890 and had fallen below one-half (48.4 percent) in 1910. Approximately a third of the workers were now in industry and handicrafts; mines and factories, which had 82,000 workers in 1873, now employed 350,000, and the industrial population had been growing since 1890 at about 2 percent a year. One important measure of industrial growth was the rapid increase in the use of coal and coke: 351,000 tons (1861–65), 1,186,000 (1881–85), 2,850,000 (1896–1900), and 4,639,000 (1906–10).[3]

Another indication that Sweden had passed beyond the limits of a developing country can be seen in the narrowing of the previously chronic trade deficit in the years before the First World War. Exports had risen from about 200 million kronor average value in 1870 to approximately 720 million in 1914, though this does not take into account a rise of about 25 percent in prices.[4] Germany passed Great Britain as Sweden's best trading partner during the first decade of the new century, and Sweden had finally ceased to be so largely an economic dependency of the United Kingdom. The trade with Germany and Great Britain together, however, made up 53.9 percent of Swedish imports-exports, followed by Denmark (8.3), France (5.94), and the United States (5.8).[5]

That other customary aspect of a developing country, large-scale borrowing abroad, was also being terminated. The Swedish foreign debt peaked in about 1910, after which more loans were being liquidated than contracted. The total debt in 1908, mostly in long-term bonds, amounted to 956.9 million kronor (about two-thirds to the French), of which nearly one-half (459.8 million) was in state bonds. By far the greater portion of the state loans had gone to complete the railroad system, whose cost of construction has been calculated at 608 million; over one-half of that had gone to build the Norrland and Lapland lines in recent years. The later loans had been floated in France with the Rothschilds, the Banque de Paris et de Pays Bas, Crédit Lyonnais, and other banks and financial institutions. Of the total Swedish debt abroad, another 254.6 million (much of it in Hamburg) had been borrowed by mortgage banks and societies and 177.6 million by the communes, these two obtaining somewhat over one-half of their borrowed capital from foreign sources. The remaining 64.9 million was accounted for by others, including private enterprise.[6] Though there were exceptions (especially in the Norrland timber industry), the use of foreign capital for railroad construction had left Swedish industry free to use its own profits and capital for further industrial expansion.

It is interesting to note that the European country with the most rapid per capita increase in GNP also had the highest per capita rate of foreign borrowing. The latter primarily reflected the high cost of providing public facilities for a relatively sparse population, but without a modern infrastructure the Swedes could scarcely have sustained their rapid economic advances. Per capita output in industry by 1914 approximated that of the Germans, and it seems to have been not far behind the British. Swedish industrial wages, higher than in Germany, were approaching the British level.[7] Measured within these terms, the long campaign to catch up to the most advanced countries had been successful.

In the broadest technological sense, the century-long struggle might be said to have consisted of three waves of innovations made possible by the successive arrival of three prime movers—the steam engine, the electric generator, and the internal combustion engine. Swedish circumstances encouraged the adoption of steam power for marine transportation, but the lack of coal helped to delay the coming of the railroad and limited its general adoption in factories. Water power, which had so largely determined the original scattered locations for industrial sites, was cheap, and the improved water turbine, evolved out of the water wheel, offered a temporarily attractive alternative to steam engines. The generator and the internal combustion engine, once in practicable form, were quite quickly adopted, a strong indication that Swedish technology and industry were approaching the level of the more advanced countries. More efficient and convenient sources of power made possible, in the long run, the adoption of machine tools, replaceable parts, and the assembly line.

Recapitulating, Sweden's iron works, manufactories, and handicraft textile industry had been rendered obsolete by the earlier stages of the British industrial revolution. The country did possess a legacy of metallurgical and mechanical skills, largely associated with the iron works, and also active and aggressive merchant houses, which were further stimulated by the arrival of a number of foreign, primarily British, entrepreneurs. Some indication of things to come had appeared in the 1840s: the founding of machine shops and their manufacture of agricultural tools and stoves, the Ekman introduction of the Lancashire process in iron, the expansion of sawmills, and the continuing mechanization of textile mills. Developments quickened in the 1850s and 1860s, a period of growth somewhat obscured by the problems of rural overpopulation, crop failures, and two financial crises, but decades when the new forces were strong enough to complete the dismantling of the state regulatory apparatus and to introduce improved banking facilities. The banks in time would come to exercise an almost paramount influence on the growth of Swedish industry, virtually taking over the role played by the state in some other countries. Also by the 1860s, agrarian reform had been nearly completed, surely a factor in preparing for an era of dramatic change, while the departure of emigrants promised to ease the burden of overpopulation on the land.

Then came the breakthrough of the 1870s with its founding of enterprises, centralization in the iron and steel industry, and the rapid construction of railroads. Financially, it had been primed by the fortunate foreign demand for timber and grain and the consequent flow of capital into the country; soon the export of wood pulp, paper, and iron ore would bring in the investment resources for further industrial expansion. Equally fortunate, Sweden's principal customers were high-income countries with an elastic demand for Swedish raw materials.[8] Though the period from the 1850s until about 1880 has been designated in these pages as one of breakthrough, a term borrowed from an older generation of economic historians, the word may not be entirely appropriate for processes more characterized by a rather constant momentum of growth patterns.

Industrial growth continued in the 1880s, though lowered prices, resulting in a seemingly lower total value of production, gave the contrary impression.[9] The restoration of a protective tariff helped to speed the growth of some consumer industries, but the more important factor was the increasing affluence of towns and cities. The agricultural sector, whose exports had previously helped to stabilize the economy, was now switching from grain to dairy products. A great expansion of industry began in the later years of the century, much stimulated by the arrival of the generator and the internal combustion engine. The electric generator, though often driven by steam during the earlier years, was ideally suited to take advantage of Sweden's water resources. Electric power created whole new industries: electric lights, the de Laval and Ljungström turbines, chemical cellulose, the chemical industry, and also the electrification of metallurgy. Even as its first full effects were being experienced, the introduction of petroleum-powered engines inaugurated another outburst of innovations. Sweden's economy and technology had reached a level conducive to authentic inventions, which in turn had great industrial potential. They appeared in relatively rapid succession and together with continued borrowed innovations from abroad cumulatively transformed industry, community facilities, and household living.

By the end of the century the Swedes were themselves going on the offensive, exporting the fruits of their own technology by finding lucrative foreign sales and establishing their own subsidiary factories abroad. They had found their place in the international market; foreign competition forced the Swedes, a small nation, to go to high-quality wares. By the 1890s their exports in general had to be more sophisticated, such as wood in more finished form, chemical cellulose, and engineering products based on their own inventions. This kind of production in turn compelled more innovations, increasing use of machine tools and replaceable parts, and the merger of domestic manufacturers into larger enterprises. Nor was Sweden large enough to sustain some of these domestically, hence these companies had to export in order to survive.

Generalizing broadly, the Swedes appear to occupy a middle position in the timing of industrialization within the context of continental Europe. The French and Germans (also the Belgians and Swiss) are customarily said to have entered a period of rapid growth in the 1830s and 1840s, while the Swedish growth pattern is perceptible by the 1850s and the momentum was accelerating in the 1870s. This would presumably place the Swedes ahead of most of Austria-Hungary, and of Italy, Spain, and Russia.

In economic histories of Europe that cover the past two centuries, the position of Sweden often seems even more peripheral than its geographic location; it is usually perfunctorily dismissed as too little to matter much. In terms of quantity, of statistical comparisons, this is quite true; even its largest enterprises, in numbers of workers and production value, have been small when measured against those of large countries. Nevertheless, the Swedes keep on reiterating that "Sweden is a small country, but. . . ," and they do have a point. In its well-developed industrial sector, reputable international companies, and an economy that has produced one of the highest standards of living in the world, Sweden would become a small-scale replica of the most successful of the large economic powers.

Whatever may be the merits of using the Swedish pattern of industrialization to test models of economic development, the country's smaller dimensions do enable one to see human faces, to become aware of individual motivations and the interplay of personalities. Seen close up, few of these men fit the image of that convenient economic construct, the profit-making automaton. Most of these nineteenth-century figures were strongly imbued with noneconomic values: an addiction to hard work that was not limited to the making of profits, the necessity of team play with their colleagues, and a strong compulsion to display civic spirit. It is tempting to ascribe their conduct, ultimately, to two fundamentals of the Lutheran ethos: the duty of fulfilling one's talents within a chosen Calling and the urge to glorify God's Creative Order by making a personal contribution to its further development. Taken together, this set of values seems to make up the mainspring that enabled the Swedes to respond to the challenge of technological and business opportunities as they opened up.

Viewed at the personal human level, several hundred individuals made contributions worthy of mention during the century. Their careers constitute an anthology of success stories, sometimes with the typical-of-the-era Horatio Alger touch; the sum of their active lives makes up the details of this peaceful conquest of nature's energies. These individuals, finding outlets for their talents, often responded valiantly and with grim determination to prevailing opportunities. It was the period when the most competent in business, engineering, and technology usually were left free to express their personal abilities and ambitions in the workshops and marketplace with minimum restraints from official authorities. Free enterprise worked wonders within the context of a great outburst of self-generating innovations that transformed the community.

Though there were exceptions, until late in the century substantial family background was decisive in securing the training, early positions, and financial means for achievement; most of them were more than one generation from the peasantry or urban laborer level. Even the most individualistic persons needed, in addition to talents, the ability to enlist the support of others. The natural networks of personalities, including family connections, helped to determine success or failure. The master-disciple relationship often was of crucial importance in securing a position where personal ability could be stimulated and fully developed. For the businessman, close personal relations with his peers were necessary for buying and selling, for investment capital, and for aid in times of economic stress; the innovator needed his patron(s) if his ideas were to be actualized. Organized groups of professionals, such as the Iron Office and the roads and waterways corps, played crucial roles in assigning posts in accordance with ability.

The warp and woof of industrialization might be said to consist of the interaction of the entrepreneurial spirit and the inventive processes, each in its own way an autonomous dynamic force; ambitious persons of ability responded to their inner drives and favorable circumstances by following one or the other pattern of behavior. Their confluence in the later part of the century and afterward brought the creation of some of Sweden's most successful enterprises. Both had their risks. The entrepreneur had to recognize the possibilities, read the market with some accuracy, and organize the financial and productive

297

means. The innovator or inventor needed to be realistic about the prospects of his devices being useful enough to be adopted. Pure chance played a part, most especially in the vagaries of the economic cycle. All too often the entrepreneurs gambled with insufficient funds and suffered disaster. And some, unable or unwilling to change in a period of accelerating transformation, lost out as one decade's innovation became obsolete in the next. The other half of innovation is obsolescence.

The Swedes, not far behind the world-leading Japanese in their increase in national product, rivaled the Japanese in their thoroughness in appropriating foreign innovations and adapting them for their own uses. Their earlier efforts, as with the steam engine or in the iron industry, might be faltering, and often, in this earlier period, it is impossible to judge whether they merely borrowed wholesale or actually invented a version capable of being patented abroad. Patent claims everywhere tended to be so loosely drafted that copying was difficult to prosecute. By the 1870s the interval between the original invention and the Swedish appropriation had radically narrowed; the technological gap, never insuperable, was approaching the vanishing point. In most fields the original borrowers were followed by a second generation capable of creative efforts; due to the constant arrival of innovations, the Swedes had come abreast of the most advanced countries in some fields while still being first-generation learners in others. Seemingly inevitably, every new technological advance abroad and every problem at home promptly attracted one or more Swedes with experience in foreign countries with just that particular device or problem.

Translating Eli F. Heckscher's *An Economic History of Sweden* into English, Göran Ohlin plucked Heckscher's phrase, "*väldiga omvälvning*" out of the Swedish text to use as the descriptive title for the 1870–1914 period.[10] "The Great Transformation" is a more felicitous term, and reflects the nuances of the changes in Sweden more precisely, than "Industrial Revolution." Probably it would be better to avoid altogether this much used—and abused—historical construct. Though the long-term effects of industrialization were indeed revolutionary, the customary implications of the term are not all that much evident in the Swedish scene, which has been far more characterized by an overriding continuity. The detailed view from close at hand, even in the decades of most rapid change, reveals a series of *evolving* innovations of varying tempo and impact within each branch of emerging industrial production and its concomitant activities. In most specific cases a sequence of problems forced a sequence of rational responses. During the Great Transformation the customary historical processes speeded up and intensified, but any phenomenon stretching the full length of a normal lifetime would scarcely qualify as revolutionary in the customary meaning of that word.

Lennart Jörberg would much later stress that Sweden has a great *om-*

vandlingskapacitet, a great capacity for handling change and for transforming itself.[11] The Great Transformation did make change seem a part of normalcy; over the century the once slow-moving Swedes in their stable society became increasingly accustomed to the incessant alterations. Some sectors of the community built up personal and group techniques for accepting and profiting from a condition of continuing flux. And the emergence of that capacity quite probably serves as a final confirmation that the Swedes had indeed joined the ranks of the advanced industrial countries.

Manifestly the history of Swedish economic and technological development cannot be told as a complete story in itself. There was (and is) a wide disparity between the political and diplomatic posture of Sweden as a compartmentalized national state and what actually was taking place in terms of the flow of innovations and market goods. Sweden's development was a fragmentary part of something much larger; it was, in the broadest sense, a province of western Europe and ultimately of the North Atlantic community. The state might to some extent succeed in channelizing the economic activities in the national interest, or on behalf of specific groups, but the incessant flow of impulses over the frontiers went on unabated, into Sweden from more advanced economies and out of the country to, especially, such less developed areas as Finland and Russia.

The Swedes early manifested a "catch-up" mentality and persisted in it longer than would seem realistically necessary. The biographers of these men diligently recorded their subjects in terms of "firsts," preferred to see them as inventors rather than borrowers, and assiduously emphasized any Swedish innovations that were used abroad. Historians of enterprises began by describing the founding years with loving care and concluded, wherever possible, with their triumphant transcending of the limited national borders to achieve the rank of a "world company" in exports and subsidiaries. When describing some specific adoption from abroad the narrator quite often blurred the episode in favor of the creative efforts of those who introduced it into the country, oblivious to the obvious fact that this same pattern of borrowing was typical of other countries also at that stage of development. The "Sweden is a small country, but . . ." sentiment was all-pervasive and served as an intensely strong motivating force in Swedish development. The Swedes continue to cherish passionately their image abroad, are continually frustrated by their failure to receive good marks when earned, rejoice excessively when they do receive good notices, and bear long resentment over bad ones even (or especially) when they may suspect that there is some truth in them.

A proud, self-conscious, tribally cohesive people, they learned to keep score in the succession of world expositions in the nineteenth century as one source of evidence of their relative success in international competition. Swedes who won awards and commendations became heroes, and such triumphs were carefully cited in their biographies. A botched national display roused general dismay and mortification. The annual Nobel competitions can be seen as a continuation of this proclivity, and serving as hosts and international score-keepers in these intellectual Olympiads constitutes a major assurance of their place in the international community. Notably, the awards are made in those fields where the Swedes, historically, have been the strongest.

Sweden's stance as an exemplary neutral supporter of international peace in the twentieth century has stemmed from its own economic realities as well as from geographical situation and a policy of keeping its powder dry. Relying on its own domestic markets, Swedish industry would have remained puny. Export sales of timber, iron and iron ore, wood pulp, and paper stimulated industrialization, and the subsequent capacity to manufacture, especially, high-quality engineering products for external markets made possible the growth of its "world companies." Offspring of relatively open frontiers before 1914, the Swedish industrial sector has good reason for being acutely aware that its own well-being remains utterly dependent upon the country's role as a small part of a greater world community.

As an insular nation living beyond the periphery of the more conspicuously dynamic peoples, the Swedes early became avid copiers of foreign models. The contrast between rooted provincialism and eager internationalism runs deep in Swedish history. In turn they imitated the Germans, the Dutch, and, in the eighteenth century, the French. Then the attractions of business and industrial technology swung attention to the British, primarily among the bourgeoisie. Though the disposition to copy foreigners has often been de-plored by their own Swedish critics, the ultimate amalgam strongly tended to become quintessentially Swedish.

In 1914 the major competing influences were German and American. To earlier cultural ties with German Lutheranism, Pietism, and Romanticism was added a sense of kinship by the Social Democrats with the strong working-class movement in Germany. The court and the upper levels of society in general tended to sympathize with and emulate the then highly successful German Empire. The conservative nationalist resurgence drew inspiration from it. After about 1870 the pattern of Swedish industrial transformation tended, in timing and sequence to parallel most closely the German, of all the major economic powers. Siemens' electric generator, Daimler's gasoline motor, the diesel engine, and sundry aspects of the chemical industry all exercised potent influence on Swedish developments, as did the German import of Swedish iron ore.

The spectacularly successful American methods of mass production and the American democratic spirit, amply reported in America Letters by Swed-ish-Americans, advertised the advantages of the "Land of Opportunity" across the Atlantic. The industrial transformation had come too late to stanch the loss of population; in 1881–95 over one-half of the natural population increase left the motherland.[12] By the 1880s most of the migrants were young unmarried men and women, and after about 1890 the proportion of industrial workers increased, the numbers varying according to economic conditions at home and in the United States. In 1910 about 820,000 native-born Swedes were living abroad, about 665,000 in the United States. Nearly 80,000 were in the neighboring Scandinavian countries and Finland, and over 40,000 in the British Isles and the dominions, 28,000 of these in Canada.

The British Isles became, in a sense, the gateway to the Anglo-American world. For Scandinavians, the United Kingdom was not all that foreign, its language sufficiently cognate to permit fairly easy learning and its social and political structure at least recognizably similar to their own. To them, the British could well seem the largest of the Scandinavian nations. Swedish experiences in Great Britain in turn made their entrance into the United States easier, almost approached as a matter of course. For the migrants, too, the British Isles became the halfway point from whence, usually traveling on British ships, they went on to the broad acres and burgeoning industry of North America.

Not that America was completely unfamiliar. The Swedes, their language and church, were there at the beginning, 1638 on the Delaware and the environs of Philadelphia. John Hanson became the President of the United States in Congress Assembled (1781–82), and John Ericsson went there shortly before the Swedish immigration of the nineteenth century commenced. Johan William Nyström, his contemporary and a former student at the Institute of Technology, designed industrial machinery, made an early calculating machine, and wrote books on mechanics and engineering. Admiral John A. Dahlgren, son of a Swedish consul in Philadelphia, devised the Dahlgren guns of Civil War fame and became chief of ordinance in Washington. The flow of America Letters over several generations made a very large proportion of Swedish families vicarious participants in the American frontier and in its industrial development. Thus began the ambivalent love-hate relationship with America, which gave some Swedes an almost proprietorial pride in American advances because of their relatives' involvement in them, but which also seemed to weaken the home country. As national feeling intensified late in the century, patriots increasingly regarded emigrants as "deserters or worse" whose departure deprived the country "of an invaluable human asset."[13]

The student technicians who spent some time working in the United States in order to apply their new knowledge later in Sweden did not necessarily find it a foreign country. Swedish could be heard on the streets of many northern cities, particularly in the Midwest; the sight of Swedish names on stores and the presence of Swedish-language congregations could be vastly reassuring.

THE SMALL GIANT

Many major American companies had at least one Swedish-born or second-generation Swedish-American in a position of some importance. The vital personal links were there for the arriving immigrant or student-worker. The arrivals rarely walked out of Ellis Island into a friendless community; they had contacts who could find work for them.

The interaction between the two countries was by no means as one-sided as it had been with Great Britain. On the contrary, this was two-way traffic in which numerous Swedish mechanics, engineers, and managers contributed to the American development. Allan Kastrup in his *The Swedish Heritage in America* has listed a long, long file of such individuals, of which the following are some conspicuous examples.[14] Alfred Stromberg learned his trade with L. M. Ericsson, during the latter's early pioneering years, before he manufactured telephones and switchboards (Stromberg-Carlson) in Chicago. John S. Gullborg worked at Husqvarna, then in the United States invented a carburetor, an automatic die-casting machine, and a grease gun for lubricating automobiles. Levin Fast (Faust) was a machinist at Motala prior to helping found the Mechanics Machine Company, later called the Mechanics Universal Joint Company of Borg-Warner; George William Borg, son of Swedish immigrants, invented a disk clutch, among other accomplishments. Carl M. Fridén studied with Karl Rudin, inventor of Swedish calculating machines, before making them himself in California. David L. Lindqvist graduated from the Institute of Technology and worked at ASEA, then became an inventor for the Otis Elevator Company. Per Torsten Berg, graduate of the Institute of Technology, became chief engineer at Andrew Carnegie's Homestead iron and steel works. The list goes on and on, perhaps culminating with Ernst F. W. Alexandersson, an Institute of Technology graduate, who had over 300 U.S. patents in radio broadcasting and other aspects of industrial and transportation electrification.

Time after time the pattern so evident in Sweden repeats itself; someone, often from a family background in metallurgy or engineering, contrives an innovation, starts a factory for its manufacture, and ultimately, as in Sweden, this company is merged into a major corporation. Not that Americans often recognized these as Swedish contributions. Quite possibly, no non-British ethnic element effaced itself so rapidly by smoothly blending into the milieu of the Yankee republic. As for Sweden itself, it would become, at least in external appearances, probably the most Americanized land—for good and for bad—in Europe. Though the history of the Swedes in America has been repeatedly narrated, no comparable history of this American influence has been written, apparently at least in part because the Swedes have not yet been able to come to terms completely with the traumatic experience of the migration and its consequences.[15]

Shortly before the parliamentary reform of 1866 Johan Gustaf Schwan had proclaimed to the House of Burgesses that the party of the bourgeoisie was becoming the citizens' party. In the long run, it was not to be. If the so-called bourgeoisie ever exercised full political power, it was a transitory phenomenon. In the next century the Social Democrats would govern, except for a few months in 1936, for forty-four consecutive years (1932–1976), sometimes in a coalition government and sometimes alone.

The three "bourgeois" parties won two extremely narrow electoral victories in 1976 and 1979. After the 1979 ministry had been formed, the cabinet members strolled over to the royal palace for the customary royal reception. When they tried to walk in a door, guards jumped out, barring the way. One bayonet glittered a few centimeters from a minister's stomach. They had tried to go in the wrong door! Meantime, the speaker of the Riksdag, a Social Democrat, had gone over by himself and entered the correct portal. Someone, writing in *Dagens Nyheter*, scoffed that the bourgeois parties had been out of power so long that they did not even know how to get into the royal palace.

The apogee of parliamentary power, if such it may be called, by the bourgeoisie, if such *they* may be called, probably occurred in the decade before the First World War during the ministries of Arvid Lindman (1906–1911) and Karl Staaff (1905–1906, 1911–1914). Staaff, a Liberal, tried to implement fully the British method of parliamentary government, but in 1914 King Gustav V (1907–1950) still manifestly considered himself to be somewhat more than a constitutional monarch. Nor did British-style Liberalism ever sink deep roots in Sweden, however much the earlier economic liberalism had influenced policy. And the Swedes, having rid themselves of a four-estate Riksdag only late and with difficulty, would, over much of the twentieth century, maintain an essentially four-party Riksdag, a parliament that never achieved, compared to the French and British, a preponderant power over other state and associational authorities. As for the political nomenclature, the political parties are still, in the public mind, divided into a dichotomy of socialist and bourgeois, this in a postindustrial society where the "workers" look and act bourgeois and the occupational spectrum has long ceased to bear much resemblance to the nineteenth-century model.

In the 1890s the authority of the state and its officials began to reemerge, originally fostered by a growing conservative and nationalist mood. The intervention in Lapland and the 50 percent takeover of its mines stemmed directly from the threat of foreign ownership; the government would later stop a British attempt to gain majority control at Boliden and in 1935 prevented a Krupp incursion. The increasing national feeling was, moreover, coupled in the 1890s with a strong conservative reaction against liberalism in favor of increasing the power of the state. During the laissez-faire period the Board of Trade had so little to do that it was repeatedly threatened with extinction, but after 1891 it gained increasing responsibilities.

A series of court cases reasserted state ownership over streams and sources of hydroelectric power. The tariff of 1888 gave some protection to the farmers against cheap foreign grain, and four years later similar help was extended to such manufactured goods as shoes, clothing, furniture, and products of engineering works; the duty on grain was increased in 1895, and the tariff rose again in 1902, though by no means to highly protective levels.

Telegraph and postal services were, of course, state-owned, to which would later be added radio and television. Privately owned telephone networks passed, one by one, into the control of the Telegraph Service. The state-owned hydroelectric network expanded over wide swaths of the country, and the state railroad began to acquire, piecemeal, the privately owned lines. Waterworks and streetcar companies lost their franchises to community ownership. In 1915 AB Svenska Tobaksmonopolet, a state company, took over the import, manufacture and distribution (but not retail sales) of tobacco. In 1917 AB Vin och Spritcentralen, largely a state company, assumed responsibility for the import of wine and hard liquor, the purchase of Swedish-made liquor, and retail distribution through state stores. All this before the Social Democrats began their prolonged reign. The nonsocialist coalition of parties would, in response to the general crisis in advanced industrial countries, nationalize more private enterprises in 1976–1982 than the Social Democrats during their whole forty-four years in power.

With the broadening of the electoral franchise, the Social Democrats, cutting into any bourgeois dominance, held 64 seats in the second chamber of the Riksdag after 1911, compared to 64 Conservatives and 102 Liberals. The Social Democratic party had been founded in 1889, and many of the descendants of those "Impoverished Sophisticates" who had not emigrated were now voting to migrate to a future utopian socialist commonwealth within the country. The Confederation of Trade Unions (LO:Landsorganisation), consisting of 350 unions, was organized in 1898 with strong Social Democratic support; employers' federations were also being established. Strikes and lockouts, which had been occurring sporadically ever since the 1870s, culminated in the famous general strike of 1909, one of the most formative episodes of the century in inducing a future spirit of compromise on both sides. Another pillar of the future commonwealth, the Cooperative Union (KF:Kooperativa Förbundet), appeared in 1899.

Sweden had the first Social Democratic government in the world, the brief Hjalmar Branting minority ministry in 1920. Once they came to power permanently under Per Albin Hansson in 1932, the remarkable achievements of a group of responsible, competent ministers had much to do with the extended longevity of the regime. The strong paternalistic state completed its return, summoned primarily by a folk impulse to collective action based on moral instincts rather than on ideological doctrines. Sweden became the "middle way", a laboratory for social experiments and the epitome of the welfare state; in the process, Sweden had also gone full circle, back to the bureaucratic state of the early nineteenth century.

Albeit that a sober, disciplined relationship prevailed between the government, the labor unions, and the industrialists, the Social Democrats did not basically tamper with the industrial sector. The mixed economy, in which about 90 percent of the productive capacities remained privately owned, continued. Too much was at stake: the world's model welfare state and the Swedish standard of living, one of the highest on the planet, had been made possible by the continued momentum of the industrial-technological legacy transmitted to posterity by the Great Transformation. Though the details of that heroic age recede in public memory, the peaceful conquest of nature's forces in that era must surely rank with those other epic stories, the exploits on the river road to Miklagård and the glory days as a Great Power, in the annals of Swedish history.

BIBLIOGRAPHY

Sources referred to repeatedly in various chapters are listed in the Bibliography; non-Swedish books dealing with the international aspects of industrialization will also be found there. Sources dealing with one particular topic have been placed in the relevant special bibliography preceding the Notes for each chapter. Non-Swedish publications used only once are cited in full in the pertinent footnote.

The basic framework for *The Small Giant* has been borrowed from standard Swedish economic historians without any attempt at reinterpretation, the focus throughout being on the role of personalities and business companies in the processes of Swedish industrialization. Most of the material has been drawn from the histories of business companies, books and articles on Swedish technology, histories of cities and provinces, and any available sources on individual persons. The company histories range from those that are models of professional competency to public relations pamphlets, which must be used with caution. The periodical *Daedalus,* issued by the Technical Museum, has, since 1931, been publishing carefully crafted articles about the development of Swedish technology; cumulatively, their authors have made a remarkable contribution to the history of Swedish technology and engineering. A number of cities have supported the preparation and publication of scholarly histories of their communities; if the specific details of *The Small Giant* tend to center on episodes in certain cities, the reason lies in the availability, in quantity and quality, of volumes about their past.

Surprisingly few book-length biographies of the major figures in industrialization have appeared. To some extent filling the gap, a number of writers published collections of short popular biographies about prominent contemporaries. The personalities and activities of the more important participants can be more confidently recreated from the pages of the *Svenskt biografiskt lexikon,* which contains lengthy scholarly assessments of these men; unfortunately, these volumes, started in 1917 and proceeding at a glacial pace, have only reached the letter L. *Svenska män och kvinnor* records, without much additional commentary, the salient features and achievements of individuals, and the nineteenth-century *Biographiskt lexicon,* published from 1835 until 1890, sometimes contains information unavailable elsewhere.

Abbreviations

GT.   See Nordenskiöld, below.
IU.   *Industriens upplysningstjänst,* a series of pamphlets and short books providing information about the industrial sector.
SBL.   *Svenskt biografiskt lexikon.*
SMK.   *Svenska män och kvinnor.*

Althin, Torsten. *Finsponga bilder. Minnesskrift till trettioårsjubileum.* Finspång: Nordisk Rotogravyr, 1943.
––––––. *Vattenbyggnadsbyrån 1897–1947.* Stockholm: Nordisk Rotogravyr, 1947.
Anderson, Ingvar. *A History of Sweden.* New York: Praeger, 1956.
Armytage, W. H. G. *A Social History of Engineering.* New York: Pitman, 1961.
Attman, Artur. *Kockumverken vid Ronnebyån. En hundraårig industriell utveckling.* Gothenburg: Wezäta, 1951.
Biographiskt lexicon öfver namnkunniga svenska män. 23 vols. Uppsala & Örebro: various publishers, 1835–1857. Ny rediverad, 8 vols. (1847–1876). Ny följd, 10 vols. (1877–1890).
Bjurling, Oscar, ed. *Malmö stads historia.* Vol. II. Malmö: Allhem, 1977.
Boëthius, Bertil, and Kromnow, Åke. *Jernkontorets historia.* 3 vols. Stockholm: Norstedt, 1947–1968.
Bonniers lexikon. 15 vols. Stockholm: Bonnier, 1966–67.
Burstall, Aubrey F. *A History of Mechanical Engineering.* New York: Pitman, 1963.
Carlsson, Sten. *Svensk historia.* Vol. II. Stockholm: Bonnier, 1961.
Chambers, Jonathan David. *The Workshop of the World. British Economic History from 1820 to 1880.* 2nd ed. London: Oxford University Press, 1968.
Clapham, J. H. *An Economic History of Modern Britain.* 2 vols. New York: Macmillan, 1932.
Clow, Archibald, and Nan L. *The Chemical Revolution. A Contribution to Social Technology.* London: Batchworth, 1952.
Colvin, Fred. *60 Years with Men and Machines.* New York: McGraw-Hill, 1947.
Daedalus. Tekniska museets årsbok. Stockholm: Tekniska museet, 1931– .
Dahlgren, Erik Wilhelm, ed. *Stockholm, Sveriges hufvudstad. Skildrad med anledning af allmänna konst-och industriutställningen 1897.* Vol. II. Stockholm: Beckman, 1897.
Dahmén, Erik. *Företagsbildningen förr och nu.* (Series C, No. 8, IU.) Stockholm: Engwall & Stråhle, 1953.
––––––. *Entrepreneurial Activity and the Development of Swedish Industry 1919–1939.* Translated by Axel Leijonhufvud. Homewood, Ill.: Irwin, 1970.

THE SMALL GIANT

Dickinson, H. W. *James Watt, Craftsman and Engineer.* Cambridge, England: Cambridge University Press, 1936.

Dodd, George. *Days at the Factories.* Reprints of Economic Classics. New York: Kelley, 1967.

Du Chaillu, Paul B. *The Land of the Midnight Sun.* 2 vols. New York: Harper, 1882.

Ekerot, Gunnar, ed. *Svenska industriella verk och anläggningar.* 14 vols. Stockholm: Vårt lands boktryckeri, 1895–1929. (Cited as *Tekniska tidskrift.*)

Elson, Robert T. *The Wallenberg Dynasty.* From *Fortune* magazine, May 1962. Stockholm: Haggröth, 1962.

Falk, Knut. *Märkesmän inom vårt ekonomiska liv.* Stockholm: Wahlström & Widstrand, 1929.

Finch, James. *The Story of Engineering.* Garden City, N. J.: Doubleday, 1960.

Fischer, Thomas. *The Scots in Sweden: Being a Contribution towards the History of the Scots Abroad.* Edinburgh: Schulze, 1907.

Forsell, Nils. *Svenska postverkets historia.* 2 vols. Stockholm: Postverkets tryckeri, 1936.

Fröding, Gustaf Hugo. *Berättelser ur Göteborgs historia under nyare tiden.* Gothenburg: Medén, 1924.

———. *Göteborgs donatorer från äldre tid intill våra dagar.* 4 vols. Gothenburg: Zachrisson, 1911–25.

Fullerton, Brian, and Williams, Alan T. *Scandinavia.* London: Chatto & Windus, 1972.

Gale, Walter K. V. *The British Iron and Steel Industry: A Technical History.* Newton Abbot: David & Charles, 1967.

Gårdlund, Torsten. *Atlas Copco 1873–1973. Historien om ett världsföretag i tryckluft.* Örebro: Ljungföretagen, 1973.

———. *Bolinders. En svensk verkstad. Till 100-års minnet av J. & C. G. Bolinders mekaniska verkstad.* Stockholm: Esselte, 1945.

———. *Industrialismens samhälle.* Vol. III, *Den svenska arbetarklassens historia.* Stockholm: Tiden, 1940.

———. *Marcus Wallenberg 1864–1943. Hans liv och gärning.* Stockholm: Norstedt, 1976.

———. *Svenska industrifinansierung under genombrottskedet 1830–1913.* Stockholm: Petterson, 1947.

Gasslander, Olle. *J. A. Gripenstedt. Statsman och företagare.* Lund, Gleerup, 1949.

———. *History of Stockholms Enskilda Bank to 1914.* Translated by M. S. Lindahl and Karin Elliott. Stockholm: Esselte, 1962.

Stor-Göteborg. Gothenburg: AB Bokförmedlingen, 1948.

308

Guinchard, Joseph, ed. *Sweden: Historical and Statistical Handbook.* 2 vols. 2nd ed. Stockholm: Norstedt, 1914.

Gullberg, Erik, and Améen, Lennart. *Jönköpings stads historia.* Vol. III. Värnamo: Fälths, 1971.

Gustavsson, Georg, and Hägg, Erik. *Stockholms ångbåtssjöfart. Anteckningar om huvudstadens ångbåtsflotta.* Stockholm: Petterson, 1932.

Hammarström, Ingrid. *Stockholm i svensk ekonomi 1850–1914.* 2 vols. Stockholm: Almqvist & Wiksell, 1930.

Hartmann, Ernst L., *et al. Jönköpings historia.* Vol. IV. Jönköping: Richards, 1921.

Hartwell, R. M. *The Causes of the Industrial Revolution in England.* London: Methuen, 1967.

Heckscher, Eli F. *An Economic History of Sweden.* Translated by Göran Ohlin from *Svenskt arbete och liv.* Cambridge, Mass.: Harvard University Press, 1954.

_____. *Svenskt arbete och liv från medeltiden till nutiden.* New ed. Stockholm: Aldus/ Bonnier, 1976.

_____. *Industrialismen. Den ekonomiska utvecklingen 1750–1914.* Stockholm: Norstedt, 1931.

_____. "The Place of Sweden in Modern Economic History." *Econ. Hist. Rev,* IV (Oct. 1932), 1: 1–22.

_____. "De svenska manufakturerna under 1700-talet." *Ekonomiska tidskrift,* XXXIX (1937), No. 6.

_____. "Svenskt och utländskt i Sveriges ekonomiska liv." *Ekonomen,* II (1931), 19–27.

_____. *Studier i ekonomi och historia. Tillägnade Eli F. Heckscher på 65-årsdagen.* Uppsala: Almqvist och Wiksell, 1944.

Heckscher, Gunnar. *Staten och organisationera.* Stockholm: Kooperativa förbundets bokföretag, 1946.

Heidenstam, Oskar Gustaf von. *Swedish Life in Town and Country.* New York: Putnam, 1904.

Helander, Olle. *Malmö stads historia.* Vol. II. Malmö: Allhem, 1977.

Helmfrid, Björn, and Kraft, Salomon, eds. *Norrköpings historia.* Vols. IV-V. Stockholm: Norstedt, 1968–1976.

Henderson, W. O. *Britain and Industrial Europe 1750–1870. Studies in British Influence on the Industrial Revolution in Western Europe.* 2nd ed. London: Leicester University Press, 1965.

_____. *The Industrial Revolution in Europe 1815–1914.* Chicago: Quadrangle Books, 1961.

_____. *The State and the Industrial Revolution in Prussia 1740–1870.* Liverpool: Liverpool University Press, 1967.

Höjer, Torvald. *Carl XIV Johan.* 3 vols. Stockholm: Norstedt & Söner, 1939–60.

Hovde, B. J. *The Scandinavian Countries, 1720–1865.* 2 vols. Boston: Chapman & Grimes, 1943.

Hudson, Kenneth. *A Guide to the Industrial Archaeology of Europe.* Edinburgh: Adams & Dart, 1971.

Humbla, Philibert, ed. *Ur Gävle stads historia.* Gävle: Westlund, 1946.

Indebetou, Govert, and Hylander, Erik, eds *Svenska Teknologföreningen 1861–1936. Biographer.* Lund: Håkan Ohlsson, 1937.

Jägerstad, Hans, ed. *Strängäs stads historia.* Lund: Berlingska, 1959.

Janson, Florence. *The Background of Swedish Immigration, 1840–1930.* Chicago: University of Chicago Press, 1931.

Jansson, John. *Underbara uppfinnarbragder. Vad stora svenskar uträttat.* Stockholm: Rydahl, 1948.

Jörberg, Lennart. *Growth and Fluctuations of Swedish Industry, 1869–1912: Studies in the Process of Industrialization.* Lund: Almqvist & Wiksell, 1961.

Josephson, Matthew. *Edison.* New York: McGraw-Hill, 1959.

Kihlberg, Leif. *Lars Hierta i helfigur.* Stockholm: Bonnier, 1968.

Kirby, Richard, and Laurson, Philip. *The Early Years of Modern Engineering.* New Haven: Yale University Press, 1932.

Kolare, Harry. *Män i täten. Svenska förgrundsmän just nu på skilda banor.* Stockholm: Åhlen & Söner, 1937.

Landes, David S. *The Unbound Prometheus. Technological Change and Industrial Development in Western Europe from 1750 to the Present.* Cambridge, England: Cambridge University Press, 1969.

Larsen, Egon. *Ideas and Inventions.* London: Spring Books, 1960.

Lazarus. See Lindahl.

Lind, Sven. *Göteborgs handel och sjöfart 1637–1920.* (Vol. X, GT.) Gothenburg: Elander, 1923.

Lindahl, Carl Fredrik (Lazarus). *Svenska millionärer. Minnen och anteckningar.* 10 vols. Stockholm: various, 1966.

Lindblom, Paul. *När maskinerna kom. Industrialismen förändrade människornas värld.* Stockholm: Bonnier, 1966.

Lindroth, Sten. *Kungl, Svenska Vetenskapsakademiens Historia 1739–1818.* Vol. II. Stockholm: Almqvist & Wiksell, 1967.

Lindroth, Sten, ed. *Swedish Men of Science, 1650–1950.* Stockholm: Almqvist & Wiksell, 1967.

Ljungzell, Nils J. *Skeppsbyggnad och båtkonstruktion.* Stockholm: Norstedt, 1931.

Lundin, Gustaf. *Trollhättan genom tiderna.* Trollhättan: Författarens Förlag, 1946.

Lundström, Ragnhild, ed. *Kring industrialismens genombrott i Sverige.* Stockholm: Wahlström & Widstrand, 1966.

Millward, Roy. *Scandinavian Lands.* London: Macmillan, 1964.

Milward, Alan S., and Saul, S. B. *The Economic Development of Continental Europe, 1780–1870.* Totowa, N. J.: Rowman & Littlefield, 1973.

Mirsky, Jeannette, and Nevins, Allan. *The World of Eli Whitney.* New York: Macmillan, 1952.

Mitchell, Brian R. *European Historical Statistics, 1750–1970.* London: Macmillan, 1975.

Modin, Karl. *Svenska uppfinnare och industrimän.* Uppsala; Lindblad, 1947.

Monkhouse, Francis. *The Geography of Northwestern Europe.* New York: Praeger, 1947.

Montgomery, Arthur. *The Rise of Modern Industry in Sweden.* London: P. S. King, 1939.

Mortenson, Johan, ed. *Sverige i England. Anteckningar samlade inom den svenska kolonien.* Gothenburg: Zachrisson, 1923.

Munthe, Arne. *Hundra år i hantverkets tjänst.* Stockholm: Nordisk Rotogravyr, 1947.

Musson, A. E., ed. *Science, Technology and Economic Growth in the Eighteenth Century.* London: Methuen, 1972.

———. *The Growth of British Industry.* New York: Holmes & Meier, 1978.

———. and Robinson, Eric. *Science and Technology in the Industrial Revolution.* Manchester: Manchester University Press, 1969.

Nordenskiöld, Otto, et al, eds. *Skrifter utgivna till Göteborgs stads tre hundraårsjubileum.* 20 vols. Gothenburg: various, 1923. (Cited as GT.)

Nordisk familjebok. Konversationslexikon och realencyklopedi. 38 vols. 2nd ed. Stockholm: Nordisk familjebok förlag, 1904–26.

Nordström, Alf, et al. *Södertäljes stads historia.* Vol. II. Stockholm: Norstedt & Söner, 1968.

O'Dell, Andrew C. *The Scandinavian World.* London: Longmans, 1963.

Orwin, Christable, and Whetham, Edith H. *History of British Agriculture.* London: Archon Books, 1964.

Rolt, Lionel T. C. *Isambard Kingdom Brunel: A Biography.* London: Longmans, Green, 1958.

———. *Victorian Engineering.* London: Penguin, 1970.

Rosman, Holger, and Munthe, Arne. *Släkten Arfwedson. Bilder ur Stockholms handelshistoria under tre århundraden.* Stockholm: Centraltryckeriet, 1929.

Samuelsson, Kurt. *Hur vårt moderna industri vuxit fram.* 4th ed. Stockholm: Prisma, 1967.

Scott, Franklin D. *Sweden: The Nation's History.* Minneapolis: University of Minnesota Press, 1977.

Seldes, George. *Iron, Blood and Profits.* New York: Harpers, 1934.

Seth, C. E. von, ed. *Kockums mekaniska verkstad AB Malmö 1840–1940.* Malmö: Lundgren söner, 1940.

Singer, Charles, *et al,* eds. *A History of Technology.* 5 vols. Oxford: Clarendon Press, 1954–58.

Sjöstrand, Erik. *Märkliga svenskar i England.* Gothenburg: Zachrisson, 1923.

Smedberg, Rickard, ed. *Kungliga väg-och vattenbyggnadskåren 1851–1937.* Stockholm: Bröderna Lagerström, 1937.

Smiles, Samuel. *Industrial Biography. Iron Workers and Tool Makers.* Reprints of Economic Classics. New York: Kelley, 1968.

Söderbaum, Henrik Gustaf. *Jac. Berzelius.* 3 vols. Uppsala: Almqvist & Wiksell, 1929–31.

Söderberg, Tom. *Norrköpings ekonomiska och sociala historia 1719–1870.* Vol. IV, Norrköpings historia, Helmfrid and Kraft, eds. Stockholm: Norstedt, 1968.

Söderlund, Ernst. *Swedish Timber Exports, 1850–1950; A History of the Timber Trade.* Stockholm: Almqvist & Wiksell, 1952.

————. *Skandinaviska banken i det svenska bankväsendets historia 1864–1914.* Gothenburg: Skandinaviska banken, 1964.

Sømme, Axel, ed. *A Geography of Norden.* Oslo: Cappelens, 1960.

Steckzén, Birger. *Bofors. En kanonindustris historia.* Stockholm: Esselte, 1946.

Strode, Hudson. *Sweden: Model for a World.* New York: Harcourt, Brace, 1949.

Svenska uppslagsbok. 2nd ed. 32 vols. Malmö: Svenska uppslags., 1947–1955.

Svenska män och kvinnor. Biografisk uppslagsbok. 8 vols. Stockholm: Bonnier, 1942–55. (Cited as SMK.)

Svenskt biografiskt lexikon. 23 vols. Stockholm: various, 1917– . (Cited as SBL.)

Taylor, Bayard. *Northern Travel: Summer and Winter Pictures. Sweden, Denmark and Lapland.* New York: Putnam's Sons, 1883.

Tekniska tidskrift. See Ekerot.

Valentin, Hugo. *Judarnas historia i Sverige.* Stockholm: Bonnier, 1924.

Welin, Gustaf, ed. *Statens järnvägar 1856–1906. Historisk-teknisk-ekonomisk beskrifning.* Vol. I. Stockholm: Centraltryckeriet, 1906.

Wertime, Theodore A. *The Coming of the Age of Steel.* Chicago: University of Chicago Press, 1962.

Wieselgren, Harald, *Ur vår samtid. Femtio porträtt med nekrologer.* Stockholm: Norstedt, 1880.

Wikberg, Sven. *Svenska uppfinnare.* Stockholm: Hugo Gebers, 1933.

Wimarson, Nils, ed. *Göteborg. En Översikt vid trehundraårsjubileum 1923.* (Vol. XX, GT) Gothenburg, Elander, 1923.

NOTES

Sources referred to repeatedly in various chapters are listed in the Bibliography; non-Swedish books dealing with the international aspects of industrialization will also be found there. Sources dealing with one particular topic have been placed in the relevant special bibliography below. Non-Swedish publications used only once are cited in full in the pertinent footnote.

Chapter 1: The Steam Engine

Althin, Torsten. *Flygkrönika. Bilder och notiser ur luftfartens historia.* Stockholm: Wahlström & Widstrand, 1931.

———. "J. E. Norbergs ångmaskinprojekt 1796." *Daedalus* (1955): 83–88.

———. "Stationary Steam Engines in Sweden, 1725–1806." *Daedalus* (1961): 96–99.

———. "Sveriges andra ångmaskin." *Daedalus* (1939): 49–60.

Birch, Alan. "Foreign Observers of the British Iron Industry during the Eighteenth Century." *J. Econ. Hist.,* XV (1955), 23–33.

Carlsson, Sten. *Gustaf IV Adolf. En biografi.* Stockholm: Wahlström & Widstrand, 1946.

Corin, Carlos Fredrik. "A. N. Edelcrantz och Eldkvarn." *Daedalus* (1961): 39–94.

———. "A. N. Edelcrantz och hans ångmaskinprojekt." *Daedalus* (1940): 72–81.

Forselles, Jenny af. *A. N. Clewberg-Edelcrantz och hans omgifning.* Helsingfors: Handelstryckeriet, 1903.

Gierow, Karl Ragnar. *Abraham Niclas Clewberg-Edelcrantz.* Stockholm: Norstedt, 1964.

Hennings, Beth. *Gustav III. En biografi.* Stockholm: Norstedt, 1957.

Johannesson, Gösta. *Helsingborgs historia.* Vol. V. Uppsala: Almqvist & Wiksell, 1979.

Johansson, Yngve. "Ångmaskinerna vid flottans varv i Karlskrona på 1700-talet." *Daedalus* (1962): 51–65.

Nyström, Per. *Stads industriens arbetare före 1800-talet.* Stockholm: Tiden, 1955.

Odencrantz, Arvid. "Höganäs och kullen år 1806." *Daedalus* (1947): 79–87.
Risberg, Nils. *Den optiska telegrafens historia i Sverige 1794–1881.* Vol. III, *Svenska telegrafverket.* Gothenburg: Elander, 1936.
Schütz, Fredrik. "Samuel Owen." *Daedalus* (1975): 93–140.
Söderlund, Ernst. *Hantverkarna. Stormaktstiden, Frihetstiden och Gustaviansk tiden.* Stockholm: Tiden, 1949.
Starbäck, C. Georg. *Samuel Owen. Lefnadsteckning.* Norrkoping: Föreningens boktryckeri, 1863.
Svensson, Nils. *Höganäs genom tiderna.* Hälsingborg: Demokraten, 1934.
Wilcke, Gust. D. *Underrättelser om Bergsunds bruk.* Stockholm: Deleen, 1830.

1. Corin, "Ångmaskinprojekt," 72–73.
2. Gierow, 221–224.
3. Risberg, 28, 246–247; Gierow, 235.
4. Gierow, 240–246.
5. (Corin) SBL, 12: 61.
6. Althin, "Stationary Steam Engines," 99.
7. Starbäck, 8.
8. Corin, "Eldkvarn," 43f.; Gierow, 228.
9. Gierow, 9.
10. Lindroth, 2: 272.
11. Lindroth, 2: 267–268; Althin, *Flygkrönika,* 32–33.
12. Althin, "Stationary Steam Engines," 96–97; Henderson, *Industrial Revolution in Europe,* 149; W. H. B. Court, *The Rise of the Midland Industries, 1600–1838* (London: Oxford Univ. Press, 1938). 32.
13. Althin, "Sveriges andra ångmaskin," 52.
14. Althin, "Norbergs ångmaskin," 86–88; Johansson, "Ångmaskinerna Karlskrona," 53–55; Lindroth, 1: 61, 66.
15. Althin, "Norbergs ångmaskin," 88.
16. Althin, "Stationary Steam Engines," 99; Schütz, 128; Gustavsson & Hägg, 72.
17. Odencrantz, 82–85; Johannesson, 5: 1–2, 343–345.
18. Svensson, 8.
19. Althin, "Sveriges andra ångmaskin," 53; Birch, 15: 29–31; Thomas S. Ashton, *Iron and Steel in the Industrial Revolution* (London: Longmans, Green, 1924), 201–204; A. E. Musson and Eric Robinson, *James Watt and the Steam Revolution* (New York: Kelley, 1965), 224–227.
20. Schütz, 97–99.
21. Starbäck, 4–7.
22. Schütz, 107–108; Ljungzell, 745–746.
23. *Biographiskt lexicon* (1844), 10: 340.

24. Schütz, 110–111, 122, 127–131; Lindroth, 2: 274.
25. Wilcke, 8–11, 20.
26. Gustavsson and Hägg, 64, 75–76.
27. *Biographiskt lexicon* (1844), 333–346.
28. Schütz, 137.
29. Munthe, *Hantverkets tjänst, 11.*
30. Lundblom, 3.
31. Jörberg, 31.
32. Jansson, 52–55, 74, 84–85, 106–116.
33. Lindroth, *Swedish Men of Science,* 24.
34. Montgomery, 39.

Chapter 2: Waterways and Steamboats

Bring, Samuel, ed. *Göta kanals historia.* 2 vols. Vol. I(2) by Herbert Lundh. Uppsala: Almquist & Wiksell, 1922–30.

Otto Edvard Carlsund. Motala: Borgström, 1931.

Church, William C. *The Life of John Ericsson.* 2 vols. New York: Scribners, 1891.

De Malé, Eric. *Swedish Cross Cut (The Gotha Canal)* Malmö: Allhem, 1957.

Ekström, Gustaf. *Baltzar von Platen och Göta kanal.* In *Natur och Kultur* series. Stockholm: Tammerfors Handelstryckeri, 1938.

Lindvall, Carl August. *En porträttsmedaljong af O. E. Carlsund.* Stockholm: Centraltryckeriet, 1896.

Minnesskrift med anledning av Motala verkstads hundraårige verksamhet 1822–1922. Stockholm: Centraltryckeriet, 1922.

Rolt, Lionel T. C. *Thomas Telford.* London: Longmans, Green, 1958.

Svenska flottans historia: Orlogsflottan i ord och bild. Vol. III. Malmö: Allhem, 1945.

Way-Matthiesen, Lennart. "John Ericssons varmluftmaskin." *Daedalus* (1932): 85–95.

Wessberg, Gertrud. *Vänersjöfarten under 1800-talets förre hälft.* (No. 6, Inst. of Econ. Hist., Gothenburg University) Gothenburg: Elander, 1966.

White, Ruth. *Yankee from Sweden: The Dream and the Reality in the Days of John Ericsson.* New York: Holt, 1960.

1. Ekström, 13–14.
2. *Ibid,* 16.
3. *Ibid,* 47–53.
4. Bring, 1(2): 249–252; Rolt, *Telford,* 93–109.
5. *Biographiska lexicon* (1845), 11: 275; Ekström, 29.

6. Ekström, 72.
7. *Ibid,* 30–31, 53, 91–92.
8. Bring, 2: 53; Ekström, 143–150.
9. Bring, 1(2): 254.
10. *Ibid,* 382, 387; 2: 73–84.
11. Bring, 1(2): 404; *Svenska män och kvinnor,* 6: 522. (Hereafter referred to as SMK.)
12. *Motala verkstad,* 292–293.
13. *Ibid.,* 322–323.
14. Bring, 1(2): 354.
15. Söderberg, 4: 7, 189; Gustavsson and Hägg, 47; (Blix) *Svenskt biografiskt lexikon,* 18: 207. (Hereafter referred to as SBL.)
16. Gustavsson and Hägg, 80–81.
17. Welin, 1: 36, quoting L. F. Rääf i Småland.
18. Lindvall, 1.
19. Ibid., 2: (Fröman) SBL, 7: 600.
20. *Otto Edvard Carlsund,* 8–9; (Fröman) SBL, 7: 602.
21. Church, 1: 21.
22. Ekström, 26.
23. Way-Matthiesen, 87.
24. Church, 1: 81.
25. Lionel T. C. Rolt, *The Railway Revolution: George and Robert Stephenson,* (New York: St. Martin's Press, 1960), 166–174.
26. Ljungzell, 132, 149.
27. White, 132, 149.
28. Church 1: 23, quoting John Ericsson.

Chapter 3: Merchants and Money

Adamson, Rolf. "Finance and Marketing in the Swedish Iron Industry, 1800–1860." *Scand. Econ. Hist. Rev, XVI (1968), 1: 47–101.*

———"Olof Wijk den äldres affärsverksamhet." In *Göteborg. Förr och nu,* Anders Bothen, ed. (Vol. IX, Göteborgs hembygdsförbunds skriftserie.) Gothenburg: Förenade, 1974.

Almquist, Helge. *Göteborgs historia. Grundläggningen och de första hundra åren.* (Vol. I, GT.) Göteborgs litografiska, 1929.

Attman, Artur. *D. Carnegie & Co. 1803–1953. En hundrafemtioårig merkantil och industriell verksamhet.* Gothenburg: John Antonson, 1953.

Behre, Göran. "Östindiska kompaniet och hattarna." *Historisk tidskrift,* 2nd Series, XXIX (1966), 31–46.

317

Bodman, Gösta. *Fabriker och industrier i det gamla Göteborg.* Gothenburg: Wettergren & Kerber, 1925.

———. *Göteborgs äldre industrie.* (Vol. IX, GT.) Gothenburg: Elander, 1923.

———. "Skotska släktnamn i svensk industri och teknik." *Daedalus* (1948): 77–88.

Furber, Holden. *John Company at Work: A Study of European Expansion in India in the late Eighteenth Century.* Cambridge, Mass.: Harvard University Press, 1948.

Heckscher, Eli F. "Ett bidrag till Alingsås manufakturverks historia." *Historisk tidskrift,* XXXVII (1917), 88–113.

Högström, Erik. S. *Barthelemy under svenska välde.* Uppsala: Almqvist & Wiksell, 1888.

Hultberg, Gösta. "Martin von Wahrendorff." *Daedalus* (1938): 87–102.

Kent, H. S. K. *War and Trade in Northern Seas: Anglo-Scandinavian Economic Relations in the mid-eighteenth Century.* Cambridge, England: Cambridge University Press, 1973.

Koninckx, Christian." The Maritime Routes of the Swedish East India Company during its First and Second Charter (1731–1766)." *Scand. Econ. Hist. Rev.,* XXVI (1978), 1: 36–65.

Olán, Eskil. *Östindiska compagniets saga. Historien om Sveriges märkligaste handelsföretag.* Gothenburg: Elander, 1920.

Ramm, Axel. *Göteborgs donationer.* (Vol. XII, GT.) Gothenburg; Göteborgs litografiska, 1923.

Samuelsson, Kurt. *De stora köpmanshusen i Stockholm 1730–1815.* Stockholm: Ekon,-Hist. Inst., 1951.

———. "International Payments and Credit Movements by the Swedish Merchant-Houses, 1730–1815." *Scand. Econ. Hist. Rev.,* III (1955), 2: 163–202.

Sinclair, George A. "The Scottish Trader in Sweden." *The Scottish Historical Review,* XXV (1928), 289–299.

Tiselius, Carl A. *Göteborg under continentaltiden. Perioden 1808–1810.* Gothenburg; Västra Sverige, 1935.

1. Almquist, 69.
2. Olán, 24–25, 32–33.
3. Olán, 64; Rosman and Munthe, 302.
4. Olán, 139.
5. Lindahl, 5: 45–46.
6. Kent, 112–125; Scott, 265–266.
7 Fröding, *Göteborgs donatorer,* 2: 80–84.
8. *Svenska uppslagsbok,* 1: 748–750.
9. Fröding, *op. cit.,* 2: 71–72.

10. Fröding, op. cit., 2: 28–39; Attman, Carnegie, 16; Adamson, "Finance and Marketing," 77–80. On the role of Hull in Anglo-Swedish commerce, see Gordon Jackson, Hull in the Eighteenth Century (London: Oxford Univ. Press, 1972).
11. Lindahl, 6: 269, 276.
12. Fischer, 17; Lindahl, 6: 283.
13. Fröding, Berättelser, 65–66; Lindahl, 6: 284–286.
14. Burton J. Hendrick, The Life of Andrew Carnegie, Vol. I (New York: Doubleday, Doran, 1932), 1.
15. Fischer, passim; Sinclair, 290.
16. SMK, 1: 171.
17. Tiselius, 1–3.
18. Ibid., 4.
19. Fischer, 192–193.
20. Fröding, Göteborgs donatorer, 4: 79–80; Lindahl, 1: 1,7–8.
21. (Söderberg) SBL, 21–66; Lindahl, 7: 339, 341.
22. Valentin, 218–219.
23. Fröding, Göteborgs donatorer, 4: 63–70; Fröding, Berättelser, 176, 258; Falk, 133–139; Adamson, "Wijk," 12.
24. Söderlund, Swedish Timber Exports, 71.
25. Taylor, 227.
26. Jörberg, Growth and Fluctuations, 14–15; Taylor, 227.
27. Samuelsson, De stora köpmanshusen, 104–105; Jörberg, 24.
28. Gårlund, Ind. samhälle, 107; Samuelsson, op. cit., 103; Samuelsson, "Swedish Merchant-Houses," 163.
29. Bodman, "Skotska släktnamn," 8.
30. Munthe and Rosman, 332; SMK, 1: 125; (Simonsson) SBL, 2: 164.
31. Lindahl, 1: 250. This story did circulate, but its basis in fact can be questioned.
32. Högström, 8, 74–76, 100.
33. Lindahl, 10: 288–289.
34. Ibid., 10: 299, 292–293.
35. Scott, 318–319; Lindahl, 2: 219–222; Höjer, 3: 79–103.
36. Hultberg, 90–96, 99–100.
37. Ibid., 92; Schütz, "Samuel Owen," 131–132 (see Chapter 2).

Chapter 4: Apprenticed to Modern Industry

Althin, Torsten. Papyrus: Sweden's Largest Fine Paper and Board Mill. Mölndal: Nordisk Rotogravyr, 1953.

Anstrin, Hans. *Sveriges pappersindustri.* (Series A, No. 8, IU.) Stockholm: Engwall & Stråhle, 1951.

_____. "Från handpappersbruk till maskindrift på 1830-talet." *Daedalus* (1935): 67–74.

Attman, Artur. *D. Carnegie & Co. 1803–1953. En hundrafemtioårig merkantil och industriell verksamhet.* Gothenburg: John Antonson, 1953.

Bergh, Thorsten. *Manufakturaktiebolaget i Malmö 1855–1930.* Malmö: Lundgrens söner, 1931.

Bergman, Gertrud. "Charles Apelquist." *Daedalus* (1962): 130–146.

Bodman, Gösta. *Göteborgs äldre industri.* (Vol. IX, GT.) Gothenburg: Elander, 1923.

Boëthius, Bertil. *Grycksbo 1382–1940. Minnesskrift.* Falun: Grycksbo AB, 1942.

Carlgren, Wilhelm. *Drag (AB) Yllefabrik 1642–1942.* Stockholm: Norstedt, 1942.

Clemensson, Gustaf. *Klippans pappersbruk med Lessebo och Böksholm.* Uppsala: Almqvist & Wiksell, 1932.

Dahl, Sven. "Travelling Pedlars in Nineteenth-Century Sweden." *Scand. Econ. Hist. Rev,* VII (1959), 167–178.

Danielson, Hilding. *Rydboholm fabrikers historia 1866–1911.* Gothenburg: Isaacson, 1934.

Ekerot, Gunnar. "Swartzarna. En industrialsläkts historia i verk." *Tekniska tidskrift* (1906).

Fagerholm, Karin. *Kvarnaktiebolaget J. G. S. J. G. Swartz Aktiebolag. En storindustri under ett sekel 1844–1944.* Stockholm: Esselte, 1944.

Falck, Albert Edvard. *Hantverksskrån och fabrikväsen i Nyköping från äldre tider.* Nyköping: Österberg, 1928.

Göth, Johan Alfred. *Bergsrådet på Lessebo och hans underhavanda.* Stockholm: Eklunds, 1925.

Hansson, Sigurd. "Antenor Nydqvist. Vid hundraårsdagen af hans födelse." *Tekniska tidskrift* (1917).

Holmens bruk och fabriks aktiebolag Norrköping. Gothenburg: Zachrisson, 1931.

Lindskog, Inga. "Lars Fresks klädesfabrik vid Elfvik pa Lidingö." *Daedalus* (1958): 105–121.

Lundmark, Efraim. *En hundraårig bomullsindustri. Norrköpings bomullsväverieaktiebolag.* Stockholm: Norstedt, 1952.

Magnell, Per. *En bok om Hov i Östergotland.* Linköping: Ostgöta boktryckeri: 1943.

Malcolm, Andrew. *Faktiska bevis att fabriks-och industri väsendet inom Sverige ej är lika tacksamt som i andra länder.* Linköping: Fridolf Wallin, 1870.

Rydberg, Sten. *Svenska studieresor till England under Frihetstiden.* Uppsala: Almqvist & Wiksell, 1951.
Rosman, Holger. *Textilfabrikerna vid Barnängen. Bilder ur Stockholms industrihistoria.* Stockholm: Centraltryckeriet, 1929.
Stålberg, Helge. *Smålands skog och träindustrier.* (Series B. No. 3, IU.) Stockholm: Engwall & Stråhle, 1949.
Sterner, Björn. *Från hemslöjd till storindustri. Sjuhäradsbygdens ekonomiska historia och geografi.* Stockholm: Liber, 1966.

1. Clemensson, *Klippan,* 49–50.
2. *Ibid.,* 58–60, 69–73.
3. *Ibid.,* 56–57; Clow, 264–265.
4. Söderberg, 4 (7): 240–241; *Holmen,* 30f.
5. Stålberg, 10.
6. Göth, 20f., 44, 66–68.
7. Althin, *Papyrus,* 57–63.
8. Clow, 521–522.
9. Attman, *Carnegie,* 90–99.
10. *Ibid.,* 253–255; Samuelsson, 75.
11. Bodman, 63–72; Althin, *Papyrus,* 62.
12. Sterner, 47.
13. Bodman, 73–75; Althin, *Papyrus,* 62; Gårdlund, *Ind. samhälle,* 43.
14. Lundmark, 38–39; Hansson, 2–3.
15. Henderson, *Industrial Europe,* 7, 14.
16. Hartwell, 3.
17. Henderson, *op. cit.,* 6–7, 63, 113.
18. Chambers, 3.
19. Musson, *Science, Technology,* 98–99; Clapham, 1: 143.
20. Sterner, 32.
21. *Ibid.,* 6–11, 28.
22. Dahl, 167–178.
23. (Danielson) SBL, 14: 383–385.
24. *Ibid.,* 14: 385–389; Sterner, *passim;* Gårdlund, *op. cit.,* 46.
25. Danielson, *Rydboholm,* 5–6; Bodman, 81; Samuelsson, 54.
26. Lindskog, "Lars Fresk," 109–113.
27. Bergman, "Apelquist," 143.
28. Rosman, 178–180.
29. Söderberg, 4(7) : 171.
30. Ekerot, *Swartzarna,* 32.
31. Lindahl, 1: 131; Magnell, 216–254; Ekerot, *Swartzarna,* 18.
32. Lundmark, 47–48; Söderberg, 4(7): 164–165.
33. Carlgren, 63.

34. Söderberg, 4(7): 175–176.
35. Bergman,"Apelquist," 143; Henderson, *Industrial Europe*, 107.
36. Söderberg, 4(7): 232–234; Malcolm, *passim;* Smiles, 267–269.
37. Gårdlund, *op.cit.,* 45–48.
38. Rosman, 179–180.
39. Söderberg, 4(7): 169.
40. *Ibid.,* 4(7): 229; Carlgren, 60, 77.
41. Söderberg, 4(7); 222.
42. Carlgren, 74, 80.
43. *Ibid.,* 68–81.
44. Söderberg, 4(7): 230, 212.
45. *Ibid.,* 4(7): 239–240, 243–244; Carlgren, 76; Lundmark, 17–20, 62, 74–78.
46. Samuelsson, 71; Gårdlund, *op. cit.,* 125

Chapter 5: Crisis in Iron

Adamson, Rolf. *De svenska järnbrukens storleksutveckling och avsättningsinriktning 1796–1860.* No. 4, Inst. of Econ. Hist., Gothenburg University. Gothenburg: Elander, 1963.

————. *Järnavsättning och bruksfinancierung 1800-1860.* No. 7, Inst. of Econ. Hist., Gothenburg University. Gothenburg: Elander, 1966.

————. "Finance and Marketing in the Swedish Iron Industry, 1800–1860." *Scand. Econ. Hist. Rev,* XVI (1968), 1:47–101.

————. "Swedish Iron Exports to the United States, 1783–1860." *Scand. Econ. Hist. Rev,* XVII (1969), 1:58–114.

Andersson, Fritz. *Surahammars bruks historia.* 5 vols. Surahammar: Surahammars AB, 1963.

Andersson, Ingvar. *Uddeholm. Värmlandsbruk med världsrykte.* Stockholm: Bröderna Lagerström, 1955.

Birch, Alan. "Foreign Observers of the British Iron Industry During the Eighteenth Century." *J. Econ. Hist.,* XV (1955), 23–33.

Boëthius, Bertil, and Kromnow, Åke. *Jernkontorets historia.* 3 vols. Stockholm: Norstedt, 1947–1968.

Boëthius, Bertil. *Gruvarnas, hyttarnas och hamrarnas folk. Bergshanteringens arbetare från medeltiden till Gustavianska tiden.* Stockholm: Tidens förlag, 1951.

————. "Jernkontoret and the Credit Problems of the Swedish Ironworks. A Survey." *Scand. Econ. Hist. Rev,* X (1962), 2: 105–114.

————. "Swedish Iron and Steel, 1600–1955." *Scand. Econ. Hist. Rev,* VI (1958), 1: 144–175.

Ekman, Gustaf. *Gustaf Ekman och järnhanteringen.* Gothenburg: Isaacson, 1942.

Hedin, Göran. *Ett svenskt järnverk. Sandviken och dess utveckling.* Uppsala: Almqvist & Wiksell, 1937.

Hendrick, Burton. *The Life of Andrew Carnegie.* Vol. I. New York: Doubleday, Doran, 1932.

Hildebrand, Karl-Gustav. "Foreign Markets for Swedish Iron in the 18th Century." *Scand. Econ. Hist. Rev,* VI (1958), 1: 3–52.

Höök, Robert. *Sveriges gruvhantering.* (Series A, No. 7, IU.) Stockholm: Engwall & Stråhle, 1950.

Hubendick, C. Edvard. "Gasgeneratorn förr och nu." *Daedalus* (1941): 37–44.

Qvist, Nils Henrik. *Ådalen. Ett bidrag till dess industri-och personhistoria.* 2 vols. Stockholm: Landby & Lundgren, 1943–1946.

Sahlin, Carl. *De svenska degelstålverken.* Reprint from *Med hammare och fackla,* IV, 1932. Stockholm: Haeggström, 1932.

Söderlund, Ernst. "The Impact of the British Industrial Revolution on the Swedish Iron Industry." In *Studies in the Industrial Revolution. Presented to T. S. Ashton,* L. S. Pressnell, ed. London: Athlone, 1960.

Svedenstierna, Eric T. *Svedenstierna's Tour: Great Britain, 1802–1803. The Travel Diary of an Industrial Spy.* Translated by E. L. Dellow. Newton Abbot: David & Charles, 1973.

Wahlund, Johan. *Dannemora grufvor. Historisk skildring.* Stockholm: Norstedt, 1879.

1. Chambers, 31; Wertime, 259; SMK, 6:193; Smiles, 101–110.
2. Birch, 23–31.
3. Gale, 44–46; Burstal, 206.
4. Smiles, 118; Singer, 4:106.
5. Steckzén, *Bofors,* 33.
6. Boëthius and Kromnow, 1: 230, 335; 3(1): 44–47.
7. Henderson, *Industrial Revolution in Europe,* 215.
8. Chambers, 22; Henderson, *op. cit.,* 49.
9. Montgomery, 17.
10. Boëthius and Kromnow, 3(1): 359–363; Gårdlund, *Bolinders,* 20–21; Svedenstierna, *passim.*
11. Boëthius and Kromnow, 3(1): 368–371.
12. *Ibid.,* 3(1): 375–388; Rosman and Munthe, 336.
13. Musson, *Science, Technology,* 125; Henderson, *Britain and Industrial Europe,* 54,154; Henderson, *Prussia,* 55.
14. Boëthius and Kromnow, 3(1): 469–470; (Althin and Forsberg) SBL, 13: 91–96; Ekman, 8; Singer, 4: 115–116.
15. Boëthius and Kromnow, 3(1): 390–394; 2(2): 499; SMK, 6: 375.

16. Boëthius and Kromnow, 3(1): 389–394; SMK, 4: 425–426.
17. Boëthius and Kromnow, 3(1) 407; Ekman, 13; SMK, 8:468.
18. Boëthius and Kromnow, 3(1):470; (Althin and Forsberg) SBL, 13: 91–96; Ekman, passim.
19. Ekman, 9.
20. Boëthius and Kromnow, 3(1): 471, 469; Ekman, 10; (Althin and Forsberg) SBL, 13: 93.
21. Ekman, 12,16–17; Singer, 4: 109–110.
22. Ekman, 16–17; Boëthius and Kromnow, 3(1): 485–488; Hubendick, 38–39.
23. Samuelsson, 15–16, 51–54; (Althin and Forsberg) SBL, 13: 95–96; Ekman, 15–16.
24. Boëthius and Kromnow, 3(1): 496–497; Qvist, 1: 69.
25. Boëthius and Kromnow, 2(2): 498; Wieselgren, 8.
26. Montgomery, 86.
27. Sahlin, 103–105.
28. Hendrick, 1: 156–159; Borstal, 292–293.
29. Hedin, 16–18.
30. Hendrick, 1: 190; Henderson, Industrial Revolution in Europe, 214.
31. Hedin, 14–20.
32. Ibid., 31
33. Ibid., 49,34,40.

Chapter 6: Timber for Export

Ahnlund, Nils. Mo och Domsjö. Deras ägare och utveckling intill 1873. Stockholm: Almqvist & Wiksell, 1911.
Ahnlund, Nils, ed. Sundsvalls historia. 5 vols. Sundsvall: Appelberg, 1921–22.
Althin, Torsten. Korsnäsbolaget 1855–1955. Gävle: Nordisk Rotogravyr, 1955.
_____. Wifsta Varf 1798–1948. Jubileumsskrift om Norrlands äldsta trä förädlande företag. Stockholm: Nordisk Rotogravyr, 1948.
Boëthius, Bertil. Robertsfors bruks historia. Uppsala: Almqvist & Wiksell, 1921.
Fagerberg, Bengt. "The Transfer of Peasant Forest to Sawmill Companies in Northern Sweden." Scand. Econ. Hist. Rev., XXI (1973), 2: 164–191.
Flodén, Nils August. Sågverks patronerna. 2 vols. Sundsvall: Sundsvall boktryckeri, 1959.
Forests, Rivers and Mills: An Introduction to Korsnäs. Stockholm: Esselte, 1956.
Mannerheim, Johan. Kramfors aktiebolag. Utveckling och organisation. Stockholm: Nordisk Rotogravyr, 1928.

NOTES

Nylén, Axel R. *Mons trävaru aktiebolag 1867–1917. Minnesskrift i anledning af bolagets femtioårsjubileum.* Stockholm: Norstedt, 1917.

Qvist, Nils Henrik. *Ådalen. Ett bidrag till dess industri-och personhistoria.* 2 vols. Stockholm: Landby & Lundgren, 1943–46.

Sallström-Nygren, Carin. *Vattensågar och ångsågar i Norrland.* (No. 10, Inst. of Econ. Hist., Gothenburg Univ.) Gothenburg: Elander, 1967.

Söderlund, Ernst. *Swedish Timber Exports 1850–1950: A History of the Swedish Timber Trade.* Stockholm: Almqvist & Wiksell, 1952.

Wik, Harald. *Norra Sveriges sågverksindustri från 1820-talets mitt fram till 1937.* (No. 21, Geografiska institut, Uppsala Univ.) Stockholm: Almqvist & Wiksell, 1950.

1. Boëthius, *Robertsfors,* 97.
2. *Ibid.,* 107.
3. Fullerton and Williams, 47.
4. Samuelsson, 47.
5. Söderlund, 23–24.
6. Heckscher, "The Place of Sweden," 4(1): 19.
7. Millward, 268.
8. Söderlund, 79.
9. *Ibid.,* 100–102.
10. *Ibid.,* 38–39; SMK, 2: 257–258.
11. Lindahl, 9: 9–10.
12. Falk, 145.
13. Lindahl, 1: 122–126.
14. Falk, 47–52; Ahnlund, *Sundsvall,* 4: 11.
15. Ahnlund, *Mo och Domsjö,* 55
16. *Ibid.,* 43.
17. *Ibid.,* 53–54; SMK, 4: 215–216.
18. Wik, 262.
19. Althin, *Wifsta Varf,* 116.
20. *Ibid.,* 84–85.
21. *Ibid.,* 14–15, 41, 45.
22. Flodén, 1:55–59.
23. Althin, *op. cit.,* 66, 97–98.
24. Wik, 120–123.
25. Althin, *op. cit.,* 101.
26. Wik, 131.
27. Gårdlund, *Bolinders,* 223.
28. *Dagens Nyheter,* Dec. 23, 1979, 30.
29. Gårdlund, *Ind. samhälle,* 249.
30. Ahnlund, *Sundsvall,* 5: 455.

31. Wik, 74; Söderlund, 67, 142.
32. Wik, 128.
33. Söderlund, 156–157.
34. Althin, *Finsponga bilder,* 6.

Chapter 7: The Gaslight Era

Ahnlund, Nils. *Mo och Domsjö. Deras ägare och utveckling intill 1873.* Stockholm: Almqvist & Wiksell, 1911.

Althin, Torsten. *Reymersholmsbolaget.* Helsingborg: Nordisk Rotogravyr, 1955.

Bodman, Gösta. "Gripsholms och Kummelnäs kemiska fabriker." *Daedalus* (1957): 93–105.

Bosaeus, Elis. *Munksjö bruks minnen.* Uppsala: Munksjö AB, 1953.

Bring, Samuel E. *Bayerska ölet 100 år i Sverige. Till minnet av pionären Fredrik Rosenquist af Åkershult.* Stockholm: Tullberg, 1943.

Brome, Janrik, ed. *Östersunds historia.* Vol. II. Östersund: Östersundspostens tryckeri, 1936.

Cederskiöld, Gunnar, and Feilitzen, Einar von. *Den svenska tändsticks industriens historia.* Stockholm: Bokförlaget Natur och Kultur, 1945.

Fritz, Martin. "Shipping in Sweden, 1850–1913." *Scand. Econ. Hist. Rev.* XXVIII (1980), 2: 147–160.

Hammarström, Ingrid. "Svenska transocean handel och sjöfart under 1800-talet." *Historisk tidskrift,* Series 2, XXV (1962), 1: 377–431.

Klemming, Sven. "Om Stockholms belysning, offentlig och privat, under perioden 1800–1850." *Daedalus* (1971): 98–107.

Liljeholmens stearinfabriks aktiebolag. Stockholm: Norstedt, 1900.

Munthe, Arne. *Tobakens och tobakshanteringen i Sverige. Minnesskrift.* Stockholm: Haeggström, 1940.

Olán, Eskil. *Svenska brännvinets historia. Från Sten Stures dagar till husbehovsbränningens slut.* Gothenburg: Elander, 1922.

Rosman, Holger, *Textilfabrikerna vid Barnängen. Bilder ur Stockholms industrihistoria.* Stockholm: Centraltryckeriet, 1929.

Sallnäs, Birger, *et al,* eds. *Jönköpings stads historia.* 3 vols. Värnamo: Fälths, 1965.

Shaplen, Robert. *Kreuger: Genius and Swindler.* New York: Knopf, 1960.

Steckzén, Birger. *Scharinska firman 1824–1924. Berättelser om ett släkt och handelshus fran Västerbotten.* Stockholm: Norstedt, 1924.

Strandh, Sigurd. "Jac. Berzelius and the Emerging Modern Chemistry." *Daedalus* (1970): 62–82.

Weibull, Waloddi. "Alexander Lagermans livsgärning." *Daedalus* (1934): 67–81.

Wollstonecroft, Mary. *Letters Written during a Short Residence in Sweden, Norway & Denmark.* Fontweld (Sussex), England: Centaur, 1970.

1. Henderson, *Industrial Revolution in Europe,* 55–56; Josephson, 180.
2. Lindroth, 2: 281–282; Klemming, 105.
3. Klemming, 105.
4. Hartmann, 4: 330.
5. Montgomery, 106; Gårdlund, *Ind. Samhälle,* 53; Fritz, 153,158; Seth, 86.
6. Humbla, 363,401,203, 420–432.
7. Ahnlund, *Mo och Domsjö,* 67–71.
8. Steckzén, *Scharinska firman,* 49–55.
9. Wollstonecroft, 44; Kirby and Laurson, 61, quoting Parnell.
10. Du Chaillu, 1: 50.
11. Wollstonecroft, 19; Taylor, 199; Du Chaillu, 1: 13–14.
12. Hammarström, *Stockholm i svensk ekonomi,* 2: 265,272; Hammarström, "Svensk transocean," 1: 419–431.
13. Hammarström, *Stockholm i svensk ekonomi,* 2: 289; SMK, 5: 615–616.
14. Bring, *Bayerska ölet,* 4; SMK, 6: 364.
15. Hammarström, *Stockholm i svensk ekonomi,* 2: 252–255; Bring, *Bayerska ölet,* 11–15.
16. Gårdlund, *Ind. samhälle* 50; Althin, *Reymersholm,* 31; Taylor, 51; Olân, 99–102; Lindroth, 2: 261–266; *Nordisk familjebok,* 4: 435–438.
17. Munthe, *Tobaken,* 14–20.
18. *Ibid.,* 88; *Nordisk familjebok,* 29: 243–244, 248–249.
19. Munthe, *Tobaken,* 106.
20. *Ibid.,* 108.
21. Lindroth, 2: 277–278; Bodman, "Gripsholm," 93–101.
22. Bodman, *op. cit.,* Söderbaum, 2: 54–57.
23. Rosman, 172; Hammarström, *Stockholm i svensk ekonomi,* 2: 280; *Tekniska tidskrift* (1895), 1: 21–24.
24. Kihlberg, 154; *Liljeholmen, passim.*
25. Cederskiöld and Feilitzen, 16.
26. Clow, 449–453.
27. Cederskiöld and Feilitzen, 20–26; Weibull, 71; *Biographiskt lexicon,* (Ny följd), 8: 115–118.
28. Cederskiöld and Feilitzen, 42.
29. *Ibid.,* 49.
30. *Ibid., passim.*
31. *Ibid.,* 46; Bosaeus, *Munksjö,* 27.

32. Cederskiöld and Feilitzen, 164.
33. *Ibid.*, 180–185; (Kjellander) SBL, 22: 165–166; Weibull, 68–81.
34. Cederskiöld and Feilitzen, 34; Gårdlund, *Ind. samhälle,* 43.
35. Shaplen, 232.
36. Elson, 79.

Chapter 8: Iron Cord, Iron Horse

Adelsköld, Claes. *Nils Ericsson. Lefnadsteckningar öfver Kongl. Svenska Vetenskaps Akademiens . . . Ledamöter (1881).* Stockholm: Norstedt & söner, 1878–1885.
Åkerman, Helge, ed. *Norsholm-Västervik-Hultsfred järnvägar 1879–1929.* Västervik: C. O. Ekblad, 1929.
Bergslagernas Järnvägsaktiebolag 1872–1922. Vol. I. Gothenburg: Bonnier, 1900.
Clemensson, Gustaf. *Nassjö-Oskarshamn järnväg 1874–1924.* Gothenburg: Isaacson, 1924.
Danielson, Hilding. *Varberg-Borås järnväg. Minnesskrift.* Gothenburg; Isaacson, 1930.
Goldkuhl, Carola. "Nils Ericsson—Mannen och ingenjören." *Daedalus:* (1966), 75–109; (1967), 31–78.
Heimburger, Hans. *Svenska telegrafverket.* 2 vols. Gothenburg: Elander, 1931–38.
Helger, Nils. *Ransäter och Munkfors. Socken beskrivning i historisk framställning.* Filipstad: Bronell, 1944.
Kjellander, Rune G:son. "Anton Henric Öller. En pionjär inom svensk elektroteknik." *Daedalus* (1955): 89–110.
Meinander, Nils. *Gränges: En krönika om svensk järnmalm.* Helsinki: Tilgmann, 1968.
Modig, Hans. *Järnvägarnas efterfrågan och den svenska industrien 1860–1914.* (No. 8, Ekonomiska-historisk studier, Uppsala Univ.) Stockholm: Norstedt, 1971.
Rosen, Adolf Eugéne von. *Anförande pa riddarhuset, den 6 December 1856.* Stockholm: Marcus, 1857.
Sundbom, Ivar. "Sveriges kapitalimport från Frankrike 1870–1912." In *Studier . . . tillägnade Eli F. Heckscher,* pp. 228–237. Uppsala: Almqvist & Wiksell, 1945.
Welin, Gustaf, ed. *Statens järnvägar 1856–1906. Historisk-teknisk-ekonomisk beskrifning.* Vol. I. Stockholm: Centraltryckeriet, 1906.
Wimarson, Nils, ed. *Göteborg. En översikt vid trehundraårsjubileum 1923.* (Vol. I, GT.) Gothenburg: Elander, 1923.

1. Heimburger, 31. 43.
2. Clapham, 1:207; Robert Luther Thompson, *Wiring a Continent. The History of the Telegraph.* (Princeton: Princeton Univ. Press, 1947), p. 254.
3. (Hildebrand) SBL, 15: 78.
4. Heimburger, 31; Dodd, 197–198; Larson, 257.
5. Heimburger, 36-43.
6. *Ibid.,* 51, 7.
7. *Ibid.,* 60-63.
8. Kjellander, "Öller," 89–110.
9. SMK, 6: 331.
10. Helger, 320; Meinander, 25.
11. Goldkuhl, 35; Adelsköld, 72.
12. Meinander, 29.
13. Meinander, 30–32; Gasslander, *Gripenstedt,* 147–153.
14. Welin, 50–51; Goldkuhl, 36; Adelsköld, 72.
15. White, 10, (see chapter 2).
16. White, 222–223; Goldkuhl, 89.
17. Goldkuhl, 93–97; (Hildebrand) SBL, 14: 86.
18. Welin, 60; Adelsköld, 74; (Hildebrand) SBL, 14: 89.
19. Goldkuhl, 39.
20. *Ibid.,* 34.
21. Lindblom, 14; Welin, 60.
22. Clapham, 1: 388–389; Larsen, 236; Kirby and Laurson, 111–112.
23. Martha Edith Almedingen, *The Emperor Alexander II* (New York: Vanguard, 1966), 119; Ralph Volney Harlow, *The Growth of the United States,* Vol. I (rev. ed., New York: Holt, 1943), 337; Richard Heywood, *The Beginnings of Railway Development in Russia,* (Durham, N.C.: Duke Univ. Press, 1969), *passim.*
24. Lindblom, 14.
25. Sundbom, 235–237; Gårdlund, *Svensk industrifinansierung,* 163–164; Heckscher, *Economic History of Sweden,* 243.
26. Goldkuhl, 42,45,47.
27. Goldkuhl, 61; (Hildebrand) SBL, 14: 92.
28. (Löfström) SBL, 3: 76.
29. Gårdlund, *Ind. samhälle,* 247; Mortenson, 19.
30. Kihlberg, 203; Althin, *Korsnäsbolaget,* 15 (see Chapter 4).
31. (Carlsson) SBL, 1: 81–83.
32. Wimarson, 1: 22.
33. *Ibid.,* 2: 235, 291.
34. *Dagens Nyheter,* Sept. 3, 1979, pp. 1,19.
35. Clemensson, 11–41 *passim*; Åkerman, *Norsholm-Västervik,* 21–37.
36. Lindblom, 14.

37. Welin, 455.
38. *Ibid.,* 440.
39. *Ibid.,* 427–429; 439.
40. Modig, 135–139.

Chapter 9: Mobilizing Capital and Talents

Axelson, Alf W. *Gällivare-verken, investerings-och spekulationsobjekt 1855-1882.* Luleå: Norrbottens Kurirens tryckeri, 1964.

Bodman, Gösta. *Chalmers Tekniska Institut matrikel 1829–1929.* Gothenburg: Elanders, 1929.

Brisman, Sven. *Sveriges affärsbanker.* 2 vols. Stockholm: Bröderna Ljungström, 1924–1934.

————. *Sveriges Riksbank: Den stora reformsperioden 1860–1904.* Vol. III, *Sveriges Riksbank 1668–1924.* Stockholm: Norstedt, 1931.

Erixon, Sigurd. *Skultuna bruks historia.* Vol. II. Stockholm: Tisell, 1921.

Gasslander, Olle. *History of Stockholms Enskilda Bank to 1914.* Translated by M. S. Lindahl and Karin Elliott. Stockholm: Esselte, 1962.

Hallendorff, Carl. *Svenska handelsbanken 1871–1921. En minnesskrift.* Stockholm: Egnellska, 1921.

Hammarström, Ingrid. "Anglo-Swedish Economic Relations and the Crisis of 1857." *Scand. Econ. Hist. Rev,* X (1962), 2: 141–164.

Henriques, Pontus. *Skildringar ur Kungl. Tekniska Högskolans historia.* 2 vols. Stockholm: Isaac Marcus, 1927.

Martinius, Sture. *Befolkningsrörlighet under industrialismens inledningsskede i Sverige.* (No. 8, Inst. of Econ. Hist., Gothenburg Univ.) Gothenburg: Elander, 1967.

Morell, Mats. "On the Stratification of the Swedish Peasant Class." *Scand. Econ. Hist. Rev,* XXVIII (1980), 1: 15–32.

Sandberg, Lars G. "Banking and Economic Growth in Sweden before World War I." *J. Econ. Hist.,* XXXVIII (1978), 3: 650–680.

————. "The Case of the Impoverished Sophisticate: Human Capital and the Swedish Economic Growth before World War I." *J. Econ. Hist.,* XXXIX (1979), 1: 225–241.

Smedberg, Rickard, ed. *Kungliga väg-och vattenbyggnadskåren 1851–1937.* Stockholm: Bröderna Lagerström, 1937.

Söderlund, Ernst. *Skandinaviska banken i det svenska bankväsendets historia 1864–1914.* Gothenburg: Skand. banken, 1964.

Thomas, Dorothy Swaine. *Social and Economic Aspects of Swedish Population Movements, 1750–1933.* New York, Macmillan, 1941.

1. Söderberg, 4(7): 211.

2. Scott, 393. *
3. Montgomery, 41; Hovde, 1: 260; Jörberg, 17; Gårdlund, *Ind. samhälle*, 60; Dahmén, *Entrepreneurial Activity*, 15.
4. Munthe, *Hantverkets tjänst*, 62; Hovde, 1: 240.
5. Hovde, 1: 231, 235.
6. Jörberg, 334. Montgomery, 133; Heckscher, *Economic History of Sweden*, 211–212.
7. Jörberg, 27.
8. Dahmén, *op. cit.*, 10.
9. Jörberg, 149–151, 26.
10. Gårdlund, *Ind. samhälle*, 163; Söderlund, *Timber Exports*, 71–72.
11. Gasslander, *SEB*, 11.
12. *Biographiskt lexicon* (Ny följd), 10: 488; Gasslander, *SEB*, 8–9,16–21.
13. Gårdlund, *op. cit.*, 119–120; Lindahl, 3: 49–50, 2: 102–106; SMK, 8: 175; Falk, 96–97; Rosman and Munthe, 511–512.
14. Lindahl, 5: 36, 86–87, 15, 55, 49–50.
15. Hallendorff, 12–21,30,109–112; Lindahl, 5: 34–35.
16. Brisman, *Sveriges affärsbanker*, 2: 128–132; Lindahl, 2: 224; Söderlund, *Timber Exports*, 173; Söderlund, *Skandinaviska banken*, 7–15, 18, 31, 34–35.
17. Gasslander, *SEB*, 277.
18. Dahmén, 15,12,6–7; Samuelsson, 105.
19. Kihlberg, 169–173, 201–202; (Wichman) SBL, 19: 28.
20. (Axelson) SBL, 21: 269–271; Kihlberg, 203; Lindahl, 10: 111–112, 4: 118–119.
21. (Högberg) SBL, 19: 214–216.
22. Axelson, *Gällivare-verken*, 130; Söderlund, *Skandinaviska banken*, 53–58.
23. (Högberg) SBL, 16: 216.
24. (Gillingstam) SBL, 16: 419; Gårdlund, *Atlas Copco*, 64–65.
25. Gårdlund, *Marcus Wallenberg*, 104.
26. (Gillingstam) SBL, 16: 417–419.
27. Gårdlund, *Atlas Copco*, 22.8; Gårdlund, *Marcus Wallenberg*, 104–105.
28. Brisman, quoted by Gillingstam, SBL, 16: 420.
29. Lindahl, 6: 79–81; Gasslander, *SEB*, 25.
30. Lindroth, *Swedish Men of Science*, 31; Guinchard, 1: 150.
31. Strode, 249–251.
32. Franklin Scott, *The United States and Scandinavia* (Cambridge, Mass.: Harvard Univ. Press, 1950), 10.
33. Heckscher, *Economic History of Sweden*, 223–224.
34. Smedberg, 74–79, 91.
35. SMK, 7:399.

36. Smedberg, 11–12.
37. Henriques, 1: 364–365, 313–315.
38. Bodman, *Chalmers, passim*; SMK, 6: 28.
39. SMK, 2: 320.
40. Gårdlund, *Ind. samhälle*, 227–228.
41. *Ibid.*, 232.
42. Althin, *Vattenbyggnadsbyrån*, 21–22.
43. Sandberg, "Banking and Economic Growth," 651–653.
44. Jörberg, 8–12.
45. Gårdlund, *op. cit.*, 14.
46. Jörberg, 13–17; Sandberg, "Banking and Economic Growth," 657, 680.
47. Michael Roberts, *Essays in Swedish History* (Minneapolis: Univ. of Minnesota Press, 1950), 5.
48. Sandberg, "Impoverished Sophisticate," 225, 237.
49. Lindahl, 10: 295–296.

Chapter 10: From Workshops to Factories

Andrén, Erik. "Rademachersmedjarna i Eskilstuna och deras arkitekt." *Daedalus* (1942): 39–48.

Bergh, Thorsten C. *Manufakturaktiebolaget i Malmö 1855–1930*. Malmo: Lundgrens söner, 1931.

Blomqvist, Ragnar. *Lunds historia*. Vol. II. Lund: Bröderna Ekstrand, 1978.

Carl Gustafs Stad. Reinhold Rademachers manufakturverk och Eskilstuna. Eskilstuna: Öberg & Son, 1959.

Dahlgren, Stellan, ed. *Nyköpings stads historia*. Vol. II. Nyköping: Almqvist & Wiksell, 1973.

Elektromekano. Hälsingborg: Schmidt, 1943.

Falck, Albert Edvard. *Hantverksskrån och fabriksväsen i Nyköping från äldre tider*. Nyköping: Österberg, 1928.

Fredholm, Johan. *Helge Palmcrantz*. From *Ny Illustrerad Tidning*, 1880. Stockholm: Haeggström, 1880.

Hallström, Carl Otto, and Hallström, Omar. *Ur Köpings mekaniska verkstads historia 1856–1942*. Köping: Esselte, 1948.

Hansson, Sigurd. "Antenor Nydqvist. Vid hundraårsdagen af hans födelse." *Tekniska tidskrift* (1917).

Hellberg, Knut. *Järnets och smedarnas Eskilstuna. Bidrag till smidindustriens historia*. Katrineholm: Författarens förlag, 1938.

Jansson, E. Alfred. *Överums bruk. Tre hundra år 1654–1954*. Västervik: E. Hultgren, 1955.

Juhlen-Dannfelt, Herman. *Lantbrukets historia. Världhistorisk översikt av lantbrukets ock lantmannalivets utveckling.* Stockholm: K. L. Beckman, 1925.

————. *Lantbruksakademien 1813–1912 samt svenska land-hushållningen under nittonde århundradet.* 2 vols. Stockholm: Fritzes, 1913.

On Keels and Wheels: Kockums Mekaniska Verkstad AB, Malmö: Esselte, 1962.

Kjellander, Rune G:son., "J. W. Bergström: Mekanikus och daguerreotypist," *Daedalus* (1953): 99–115.

Kuuse, Jan. "Foreign Trade and the Breakthrough of the Engineering Industry in Sweden, 1890–1920." *Scand. Econ. Hist. Rev,* XXV (1977), 1: 1–36.

————. *Från redskap till maskiner. Mekaniseringsspridning och kommersialisering inom svenskt jordbruk 1860–1961.* (No. 20, Inst. of Econ. Hist., Gothenburg Univ.) Gothenburg: Elander, 1970.

————. *Interaction Between Agriculture and Industry. Case Studies of farm mechanization and industrialization in Sweden and the United States 1830–1930.* (No. 34, Inst. of Econ. Hist., Gothenburg Univ.) Gothenburg: Almqvist & Wiksell, 1974.

Lönnberg, Egil, ed. *NOHAB 100 år.* Karlstad: Nerman, 1947.

Minnesskrift med anledning av Motala verkstads hundraårige verksamhet 1822–1922. Stockholm: Centraltryckeriet, 1922.

Modig, Hans. *Järnvägarnas efterfrågan och den svenska industrien 1860–1914.* (No. 8, Ekonomiska-historisk studier, Uppsala Univ.) Stockholm: Norstedt, 1971.

Modin, Karl. *Atlas Diesel 1973/1898/1948. Minnesskrift.* Stockholm: Nordisk Rotogravyr, 1949.

Morén, Fredrik Wilhelm. *Ystads historia.* Vol. II. Ystad: Aurora, 1953.

Nilsson, Knut. *Eskilstuna som industristad.* Eskilstuna: Eskilstuna tryckeri, 1939.

Olsson, Erik Wilhelm, ed. *Nydqvist & Holm AB. Trollhättan. Det 2000: de lokomotivet: Jubileumsskrift.* Stockholm: Petterson, 1936.

Överums bruk. En modern industri med anor. Gothenburg: Weżata, 1962.

Pollock, Walter. *The Bolinder Book.* London: Jones, Roberts & Leete, 1930.

Rennerfelt, Ivar. "Flytande tillverkning av hästskor." *Daedalus* (1944): 73–82.

Rolt, Lionel T. C. *A Short History of Machine Tools.* Cambridge, Mass.: M.I.T. Press, 1965.

Seth, C. E. von, ed. *Kockums mekaniska verkstad AB Malmö 1840–1940.* Malmö: Lundgren söner, 1937.

Thermaenius-tröskverken. Torshälla 1847–1868, Hallsberg 1868–1918. Linköping: Linköpings lithogr., 1918.

Tisell, Gunnar. *Bultfabriks-Aktiebolaget 1873–1923. Minnesskrift.* Stockholm: Nordisk Rotogravyr, 1923.

THE SMALL GIANT

Way-Matthiesen, Lennart. "John Ericssons varmluftmaskin." *Daedalus* (1932): 85–95.

1. Hallström and Hallström, 15–16; Gustavsson and Hägg, 100–101,106; Falck, 437–442; Dahlgren, *Nyköping,* 2: 498–500.
2. Dahlgren, *op. cit.,* 2: 495, 499–502; Modig, 39–40.
3. *Motala,* 74–75.
4. Gårdlund, *Ind. samhälle,* 88; Gårdlund, *Bolinders,* 28.
5. Seth, 25; Juhlen–Dannfelt, *Lantbruksakademien,* 1: 304–306.
6. Seth, 20–22,30,35,301; Nilsson, 59; Juhlen-Dannfelt, *op. cit.,* 1: 306.
7. Kuuse, *Redskap till maskiner,* 47,65,113.
8. Juhlen-Dannfelt, *op. cit.,* 1: 303, 2: 87; William T. Hutchinson, *Cyrus Hall McCormick. Seed Time, 1809–1856* (New York: Century, 1930), *passim.*
9. Kuuse, *Interaction,* 89,190.
10. *Överums bruk,* 1; Juhlen-Dannfelt, *op. cit.,* 1: 307.
11. Jansson, 150,148,165–166; Kuuse, *Interaction,* 56,54.
12. Jansson, 191–198; Kuuse, *Interaction,* 60–77.
13. Kolare, 123–126; SMK, 1: 89; Kuuse, "Foreign Trade," 18–20.
14. Silfverstolpe (in *Carl Gustafs Stad*), 197–201; Andrén, 40; Nilsson, 6–16.
15. Silfverstolpe, *op. cit.,* 124–126, 144–152; Nilsson, 26–57; *Tekniska tidskrift* (1903/1904); Boëthius and Kromnow, 3(1): 363.
16. Hellberg, 2: 115–125; Modig, 83; *Tekniska tidskrift* (1903), 51–66; SMK, 5: 347–348.
17. Gårdlund, *Bolinders,* 8f.
18. Gårdlund, *op. cit.,* 35–37; Pollock, 1–2; (Fröman) SBL, 5: 290–291.
19. Dahlgren, *Stockholm,* 3: 28; Hammarström, 303; SMK, 4: 614–615; Hallström and Hallström, 79.
20. Hallström and Hallström, 30–37, 82–83.
21. Bergh, 20; Morén, 2: 107–114.
22. Seth, 1–5,55; Attman, *Kockumverken,* 50,178.
23. Seth, 63; Attman, *op. cit.,* 50.
24. Blomqvist, 2: 349–350; *On Keels and Wheels,* 39–49; *Elektromekano,* 1–3.
25. Hansson, 9.
26. Olsson, 5.
27. Hansson, *passim;* Olsson,10–11; *Tekniska tidskrift* (1896), 71–94.
28. Althin, *Vattenbyggnadsbyrån,* 6, 16, 21–22; Olsson, 8–9; (Henriques) SBL, 3: 593.
29. Way-Matthiesen, 87–94.
30. Modin, *Atlas Diesel,* 20–22; Gårdlund, *Atlas Copco,* 15.
31. Gårdlund, *op. cit.,* 17.
32. Nordström, *Södertälje,* 2: 635–637.

33. Gårdlund, *op. cit.*, 9; Gasslander, *SEB*, 129–131.
34. Gårdlund, *Ind. samhälle*, 247.
35. Mirsky and Nevins, 185, 216–222; Gårdlund, *Ind. samhälle*, 93; Paul Clements, *Marc Isambard Brunel* (London: Longmans, 1970), 25–36.
36. Kjellander, "Bergström," 110.
37. Nilsson, 24; Hellberg, 2: 233–234; Gårdlund, *Ind. samhälle*, 92–93, 244–245.
38. *Tekniska tidskrift* (1903), 4; Indebetou and Hylander, 1: 35.
39. (Åhman) SBL, 16: 452–453; Gårdlund, *Ind. samhälle*, 245–246.
40. Gårdlund, *op. cit.*, 245; Nilsson, 29–31; Hellberg, 2: 185, 256–258.
41. Hellberg, 2: 198–199,269,357.
42. Fredholm, 1–2; Hammarström, *Stockholm i svensk ekonomi*, 1: 316–317.
43. Rennerfelt, 74–75, 82; Tisell, 12–26, 34. Gasslander, *SEB*, 33–34.
44. Hallström and Hallström, 94–103.
45. *Ibid.*, 173,195,104; Finch, 355.
46. *Ibid.*, 179,191; Finch, 353–354.
47. Gårdlund, *Bolinders*, 131–134.
48. Hovde, 2: 253; Lundström, 105; Jörberg, 132; Modin, *Atlas Diesel*, 17.
49. Gårdlund, *Ind. samhälle*, 94. For the American counterpart, see Colvin, 42f.
50. Sir Arthur Hezlet, *The Submarine and Sea Power* (New York: Stein & Day, 1967), 9–12.
51. Sjöstrand, 44–45; Mortenson, 1; N.C. Engelbrecht and F. C. Hanighen, *Merchants of Death; A Study of the International Armament Industry* (New York: Dodd, Mead, 1934), 97,86.
52. SMK, 5: 487.
53. Seldes, 43, 181–183.
54. Kuuse, "Foreign Trade," 5–6.

Chapter 11: Ancient Companies, Modern Industry

Åkerman, Helge. *Ankarsrum: Minnesskrift.* Stockholm: Bröderna Lagerström, 1933.
Almquist, Johan Axel. *Graningeverken. Historisk skildring.* Stockholm, Tullberg, 1909.
Althin, Torsten. "C. A. Wittenström 1831–1911. Järnverksbyggare och uppfinnare." *Daedalus* (1959): 73–88.
Andersson, Ingvar. *Uddeholm. Värmlandsbruk med världsrykte.* Stockholm: Bröderna Lagerström, 1955.

Attman, Artur, ed. *Fagerstabrukens historia.* 4 vols. Uppsala: Almqvist & Wiksell, 1957.

Collin, Karin. *The Great Spinning Wheel: Historical Sketches and Legends in the History of Iggesund Bruk.* Uppsala: Almqvist & Wiksell, 1935.

Domnarvet 100 år. Gothenburg: Wezäta, 1978.

Ekerot, Gunnar. *Erik Johan Ljungberg.* Reprint from *Tekniska tidskrift,* 1915. Stockholm: Centraltryckeriet, 1915.

Fagersta bruks aktiebolag. Falun: Falu nya boktryckeri, 1929.

Forsslund, Karl-Erik. *Falu gruva och Stora Kopparbergs Bergslag.* Stockholm: Åhlen & Akerlund, 1936.

Göransson, Edward. *Husqvarna Vapenfabrik 1689–1939. En historia över dess utveckling under tvåhundrafemtio år.* Stockholm: Nordisk Rotogravyr, 1939.

Helger, Nils. *Ransäter och Munkfors. Socken beskrivning i historisk framställning.* Filipstad: Bronellska, 1944.

Hellgren, Olof. "J. F. Lundin och hans ungskonstruktioner." *Daedalus* (1946): 51–63.

Hildebrand, Karl-Gustaf. *Erik Johan Ljungberg och Stora Kopparberg.* Falun: Almqvist & Wiksell, 1970.

Hofors bruk genom tiderna. Gothenburg: Zachrisson, 1934.

SKF Hofors Bruk. A Modern Swedish Steelworks. Gothenburg: Antonson, 1946.

Holmström, Algot. Karlskoga. En bruksbygd blir industriort. Kumla: Kumla tryck., 1978.

Kjellson, Birger. *Husqvarna Vapenfabriks Aktiebolag. Dess tillkomst och utveckling samt något om Huskvarna stad.* Stockholm: Petterson, 1935.

Kjellström, Nils. *Uddeholm 1668–1968. A Jubilee Sketch 1968.* Stockholm: Esselte, 1968.

Langenskiöld, Karl Johan. *Erik Johan Ljungberg, Minnesteckning.* Reprint from Lefnadsteckningar över Kungl. Sv. Vetenskapsakademiens ledamöter. Stockholm: Almqvist & Wiksell, 1923.

Pauli, Herta. *Alfred Nobel: Dynamite King–Architect of Peace.* New York: Fischer, 1942.

Sahlin, Carl. *Stora Kopparbergs Bergslags Aktiebolag.* Falun: Falu nya boktryckeri, 1897.

Simons, Rodger L. *Fagersta: Six Centuries of Swedish Steel.* Stockholm: Fagersta bruk AB, 1945.

Söderlund, Ernst & Wretblad, P.E. *Nittonhundratalet Fagerstabrukens historia.* Vol. III, *Fagerstabrukens historia,* Artur Attman, ed. Uppsala: Almqvist & Wiksell, 1957.

Steckzén, Birger. *Bofors. En kanonindustris historia.* Stockholm: Esselte, 1946.

_____, ed. *Hofors bruks historia.* Gothenburg:: Wezäta, 1957.

Stora Kopparberg under 800 år. New ed. Gothenburg: Wezäta, 1962.

Stora Kopparberg: A Chronicle from the beginning to the Present Day. Gothenburg: Wezäta, 1971.

Tunberg, Sven. *Stora Kopparbergs historia.* Vol. I, Uppsala: Almqvist & Wiksell, 1922.

Ugglas, Samuel af. *Husqvarna 1689–1917. Historisk översikt af gevärsfaktoriets uppkomst och utveckling.* Jönköping: Jönköpings litografisk, 1917.

1. *Stora Kopparberg: Chronicle,* 51.
2. *Ibid.,* 13–14; Langenskiöld, 7.
3. *Ibid.,* 35–36; Forsslund, 141–142.
4. Hildebrand, 62–63.
5. Althin, "Wittenström," 76–81.
6. *Domnarvet 100 år,* 9; Hildebrand, 79; Forsslund, 190; Gårdlund, *Atlas Copco,* 20.
7. Hildebrand, 76.
8. *Domnarvet 100 år,* 9; Althin, "Wittenström," 74.
9. Ekerot, 2; Langenskiöld, 19–20.
10. Langenskiöld, 23.
11. Andersson, 13.
12. Steckzén, *Bofors,* 40; Andersson, 21–26.
13. Helger, 321.
14. *Ibid.,* 322; Hellgren, "Lundin," 52–60; Finch, 247.
15. Helger, 323–324; Andersson, 22; Sømme, 326–327; SMK,4: 43.
16. *Hofors genom tiderna,* 8–10; SMK, 6: 90–92.
17. Steckzén, *Hofors,* 165.
18. Gårdlund, *Marcus Wallenberg,* 111–112; Gasslander, *SEB,* 31–34; Lindahl, 5: 38–42.
19. Steckzén, *Hofors,* 275.
20. *Ibid.,* 265–266, 273–274, 281; Lindahl, 5: 85, 44.
21. Gårdlund, *op. cit.,* 113, 116; Gasslander, *op. cit.,* 122–128.
22. *Hofors genom tiderna,* 36–37.
23. Althin, *Finsponga bilder,* 14; Steckzén, *Bofors,* 17.
24. Althin, *Finsponga bilder,* 213.
25. Steckzén, *Bofors,* 44–45, *passim;* Holmström, 32–46.
26. Steckzén, *Bofors,* 51–85.
27. *Ibid.,* 111–112; SMK, 7: 20.
28. *Ibid.,* 48.
29. *Ibid.,* 143; Pauli, 246–249. For brief account of the later Bofors, see Holmström, 241–256.

30. Göransson, 24.
31. *Ibid.,* 113–125, 158–159.
32. Kjellson, 63; Colvin, 60.
33. Göransson, 120; af Ugglas, 68; Kolare, 158; SMK, 7: 495.
34. (Brinell) SBL, 2: 393.
35. (Benedicks) SBL, 6: 240; SMK, 1: 465.
36. Söderlund and Wretblad, 3: 156–157; Seldes, 69–70; Gasslander, *SEB,* 346–347.
37. Seldes, 69–70.
38. Collin, 219.

Chapter 12: Networks: Telephones and Electric Power

Åkerman, Johan ed. *Ett elektriskt halvsekel. Översikt över Aseas utveckling 1882–1933.* Västerås: Västmanlands Allehanda, 1933.

ASEA: *A Presentation in Words and Pictures.* Västerås: ASEA, 1962.

Blomqvist, Erik. *Sveriges energisförsörjning.* (Series C, No. 7, IU.) Stockholm: Engwall & Stråhle, 1951.

Drakenberg, Sven. *Västerås genom tiderna. Stadens byggnadshistoria från 1800-talets mitt.* Vol. V(2), *Västerås genom tiderna.* Västerås: Vestmanlands Tidnings tryckeri, 1962.

Heimburger, Hans. *Svenska telegrafverket.* 2 vols. Gothenburg: Elander, 1931, 1938.

Helén, Martin. *Asea: s historia 1883–1948.* Västerås: Västra Aros, 1955.

Hjulström, Filip. *Elektrifieringens utveckling i Sverige. En ekonomiska-geografiska översikt.* (Series 2, No. 29, Geografiska institut, Uppsala Univ.) Almqvist & Wiksell, 1941.

Kjellander, Rune G: son. "Anton Henric Öller. En pionjär inom svensk elektroteknik." *Daedalus* (1955): 89–110.

———. "J. E. Erikson. En bortglömd konstruktör och industriman." *Daedalus* (1947): 89–116.

———. "Wilhelm Wiklund 1832–1902." *Daedalus* (1957): 127–154.

Lundström, Ragnhild, ed. *Kring industrialismens genombrott i Sverige.* Stockholm: Wahlström & Widstrand, 1966.

Svensson, Nils. *Borås stads elektricitetsverk 1894–1944.* Borås: Tryckericentralen, 1944.

1. Montgomery, 161, 135; Jörberg, 16, 19, 38, 42; G. Heckscher, 33; Jörberg in Lundström, 47.
2. Heimburger, 1: 8; Josephson, 139; Herbert N. Casson, *The History of the Telephone* (Chicago: McClurg, 1910), 43; S. P. Thompson, *The Life of*

William Thomson, Baron Kelvin of Largs, Vol. II. (London: Macmillan, 1910), 674.

3. Heimburger, 1: 8–9; Kjellander "Öller," 105.
4. (Roosval) SBL, 7: 799.
5. (Hubendick) SBL, 14: 146–148; Kjellander, "Öller," 105.
6. Jansson, 26.
7. Heimburger, 1: 69.
8. *Ibid.*, 1: 36–41.
9. *Ibid.*, 1: 10; Modin, 239.
10. *Ibid.*, 1: 36.
11. *Ibid.*, 1: 42–49, 72–75, 141–142.
12. Casson, *op.cit.*, 257.
13. SMK, 1: 297.
14. (Roosval) SBL, 7: 802; Casson, *op. cit.*, 263. Gasslander, *SEB*, 456–461.
15. Elson, 3.
16. Jansson, 21; Falk, 68; (Hubendick) SBL, 14: 153; Guinchard, 2: 643–660.
17. Åkerman, 33.
18. Svensson, 8.
19. Kjellander, "Wiklund," 137.
20. Kjellander, "J. E. Erikson," 89–115; Svensson, 8; Åke Ortmark, *De okända makthavarna* (Stockholm: Wahlström & Widstrand, 1970), 91.
21. Lundström, 110; Wimarson, 568.
22. Åkerman, 29.
23. Bodman, "Strehlenert," 48–59; Nordström, 2: 763.
24. Kjellander, "Wiklund," 136–139, 143.
25. (Gillingstam) SBL, 16: 456–457.
26. Åkerman, 36.
27. Mirsky and Nevins, 82; Åkerman, 38–39; Smiles, 315.
28. Åkerman, 45–49, 53–55.
29. Althin, *Vattenbyggnadsbyrå,* 22–23; Way-Matthiesen, 92–94 (see Chapter 10).
30. Åkerman, 126f.; Jansson, 127; Edlund (Meddellanden), *Daedalus* (1934): 102; Singer, 4: 191.
31. Lundstrom, 144–145; Åkerman, 27–31; (Boëthius and Lindström) SBL, 10: 212.
32. (Boëthius and Lindstrom) SBL 10: 207–213.
33. Lundström, 145–148; Åkerman, 63–64; O'Dell, 462.
34. Lundström, 150–154; Hjulström, *Elekt. utveckling,* 126; Samuelsson, 88–89.
35. Åkerman, 169, 85; Lundström, 157–186; Gårdlund, *Marcus Wallenberg,* 221–239.
36. *Stor-Göteborg*, 390–392; (Kjellander) SBL, 21: 174–175.

37. Hylander, "Lavalturbinen," *Daedalus* (1973): 34–35.
38. Hjulström, *Elekt. utveckling*, 124; Althin, *Vattenbyggnadsbyrå*, 121. On later developments, see Millward, 280–304.

Chapter 13: Cellulose and Chemicals

Althin, Torsten. "Carl Daniel Ekmans liv och person." *Daedalus* (1935): 47–66.

————. *Papyrus. Sweden's Largest Fine Paper and Board Mill.* Mölndal: Nordisk Rotogravyr, 1953.

————. *Reymersholmsbolaget.* Helsingborg: Nordisk Rotogravyr, 1955.

————. *Stockholms Superfosfat Fabriks Aktiebolag 1871–1946. Minnesskrift.* Stockholm: Nordisk Rotogravyr, 1946.

Bodman, Gösta, "Klippans superfosfatfabrik" 1857–1875." *Daedalus* (1947): 41–58.

Bosaeus, Elis. *Utveckling av produktion och teknik i svensk massindustri 1857–1939.* (No. 4, Industrihistorisk skriftserie utgiven av Sv. cellulosa-och trämassaföreningarna.) Uppsala: Almqvist & Wiksell, 1949.

Clemensson, Gustaf. *Klippans pappersbruk med Lessebo och Böksholm.* Uppsala: Almqvist & Wiksell, 1932.

I Styrkans deglar. Aktiebolag Ferrolegeringar. Stockholm: Esselte, 1963.

Ekerot, Gunnar. "Erik Johan Ljungberg." *Tekniska tidskrift* (1915).

Gelhaar, Julius. "Karbidindustriens begynnelse i Sverige." *Daedalus* (1954): 81–104.

Lundin, Gustaf. *Trollhättan genom tiderna.* Trollhättan: Författarens förlag, 1946.

Spaak, George. "Männen kring Carl Daniel Ekman." *Daedalus* (1951): 109–124.

1. Althin, *Papyrus,* 66–67; Lundin, 312.
2. Clemensson, 83f.; Gårdlund, *Ind. samhälle,* 250; Bosaeus, 42.
3. Gårdlund, *op.cit.,* 115; Bosaeus, 46; SMK, 4: 545–546.
4. Spaak, 113–121; Althin, *Papyrus,* 69.
5. Althin, *Papyrus,* 72–74; (Spaak) SBL, 16: 212–213; (Gillingstam) SBL, 16: 421.
6. Gårdlund, *op.cit.,* 116; Bosaeus, 46; Jörberg, 86.
7. Gårdlund, *op.cit.,* 84, 116–121; Bosaeus, 15–18; Jörberg, 83–87; Althin, *Papyrus,* 68.
8. Jörberg, 84–87; Samuelsson, 65.
9. Langenskiöld, 15–16 (see Chapter 11).
10. Bosaeus, 50–53, 82, 84; SMK, 2: 377.

11. *Ibid.,* 77.
12. Heckscher, *Economic History of Sweden,* 228; Jörberg, 38.
13. Millward, 441–442.
14. Musson, *Science, Technology,* 165; L. F. Haber, *The Chemical Industry during the Nineteenth Century* (Oxford: Clarendon Press, 1958), 61–62.
15. Althin, *Stockholm superfosfat,* 34, 40; Bodman, "Klippans superfosfat," 46–50.
16. Althin, *Stockholm superfosfat,* 66–68, *passim.*
17. *Ibid.,* 48–54, 175.
18. *Ibid.,* 289; Gelhaar, 83, 90–91.
19. Gelhaar, 86–88.
20. *Ferrolegeringar,* 1–3.
21. Althin, *Reymersholm,* 28–45.

Chapter 14: Iron Ore and High Finance

Axelson, Alf W. *Gällivare-verken investerings- och spekulationsobjekt 1855-1882.* Luleå: Norrbottens Kurirens tryckeri, 1964.
Flinn, Michael. "Scandinavian Iron Ore Mining and the British Steel Industry, 1870–1914." *Scand. Econ. Hist. Rev,* II (1954), 1: 31–46.
Fritz, Martin. *Järnmalmsproduktion och järnmalmsmarknaden 1883–1913. De svenska exportföretagens produktionsutveckling, avsättningsrikting och skeppnings förhållanden.* (No. 11, Inst. of Econ. Hist., Gothenburg Univ.) Gothenburg: Elander, 1967.
Jonsson, Bo. *Staten och malmfälten. En studie i svensk malmfältspolitik omkring sekelskiftet.* Stockholm: Almqvist & Wiksell, 1969.
Ljung, Sven, with Sigurd Erixon. *Skultuna bruks historia 1607– 1860.* Stockholm: Nordisk Rotogravyr, 1957.
Meinander, Nils. *Gränges. En krönika om svensk järnmalm.* Helsinki: Tilgmann, 1968.
Westin, Gunnar, ed. *Övre Norrlands historia.* Vols. III–IV. Umeå: City, 1974.

1. Heckscher, "The Place of Sweden," 20; Henderson, *Industrial Revolution in Europe,* 214; Finch, 247; Samuelsson, 53–54.
2. Meinander, 34–35, *passim.*
3. *Ibid.,* Söderlund, *Skandinaviska banken,* 267–283.
4. Meinander, 63.
5. Fritz, 52.
6. The *Times,* Sept. 23, 1921 (No. 42,833), p. 5.
7. Falk, 73.
8. Lindahl, 10: 107.

9. (Hildebrand) SBL, 18: 162–163; Ljung, 243–252; Attman, *Kockum,* 49; Andersson, *Surahammar,* 2: 23–28 (see Chapter 17).

10. Axelson, 24–34, 54–56; Lindahl, 4: 115–119; (Axelson) SBL, 21: 181–182.

11. Axelson, 112; (Gillingstam) SBL, 21: 271; (Axelson) SBL, 16: 417.

12. Axelson, 218.

13. Jonsson, 26–27; Fröding, *Berättelser,* 337–380.

14. Jonsson, 28–33, 40; Gasslander, *SEB,* 140–143.

15. Axelson, 261, 281; (Lagergren) SBL, 3: 615–617; Flinn, 38; Gasslander, *op. cit.,* 336–344.

16. Jonsson, 61.

17. Quoted by Axelson, 220.

18. Fritz, 10; (Boëthius) SBL, 6: 411–414; (Lagergren) SBL, 3: 616; Flinn, 41.

19. Fritz, 13; Gårdlund, *Marcus Wallenberg,* 151, 73.

20. Fritz, 13, 17, 25–26; Gårdlund, *op. cit.,* 168–169; Gasslander, *op. cit.,* 345–357.

21. Fritz, 37, 56; Jonsson, 370; Gårdlund, *op. cit.,* 173.

22. Fritz, 25–48, *passim.*

23. Jonsson, 371–373.

Chapter 15: The Urban Community: A Miscellany

Adelswärd, Gösta. *Varaktigare än kopparn. Åtvidaberg 1413–1963.* Åtvidaberg: AB Åtvidaberg Facit, 1963.

Ekerot, Gunnar. *Minnesskrift över Halda fabrik.* Gothenburg: Zachrisson, 1917.

Fritz, Martin. "Shipping in Sweden, 1850–1913." *Scand. Econ. Hist. Rev,* XXVIII (1980), 2: 147–160.

Götaverken 1841–1941. (No. 8, Götaverken skrifter.) Gothenburg: AB Götaverken, 1941.

Grenander-Nyberg, Gertrud. "Sömnadsindustri. En översikt av dess uppkomst och utveckling i Sverige." *Daedalus* (1946): 75–132.

Helmfrid, Björn. *Åtvidaberg. Kopparen—Baroniet—Industrierna.* Malmö: Landby & Lundgren, 1955.

Kjellander, Rune G: son." J. W. Bergström. Mekanikus och daguerreotypist." *Daedalus* (1953): 99–115.

———. "J. E. Erikson. En bortglömd konstruktör och industriman." *Daedalus* (1947): 89–116.

———. "Wilhelm Wiklund 1832–1902." *Daedalus* (1957): 127–154.

———. "J. G. Wikström och den första symaskinstillverkningen." *Daedalus* (1956): 131–140.

Kock, Birger, and Schütz, Fredrik. "Knut Lundmark. En pionjär inom kommunikationstekniker." *Daedalus* (1973): 61–85.

Kock, Karin. *Skånska cement aktiebolaget 1871–1931. Minnesskrift.* Uppsala: Almqvist & Wiksell, 1932.

Lahnhagen, Rolf. *Sveriges cementindustri.* (Series A, No. 6, IU.) Stockholm: Engwall & Stråhle, 1950.

Lindgren, Michael. "Georg och Edvard Scheutz' första differensmaskin återfunnin." *Daedalus* (1980): 97–102.

Lundmark, Efraim. *Rederi-Svea. Ett svenskt storrederi och dess insatser i handelssjöfarten.* Stockholm: Petterson, 1951.

Rönnow, Sixtén. *Skånska cementgjuteri 1887–1947. 60 årsjubileum.* Stockholm: Nordisk Rotogravyr, 1947.

Sönnerberg, Sven, ed. *Kampen mot elden. Brandförsvaret genom tiderna.* Malmö: Bernce, 1951.

Stålberg, Helge. *Smålands skogs och träindustrier.* (Series B, No. 3, IU.) Stockholm: Engwall & Stråhle, 1949.

Wassén, Henry. *Odhners historia. Illustrerad krönika över en maskin att räkna med.* Gothenburg: Wezäta, 1945.

Wiberg, Helge. "Några av Martin Wibergs uppfinningar." *Daedalus* (1955): 112–118.

1. Dahlgren, 327–328; SMK, 4: 512; Söderbaum, 3: 163–181; Hartmann, 4: 318–319; Heckscher, *Economic History of Sweden,* 145–147.
2. Kjellander, "J. E. Erikson," 108.
3. Kjellander, "J. E. Erikson," 108; Kjellander, "Bergström," 100; Kjellander, "Wiklund," 129; Kjellander, "Wikström, 132.
4. Kjellander, "Bergström," 113–114.
5. (Kjellander) SBL, 15: 85–86.
6. Sönnerberg, 37.
7. *Ibid.,* 48.
8. Kock, 13, 20, 40, *passim.*
9. Rönnow, 10–17.
10. Dahlgren, 157f.; Gårdlund, *Atlas Copco,* 79; John P. Mckay, *Tramways and Trolleys: The Rise of Urban Mass Transport in Europe* (Princeton: Princeton Univ. Press, 1976), 30–32, 50–51, 71.
11. Wimarson, 592, 598.
12. Modin, 31–53; Åkerman, 80–81 (see Chapter 12).
13. Kock and Schütz, 62–68, 75–84.
14. Fritz, "Shipping in Sweden," 159–160.
15. Dahlgren, 14–16.
16. *Götaverken,* 22–30.
17. *Götaverken,* 39; Lindahl, 1: 31–33.

18. *Stor-Göteborg,* 50–52; Lundmark, 10.
19. Lundmark, 67.
20. Falk, 33–43; SMK, 1: 483.
21. Modin, 131–133; SMK, 4: 100–102.
22. *Götaverken,* 23–29, 38.
23. Grenander-Nyberg, 75f.
24. Grenander-Nyberg, 80–93; Grenander-Nyberg (Meddelanden), *Daedalus* (1942): 102–105.
25. *Ibid.,* 84; Victor S. Clark, *History of Manufacturing in the United States,* Vol. I (New York: McGraw-Hill, 1929), 416, 521–522.
26. Kjellander, "Wikström," 132–134, 137.
27. *Ibid.,* 138–139; Grenander-Nyberg, 89.
28. *Ibid.,* 138; Jansson, 162.
29. Lindblom, 3–4.
30. *Ibid.,* 29–32.
31. Jansson, 154–164.
32. *Ibid.,* 143–150; Strode, 286; Sømme, 334; Stålberg, 6–9, 60.
33. Helmfrid, 3–5; Adelswärd, 12–13.
34. Adelswärd, 23–25.
35. Du Chaillu, 2: 392–398.
36. Helmfrid, 15; Adelswärd, 45.
37. Adelswärd, 57.
38. Norén, 359 (see Chapter 17).
39. *Tekniska tidskrift* (1916–1918), 157–168; Ekerot, *Halda,* 18–22, 38–40; SMK, 3: 288–289; Maboth Moseley, *Irascible Genius, The Life of Charles Babbage* (Chicago: Henry Regnery, 1964), 233–234.
40. Wieselgren, 94–101.
41. Wiberg, 112–118; SMK, 8: 325.
42. Wassén, 25–41.
43. *Ibid.,* 42–50.

Chapter 16: Technologists Triumphant: The Inventors

Althin, Torsten, ed. *Gustaf de Laval 1845–1913. De höga hastigheternas man.* Stockholm: Nordisk Rotogravyr, 1943.
_____. *C. E. Johansson, 1864–1943. The Master of Measurement.* Stockholm: Nordisk Rotogravyr, 1948.
_____. "Gustaf Dalén. En minnesteckning." *Daedalus* (1945): 37–46.
Blomqvist, Erik. *Sveriges energisförsörjning.* (Series C, No. 7, IU.) Stockholm: Engwall & Stråhle, 1951.

Cronquist, A. Werner. *Alfred Nobel. Hans fader och hans bröder.* From *Ord och Bild,* 1894. Stockholm: Wahlström & Widstrand, 1898.

Gustaf Dalén. Centennial Commemoration. Stockholm: AGA, 1969.

Dickinson, H. W. *A Short History of the Steam Engine.* Reprints of Economic Classics. New York: Kelley, 1966.

Ekeberg, Birger. "Alfred Nobel. Tal vid Nobelfesten, 1956." *Daedalus* (1957): 47–51.

Gelhaar, Julius. "Karbidindustriens begynnelse i Sverige." *Daedalus* (1954): 81–104.

Hagelin, Ernst. *Striden om Trollhättefallen* Vol. II(1), *Trollhättan, dess kanal och kraftverk.* Stockholm: no pub., 1916.

Halasz, Nicholas. *Nobel. A Biography of Alfred Nobel.* New York: Orion Press, 1959.

Hjern, Kjell, ed. *Gamlestadens aktiebolag.* Gothenburg: Isacson, 1965.

Hylander, Hans. "Lavalturbinen i historiskt perspektive." *Daedalus* (1973): 33–60.

On Keels and Wheels: Kockums Mekaniska Verkstad AB. Malmö: Esselte, 1962.

Kuuse, Jan. "Foreign Trade and the Breakthrough of the Engineering Industry in Sweden, 1890–1920." *Scand. Econ. Hist. Rev,* XXV (1977), 1: 1–36.

———. *Från redskap till maskiner. Mekaniseringsspridning och kommersialisering inom svenskt jordbruk 1860–1961.* (No. 20, Inst. of Econ. Hist., Gothenburg Univ.) Gothenburg: Elander, 1970.

———. *Interaction Between Agriculture and Industry. Case Studies of farm mechanization and industrialization in Sweden and the United States 1830–1930.* (No. 34, Inst. of Econ. Hist., Gothenburg Univ.) Gothenburg: Almqvist & Wiksell, 1974.

Pauli, Herta. *Alfred Nobel: Dynamite King—Architect of Peace.* New York: Fischer, 1942.

Sohlman, Ragner, and Schück, Henrik. *Nobel: Dynamite and Peace.* Translated by Brian and Beatrix Lunn. New York: Cosmopolitan, 1929.

Tolf, Robert W. *The Russian Rockefellers. The Saga of the Nobel Family and the Russian Oil Industry.* Stanford: Hoover Institute Press, 1976.

Unger, Gunnar. *Axel Wenner-Gren. En vikingasaga.* Stockholm: Bonnier, 1962.

1. Althin, *Vattenbyggnadsbyrå,* 27.
2. Those not listed in this paragraph include: J. S. Bagge, Ansgar Betulander, Gustaf Dalén, Gustaf de Laval, K. Jones Hesselman, C. E. Johansson, J. P. Johansson, Birger and Fredrik Ljungström, Frans Lundgren, Carl Nyberg, Ernst Nyberg, Martin Wiberg, and Sven Wingquist.

3. Wikberg, 107. For a detailed account in English about Gustaf de Laval, see Kuuse, *Interaction,* 116–215.
4. Dickinson, 207; Henry G. Prout, *A Life of George Westinghouse,* reprinted. (New York: Arno Press, 1972), 185.
5. Althin, *Gustaf de Laval,* 64, 67–69; Jansson, 63–68, 72.
6. Wikberg, 112–113.
7. Quoted by Althin, *op. cit.,* 69.
8. Magnell, 248 (see Chapter 4).
9. Kuuse, *Interaction,* 169; (Forsberg) SBL, 4: 10.
10. Althin, *op. cit.,* 236.
11. Althin, *op. cit.,* 91–92; Dickinson, 207–211; (Lindmark) SBL, 11: 26.
12. Hylander, 48–49.
13. Althin, *op. cit.,* 213, 223–227; Althin, *Finsponga bilder,* 30; Hylander, 38.
14. Althin, *Gustaf de Laval,* 278–281; Singer, 5: 150.
15. Quoted by Althin, *Gustaf de Laval;* 223, 128–137.
16. Gårdlund, *Marcus Wallenberg,* 106.
17. Althin, *Gustaf de Laval,* 137, 274.
18. *Ibid.,* 284, 289; Gelhaar, 90–91.
19. Gårdlund, *op. cit.,* 224; Lundström, 157–178 *passim*; Gasslander, *SEB,* 212–216, 223–227; SMK, 7: 506.
20. Hagelin, 109–151 *passim*; Blomqvist, 46–47.
21. Kuuse, 13, 26; (Lindmark) SBL, 11: 29.
22. Jansson, 73; SMK, 15: 63.
23. Jansson, 77–82; SMK, 5: 63–65; Althin, *Finsponga bilder,* 29–33; Dickinson, 218–220.
24. (Hubendick) SBL, 10: 37–50.
25. *Dalén: Centennial,* 2; *Tekniska tidskrift* (1916/1918), 9–20.
26. (Hubendick) SBL, 10: 45–46; *Dalén: Centennial,* 3; Falk, 16–17; Jansson, 15.
27. Althin, *Johansson,* 35–45; Colvin, 42–43.
28. Althin, *Johansson,* 68–71.
29. *Ibid.,* 91–92.
30. *Ibid.,* 11.
31. Jansson, 45–59; SMK, 3: 474.
32. Jansson, 52.
33. Hjern, 1–2.
34. Modin, 254–255.
35. Jansson, 133; Hjern, 2–3; Modin, 253–266.
36. Unger, 16–17.
37. *Ibid.,* 21–27.
38. *Ibid.,* 31.
39. Sohlman and Schück, 35; Tolf, 13.

40. Cronquist, 15; SMK, 5: 464–465; Tolf, 13–14.
41. Sohlman and Schück, 31–32; Tolf, *passim*.
42. Tolf, 39–49; Cronquist, 32–33; Henderson, *Industrial Revolution in Europe*, 219; Halasz, 44.
43. Tolf, 75; Henderson, *op. cit.*, 219.
44. Tolf, 53–66; Sohlman and Schück, 71–72; Pauli, 165–172.
45. See Tolf, 84–121, for details.
46. Sohlman and Schück, 79–80.
47. Tolf, 192.
48. Kuuse, "Foreign Trade," 10, 19, 27–28.
49. *On Keels and Wheels*, 11; Pauli, 33–34.
50. Sohlman and Schück, 101; Jansson, 87.
51. Wikberg, 87–88.
52. Edwin E. Slosson, *Creative Chemistry; Descriptive of Recent Achievements in the Chemical Industries* (New York: Century, 1919), 117.
53. Cronquist, 24; Halasz, 109–110; on the politics, see Pauli, 182–211.
54. Wikberg, 89–90; Cronquist, 28; Ekeberg, 49.
55. Sohlman and Schück, 2.
56. Pauli, 69–70; Ekeberg, 50.
57. Steckzén, *Bofors*, 148.
58. Wikberg, 90–91, 99–101; Ekeberg, 51.
59. Tolf, 126–128.

Chapter 17: The Petroleum Age Begins

Ågren, Per. "Engelsberg's Oil Factory. An Early Petroleum refinery." *Daedalus* (1967): 19–29.

Althin, Torsten. *Flygkrönika. Bilder och notiser ur luftfartens historia.* Stockholm: Wahlström & Widstrand, 1931.

Andersson, Fritz. *Surahammars bruks historia.* 5 vols. Surahammar: Surahammar AB, 1963.

Andrén, Erik. *Aktiebolaget Arvid Böhlmarks lampfabrik 1872–1937.* Stockholm: Nordisk Rotogravyr, 1937.

Hjern, Kjell, ed. *Gamlestadens aktiebolag.* Gothenburg: Isacson, 1965.

Hult, Jan. "Cykeln mitt ibland oss." *Daedalus* (1978–1979): 75–79.

Josephsson, Robert, ed. *Marcus Wallenberg 1864–1939.* Stockholm: Bonnier, 1939.

Lindh, Björn-Eric. "Sveriges första 'kungliga' bil och Stockholms första automobildroska." *Daedalus* (1975): 141–151.

——. "Volvos tidiga år." *Daedalus* (1977): 134–169.

THE SMALL GIANT

Modin, Karl. *Atlas Diesel 1873/1898/1948. Minnesskrift.* Stockholm: Nordisk Rotogravyr, 1949.

———. *Svenska uppfinnare och industrimän.* Uppsala: Lindblad, 1947.
Nachmanson, August and Sundberg, Karl, eds. *Svenska diamantbergborrnings aktiebolag 1886–1936.* Uppsala: Almqvist & Wiksell, 1936.
Nerén, John. *Automobilens historia.* Stockholm: Thule, 1937.
Nilsson, Knut. *Eskilstuna som industristad.* Eskilstuna: Eskilstuna tryck. Folket, 1939.
Nordström, Alf. *et al.* Södertälje stads historia. Vol. II. Stockholm: Norstedt, 1968.
Pollock, Walter. *The Bolinder Book.* London: Jones, Roberts & Leete, 1930.
Sandklef, Albert. *Varbergs historia.* Varberg: Bröderna Carlsson, 1963.

1. Hult, 75–76; Sandklef, 443.
2. Egon Larsen, *Ideas and Inventions* (London: Spring Books, 1960), 96f.; Harmon Tupper, *To the Great Ocean: Siberia and the Trans-Siberian Railway* (Boston: Little Brown, 1965), 110, 228.
3. Modin, *Uppfinnare,* 211–212; Hult, 75.
4. Modin, *Uppfinnare,* 207–213; Sandklef, 443–450; SMK, 7: 389.
5. Andrén, 14–15, 20; Hammarström, 285; Ågren, 11; Nordström, 2: 634, 638.
6. Ågren, 12, 28.
7. *Nordisk familjebok,* 12: 107, 32: 838; *Svenska uppslagsbok,* 13: 149–150, 29: 869–870; 12: 317.
8. (Kjellander) SBL, 20: 471–472; *Tekniska tidskrift* (1916/1918), 129–136.
9. Hammarström, 273, 284–285.
10. Andrén, 24, 32–33, 36.
11. Jansson, 95–103; SMK, 5: 560, 7:8.
12. Modin, *Uppfinnare,* 111–125; SMK, 7: 386–387, 3: 474.
13. Nerén, 325.
14. Gårdlund, *Bolinders,* 224, 133–134; Pollock, 31.
15. Modin, *Uppfinnare,* 123–124; SMK, 4: 358, 7: 387.
16. Pollock, 32–34.
17. Modin, *Atlas Diesel,* 75; Gasslander, *SEB,* 216–223; 379–385.
18. Modin, *Atlas Diesel,* 80–87; Ljungzell, 768.
19. Gårdlund, *Atlas Copco,* 46–48, 138, 199–206.
20. Nachmanson and Sundberg, 167–170.
21. Nerén, 313–314; Colvin, 110.
22. Nerén, 325.
23. Lindh, "Kungliga bil," 141–151.
24. Nerén, 316–317.

25. Nerén, 338; Andersson, 1: 11–12, 4: 54–58, 4: 38–40; Nordström, 2: 766–775, 778.
26. Nerén, 350–354; *Tekniska tidskrift* (1914/1915), 43–58.
27. Nerén, 347–348; Nilsson, 30; SMK, 7: 427.
28. Lindh, "Volvo," 141.
29. Jansson, 102–103; SMK, 5: 560.
30. Nordström, 2: 778; (Jacobson) SBL, 8: 195–196.
31. Modin, *Uppfinnare*, 236–237; Althin, *Flygkrönika*, 59.
32. Lindh, "Volvo," 134–135.

Chapter 18: In Summary (1914)

1. Samuelsson, 61; Gårdlund, *Ind. samhälle*, 22.
2. Jörberg, 18; Lundström, 47.
3. Arthur Montgomery, *How Sweden Overcame the Depression* (Stockholm: Bonnier, 1938), 136.
4. Samuelsson, 64.
5. Guinchard, 2: 524–525.
6. Sundbom in *Studier . . . tillägnade Heckscher*, 231–237.
7. Milward and Saul, 500–502.
8. *Ibid.*, 490.
9. Montgomery, *op. cit.*, 135.
10. Heckscher, *Economic History of Sweden*, 209; Heckscher, *Svenskt arbete*, 246, 250.
11. Lundström, 47.
12. Heckscher, *Economic History of Sweden*, 256.
13. O. Fritof Ander, *The Building of Modern Sweden. The Reign of Gustav V, 1907–1950* (Rock Island, Ill.: Augustana Book Concern, 1958), xvii.
14. Allan Kastrup, *The Swedish Heritage in America. The Swedish Element in America and American-Swedish Relations in their Historical Perspective* (St. Paul, Minn.: Swedish Council of America, 1975), 390–396, 514.
15. However, see three articles in the *Journal of Modern History*: J. M. H. Hovde, "Notes on the Effects of Emigration upon Scandinavia," VI (1934), 3: 253–279; and two by Franklin D. Scott, "American Influences in Norway and Sweden," XVIII (1946), 1: 37–47; and "Sweden's Constructive Opposition to Emigration," XXXVII (1965), 3: 307–335.

REGISTER OF PERSONS

INDEX